Business Multimedia
Explained

BUSINESS MULTIMEDIA EXPLAINED

A MANAGER'S GUIDE TO KEY TERMS & CONCEPTS

PETER G.W. KEEN

Harvard Business School Press
Boston, Massachusetts

To my wife, Sherry, with thanks for such wonderful years with so many more to come.

Copyright © 1997 by Peter G. W. Keen
All rights reserved
Printed in the United States of America

01 00 99 98 97   5 4 3 2 1

Library of Congress Cataloging-in-Publication Data

Keen, Peter G. W.
    Business multimedia explained : a manager's guide to key
terms & concepts
        p.   cm.
    Includes index.
    ISBN 0-87584-718-8 (hc : alk. paper).
    ISBN 0-87584-772-2 (pb : alk. paper)
    1. Management information systems.   2. Multimedia systems.
3. Business enterprises—Computer networks.
4. Internet (Computer network)   5. Telecommunication systems.
    I. Title.
HD30.213.K43 1997
                                                                96-41594
                                                                    CIP

The paper used in this publication meets the requirements of the
American National Standard for Permanence of Paper for Printed
Library Materials Z39.49-1984.

Contents

Preface

Goering's famous gesture to anyone who used the word "history" was to reach for his pistol. Many managers exhibit a similar response to mention of the word "multimedia"—they reach for an antihype gun or for earplugs.

When I began researching the business uses of multimedia, I thought I was investigating a field that would be important sometime in the future but that today entailed gimmicky graphics, promising experiments, and hype. What I found was anything but hype: I found solid evidence that multimedia is for *now* and will have an enormous impact on many areas of business well within the next three to five years. Hundreds of business case examples show that its use is already widespread. As yet, though, there's no one exemplar organization or industry in which its use stands out as the basis of new competitive forms and sustained advantage in the way that airline reservations and point-of-sales technology stood out among airlines and retailers.

I hope and believe that I have a reputation for being hype-free in my fifteen books, my public speaking, my management and university teaching, and my consulting across the world. I distrust "the future is now" tone of so much evangelism and technobabble in the information technology field; if anything, I'm biased toward skepticism and caution in evaluating new technology. But as a student of multimedia in business over just the past year, it has become clear to me that multimedia will live up to its claims of great opportunity and impact. And that will be so not because of its eye-catching technological glamour, but because of people.

In some ways, multimedia is a step back, not forward. It steps back to bring into the Information "Age," "Society," or "Economy" (or whatever it's called this week) information in forms natural to human beings. For decades, we have been inundated with more and more "information," essentially a very narrow stream of text and numbers and corresponding analytic tools that crunch and display them. It's information that has been useful but that has required us to learn specific skills to adapt to it. It is *not* innate to the ways in which we wander through our daily living.

Multimedia restores the human dimension to information. We naturally rely on our three-dimensional sight and our acuity of hearing. We use visualization rather than numbers for much of our decision making. We respond rapidly to animation in entertainment and on TV news. So the technology of multimedia, so often striking and dramatic when used to create films and games, is perhaps less immediately striking but certainly more far-reaching in its potential business uses. I am convinced that multimedia will soon be the base for information in organizations and thus must now be at the base of business planning and technology infrastructures. In reviewing all the case examples I could locate in my reading, on the Internet, and in my consulting work, I find four main areas of impact, discussed in the Introduction to this guide: knowledge—rather than information—management, customer interaction, natural decision input, and shared understanding.

This is the third of my "every manager's guide" books published by the Harvard Business School Press. The first was on information technology and the second on business processes; two others, on electronic commerce and the business Internet and intranets, will soon be in press. I write these guides for several purposes. One is to make sure that I keep up with technology, a growing challenge; I believe that if you want to be a great teacher, you'd better be a great student. But my primary reason for writing them is to address what I see as the most fundamental problem in the effective use of information technology: language and shared understanding. Managers simply cannot follow all the jargon and technicalities of the IT field, yet they need a grounding in its main terms and concepts. Too often, though, managers have no idea which terms and concepts matter for their own planning and decision making, and how they are relevant to business. The further technology gets ahead of everyday management understanding, the more managers tune out, despair about keeping up, or feel at the mercy of their consultants, their information systems, or their teenagers. They don't know what they don't know, or why they need to know it. In these guides I provide a map to the territory by highlighting the key concepts and terms, offering plenty of business examples, and focusing on the terms' meaning for business.

Multimedia is the fastest-changing element in an always fast-changing field. There's a lot of jargon associated with multimedia because there's a lot of technology, and the technology changes. Over time, much of today's jargon will work its way into the everyday vocabulary of managers. When the first edition of *Every Manager's Guide to Information Technology* was published in late 1991, for example, many managers were completely unfamiliar with terms such as "Internet," "Windows," or "EDI"—terms that most of them routinely accept and understand today. I work hard to demystify the terminology and relate the technology to the world of management action, and I hope that *Business Multimedia Explained* will help managers keep ahead as multimedia moves into the business mainstream.

Business Multimedia
Explained

Introduction

This is a guidebook to territory as yet unmapped for most business managers: that of information technology's new and accelerating capabilities to process just about any type of media that your ears and eyes can take in and your mind can use. Multimedia in today's business is at about the same stage as personal computers (PCs) in the early 1980s. Relatively few managers realized then what PCs would soon mean for business or how the combination of PCs and telecommunications would reshape customer service and organizational coordination. So, too, most businesspeople may not be aware of just how much and how soon today's multimedia is likely to have similar impacts.

The business effects of multimedia have been less dramatic than the technology itself, which is dynamic and eye-catching, but they are growing rapidly. Here are some representative examples:

- *Multimedia typically cuts training time in half,* while increasing retention of what is learned by 20 to 40 percent. This finding is reported by company after company, reflecting the fact that multimedia is a major resource for building the knowledge-driven, learning organization that just about all commentators see as key to competitive positioning—an organization where education is not a single event but an ongoing commitment. Multimedia tools facilitate self-paced learning at the employee's own location, instead of dependence on travel to teacher-paced classroom programs. Multimedia cuts overall costs by creating systems that can be reused and distributed either on CD-ROMs or over telecommunications networks. More substantively, well-designed video and animation, interaction and simulation, augment learning. In the words of one expert, multimedia lets employees learn by virtually doing, in training programs that look like real work and use real tools that allow learners to see the real consequences of their actions, with the opportunity to repeat that work until they are fully comfortable with and competent at it.

A comprehensive survey of 7,000 people in 50 countries, by the accounting and consulting firm of Price Waterhouse, estimates that, over five years, the cost per learner of audit training dropped from $760 for traditional methods to $106 for multimedia. Storage Technology, Inc., calculates that the annual cost of its training course for field technicians fell from $3.2 million (lectures plus labs) to $1.7 million, and course time per student, from 28 hours over four days to 11.2 hours. Union Pacific Railroad reports that it cut training costs by 35 percent, while reducing training time by 30 percent and increasing student retention by 40 percent. With training budgets in the United States now amounting to over $200 billion, multimedia is clearly a powerful tool for knowledge management and for making knowledge a real business asset.

- *Multimedia greatly facilitates interaction with customers.* In the auto industry, it has contributed to rapid and marked changes in how people buy cars, reducing the dominant role of the dealer and salesperson by making it easy for customers to see before they buy. CarMax, a fast-growing start-up subsidiary of Circuit City, sells used cars via electronic kiosks—private booths with a personal computer, CD-ROM, and telecommunications links—where customers can enter information about the car model and their financing needs. The system prints out photographs and data about cars on the lot that meet their criteria. The entire selling process takes less than two hours on average, with buyers reporting more comfort, satisfaction, and trust than with the typical used-car dealership. Daewoo, the Korean manufacturer, saves 5 percent of the price of a car through not having to pay a commission, by direct selling via multimedia kiosk. Toyota markets a free CD-ROM that provides more vivid information about every model than brochures can; the disk lets potential buyers try out different colors and configurations on the screen. GM has implemented its own multimedia service on the Internet, offering 16,000 pages of information on its cars and linking customers to its car divisions.

In another industry, Florsheim, the shoe retailer, reports that sales per store employee went up 20 percent when it introduced kiosks in 550 stores, starting in 1985. Its Express Shopper lets customers choose from an electronic catalogue of over 400 styles in 24,000 size and width combinations, then order them at the kiosk. Some 30 percent of Florsheim's business is now handled through these new outlets.

- *Three-dimensional computing transforms any area of design* in which visualization, depth perception, and simulation of movement are integral. The designers of the New

Zealand craft that won the America's Cup used it to evaluate over 10,000 alternatives in just two months. Engineers responsible for managing the safety and environmental impact of chemical plants, who used to work with two-dimensional diagrams and computer simulations, backed up by frequent visits to the site and reams of documentation, now bypass all of these. Instead, they use 3-D photographic displays of a plant, built up from a library of camera shots, which allow them to pinpoint the exact locations of specific pipes, joints, and openings. They can electronically "walk" around the plant; the software rotates the selected area, provides close-ups, and shows the effects of changing any component. Wherever visualization is key to analysis and decision making, the increasingly affordable tools of 3-D multimedia allow new ways of simulating and displaying information in more meaningful ways.

- *Virtual reality (VR) software and hardware* create simulations of physical reality that users can enter and interact with as if they were in the real world. Virtual reality enabled McDonnell Douglas engineers to maintain a fighter plane that did not yet exist. They created an animation of the plane from design documents. They used virtual tools to try out maintenance procedures and test virtual equipment. In one instance, the simulation alerted them to problems in removing an engine within a confined space; they redesigned the equipment and now will never encounter the problem when the plane is made operational. Caterpillar uses virtual reality for workers to operate the controls of a simulated backbone forkloader. The company reports that, whereas it took anywhere from six months to a year to build a physical prototype machine for evaluation, designers can create a VR machine in a week. Rolls Royce has replaced models of submarines with VR versions, which engineers can "walk through" to check out design features.

- *Animation gets ideas across quickly and simply,* as its wide use in television news programs and instructional videos shows. It has become a standard courtroom tool for communicating to jurors, who can "see" events rather than merely hear them described. Attorneys can freeze shots, show the implications of, say, a car hitting someone at different speeds, including slow motion, and make evidence concrete to viewers. Animation is widely used in medical and technical training as well. It is communicative, far cheaper and easier to produce than video, and in many instances even more effective than video, in that it strips away extraneous background and detail, and can speed up or slow down time to capture the growth of a city or the flow of traffic through a telecommunications network.

- *Computer-telephony integration (CTI),* the incorporation of telephone functions in personal computer hardware, *meshes the natural information medium of voice with the media of computers.* CTI has enabled an insurance firm to add many features to its customer service systems. Callers can access forms, hear information on the progress of their claims, and have the PC software automatically page specific people to help them. Claims adjusters can phone in reports that are automatically appended to documents, together with handwritten annotations and copies of photographs. These can be automatically accessed by phone and automatically faxed. Phone services become just another type of PC application. The full customer history resides in a multimedia file that can be directly accessed by phone as well as by computer.

- *Every major new development in the Internet since 1994 has been in multimedia.* The Internet, the massive set of telecommunications links and computers to which other networks and computers can connect, is now fully established as the single most widespread and influential information and communication resource in the world. Adding multimedia to its capabilities makes it even more so. The Internet's telecommunications technology allows any computer anywhere in the world to link to any other computer. That is the main reason for its explosive growth. The software technology of the World Wide Web, one of the main services provided through the Internet, provides the vehicle for these computers to organize, access, and share information simply. Until recently, that information was largely in the form of text and numbers, the staple diet of computers. Now, demand and supply on the Internet are rapidly moving to add video, graphics, radio, telephone, 3-D, virtual reality, and every other type of multimedia to its capabilities.

What's Special about Multimedia?

Multimedia is a catchall term for the next major wave of innovation in the *routine* use of computers and telecommunications. Fundamentally, multimedia moves information technology from being limited to electronically processing the type of information that typewriters have been able to process for over a century to *routinely* handling almost the full range of information and communication that humans can experience through sight, hearing, and—though to a far lesser extent and not yet routinely— touch. Multimedia brings to the PC the photographs, VHS-quality video (higher quality is practical but far more expensive), CD-quality music, book illustrations, color pictures, animation, and 3-D depth perception that surround us in everyday life. What it adds to everyday life is that, without the enabling technology of multimedia, all these are available only in a form that does not permit their easy reproduction; their transmission from one location to another; their compact and cheap storage; their editing, augmentation, and even transformation; and their rapid access by anyone.

By so radically expanding the range of information that can be created, communicated, and manipulated, multimedia expands the opportunities for business innovation by at least as much as personal computers and telecommunications networks did in the 1980s. By presenting information in the forms most natural to human understanding—its single most distinctive feature—multimedia goes well beyond anything computers have to date made practical. By making it easier and cheaper to process and share such information, multimedia offers businesses proven opportunities for building and using knowledge, interacting with customers, making effective decisions, and working together to build a shared understanding.

The available price-performance options are now so wide in range that high-quality multimedia systems can be developed on home computers; professional-quality ones, on hardware and software that is well within the budget of even small departments; and Hollywood-quality ones, on the most advanced machines. The capital cost of a professional-level combination of fast PC hardware, the large disk storage needed for multimedia, scanners, color printers, authoring and editing software, video camera, and the add-on hardware needed to speed up processing of video and audio is between $20,000 and $80,000. Top-of-the line multimedia software typically costs just under $3,000. CD-ROMs cost under a dollar to produce in quantity. Development of training programs, electronic customer brochures, interactive kiosk systems, advertising, and the like can obviously be very expensive. One 1995 survey of the cost of multimedia training per minute yielded the following:

Low	Midrange hardware and software, limited size, speed, and resolution of video and audio; limited use of full-motion video; delivered through CD-ROM	$1,000–1,500
Medium	Midrange hardware and software, but with more and higher resolution use of video and more complex interactive menus for the user	$1,500–2,200
High	Professional-studio quality, delivered through CD-ROM or over a network	over $2,200

That means that a typical training program will cost around $35,000 per half-hour, and a customer service interactive system, anywhere from $50,000 to several million dollars. Tulare County in California spent $2.5 million on its Tulare Touch multimedia system for welfare applications. That's obviously expensive, but for many multimedia applications, the payoff comes from the savings *per user.* The larger the base of users—students in training programs, customers, or in this case welfare applicants—the greater the overall benefit, even though that may amount to just a few dollars per person. One example is Storage Technology's saving of $654 in training costs per field technician ($760 minus $106). That may not seem to be much, but it compounds rapidly when 1,500 technicians must be trained every year. In Tulare's case, the savings added up to $20 million a year, and application time has been cut from 2 hours to 15 minutes, with the near elimination of the 38 percent error rate in applications.

Apart from enabling such savings, perhaps most important of all for the future of multimedia is the shifting of much video, publishing, and customer service development from outside agencies into the firm itself and onto the desktop instead of in the studio. Up until now, the use of equivalent media has relied heavily on expert intermediaries; most people do not have the tools or expertise to create their own movies, search the world's libraries for information on individual topics, generate music, improve or edit photographs, or produce their own CDs containing combinations of video, speech, documents, numeric data, and music.

Nor can they interact with photographs, videos, or documents to change colors, clip out sections, remove or add features, or link them together (to create an electronic book, insert a video into a word-processed document, or add voice annotation to an electronic mail message).

Multimedia transforms the creation and use of all the media that have historically required expensive studios. The desktop PC studio is now commonplace. Although managers are still unlikely to produce their own training videos, those who use today's software to produce their own management presentations are already positioned to create more powerful, communicative, and information-rich multimedia presentations with minimal effort. The sales reps who travel with a briefcase full of brochures can carry the equivalent of literally a truckload of material, including videos, promotional material, manuals, photos, and packaged presentations, all on a laptop computer with a built-in CD-ROM drive. Such machines are no longer the Porsches or Maseratis of the PC field, but the Ford Tauruses or Grand Cherokees, a little pricier than compacts but well within the reasonable price for a midrange car.

Companies will still rely on expert intermediaries for their training and marketing videos, which can cost $50,000 to $5 million to produce and edit, but many of those intermediaries will now be on staff. Human resources, finance, marketing, and engineering can and should have their own small teams working on what is now a standard PC application on standard PCs—a training video, Internet Web page design, 3-D engineering simulation, or marketing animation, for instance. These groups can now bring multimedia into the mainstream of the firm's PC use and, over time, into the mainstream of their use of telecommunications networks.

The Need for a Business Map of Multimedia

Multimedia technology obviously creates business opportunities, but it is not in itself the opportunity. It is so recently a practical and cost-effective tool for business use (rather than confined to

Hollywood studios and computer research labs) that there is no reliable *business* map to help orient managers to its impacts and opportunities. Multimedia maps are all technological ones, with plenty of examples of the tools themselves, but mainly used for prototypes or entertainment, the primary application areas of multimedia to date.

Managers have plenty of reason to distrust such maps. Throughout the roughly 30 years in which computers have been an integral part of business operations, and the 20 in which telecommunications has played a growing role in them, technology innovation has too often failed to lead to the business innovation its enthusiasts predicted for it. Time and time again, firms invest heavily in promising new ideas that turn out either to be duds or to take much longer than expected to generate customer demand, organizational value, and economic payoff. Examples are the 1970s forecasts of a cashless society, paperless office, home banking, and artificial intelligence replacing managers' decision making. Twenty years later, progress toward these technology-driven goals has been at most incremental, not the promised revolution.

The gap between technological promise and business payoff is a particular risk with multimedia. The technology is both revolutionary and glamorous; it is designed to be dramatic. For example, images of goods for sale seem to float in the air above the sidewalk in front of a department store in New York. The 3-D displays look realistic and solid. Shoppers have been "bewitched" and "astounded" by them. That's impressive, but what does it mean for advertising in the future? Is this just one of the many multimedia gimmicks that flashy technology offers, or does it signal a long-term change in the role of technology in customer communication?

The same basic question—what does this mean for *business*?—has to be answered convincingly for managers to have any reason to factor the major developments in multimedia into their thinking and planning. Interactive television has to date been the

1990s' equivalent of the paperless office, with billions of dollars invested on the basis of promises of multibillion-dollar returns resulting in over a billion dollars of losses. Will this in the end make home shopping more than a minor niche, or is it a technology solution in search of a problem? Digital video tools have transformed the economics, production, and even content of film making. *Jurassic Park* set a new standard for special effects, generated and processed by multimedia software and hardware. *Toy Story* created a new medium of full length 3-D animated films. *Forrest Gump* created the illusion of large crowds from multimedia processing of images of just a few actors. *Twister* showed that even a film with the thinnest of plots could be a major hit through dramatic multimedia special effects. Less powerful but less costly versions of the technology of digital filming are available for businesses to film their own ads, training programs, investor relations communications, and the like. Virtual reality, morphing, 3-D, animation, and first-rate digital editing tools are now available to businesses large and small. But what business opportunity do they offer? Where, if at all, they will transform customer service, product innovation, and organizational coordination? Will the Internet truly turn out to revolutionize business and society? Do the Internet and CD-ROM mean the slow but certain death of printed books and newspapers?

  In addressing these questions, it isn't enough to focus on the technology itself. What's needed to create a business map of multimedia opportunities is to organize the lessons from experiences in applying the wide range of technologies across a wide range of operational business contexts in *real* organizations, not labs and prototypes. This may run the risk of overlooking a breakthrough new technology, but it has the advantage of showing, not claiming, the impacts of multimedia. I've read at least 2,000 articles, cases, surveys, and books on multimedia over the past year, trying to tease out from them evidence of business impact. I've looked for common patterns across organizations, industries and technologies and have found four that comprise the basis of a business mapping of multimedia. I use these four categories as the basis in the Glossary for assessing the likely impacts of emerging and new technology. My logic is first to make sense of the business impacts and then to use that knowledge to make sense of the implications of existing, emerging, and new technology.

Mapping the Business Opportunities of Multimedia

The four categories of opportunity are knowledge management, customer interaction, natural decision input, and shared understanding.

These four categories are just that—opportunities. Realizing the opportunity is not a technical issue, but one of business leadership and innovation, backed up by technical expertise. These are not futuristic concepts, but proven applications of multimedia, based on established technology. As the technology improves in cost and performance, the opportunities become easier to turn into cost-effective implementation.

Knowledge Management

Knowledge is information put to use. Multimedia offers the opportunity to manage knowledge rather than just information. Fundamentally, multimedia is about making information natural by appealing to our senses of sight, hearing, and touch. Historically, computers have limited information to that to which our *intellects* can respond. By making information more naturally absorbed and by extending the types of information that can be captured, stored, and communicated, multimedia marks as radical an advance in the value of information technology as personal computers were to centralized mainframe computers.

Knowledge is the currency of business in a time of change. Companies recognize that learning, adaptation, speed, and flexibility are critical to organizational success. We talk routinely about the learning organization, but information technology is not routinely seen as part of building it, because "knowledge" and learning haven't been embodied in our computerized information systems. It is estimated that less than 2 percent of the basic information used in a company is stored on computers. The rest is in filing cabinets, on paper, and in people's heads. *If multimedia raised that figure from just 2 percent to just 4 percent, a very practical target today, or 10 percent, a very practical target five to ten years out, think of what it could mean for managing knowledge as a corporate asset.*

Information is not at all the same as knowledge, but it enables knowledge. As many people have commented, our society is flooded with information that we don't know how to access or use. Adding more information may not add more knowledge. However, adding more information *in the form most natural to human understanding* may help people to build knowledge. Multimedia definitely reduces the time and effort needed to interpret many types of information. By including documents, video, and audio in the range of information that PCs can easily and quickly access, it also immediately extends the 2 percent of information available for building and sharing knowledge. Some of the business leaders mentioned here have been those insurance companies that are the most customer focused. For these firms, customer service is not the complaints department; responsive customer claims processing is the basis of service and personal interaction. These companies were pushing the edge of multimedia technology before the term came into vogue and before the available tools matured enough to merit their own label. USAA, an insurance company, was the first firm to use scanners to incorporate any type of document, including handwritten letters, in the files that captured the entire customer relationship. Progressive Insurance used mobile vans, radio communications, computers, cameras, scanners, and audiotapes to speed up claims processing, to the extent that on occasion it has issued a payment check to the policy holder as the damaged car was being towed away.

Through its use of *hypertext* and *hypermedia*—tools that link one piece of information to other relevant information items stored on other computers—multimedia helps people make much more effective use of all the information available to them. By making it easy and cheap to browse through large volumes of information, it encourages exploration that might be possible but not practical otherwise. CD-ROMs are an example. People who wouldn't think of buying every telephone directory in the United States in order to track down old high school friends don't have to take this expensive and active a step. They can instead, for around $15, buy a CD-ROM containing every phone number in the country. They may leave it unopened for months and then, any day they feel like it, start playing around with it.

The success of the World Wide Web shows how thirsty people are for information they can assimilate and use, and how wide a market there is for communication and the building of new electronic communities. One of the most interesting aspects of the Internet phenomenon is that its explosive growth has come almost in spite of the technology, rather than because of it, in the sense that it is slow and unreliable, with constant electronic traffic jams. But millions of new users put up with its aberrations because it provides something of great value to them. The very same communities have been unresponsive to many other far more "elegant" technologies because they don't see the value of those technologies.

Much of this value comes from telecommunications. The growing reach of networks across the organization and to the outside world make information easily shared. The explosive growth of the Internet and the equally rapid use of its technology within companies ("intranets") demonstrate the role of networks as the information carriers of our age. Networks move information. Multimedia humanizes it. It also augments much of the everyday media we use. Videos capture reality; virtual reality simulates it and even creates realities that may never exist in the real world. Photos capture images; software tools for morphing, 3-D, and animation take those same inputs and create entirely new ones.

Perhaps the single highest-payoff opportunity of multimedia in the area of knowledge management lies in training. Study after study comes up with the same conclusions: multimedia halves training time and increases retention by around half. Five years ago, the investment needed was too much to justify even these impressive benefits. Now, the investment is on the desktop computer, not in an outside studio.

Such innovations are providing substantial contributions to building the type of organization that companies see as the blueprint for success in the 1990s and beyond—customer centered and built on communication and learning, with a labor force slimmed down by the downsizings of the past few years but leveraged by training, technology, focused management, and true empowerment. The technology of multimedia is proven and getting cheaper and more powerful every few months. If the old adage that knowledge is power is to become a truth rather than a truism, multimedia will be a cornerstone of knowledge management.

A Caveat: Knowledge and Information Fallacies

Multimedia brings information to people in forms that are natural for them to assimilate and respond to, because it so directly corresponds to the media of our everyday life and to our innate senses. This naturalness can help build knowledge and expertise. *This is not the same as just bringing information to people.* For businesses to get value from multimedia, they need to avoid the knowledge fallacy: that information directly translates to knowledge. It underlies phrases such as "the Information Superhighway," "the Information Age," and "the Digital Society." The knowledge fallacy is very similar to the information fallacy that did so much damage to the credibility of the management information systems (MIS) profession in the 1970s. That fallacy holds that data translate directly to information. The data processing (DP) field renamed itself MIS in the 1970s and used the power of its centralized computers and transaction processing systems—payroll, accounting, sales, and inventory—to produce voluminous reports. The DP field assumed that the data in those systems constituted the base for management information, which they saw as their organizational mission; hence the widespread adoption of MIS as their signal of identity. The academic journals, professional societies, and leading conferences reflected this: *MIS Quarterly* was through the 1980s a leading journal partially funded by the business Society for Information Management, for instance.

MIS too often turned out to have little to do with management or information, and far more to do with accounting and data. It provided detailed historical reports about internal operations but could not provide more useful external competitive news, customer feedback, or reports customized to individual users' needs. Generating information of real value in management planning and decision making came from new tools of (1) computer terminals with software that accessed the data on central "host" machines and manipulated it to turn it into information—data with meaning—and (2) PCs, which both transformed the costs of information management and provided user-friendly software that removed the need to rely on expert intermediaries, such as systems analysts and computer programmers. We are now an information-rich society as a result.

Are we a knowledge-rich society, though? Companies are recognizing that just providing information is not the same as creating knowledge or turning knowledge into expertise. People do that, helped by training, experience, support, and reward. Data are not information. Information is not knowledge. Knowledge is not professional expertise. Data enable information. Information enables knowledge. Knowledge enables expertise. Knowledge management is thus the link between the information resources that an organization can build and how it uses those resources to help grow professional expertise. If the learning organization, empowerment, teams, and the like are to be more than just slogans, companies must exploit the sequence of adding value: that sequence builds from data to information to knowledge to expertise.

Multimedia can amplify *all* the links in this chain. Its technology allows cost-efficient generation and processing of data that previously could not be handled in digital form; video is an example. This in turn allows firms to expand the range of information they can include in their information technology base, gathered from a range of external and internal sources. The multimedia presentation of information in visual, tactile, and auditory form makes it easier for people to derive knowledge from it; the widely reported halving of training time and increase in retention are evidence of this. Giving capable people the best information in the best form for them to use it in their work gives them the best chance to build new expertise.

Most of the discussion of multimedia today focuses on the data element in the data to information to knowledge to expertise value chain, mainly because it is the liberating and enabling force. It is liberating in the sense that it removes the many constraints on the creation, storage, and movement of data and hence on its use of data to provide information. It's enabling in that it makes practical and cost-effective (the two are obviously not equivalent) many business and organizational innovations. It is the astonishing and increasing data capabilities of multimedia that create the technical opportunity to transform information management. It is management and worker acumen that will exploit this information opportunity to create knowledge and then apply that knowledge, but they need the data in the first place to turn the opportunity into payoff.

That opportunity is sitting there waiting for the firms that can grasp it. Today, multimedia is discussed mainly in terms of data—the raw processing capabilities of the technology. Many of the terms and concepts defined and discussed in the Glossary address these capabilities. Without these purely technical enablers, multimedia is impractical or even impossible. Each innovation in the technology is fundamentally an innovation in data handling. Each

Mgmt makes it happen

innovation in its use is just as fundamentally one of using the information multimedia provides from the data to build knowledge and expertise. The link from technology to use is not automatic. That means that the wonders of multimedia will not automatically generate value; management does that.

② Customer Interaction

Customer contact—advertising, selling, education, service, and support—is a process of interaction. Just about any mode of human interaction is obviously enhanced by shifting from the impersonal, abstract, and artificial to their opposites. Because multimedia reduces the cost of creating and accessing the natural media of everyday life, such as videos, photographs, sound recordings, animations, and so on, it has opened up many ways of interacting with customers, whether through electronic catalogues, low cost CD-ROMs packed with interactive information on products, or more complex and uncertain new shopping and information channels, such as the Internet.

The basic logic of multimedia for customer interaction is "show," not "tell"—show the product, let people select what to look at, and give them the opportunity to ask their own questions and get answers in the form of videos, photos, animations, and the like, instead of just words. Let them then interact with your sales staff with clear pictures in their minds of what they want and what they will get.

Despite the growing successful uses of multimedia for customer interaction, there are so many innovations that have failed to generate payoff that it is clear there is no guaranteed road to success. The allure of the Internet and interactive television as electronic channels for selling goods and services faded quickly when an encouraging 2,000 accesses to the information per day resulted in a discouraging 20 orders (the Internet). Instead of the heady predictions of interactive TV's generating profits of $8 to $10 billion by 1990, the accumulated losses were over $1 billion.

There are, though, enough successes for many lessons to

be learned from the growing numbers of firms that use multimedia to interact with customers, not just broadcast to them. Kiosks, for instance, help customers explore options and information *before* interacting with sales staff. *Skilled* development of interactive menus on the Internet's World Wide Web provides customers with contact with knowledgeable staff, something too often missing in large, warehouselike retail stores. As mentioned earlier, multimedia is a major force in the ongoing and rapid transformation of car sales. Early 1996 saw a flood of articles in such publications as *Business Week, Fortune,* and *The Wall Street Journal* talking about the inevitability of the collapse of the dealer as the controlling channel. The theme emerging from these articles is that customers find the interaction with the new channels, of which multimedia is a core component, much better: simpler, less worrisome, faster, and under their control, not the salesperson's.

Examples of the payoff from providing customers with multimedia kiosks have been given earlier in this introduction—Florsheim's estimated 20 percent increase in sales productivity, Daewoo's saving 5 percent commissions on car sales, and CarMax's creation of an entirely new way of selling used cars. To this may be added Consumers' Catalog Showroom, which reports a 50 percent increase in accessories purchased with items such as cameras—all as a result of kiosks. The system allows people to locate specific products by name, shows pictures and videos, and identifies alternatives. Once the sale is made, it suggests add-on accessories, such as film, tripods, and filters to go with the camera.

Over time, multimedia will obviously have major impacts on the core of customer interaction: advertising. So far, though, large firms that have rushed onto the Internet to set up World Wide Web sites have been disappointed by the results. Simply providing electronic versions of corporate public relations handouts and static on-line ads is not at all the same as customer *interaction*. Smaller firms have shown that, by focusing on a two-way dialogue with customers rather than providing a passive one-way information flow, they can generate incremental revenues, albeit relatively small ones. For example, Virtual Vineyard, one of the best-known successes in selling over the Internet, offers customers a variety of discussion groups, facilities for sharing evaluations on the wines they purchased from the firm, and on-line lessons from experts about wines. Ford and Volvo have set up Internet sites where people can evaluate their products and provide input about designs. Multimedia is only a small element of these and similar services; it is the interaction, not the media, that seems to explain their successes and other firms' relative failures.

Natural Decision Input

The limitations of computer information mean that, in many instances, when decision making would naturally benefit from visualization, only numbers are available. Foreign exchange trading rooms are packed with screens showing changing exchange rates; traders really want to see how the market is moving. In one bank, the numbers are displayed literally in the air, as three-dimensional graphs dynamically animated with highlights of color and movement. Our everyday world is naturally three-dimensional, but engineers and designers who rely on CAD/CAM simulations (computer-aided design and manufacturing) have been limited to a 2-D flatland. Multimedia makes these three-dimensional—and more natural.

Multimedia facilitates visualization, through animation, 3-D graphics, virtual reality, interactive video, and fast display of graphical information as part of decision processes. Visualization is central to everyday human thinking and to synthesizing large volumes of data. In engineering, medicine, foreign exchange trading, facilities planning, real estate, and many other areas, the old adage that "A picture is worth a thousand words" becomes "A multimedia organization of pictures, words, animation, movie, and sound can be worth a thousand pictures, graphs, tables of numbers, and words." It is for this reason that animated simulations are being used more and more (and more and more controversially) for reenacting events in court cases to help jurors assess evidence. Three-dimensional graphics and simulation are of growing value in design and engineering. Visualization through multimedia is becoming important to financial traders, who are using it to organize the welter of numbers that flows across the foreign exchange, securities, and bond markets, in order to better see market patterns and movements in a business where 20 seconds may see a shift that demands immediate decisions.

It is only within the past few years that computers have supported visualization at all, through software that can turn spreadsheets into graphs and wordy transparencies into color presentation graphics. Multimedia offers a step-shift improvement in every area of information management relevant to visualization, making it the base for the next generation of decision support, executive information, simulation, and modeling systems. You can guess at the difference between the systems of today and just five years from now if you can find in your files a management presentation from five years ago. It's almost certain to have been a black and white collection of bullet points, shown on transparencies. Today's equivalents are almost certain to be in color and much more graphical; they may include "clip art" symbols or use one of the slide layouts provided by such graphics presentation packages as Microsoft's PowerPoint. Five years ago, a top-quality presentation meant paying an outside company $20 to $50 each for 35-millimeter slides. Now, it more often means displaying your PowerPoint slides from a laptop computer.

Look ahead five years. The differences will be at least as great. Obviously, just as color, clip art, and transition effects—fade ins, zooms, and the like—are sometimes used as gimmicks and can detract from the ideas, multimedia may often be used to dress up a poor presentation by adding garish overkill. However, just as the color graphics of today's management presentations are more communicative, memorable, and meaningful than those of the black-and-white word era, multimedia will add to the communication of meaningful information that is a foundation for effective decision making.

In manufacturing, there have been many successful uses of multimedia to help technicians diagnose problems. Xerox's General Fault Analysis system walks them through the process of analyzing electronic faults, with schematic diagrams, scripts, photos, and video clips on what to do and when. Nortel, the telecommunications equipment manufacturer, uses a multimedia system that shows technicians which tools to use in handling delicate microelectronic components, how to position them, and even what hand motions to make. Technicians can repeat the video clips and call up more detailed diagrams. One interesting common feature of the many multimedia systems of this type is their multiple uses, as well as multiple media. They are used in training as well as decision support. AT&T can't train its 2,000-specialist staff in how to manage blackouts by using live equipment, so they used to fly them into corporate headquarters. Now, they train by using a diagnostic multimedia system that breaks problems down into dozens of subtasks and provides instructions on what to do. Alyeska, an oil pipeline company, uses a comparable multimedia system to prepare staff to deal with leaks and fires—which valves to open and close and which alarms to set off.

Many of the systems used for such internal training and decision-making help are being given to *customers* to use. The Nortel system has been modified so that technicians on customer sites can handle their own diagnostics and limited repairs. This eliminates dependence on Nortel's own staff, who must travel to the customer's location, speeds up diagnosis and repair, and of course saves money for both Nortel and the customer. In many instances, multimedia itself is being used to augment decision analysis. McCaw Cellular's service staff troubleshoots phones over the phone by playing audio tones digitally stored on their workstation until the customer recognizes the sound that indicates the problem. They can then provide the customer with information about how to solve it.

Shared Understanding

When people meet to collaborate or form teams, some of their main tools for working together are blackboards and pencils. When you try to explain your ideas, you are likely to reach for a piece of paper or a restaurant napkin on which to sketch a diagram. However much you may read the newspapers, it's CNN news or CBS's *60 Minutes* that you most often remember. You ask friends, "Did you *see*...?" Multimedia can greatly improve shared understanding through shared seeing, as a group of citizens and town planners together watch a visual simulation of traffic flows through a planned shopping mall; as customers and marketing staff work with engineers by "driving" a new car on the screen; or as executives present their plans to an audience of financial analysts or staff through video, animation, and sound. Two minutes of a video of customer comments plus animated product photographs and video simulations of new stores may immediately bring to life a lengthy market survey report, for instance.

The use of animation in court cases, mentioned earlier, illustrates the value of multimedia in creating shared understanding. In 1985, it cost around $250,000 to produce a five-minute animated video simulation of some event that was acceptable as evidence. Now the cost is just $5,000. Think of yourself listening to an attorney describe what happened in an accident in a hotel diving pool (a real case in which animation played a major role). You hear from the plaintiff's counsel how the diving board was too short, so that when his client slipped as she was making her dive, she caught her head against the side of the pool. The defense counters that she could have fallen this way only if she were fooling around. Counsel for the plaintiff argues that, if she slipped as she were about to tuck up her knees and roll forward, her panicked effort to recover her balance would have thrown her body weight back and to the side. Other points of contention concern the design of the pool and access to it, mistakes made in pulling her out, and the nature of her injuries.

The actual animation in this case was built up from photographs and videos of other people diving from the board. It simulated the client's dive, as well as what would have happened had the board extended farther out. It showed how the gap in height between the edge of the pool and the water contributed to her neck's being paralyzed as a result of how she was pulled out. The animation gave jurors a clear illustration of both the accident and what might otherwise have happened if the pool and board were designed differently. They had a common and concrete set of images in their minds, and the attorneys had equally concrete images to show in support of their own arguments. It is difficult for ordinary people to envision such a situation from words alone; the animation did the work for them. The power of such animations is so strong, in fact, that some jurists are concerned that simulations confer "pseudomemories" on jurors, giving them the feeling that they witnessed the event and that this can be the source of shared *mis*understanding. That concern acknowledges the effectiveness of this multimedia tool (the woman won her case).

Another striking example is a government agency's "morphing" photographs of children who have been kidnapped or reported missing when they were very small. In this instance, photographs of a very small child plus those of parents and siblings were morphed to show what the child was likely to look like 10 or more years later. In one instance, in which the morphed photo directly led to a child's being located by an immigration official who recognized the likeness, FBI agents wanted to know how the agency had gotten the photo; it was so accurate they were convinced it was real.

In many areas of business, effective understanding between salesperson and client or between designer and producer similarly rest on each being sure that the other has a clear picture of what is involved. If you look at the ads in suburban newspapers, you will find more and more landscape gardeners offering multimedia simulations. They take a photograph of a home using a digital camera like the ones offered by many consumer electronics firms such as Canon and Sony and overlay on it photographs of plants and trees the customer is interested in. Denmark's largest real estate firm similarly uses a multimedia personal computer to enable customers to browse through its listing of available houses. Customers can look at interior and exterior photographs, location on maps, and floor plans. One executive comments that, without the system, potential buyers typically look at 15 houses before deciding to buy. With it, they look at 7 or 8. The company has reduced its overhead while increasing sales by 50 percent; the executive directly attributes this to the multimedia system.

Similarly, a sporting goods retailer uses a multimedia expert adviser to help a customer select the right-size tennis racket and the right grip; that choice significantly affects a player's performance but is often made on the basis of either a sales rep's recommendation or an uninformed response to the look and feel of a racket. The multimedia system analyzes the customer's replies to 10 questions and then demonstrates via video 5 recommended models from a database of over 100 from all manufacturers.

Summary: The Business Opportunity Checklist

In all these examples of knowledge management, customer interaction, natural decision input, and shared understanding, two distinctive features of multimedia emerge: simulation and a common base of images. *Simulation* has always been one of the main tools that modern computing uses to facilitate *what if?* analyses. Examples are the use of spreadsheets for evaluating the impact of higher interest rates, sales volumes, or price changes, and the widespread reliance on CAD/CAM modeling in manufacturing design. Multimedia is a natural extension of these, which goes beyond them in the variety of what it can simulate and how that simulation can be presented. The core of its presentation is sensory, rather than intellectual. The sensory element of multimedia is most often exploited for games and entertainment: virtual reality, 3-D, animation, and the addition of music and vivid images. *Images* are thus the core of shared understanding in simulations, in the types of diagnostic and training systems described above, and in the tools used for customer interaction. With games and entertainment, the goal is often to invent a new sense of reality; films like *Terminator, Jumanji,* and *Jurassic Park* are striking examples. For business, the opportunity is not to invent a reality but to communicate a sense of a reality relevant to the business *purpose,* whether it be knowledge management, customer interaction, or another goal.

Viewed in this light, all the multimedia technologies in all their applications open up business opportunities. The morphing tools used in *Terminator* to turn human flesh into flowing metal can also be used to simulate what a patient's face will look like after plastic surgery, what a missing child looks like now, or how a chemical reaction will affect materials. The animation tools of *Jurassic Park,* scaled down in power and cost, can simulate what it would feel like to work in a planned new building, so that the client and the designer can communicate with each other about proposed changes. The animations of *Toy Story* point toward low-cost training program material that can get ideas across easily and quickly. The virtual reality tools that create games like *Starwave* can also create down-to-earth simulations of backhoe loaders and submarine interiors.

The very flashiness of much multimedia and its heavy focus on entertainment gives it both an immediacy and a distance. The immediacy lies in its vividness, which can also obscure its business potential. Most of my examples of successful company applications of multimedia are in no way as glamorous and exciting as *Jurassic Park;* many are quite boring—training programs, kiosks in shoe stores, and diagnosis of cellular phone problems. In the short term, multimedia dominates awareness through the drama of its technology and its entertainment focus. In the long term, it is equally easily seen as a "gee-whiz" development that points the way toward a brave new cyberworld.

The management challenge in handling multimedia as a business resource is less the short term or the long term than the intermediate term—in particular, the three- to five-year time span between being there when demand takes off and either moving too early and ending up at the famous "bleeding edge" of information technology, or moving too late and being forced into a catch-up position by competitors. The short-term approach is simply to be opportunistic. Because there is no clear basis today for targeting multimedia opportunities, most companies' pilots and applications are fairly ad hoc. They are unlikely to get out on an expensive limb by moving too early, but they are also unlikely to locate more than obvious, small-scale opportunities. For the long term, it seems reasonable to assume that, at some stage, interactive television, home shopping, home banking, the Internet, and other telecommunications and multimedia vehicles will substantially change business and society. That assumption either pushes toward the ambitious investments of firms such as Bell Atlantic and Time Warner in interactive TV or toward a wait-and-see approach—wait until someone else provides the market and then follow as fast as is practical.

The intermediate-term strategy requires making decisions now in order to get value soon, carefully piloting technology and applications where needed, but within the framework of the wider business opportunity map. Piloting the technology for its own sake just to see what happens is the more reactive, short-term approach. On page 28 is my own simple checklist grid for identifying high-payoff opportunities for multimedia, based on the four areas of business opportunity I've identified. Take any key operation, activity, decision process, customer service or management responsibility in your organization, and jot down a simple yes-no classification in the grid. I suspect that you'll be surprised at how many yesses there are.

The Multimedia Opportunity	The Business Opportunity			
	Knowledge management	Customer interaction	Natural decision input	Shared understanding
The ability to visualize information is key.				
Effective interpretation of information is enhanced by how it is presented.				
The more variety of information you have access to and the more you browse it, the better job you can do.				
How information is displayed affects your willingness to look at it.				
Multimedia can change the economics of the creation, access, movement, storage, and manipulation of information essential to this activity.				
Presentation is key to communication of *substantive* meaning.				

Wherever there is a match between the columns of this checklist that identify areas of business opportunity and the rows that identify the relevance of multimedia, this is a multimedia opportunity.

The Role of the Internet in Multimedia

From E-Mail to Multimedia: The Evolution of the Internet

It is nearly impossible today not to include the Internet in any discussion of computers and telecommunications. It is also hard to sort out likelihood from fantasy and claim from reality in evaluating its current and potential impacts on business, politics, society, and individuals. The Internet was for decades a specialized network used only by academics and researchers, who had to understand its complex and cumbersome procedures for accessing services. In a very short time, it has been transformed into something for use by anyone, anywhere, for nearly anything any computer can handle. And that transformation is accelerating.

Initially, the main uses of the Internet by its community of academics and technical professionals were electronic mail, online discussion groups, and sharing of computer files, such as research data, draft publications, and library resources. When individuals and organizations began to use it on personal computers, electronic mail became by far the largest use, followed by the World Wide Web. Internet e-mail allowed PC users to contact anyone else on the Net, no matter what their country or their PC. Hitherto, electronic mail systems were limited in reach, with each service a bounded community and private facility, not open to the general public. By 1995, Web usage had overtaken all other Internet services combined. The Web provides a simple means of organizing and displaying information. Initially, that information was largely static text with low resolution graphic images, such as photographs. Very rapidly, a variety of forces shifted the Web to multimedia, not text. Those forces included the demand for pornography and music, the need for companies advertising on the Web to differentiate their own home pages from the hundreds and thousands that look just like theirs, and PC users' expectations for multimedia. CD-ROMs have provided them with a

Java. 3-D

growing range of multimedia information and entertainment, as well as innovations in Internet technology, including almost free worldwide phone calls, radio, and a software development programming language called Java that, among many other features, has made it practical to incorporate three-dimensional graphics into the previously two-dimensional Web page. Other technical developments include the provision of features for virtual reality on the Web, improved security, and user-friendly browser software—most notably, Netscape's Navigator.

All these open up the multimedia opportunities of the Net. The Internet is *essentially* multimedia in conception and in evolution. It has only gradually become multimedia in implementation. The reason for this is that, for reasons explained later in this Introduction and illustrated throughout the Glossary, multimedia data require exponentially more digital bits to code and format information, such as video and high-resolution photographic images, and to reproduce audio, including speech and music, than is needed to handle the numbers and alphabetic characters that have for decades been the main medium of computers.

Prices are falling so rapidly that, for just about every element of multimedia, there is a spectrum of choices, from less than a thousand dollars up to many thousands, with the cheapest offering adequate performance and the best offering professional level multimedia. The PC world is thus already multimedia. The blockage to the Internet being so is the slow telecommunications speeds to which the majority of World Wide Web users have access. They dial up an Internet "node" over the public phone system. The highest speed available without investing in special services and equipment is the equivalent of moving a single typewritten page (28,800 digital bits) per second, and many PCs are limited to half a page per second. The practical upper limit on nondigital public telephone lines is just 56,000 bits per second. To put that in context, whereas a simple electronic mail message can be sent and received in a few seconds at these speeds,

Not w/ RealAudio

including telecommunications overhead, it can take 15 minutes to several hours to download video and music clips over the Internet.

Business Multimedia Explained is not about the Internet. Multimedia is much more far-reaching, even if the Net does become its main delivery mechanism. I include the Internet as an emerging business multimedia resource that is fundamentally multimedia in nature, development, application and user interests. Until users can routinely get at least the speeds of 5 pages per second (128,000 bits) provided by the integrated services digital network (ISDN) service, which, after 20 years local phone companies are making widely available, the Internet will not be *basically* multimedia. When they can, then it will be so, for the simple reason that just about every driving force of supply and demand is pushing in that direction. Advertisers want to use graphics and video to get their message across, and Net surfers of every description want music, video, photos, maps, animation, and 3-D as well as text and numbers. (ISDN, described in the Glossary, is an intermediate speed transmission technology, defined in the 1970s but only gradually rolled out by local phone companies. It fills the gap between today's slow analog phone lines and the emerging high-speed digital links that will use television cables, fiber optics, and special software to provide transmission rates hundreds and even thousands of times faster.)

A key assumption underlying this Glossary is that the "when" of the telecommunication capabilities needed for the Internet to move from caterpillar to multimedia butterfly is "very soon." The year 1995 showed the demand and fragmented improvement in supply; 1996 has seen expansion of supply. By 1999 at the latest, it seems certain that most businesses and consumers will be using the Internet predominantly as a multimedia resource.

On page 32 is a simplified summary of the evolution of the Internet and the forces moving it; it shows the mainstream of Internet technology and use over the past two decades.

Early Internet	Mid-1980s	Early 1990s	Mid-1990s	Now	Soon
Telecommunications	Special nets provided by government agencies sponsoring research	Consolidation of separate nets through a shared "backbone" analogous to the interstate highway system	Expansion of reach and upgrading of capacity	Dial-up access and links to Net from on-line information services, such as America Online and Intranets	Wireless, ultrahigh-speed transmission links, cable modems
User hardware	Workstations, specialized hardware devices	Workstations and PCs with specialized software	Business PCs with networked multimedia	Consumer PCs with multimedia chips built in	Low cost Internet "appliances"
User software	Technically focused UNIX systems*	Electronic mail	World Wide Web Internet browsers	Internet browsers with security, Java**	Internet browsers that are full operating systems
Knowledge required	Computer scientist level knowledge of basics	PC expertise, telecommunications basics	PC expertise	Commonsense PC level	Internet and multimedia savvy
User community	Technical researchers and graduate students	General academic community	Entire school population and technical businesspeople	Anyone, anywhere, but within limited demographics	International, anyone, anywhere, with any level of PC
Main uses	E-mail and file sharing	E-mail, file sharing, and information search	Net "surfing," discussion groups	Surfing, sex, education, company PR, advertising, news	Virtual reality, intranets, financial transactions
Driving trends	Graduate student creativity	Research and telecommunications innovation	PCs and Web	Easy-to-use browsers, press, critical mass of users, intranets	Multimedia (tools for 3-D, virtual reality, animation), Internet radio, music widely used

* UNIX is the software operating system that is to technical users of computers what Windows is to most PC users.
** Java is the computer programming language that has redefined the possible direction of both the Internet, the mainstream of PCs, and the competition between Microsoft and the rest. It is discussed in the Glossary.

Some of the general trends in the evolution of the Internet that are most relevant to business are:

- *Telecommunications.* The Internet is not a network or even a network of networks—as it is frequently described. It is now the main traffic hub for any network to link to. That means that such on-line information services as America Online (AOL) and Microsoft Network are Internet "gateways" and that more and more companies use the Internet as a means of creating their own intranet internal network services. The usefulness of all these is paced mainly by the speed of telecommunications transmission available through their own part of this complex and by the reliability and traffic capacity of the Internet components.

- *User hardware.* Today, the main vehicle for accessing Internet services is a PC. The variety of services depends on the features of the PC operating system and on hardware performance and capacity. The next likely wave of innovation will be in reducing the cost and complexity of the access tools, with many firms in 1996 launching low cost Internet "appliances" ranging from specialized, stripped-down PC-type machines to attachments to television sets to game machines adapted for Internet use. Their goal is a system that retails for $500. The success or failure of these appliances is a major competitive issue for the entire computer industry for the coming years.

- *User software.* More and more software is being designed to provide access to the Internet, to design Web pages, and to include multimedia. Ease of use is the primary driver of innovation here. Today, Windows, the main operating system on PCs, is a computing environment into which Internet features can be fitted. Thus Netscape, the main Internet software browser, runs under Windows (as well as under all other major operating systems). Within a few years, it will be close to impossible to distinguish the Internet browser from the PC operating system.

- *Knowledge required.* Browsers and the World Wide Web have humanized the Internet and simplified the previously complex and cumbersome procedures involved in using it. Today, anyone with basic PC skills can use the Web, Internet e-mail, and on-line information systems that link to the Net, such as AOL. As more and more of the Web shifts to multimedia, there will be a period during which users will need to build a new level of comfort and understanding of multimedia tools. That transition may be difficult, as multimedia hardware is often complex to install and operate, and multimedia software demands new skills. Today, there are plenty of simple software tools to help individuals design their own Web pages, for instance. There are also more and more tools coming onto the market for adding 3-D, video, and virtual reality to those pages. Those tools are far more complex to master, however.

- *User community.* The demographics of the Internet are not yet representative of the wider society. The majority of users remains male, professional, academic, and technical, though more and more women are moving onto the Net. An October 1996 Louis Harris Poll survey found that twice as many Net users saw President Clinton as doing a poor job compared with a national phone survey. They were six times more likely to think Republicans were doing an excellent job. The main concentration of Internet services and facilities is in North America and Northern and Western Europe. International telecommunications links, intranets, low-cost network appliances, and such on-line services as

AOL are extending the demographics of the Internet. Basically, anyone with above average income who lives in a country where phone service is reliable, modern and cheap is likely to become an Internet user either at home, at work (intranets), or in school.

- *Main uses.* Given the rapid extensions in telecommunications, user hardware, user software, user knowledge, and user community, purely technical barriers to business exploitation of the Internet become fewer and fewer. It is already clear that people will make their own distinctive uses of the Net and that there is no guaranteed mass market, but a wide set of niches. Finding and filling the niches is both the opportunity and the challenge.

- *Driving trends.* It is multimedia that drives now, but electronic mail and the Web that have been the foundation of demand growth. Multimedia is the natural evolution of the Web, improving on everything that the Web now provides: better information display; better graphics; better audio; better options for radio, television, film, and music; better communication of all media via high-speed telecommunications and intranets; better content choices and variety.

The Glossary describes in more detail the main forces and tools behind the shift of the Net to multimedia. The most important of these are the programming language called Java, explicitly designed for the Internet and for multimedia; the next generation of computer chips designed by Intel for multimedia; and, above all, user demand for more graphics, more video, more display, more interaction, more color, and more communication.

The Internet as a Business Resource

Five years ago or even more recently, hardly any business managers had heard of the Internet. Now, hardly any have not.

There's a whole new Internet vocabulary: surfing the Web, cyber-space, home page, Java, Yahoo!, e-cash, Netscape, and many oth-ers. If their firm doesn't already have a home page on the World Wide Web, people inside the firm are sure to be asking why not. If it does have one, they are sure to be asking what comes next. The Internet moved so suddenly out of its long-established aca-demic and technical niche into the world of personal computers that there is little business experience to draw on in defining effective strategies for exploiting it.

The general consensus among business observers is that, to date, successful innovations in marketing, advertising, and cus-tomer service via the Internet have been sporadic, with no critical mass of successes. Expectations of making money through adver-tising, on-line selling, and publishing have not been met. Reve-nues have been small and profits, smaller. Many companies simply put electronic versions of their existing services and informa-tion on the Net, adding them to the literally millions of pages on the World Wide Web. They have found, for example, that "webzines"—Internet magazines—are cumbersome to read on-line and don't meet the preferences of Net users for short snip-pets of information. They have found that Net surfers who have such a proliferation of free information are reluctant to pay even a few dollars for other information. The issue of Internet security has become a growing barrier to people's willingness to give their credit card numbers for Internet payments.

Most of these largely unexpected barriers to business on the Internet may turn out to be just matters of timing. Many smaller businesses have found profitable niches on the Net. There are signs that the big players will learn how to use it as a new base for customer contact, once they recognize that the Net is basically driven by interaction and that the traditional broadcast-your-ad-over-CBS approach is totally unsuited to the Web.

The main news in 1996 was the rapid emergence of intranets: companies using the Net as the base for low cost, easy to develop, easy to use services within their own organizations. This may well be the single most important managerial use of the Net, in that it creates the same democratization and diffusion of information and communication inside the firm that the Net has created for the general population of PC users. Intranets exploit the reach of the Net and its unique technical feature, which allows any computer of any type to communicate with any computer of any other type without either one having to know anything about the other. They use the growing range of Net browsers that make it easy to use the Net, organize Web sites that provide information, and operate the services. They install "firewalls," complexes of hardware and software that ensure security. Examples of intranets are in-house Web pages with information on internal job opportunities, department news, software support, and project coordination.

Eli Lilly, the pharmaceutical firm, illustrates the value of Internet technology for building an intranet. For an expenditure of just $80,000, an entrepreneurial staff member built a system linking 3,000 of the firm's PCs and workstations to access and share information on clinical trials scattered across 120 countries and stored on separate technology bases that could not link to each other. The cost of converting them to a common technical platform was prohibitive, but an intranet allows all these separate data bases to appear as one, via Web pages.

Good intranet example

The Internet is so complex in its many dimensions—technical, social, political, economic, geographic, and demographic, to name just a few—that it is hard to step back and look at it through a business lens. It has become a living organism and a social force, not just a technological artifact. That doesn't in any way mean that the Net will change life as we know it. The aggressively assertive tone that marks many predictions about the Internet usually has little foundation, and much of the discussion is driven by writers' interpretations, politics, wishes, and technical biases rather than by reflective observation and dispassionate analysis. The Internet is a focal point for radicals of every sort. *Details* magazine listed in its November 1995 issue predictions about the telephone made in the late nineteenth century, comparing them with "cyberhype." What's intriguing about the predictions is that they are at the same time both silly and essentially correct. So, too, may cyberhype turn out to be. Here are a few of *Details'* examples:

The Telephone (1890s)	The Internet (1990s)
"All the corners of the earth are joined, kindled, fused. Just as in a theater you speak face-to-face with five or six hundred persons crying with the the same pang of emotion. So the poetical telephone speaks to the whole world—now become a theater—and brings us joy and sorrow, exultation and remorse. And every kind and race of man."	"In cyberspace, we'll be able to test and evolve rules governing what needs to be governed. . . . We are liberated from the tyranny of government, where everybody lives by the rule of the majority."
"More wonderful still is a scheme . . . which looks to provide music on tap at certain times every day, especially at mealtimes. The scheme is to have a fine band perform the choicest music, gather up the sound waves, and distribute to any number of subscribers. . . . We have perfected the distribution and have over a hundred persons who have certified their anxiety to be subscribers."	"There will be little waste, few unsold goods, almost no friction. . . Nothing is illegal because there is no law. . . . The telescreen, the most perfect communicator, is also the most perfect police force."

Cyberhype creates its own backlash, as people tire of all this. Quite a number of managers who were intrigued in 1995 by the possibilities of the Internet, without fully understanding what it is and means, tuned out in 1996. The title of a best-selling book published in 1995 captures the worries of many managers and social commentators about the Internet and multimedia: *Silicon Snake Oil.* The most frequent metaphors for the Internet are not just those of science fiction and "cyberspace," but those of biology and chaos. Two 1996 best-sellers have been *Out of Control: The New Biology of Machines, Social Systems and the Economic World,* written by a strong Internet believer, and *Why Things Bite Back: Technology and the Revenge of Unintended Consequences.* Making predictions about the future of the Internet and its impacts is a mini-industry, with opinions ranging from euphoric optimism to suspicious caution to downright pessimism. Meanwhile, managers have a business to run today.

Overall it's clear that the Internet is an important social force that seems likely to have the same impacts on everyday life as has electricity, the car, television, and the telephone. We now take these for granted, but none of them immediately and completely changed the basics of our society in and of themselves. The Net will not either, though it will quickly generate the equivalent of drive-in movies, "CBS News," obscene phone calls, and Domino's pizza. Obviously, the businesses, political groups, educators, and public sector organizations that best understand and exploit the emerging opportunities of the Internet will create innovations we can't even guess at. In that regard, the hypesters are surely right about its implications. But meanwhile, it's just part of the context of society and thus of change, not the context that will drive them.

One thing I am sure of is the basic multimedia nature of the Internet. That's not hype, just common sense. So, in this guide to multimedia for business managers, I include the Internet as *part* of multimedia. I believe that multimedia is the broader context and that the Internet is an enabler within that context. I believe, too, that skilled business managers can and should absorb both multimedia and the Internet as opportunities to drive change.

The Technology of Multimedia

Making Sense of Multimedia Measurements

What makes multimedia different from other uses of information technology is the number of digital bits involved. A bit is either a 0 or a 1, the fundamental units of coding for *everything* in a computer. Bits are grouped together in groups of eight called "bytes," to code numbers and characters (*1* or *a*, for instance) and in multimedia to code information about a picture or video image ("This next byte defines a pixel—a dot on the PC screen display—

More bits

as color 129"), sound ("this byte shows the pitch and volume of the next note"), and the like. Think of bits as information atoms and bytes as information molecules. Everything in multimedia is measured in bits and bytes.

With numeric and text information (units such as a message, customer number, credit card transaction, airline reservation, or electronic mail message), the number of bits amount to a few hundreds up to a few thousands. Multimedia is very different. Graphic images used in management presentations are coded in just thousands of bits, but high-resolution photos, in millions and full-motion video, in billions. Tricks of the multimedia hardware and software art and trade-offs between quality and storage size and speed of transmission allow you to choose between audio in thousands or millions of bits and video in millions or billions. Multimedia could be redefined as the economics of bits—how many can be processed cheaply and quickly. Until the 1990s, the answer was "a few thousand at a time." Now, it's a few million, and many millions and even billions using emerging high speed telecommunications options and fast computers. Multimedia technology is the management of bits—lots and lots of them.

A major problem in making sense of multimedia is making sense of these measurements. Consider the following (don't let your eyes glaze over—I offer a way to make the figures much more meaningful just a few pages from now):

- *A page of printed text* in a business book is typically equivalent to 3,000 bytes. Although this obviously varies according to page and font size, it's a reliable general estimate. A spreadsheet that takes up 750,000 bytes of data is a very large file for a PC application; it would be something like 1,000 rows and 100 columns in size. An entire 300-page book occupies under 1 million bytes. A straightforward management presentation with 30 color slides, enough for around two hours of nonstop lecturing, requires about 100,000 bytes, unless it incorporates images, in which case each slide may take up 1 million bytes.

- *Software programs* and operating systems typically consume 2 to 40 million bytes. Microsoft Excel spreadsheet application, for instance, takes 5 MB. The programs for Corel Draw, a multimedia package, occupy over 30 MB. The Windows 95 operating system requires 40 to 60 MB.

- A *15-minute video,* which uses only half the available PC display screen and runs at half the speed of full-motion TV-quality transmission: 300 MB (300 million bytes).

- *Full-screen, full-motion video:* 3 GB (gigabytes, or billions of bytes). Showing the movie requires a transmission speed of at least 3 mbps (million bits per second).

- A *professional-quality photograph:* 2.4 mb (million bits).

- A *full-page magazine ad* from a high-quality color image: 7.2 MB (million bytes).

- An image of what is displayed on a *typical laptop computer color screen:* 300 KB (thousand bytes).

This isn't just an issue of size. It obviously takes longer to move a single 2.4-MB photo from disk storage to computer memory, or from a CD-ROM or a scanner that makes a digital image of it, than to move a 20-KB (thousands of bytes) spreadsheet. A standard **CD-ROM** drive moves data at 600,000 bits per second. That means that moving 4 million bytes takes almost a minute.

All this is accurate, but not very meaningful for managers— it's data to them, not information, and it doesn't help them build knowledge of multimedia. What makes things even more difficult is that there is no common base of measurement. **Telecommunications** speeds are measured in bits per second, but the files transmitted are measured in bytes. A thousand bits or kilobits is 1,000, but a kilobyte is 1,024 (because bytes are measured in powers of 2—2^8 is 256, and 1,024 is 2^{10}). The sequence of size and speed goes from single units of bits/bytes; to thousands, or kilo-bits/bytes, shown as kb and Kb; to millions, shown as mega-bits/bytes (mb and MB) and billions (gb and Gb). Subsets of these may be shown in decimals, so that 14,800 bps is 14,800 bits per second. However, it is more likely to be shown as 14.8 kb. Common units of telecommunications speeds are 9.6 kb, 14.4 kb, 28.8 kb, 64 kb, 128 kb, 1.54 mb, 45 mb, and 2.4 gb. Of course, for videoconferencing, you need 384 kb.

Multimedia is fundamentally about the management and transmission of bits and the storage of bytes. As these examples show, there are huge variations in the ranges of each for differ-ent media. Those differences are the key issue in the choice and capabilities of hardware and software. The problem is that the figures often mean very little to managers. The sheer scale makes them rather like units of measurement for astronomical dis-tance. Light travels 186,000 miles per second. That's something we can at least relate to. But how about 11,160,000, 669,600,000, or 16,070,400,000? They are the distances light travels in a min-ute, an hour, and a day. A light year is about 6 trillion miles. If you know that a star is 120 light years away, you have at least a sense of what that means. When I add that another is just 60 light years away, you understand the difference.

In this guide, I've created my own equivalents of light min-utes, hours, and days. Instead of translating the units of informa-tion technology measurement into time equivalents, I use printed page, book, and movie equivalents to make the scales more mean-ingful. My approximations are based on a book's being 300 pages long, with each page having 30 to 40 lines of print and 70 char-acters per line. A movie is two hours long. Obviously, these are not exact measurements, but they give a reasonable sense of relative speed and size, which is what managers need. Because I want this book to be accurate about the technology, I add the exact figures in parentheses. So, for instance, I recast the figures shown earlier in terms of:

	Bits		Bytes		
	Number	Abbreviation	Number	Abbreviation	Unit
Page	25 thousand	25 kb	3 thousand	3 KB	k kilo
Book	7.5 million	7.5 mb	1 million	1 MB	m mega
Movie	25 billion	25 gb	3 billion	3 GB	g giga

I've rounded the figures up and down to make them correspond to units that result in the most comprehensible relative scales. For instance, I could have chosen 24,000 bits as a printed page equivalent, but 25,000 divides more tidily into such units as 1 million (40 page equivalents). I chose 7.5 million bits and 1 million bytes as the measure of a book and 25 billion bits and 3 billion bytes as that of a film, so that all my figures have a common denominator of 3 and 5 and are also fairly easy for you to remember.

Using these measures, here's how I present multimedia telecommunications speeds and storage requirements, rephrasing the examples given earlier:

- A spreadsheet takes up 250 printed pages (750 KB) of data.

- A straightforward management presentation with 30 color slides requires about 30 printed pages (90 KB).

- Software programs and operating systems occupy around 3 to 10 printed books (3 to 10 MB).

- A 15-minute video: 300 printed books (300 MB).

- Full-screen, full-motion video: 120 printed pages per second (3 mbps).

- A professional-quality photograph: $2\frac{1}{2}$ printed book equivalents (2.4 MB).

- A-full page magazine ad from a high-quality color image: 1 printed book (7.2 MB).

- An image of what is displayed on a typical laptop computer color screen: 12 printed pages (300 KB).

I'm not entirely comfortable converting the exactitude of technology to these approximations; it's a little like describing the speed limit as "50 miles per hourish but 70-plus is fine on major highways" or specifying a person's "normal" temperature as "in the 90- to 100-degree range." It is, after all, the precise figures that determine the many technology choices and trade-offs. But to allow managers to make technology decisions without becoming overwhelmed by measurements of bits and bytes, I use page and book equivalents, with exact numbers of bits and bytes in parentheses.

The Technical Foundations of Multimedia

Multimedia *technology* moves forward by combining speed of processing, massive storage capacity, and high-speed telecommunications transmission. Multimedia *usage* moves forward only when that combination leads to easy-to-use software on low-cost hardware via easy-to-access telecommunications services. That movement is becoming increasingly rapid because all the needed technical enablers are progressing together: digitization, chip performance, storage capacity, data compression, and transmission speed in new network services. These are the five basic technical foundations of multimedia. None of them is new; it is their continued and largely predictable pace of change, in terms of raw performance and cost per unit of performance, that drive the market.

Digitization. Digitization is the foundation of computers and modern telecommunications: the ability to represent *any* information as a series of 0s and 1s—digital bits. It has long been *possible* to represent music, video, voice, handwriting, and photographs in digital form. It is now *practical* and *cheap* as well. Video remains the most expensive medium, with tools for developing professional quality still very expensive, but tools for producing and editing VHS-quality tape cost about as much as the PC they are edited on. Once information of any sort is digitized, it can be manipulated by computer hardware and software. That requires masses of processing power and ultrafast speed of data movement between devices such as cameras, computer memory, disk storage, and CD-ROMs.

Chip performance. That power and speed is provided by the doubling of microchip performance every 18 months that has been the case now for over 20 years and continue for the next 20 (although some experts are predicting a slowdown around 10 years from now). Multimedia rests on being able to process digital information as fast as it is needed; for photographs, that may mean in seconds, but for full motion video, it means now. Only in the past 3 years has that been practical within the $5,000 to $15,000 cost range of standard high level PCs. In the past year it has become practical within the $2,000 to $5,000 price range of home and small office PCs (this new market is often referred to in the industry as SOHO—"small office, home office"—and is one of the fastest growing for multimedia). This opens up new options and capabilities at the high end. Yesterday's incredibly expensive multimedia environment is today's $8,000 machine. Today's $8,000 machine is tomorrow's home computer. $8,000 today buys you what was a major capital item 3 years ago. This is not at all "gee-whiz," but the pattern of the past 30 years.

Historically, the main areas of innovation, application, competition, and acceleration in chip price performance have been in the CPU (central processing unit) chips that are the heart of computers and in the memory chips that determine how much storage the CPU has to work with. Fast CPUs slow rapidly, like racehorses trying to run through a hotel, if they don't have immediate access to program instructions and data but must wait while these are loaded into memory from secondary storage, such as a PC's hard disk.

The chips in PCs and larger computers are general purpose ones designed to handle computation and the movement and processing of numbers and text. Multimedia is driven more and more by special-purpose chips specifically designed to mediate between the world of our senses and that of computers. These digital signal processors (Intel's versions are called "native signal processors") are chips that, as their name suggests, convert and process the nondigital signals of voices, music, and the chemical emulsions of photographs into digital bitstreams (DSPs)—flows of electrical pulses that correspond to the 0s and 1s of digital coding. DSPs are crucial to communication between multimedia hardware input and output devices. They are crucial to future competition in the volatile, almost frantically innovative chip industry, with Intel targeting them as a priority for growth—and hence targeting multimedia as a priority opportunity—and companies like Motorola and Texas Instruments positioning for leadership. Intel faces new competitors, too, with AMD the most aggressive and visible. These innovative companies are hardly likely to slow down their innovation and aggression in an era of intensified competition. The doubling of chip performance every 18 months is a historical pattern from which multimedia will continue to benefit.

3. **Storage capacity.** What hasn't been the historical pattern is storage media's keeping up with chip performance. It makes little sense to digitize a video that takes up gigabytes of data if it can't be stored. Whereas spreadsheet and word processing files are measured in thousands of bytes, multimedia files can be many millions, even billions.

The breakthrough in storage has been CD-ROM technology, computer versions of the music compact discs that have displaced long-playing records. Available for a decade, it took off only in the mid-1990s and now is as basic to PCs as hard disks are. CD-ROMs cost less than a dollar to copy, making them the most cost-effective medium today for multimedia. A single CD-ROM disk holds close to 100 printed book equivalents (650 million bytes of data), enough to store an entire encyclopedia set or around 200 high-quality photos. Note the difference. To hear that a single CD-ROM holds the equivalent of a hundred novels impresses most people. To be told that it holds just 200 photos is not at all impressive. Multimedia is counterintuitive in that what

looks small for humans is often giant for computers, and vice) paradox
versa. The same is true for speed and for complexity. Humans
absorb and process pictures quickly. Computers carry out mathematical calculations with ease.

There has been less progress in the storage capacity of hard
disk technology than in that of CD-ROM and related optical
media (so called because they rely on lasers that use light beams,
not on electronics, as their technology base). This is mainly because, unlike chips, which operate in millionths and billionths of
a second (microseconds and nanoseconds), hard disks contain
moving parts that run in milliseconds—the equivalent of 100
years of delay for a nanosecond-speed chip waiting for input. In
addition, the electromechanical nature of hard disks makes it
difficult to pack bits close together. On the other hand, lasers can
mark 0s and 1s on optical storage almost down to the atomic level.

Although optical storage devices offer improved capacity and
speed, they are presently too expensive for most PC users to consider for on-line use. That makes hard disks the most cost-effective
PC on-line storage medium today, with CD-ROMs increasingly
the most cost-effective off-line medium. Hard disks transfer data
faster than CD-ROMs but are more expensive. The cost of storage
per megabyte (million bytes) in early 1996 was around $1 for hard
disk and under 5¢ for CD-ROM.

On-line storage is immediately accessible by the computer's
software. Off-line storage media have to be inserted into a drive.
Floppy disks and CD-ROM are examples of off-line media. A PC
hard disk stores anywhere between 200 book equivalents (200
MB) and 300 (2 GB, or billion). That's a huge amount of storage
for text and numbers, but not much for multimedia, especially if
half the disk is already taken up by software and data files.

Data compression. Data compression eases the storage problem. It typically reduces file sizes by 10 to 80 percent depending
on the nature of the data. Hardware chips or software examines
a stream of bits and uses a wide range of mathematical tricks to
cut down the amount of data that must be passed on to accurately

reproduce the original. So, for instance, when a photograph shows an expanse of white shirt, the chip compresses the signal "Color 123, 123, 123 . . ."to the equivalent of "Next 5,000 pixels (picture elements) are all 123." As well as cutting down on storage requirements, data compression cuts down on transmission time. In the artificial example above, about 10 bits are needed instead of 5,000, an extreme of compression. More typical rates are from 20:1 to 400:1, but every little bit helps.

Transmission speed. Transmission time amounts to waiting time. On the Internet, you use your phone and a modem to input a request to download a file such as a photograph. You wait. The digital coding that represents the original photo moves at gigabit-per-second speeds over the "backbone" network, the Internet equivalent of the interstate highway system, but slows down on your local phone system byway. You wait. You go off to make a sandwich. You come back and wait some more.

More than any other single factor, telecommunications speed can be either the blockage to or the enabler of multimedia use and innovation. If all data sent over telecommunications networks went via today's phone lines, there would be very little on-line multimedia and lots of sandwich making. It doesn't have to be that way and won't be so around five years from now, as fiber optics and digital cable TV links bring high-speed communications into more and more homes. In the past five years, there has been as dramatic an improvement in transmission speeds on business networks as in PC hardware speeds. The local area networks that are the basic building blocks of today's corporate communication systems can move data at printed books—megabits—per second versus the single page per second of the public phone line. You don't have time even to think about what sandwich you want.

Putting it all together. It is the interaction of these five factors, not any one of them alone, that moves computers and telecommunications more and more into multimedia. In other words, multimedia is a natural evolution of the entire information technology field. Digitization allows new forms of media to be handled. Chip performance provides the processing speed and power to handle the huge volumes of bits that this digitization generates. Improvements in storage capacity make it practical to handle them on PCs. Data compression reduces their size, making it cost-effective to store them. Increases in telecommunications transmission speed make it practical to share multimedia files.

Multimedia hardware systems are packed with devices that combine storage and chip speed. There are cards that capture and store an entire TV or video frame (a frame is a single image). They compress it quickly enough to pass it on or display it before the next frame arrives. There are cards that do the same for audio. Some systems offer ultrahigh-quality displays directly equivalent to large-screen TV sets; the extra screen size and its quality and resolution (detail and clarity of image) add to the number of bits required, the speed of the chips required, and the amount of processing involved. The same is true for audio; to get compact disc–quality sound places too much demand on the typical system's storage, speed, and rate of data transfer to be practical; low-cost game machines thus use much lower fidelity.

All the components of a multimedia system must work in concert. The slowest one can become the equivalent of a toll booth on a congested turnpike. At a busy Friday rush hour on the New Jersey Turnpike, it doesn't make any difference if your car can go from 0 to 60 in two seconds; you'll still be traveling at the same average speed as a Yugo or even a pedestrian strolling along the verge of the highway. One key electronic tollbooth is the computer modem that links consumers to the Internet over the public telephone system. Telephone transmission links have until recently been nondigital; they use analog transmission. They send an electronic copy—analog—of the sound wave created by your voice when you speak. A digital transmission link is like a strobe light that pulses 0s and 1s. The faster the strobe, the more data are sent per second. The digital telecommunications systems of today can pulse at hundreds of millions and even billions of bits per second—college libraries a second. At these speeds they keep up with the processing capabilities and storage demands of multimedia.

Businesses routinely have access to such ultrafast transmission. Consumers in general don't. They need a modem in or attached to their PC that converts its digital computer signals to those of an analog telephone line and converts incoming analog signals back. Until recently, the typical transmission speed over a modem was around one-third of a printed page per second (9.6 kb). Half a page is now the standard, and one page is rapidly emerging as the next standard; one and a half pages per second (34.4 kbps) is the practical, cost-effective upper limit on today's nondigital telephone lines. A strobe can pulse at ever-faster rates, with each pulse clearly separate, but if you speed up an analog wave, it's like speeding up a tape—your voice gets squeakier and squeakier, until it becomes unrecognizable.

Sending multimedia at half a page per second over the Internet may sound impractical. Yet it is sort of practical, if frustrating. Users of the Internet routinely download short music and video clips. If you use an on-line information service such as America Online or CompuServe, you'll be able to download fair-quality photographs in 5 to 20 seconds. Data compression permits all this.

And so does ingenuity. Multimedia technology is a bag of tricks. Because the price performance of chip technology improves at a rate of 20 to 40 percent a year and because the PC industry is increasingly competitive, with ferocious price wars, the base technology gets better and better and cheaper and cheaper. The innovators in multimedia software and hardware thus have more to work with. For instance, MPEG is a recent key standard for compressing multimedia data. An MPEG board that compresses and decompresses video contains dozens of chips that together add up to far more computing power than an entire PC of five years ago. The producers of such a board, which is one of the most important recent developments in bringing TV-quality video to PCs, could have designed the MPEG data compression techniques ten years ago, but there was no point because the enabling low-cost, high-performance chips were not available. Now that they are, innovators are free to push new limits of design.

The Business Technology Key: The Enterprise Multimedia Network

A large business uses many types of telecommunications: local area networks, "private" leased lines, public networks, the Internet, and "value-added" networks. The "enterprise network" is the combination of all of these components working together—a network of networks—and it provides the base of more and more customer service, organizational coordination, and relationships with suppliers, banks, and other parties.

What matters most for the progress of multimedia in business is seen the least: these telecommunications networks. It is natural that computer users in business and personal life focus on what they do see and what they need to know most about: the PC, its software operating system, and application packages. They don't pay much attention to the telecommunications systems that link the PC to information resources and other PCs. The direct analogy here is with electrical appliances, where you take the power supply for granted. Very few people who use VCRs, hair dryers, and stereo systems ever need to know anything about electrical power generation. The only time they are aware of the electrical infrastructure is when it's out of service or short circuits.

The electrical system has evolved over a century of continued investment. When PCs began their proliferation across, first, the office landscape and now the home living room and the briefcase, manufacturers and users did not have to wait for electrical utilities' voltages and plug sizes to be debated and agreed on, or special wires to be installed across the nation. You simply plugged in and turned the machine on. Things are totally different with telecommunications, the information equivalent of the electrical utility. Here, the technology is not stable; there is constant competitive, regulatory, and technological change; and today what is practical and cost-effective for a PC frequently depends on what is practical and cost-effective for telecommunications. Telecommunications is the key element in making computers and information an enterprise business resource.

That resource has four main types of components:

- *Access tools.* These include PCs, phones, bar code readers, ATMs, and point-of-sale registers in stores. They access services and information. Many new tools are specifically multimedia in nature: digital cameras, music synthesizers, image scanners, and CD-ROM players. The services they access may be local ones on PC; the scanner accesses the software that runs it, and the camera accesses software to input, store, and edit a photograph, for instance. But many of the services will involve telecommunications.

- *Telecommunications links.* Telecommunications links determine the variety of services that can be accessed by someone, somewhere, with the goal being anyone, anywhere. There are many different types of telecommunications networks, transmission methods, "protocols" for ensuring synchronization of sending and receiving devices, plus a bewildering variety of design and operational issues to ensure that the many individual network links work as seamlessly as the many components of the electrical supply do. Most business networks were configured to handle nonmultimedia traffic. Adding multimedia pushes the limits of today's capabilities at a time when demand for high speed, low cost transmission of multimedia is growing rapidly.

- *Transaction processing engines.* These are the systems that process your ATM cash withdrawal, airline reservation, bill payment, and so forth. They are often massive complexes of computer hardware and software that handle as many as 2,000 transactions per second, ensure security, and update records on line.

- *Information stores.* These are the data bases of largely numeric information that are accessed by transaction processing engines, plus multimedia files that include World Wide Web pages, libraries of photographs, video clips, and the like. Multimedia files are hundreds, thousands, even millions of times larger than those contained in the data bases built up as part of the firm's everyday transaction processing. Most firms are moving rapidly to augment their traditional alphanumeric data bases with libraries and archives of electronic documents and, more cautiously, toward the fully multimedia "object" data bases that will include in one electronic filing cabinet all relevant information regardless of medium.

All the components of the business multimedia resource have to work together. In the jargon of information technology, the goal is "integration." The enemy is "incompatibility," which means that this device, software, or file logically ought to be able to be used with this other device, software, or file, but can't. Incompatibilities are the norm, not the exception. That may not matter to an individual who uses his or her PC for personal applications, but in a business environment, it blocks resource sharing and communication. Dominant designs often become so because they are adopted by companies, software developers, and hardware manufacturers as standards that ensure compatibility. An example is the 1995 agreement by two competing consortia on a common format for digital video discs. Each felt it had a better design than the other but knew that market growth would be badly stalled if buyers had to deal with two incompatible systems. The cooperative truce was made not for reasons of social altruism but for the sake of competitive realism.

Telecommunications binds together access tools, transaction

processing engines, and information stores. Compatibility is essential here. The main reason the Internet took off is that the telecommunications protocol on which it is built is the only one *ever* to allow any computer of any type to connect to any computer of any other type. (This protocol, discussed in the Glossary, is called TCP/IP, often abbreviated to TCP or IP.) Think of telecommunications as the electronic equivalent of the electrical utility. General Electric used to advertise better living through electricity. The foundation of much of modern business is better living through telecommunications.

That means that telecommunications network design and operations will almost certainly be the most important and, alas, difficult issues concerning multimedia in large organizations. They are issues of which business managers need to be very aware if the network is to enable payoff from using multimedia to leverage knowledge management, customer interaction, natural decision input, and shared understanding. If managers and their information services planners and professionals are not fully aware of the immense impacts of multimedia on the enterprise network, then telecommunications can become a block instead of an enabler.

There are three levels of telecommunications demands that multimedia creates: simple dial-up, fast bitstream, and complex communications processing.

1. *Simple dial-up.* You use the public dial-up telephone system, typically to access information on remote computers that is provided by on-line information providers or over the Internet. The user of these services doesn't have to handle the telecommunications component. Receiving electronic mail messages or short text, accessing items in a data base, or sending a spreadsheet to another PC require only that the transmission link be able to move data at speeds of around $\frac{1}{3}$ to 1 page per second (9,600 to 28,800 bits). A few seconds' delay in receipt may be mildly irritating, but you hardly notice it if your e-mail message takes an extra second to transmit. Existing business and public networks have no problems whatsoever in handling such standard applica-

tions. The success of the Internet rests on its provision of simple dial-up; the many inefficiencies, delays, and limitations of dial-up are offset by its convenience and simplicity of use for most individuals.

2. *Fast bitstream.* Delays are not acceptable, though, for more and more people or most businesses. Simple dial-up access constrains the number of bits that can be transmitted and hence the range of media that can be easily and cheaply used. Multimedia raises the demand for raw transmission speed, simply because it so dramatically increases the number of bits per message. Video, audio, and high-resolution images take up millions and even hundreds of millions of bits. The transmission links thus need to operate in millions or billions, not thousands, of bits per second. Each may carry hundreds of messages simultaneously. The bigger the digital pipeline, the more traffic that can flow through it, and the faster each piece of traffic can be moved.

New telecommunications services and tools provide the needed raw transmission speed. Traffic over the public telephone system is no longer limited to a page per second. In many parts of the country, consumers can obtain 5-page-per-second transmission speed (through a service called ISDN). That's still very slow in comparison to what is routine for large businesses. Companies can access services with somewhat exotic names that offer increasing units of speed for long-distance transmission: T1 lines provide 50 pages per second (1.54 mbps) and frame relay speeds of from 2 pages up to 50 pages per second. ATM provides 7 to 80 printed book equivalents (45 to 600 mbps), with speeds of from 1 to 3 full-length movies per second being fully practical (gigabits a second, billions of bits). The backbone of the Internet is packed with fiber optics pulsing information at gigabit speeds. The new transmission technologies also offer bandwidth on demand, so that, for instance, on a university's research network, the scientific particle simulation that requires 100 book equivalents per second gets allocated the needed bandwidth for the seconds when it needs it, while the weather forecasting application, which needs only 6 book equivalents, the chemistry data base that requires 20 page equivalents, and the flood of other images, e-mail, audio, and perhaps video are all independently allocated capacity as needed.

Without all these, multimedia would be limited to applications that do not involve telecommunications or to low-quality images and audio. CD-ROMs are the main multimedia tool that does not depend on telecommunications. Businesses can go beyond off-line CD-ROMs and slow dial-up access to information through the local area networks that are the building blocks of departmental and enterprise communications resource. These work at transmission speeds of 80 to 400 printed pages (2 to 10 mbps), without pushing the commercially available state of the technology. Only very large firms could afford high-speed lines for metropolitan and wide area communication—distances measured in miles, not feet—through the late 1980s. New services offer high bandwidth on demand instead of high bandwidth by monthly rental, allowing small firms to compete on equal electronic terms with giants.

3. *Complex communications processing.* There would seem to be no problem in managing large and fast bitstreams. In fact, there are very big problems, of which the multimedia community that develops desktop PC tools is largely unaware, for the very reason that experts in this area are not involved in building and running large-scale business telecommunications networks. *When large bitstreams have to be transmitted in real time across a network of "nodes," the throughput is determined by many factors other than raw transmission speed.* The basic design of local area networks (LANs), wide area networks, the many devices such as servers that coordinate the flow of traffic, and the configuration of the network (exactly how devices are clustered to balance efficiency, service, and cost) has been based on the network traffic being entirely different in volume, size of messages, and performance demands from that of networked multimedia. The differences and their impacts on network requirements are discussed in Glossary entries that ad-

*time sensitive

dress telecommunications. The main point to grasp is that inter-active multimedia is largely time-sensitive. A tiny delay or added "latency" breaks up voice and video. A LAN with 20 users that can easily accommodate all of their needs to send and receive short, "bursty" messages, such as electronic mail, congests very quickly when just a few of them are simultaneously using interactive videoconferencing, for example.

All three of these levels of telecommunications complexity—simple dial-up, fast bitstream, and complex communications proc-essing—are widely used in networked business multimedia. The main problem is one of fitting all the pieces of a telecommunica-tions resource together to ensure a smooth flow of traffic across the entire system. Today's designs do not easily accommodate the massive increases in volume, type, and size of messages intrinsic to multimedia. Some of their most basic principles get in the way of this. For instance, many local area networks speed data to and from PCs at speeds of 70 to 300 page equivalents per second (2 to 10 million bits), at very low cost, through a "contention" traffic management system. In the most widely used type of LAN, called Ethernet, each device that wants to send a message is like a car trying to get on the freeway in rush hour. The devices in essence are drivers who close their eyes, pray, and accelerate, hoping they don't get hit. If they are hit, they back off and try again. Another common LAN technique, called "token ring," has a token that is sent around the network; only the holder of the token can trans-mit data. A device that wants to send traffic waits and grabs the token, releasing it when the transmission is complete. Since only one device holds the token, the rest wait their turn. Ethernet collisions and the waiting time for getting the token create delays. Those may be just a few milliseconds (thousandths of a second), though, as users of large-scale corporate networks, busy depart-mental LANs, or the Internet all too often experience, they can create lengthy traffic jams amounting to many seconds or even minutes.

Delays and overhead add up quickly in complex networks.

Ethernet
Token Ring

These are inherent in the standard transmission techniques that break long messages up into shorter "packets," which are given a header that identifies the sending and receiving destination, add error control and format information, and route the pieces of the message through as many as 100 different hardware links, perhaps across wide area domestic and international networks, with each link involving some type of processing, conversion, traffic flow management, administration, and network management control. Typically, each message may add 100 milliseconds of such "latency." *Latency* is the total time added "end to end" as a message is routed from sender to receiver. You often encounter latency when your long-distance phone call is handled by satellite links. It takes one-fourth of a second for what you say to be sent up to the satellite 22,800 miles above the earth and to come back down; this delay occasionally leads to a distinct breaking up of the continuous flow of conversation. It's irritating, but you easily adjust to it.

That's not so with many multimedia applications. One hundred milliseconds equal just one-tenth of a second and may not sound like much of a problem. Imagine, though, watching TV. If each frame were delayed by that tenth of a second, you would get no picture. TV frames are updated 30 times per second and take up millions of bits per frame. When a complex video image is broken up into packets, some may be lost as the intermediate nodes drop them because they can't process them fast enough, and latency is added along the routes, it doesn't matter that the backbone network operates at a jillion bits a second or that the workstation display is the most clear and detailed on the market. The traffic flow at the equivalent for cars of 55 mph is brought to a halt by electronic tollbooths.

All the challenges of upgrading today's networks to meet the demands of multimedia can be met, but not at all easily. Because users of multimedia PCs don't see the network, they take it for granted. They may not have any sense of how a planned interactive video application, use of networked kiosks for customer service, on-line shared CD-ROM and video data base servers, networked training resources, and the like affect the departmental or business network. The multimedia software developers who create the applications may similarly be unaware of the telecommunications implications of their work. Telecommunications specialists who are wrestling with today's operational demands may have little understanding of or interest in multimedia. Business managers who see telecommunications as an expense may underestimate the vital importance of viewing the network infrastructure—what is termed an "integrated architecture"—as almost surely the technical key to getting real value from multimedia. You can buy CD-ROMs off the shelf, get onto the Internet as a new subscriber in a few hours, purchase multimedia software and hardware three months from now that is even more powerful and easy to use than those you bought three months ago. Companies can order from AT&T, MCI, and others all the bandwidth they can fill up. An ad hoc, take-it-as-it-comes approach to multimedia in this regard, via experiment and opportunism, is very practical.

What companies can't do is put all the pieces together opportunistically and ad hoc.

Conclusion: The Future of Multimedia

The Promise of Multimedia

Many of the most productive and profitable business opportunities opened up by multimedia are not yet apparent. They will emerge as the technology matures, as organizations experiment and gain experience, and as expectations become more realistic, sorting out pragmatism from hype and hope. The timetable for multimedia's reaching the same degree of impact on everyday business as personal computers have will obviously vary widely for specific types of applications and specific areas of use. We can expect it to become widespread for training within the next year or so (it's pretty widespread already in some firms), for the obvious reasons that interactive video, CD-ROM, graphics, and animation are powerful tools for instruction and the low cost of reproducing and using these on a PC opens up many opportunities for learning outside the classroom. We can also expect multimedia very quickly to become a key part of firms' marketing and selling activities; there are many examples today of car companies' producing CD-ROMs that provide video, photographs, and product information that potential customers can browse through, of sales reps using laptop computers with CD-ROM drives for presentations to customers, and of firms using the reach of the Internet to provide product information and customer service. All these are obvious uses of today's multimedia technology, which every firm needs to investigate in depth.

Multimedia will, *in the long term,* surely have as profound and far-reaching an effect on individuals, business, and society as telephones and personal computers have had over the past decades. Like them, multimedia tools will *over time* become so embedded in the fabric of everyday life that we will take them as much for granted as the fax machines we routinely use to order a pizza, the PC word processing package that can turn even the most leaden prose into elegantly formatted, correctly spelled text, or the 1–800 number that has become the norm for ordering just about any item over the phone. Ten years ago, these were neither inexpensive, simple to install and use, nor part of the repertoire of standard business tools. It was as difficult—or foolish—for firms to adopt them 20 years ago as it is now for them not to have already done so.

In the long term, then, it seems easy to agree with statements like that of a teacher who has made multimedia part of his own everyday work that "multimedia is fast emerging as a basic skill that will be as important to life in the twenty-first century as reading is now." In the shorter term, too, multimedia is already generating substantive innovations in how films are made, how information and entertainment are provided to consumers, and the ways people use their personal computers. CD-ROMs are now a standard component of home PCs. The Internet has become the base for an explosion in communication by computers and for "surfing" for information across the world and, most recently, for new channels for business and publishing. America Online, CompuServe, and the Internet have created new forms of electronic communities, where people interact intimately without ever meeting. The short-term picture is one of intriguing experiment. The long-term picture is one of profound social and business change.

Dominant Designs

It's also a picture of often-bewildering technical and market change. Every few months, new multimedia products come onto the market. There's constant experimentation with existing ones. The technology is unstable in many areas, with individual manufacturers and software providers developing their own "proprietary" systems in situations where there are no established standards. That means that many of the components of the multimedia technology resource do not work with each other well, if at all. There are many competing designs. Firms are naturally reluctant to bet their future on designs and companies that may not be in business a few years from now, or to be locked into obsolescent products that are not within the mainstream of the market. At the same time, they want to exploit innovations in technology, application, and price performance. As with PCs and telecommunications equipment, many of the innovators are recent start-ups. Just as Microsoft, Compaq, and Dell became powerful forces in PCs, and Cisco and Cincom did the same in telecommunications, there are many rapidly emerging firms that are playing the same role in multimedia as these. It's almost certain that some of the most successful firms in the multimedia market of 2007 do not yet exist.

The concept of dominant designs is useful for making some sense of all this turbulence in multimedia technology and competition. A dominant design is one that emerges from the competitive offerings to take what may initially be a relatively small share of the overall market. Quickly, though, that share grows as the wider industry adapts its own offerings to that design. Examples of such dominant designs are Microsoft's MS-DOS and Windows, the QWERTY keyboard, VHS, screw-in lightbulbs and $8\frac{1}{2}$-by-11-inch paper. The VHS story is well known. It competed with a technically superior design, Betamax, promulgated by Sony, the strongest company in consumer electronics. VHS gradually took the lead. When it did so, consumers started buying VHS players and recorders, which got cheaper because of economies of scale, which increased the relative gap between VHS and Beta, which moved tape providers to focus on issuing their products for VHS, and so on.

Dominant designs thus stabilize the market and establish the blueprints other providers follow. The $8\frac{1}{2}$-by-11-inch paper standard freed up makers of photocopiers to build machines without having to worry about paper. Intel's 80XX chips helped standardize the entire PC market. Once, there were many software operating systems. Then, DOS established the PC hardware and software market. Software developers wrote their packages to run under DOS. Manufacturers of printers and telecommunications devices announced that their products were DOS "compatible." Once a market is driven by dominant designs, prices drop quickly by the very fact that a producer is selling into a proven market and can be sure that an incremental improvement in product or price will capture sales. Elements of the market then become commoditized, creating price competition, because there are fewer opportunities to compete on features. Developers hold off on supporting products that are losing out to dominant designs. They thus, for instance, build software for Windows before they provide versions for the Apple Macintosh. It was once the other way around. All the high-end desktop publishing, multimedia authoring, and video management packages were originally built for the Mac. That's no longer the case; Windows is the dominant design for PCs. Developers have thus moved with the market—which means away from the Mac. The shift from the Mac as the artistic multimedia base to Windows as the commercial base reinforces Windows' dominance, which reinforces the developers' strategy, which reinforces Windows, and so on.

Multimedia will be paced by dominant designs. Some of these will be generated by the success of a market innovator. Creative Labs' Sound Blaster audio card is one such instance. It is the brainchild of a single individual who preempted large vendors of computer hardware with a product that captured the market. The most striking dominant design in information technology outside Microsoft has been Netscape, a relatively simple piece of software which has become the window to the Internet Web.

Some dominant designs will be created by committees of standard-setting organizations or groups of vendors working together. But such standards are successful only if users want the products that implement them, which is not always the case. Examples are, in the computer field, the complete failure of Japanese computer hardware manufacturers to impose their System X operating system on buyers, the failure of Betamax in videos, and the unexpectedly slow take-up of DAT (digital audiotape).

In multimedia, MPEG, the rapidly emerging standard for coding and compressing digital video, is almost certain to be a dominant design. Several multimedia software packages have already become such designs; they include PhotoShop and MacroMedia, which are multimedia equivalents of Microsoft Word or Lotus 1–2–3. As with those packages, there will always be competing products and variants, but it is the dominant designs that set the rules for competition and variation.

Dominant designs can emerge quite suddenly. A recent example is the Java programming language created by a team at Sun Microsystems, a manufacturer of high-end computer workstations. Java opens up an entirely new direction for the use of the Internet. Today, the PC stores the software needed to handle applications such as displaying graphics or editing text, to access and process information over the network, and to handle multi-media. The growing range of software capabilities and needs has increased the complexity of the operating systems that manage them, most especially Windows 95, the most recent version of Microsoft's dominant design for PCs. This adds to the hardware cost and complexity. Java may change this entirely by allowing software "applets" to be accessed on demand over the Internet. A multimedia application such as playing a music clip will not draw on stored software on the PC hard disk but will download the applet. Once announced, Java was immediately licensed for use by such firms as Netscape, whose Internet browser became a dominant design in just a year—its market share grew from around 14 percent in early 1995 to 75 percent at the start of 1996. Within a few months, Microsoft had completely turned its strategy for its Microsoft Network service upside down and refocused its entire development plan, including licensing Java.

The more immature a field, the more the range of designs that will compete for dominance. Now that Microsoft's Windows dominates PCs, it is easy to forget that its dominance was not predicted. CP/M, Pascal, and even Sony's System X looked more likely to succeed. Sometimes, as with Java, fortuitous timing, competitive jostling, and the leaders in the development community determine the outcome; consumers didn't suddenly adopt Java— there's nothing yet for them to adopt. It will be mid-to-late 1997 before they will see many Java-based Internet services or the stripped-down Internet "appliances" promised by a number of companies including Sony. But Java is already pacing and shaping a new market.

The way to watch the technology is to look for emerging dominant designs. Experiment with the new designs. Pilot with the best designs. Invest in large scale applications only when they can be built on dominant designs. One of my priorities in the Glossary is to identify dominant designs and to be very clear in acknowledging where such designs are not yet apparent.

Glossary

3-D Computing Three-dimensional graphics and videos display information on a computer screen so that it looks as if it shows objects in the three-dimensional space that we take for granted in everyday life but lose when we look at a two-dimensional book, television screen, photograph, or computer monitor. Efforts to add back the missing third dimension without computers have been primitive and cumbersome, such as 3-D movies that required you to put on special cardboard glasses with one red and one green eyepiece.

Applications of 3-D computing are growing rapidly, to the extent that *Business Week* made the topic its cover story in Septem-

Note: One puzzling or irritating feature of many terms in my Glossary may be the number of strange-looking names of computer products and information technology jargon that take the form of single words, with no spaces: CompuServe, IntelliWeb, MetaTools, MacroMedia, NetWare, and the like. There's a reason for this—sort of. Spaces matter to computers, in that software on the Internet, operating systems, and telecommunications systems read a block of text looking for a space or special symbol, such as @ or /, that marks the end of a command or file name. They can't handle Macro Media and instead need something like Macro_Media, Macro@Media, Macro.Media, or Macro/Media. Techies are used to connecting words with dots, dashes, and slashes in this way and are cavalier about upper and lower case. You see the vestiges of this practice on the Internet, where addresses on the World Wide Web are full of dots and other connecting symbols that never, ever follow or are followed by a space—for instance, "http://www.choices.client/server.uiuc.edu/research/Vosaic/vosaic2.html" (a real address, for NCSA's Vosaic site. Vosaic actually stands for Visual Mosaic, but no spaces, please).

ber 1995, with the somewhat breathless subheading "From medical imaging to virtual reality games, the race is on to capture computing's next dimension." The article is thin on examples, suggesting that 3-D is still in the take-off stage. It includes a military flight simulator, the "biggest ever" simulation, which left an Air Force officer saying, "You got sweat beading up on your forehead . . . you could hear anxiety in your wingman's voice when you got separated." It later states that "like no other field of computing, 3-D hits people in the gut." It cites engineering applications such as use of 3-D by the designers of New Zealand's winning entry for the America's Cup yachting competition, X-ray crystallography, architecture, radiology, and computer games, the single area in which it is expected to have most immediate impact.

It is as easy for a multimedia computer to process and display 3-D as any other type of graphic image, given enough processing power, speed of data transmission, and storage capacity. Those were not at all givens until the mid-1990s. Even today, although generating 3-D still graphics can easily be done on a PC, creating 3-D *video* graphics requires a powerful and expensive computer workstation, typically a Silicon Graphics machine. Silicon Graphics has become Hollywood's favorite enabler of ultraspecial effects; its sales tripled between 1991 and 1994. To some extent, it's a prestige item, equivalent to a Porsche. Half a million dollars can be the entry fee for this top end of special effects. You know you've arrived when you drive a Silicon Graphics.

You can make do with less (and Silicon Graphics sells machines for a few thousand as well as a million dollars), with many competitors such as Hewlett-Packard driving prices down rapidly, but the cost is still high in comparison with that for basic personal computers. The first commercially available plug-in card for PCs that offers full 3-D video graphics capabilities, introduced in late 1995, cost $24,000. (The feature "set" includes "24-bit texture acceleration, scaleable textual memory, bilinear and trilinear MIP-mapping, specular highlights, full-score antialiasing, transparency and depth cue.")

The top end of the top end of the PC hardware range rarely costs more than $12,000, fully loaded with monitor, high-quality printer, and multimedia goodies. Spending $24,000 for a card to plug into a PC may not look like much of a deal. It may well be an excellent deal for such applications as engineering design; simulation of physical operations, including store design, manufacturing facilities, and office layout; and any planning or decision process that *fundamentally* depends on effective visualization of movement. Training pilots is an obvious example. Wherever visualization of movement in physical space is natural in decision making, 3-D computing is a productive direction for companies. As one expert comments, "The brain absorbs three-dimensional information like a sponge. We've been doing it since birth."

The real world is three-dimensional. Depth perception is a critical element of how our brains work. It's natural to us. We have been denied it by available media and perhaps as a result we don't expect to get out of Flatland. Given that the $24,000 will cost at most $5,000 five years from now (that figure assumes just a 25 percent-per-year drop in price, routine in the PC hardware field), this may be a technology worth exploring today to locate opportunities that can be realized when the costs make them affordable or to locate ones for which $24,000 is well worth paying for now.

One very successful example of how 3-D can augment existing business processes comes from physical plant operations. Safety and environmental legislation increasingly requires full and frequent surveys of manufacturing plants, hazardous materials storage centers, oil refineries, utilities, and many others. In addition, how a plant changes as it is being built, modified, and upgraded has to be carefully documented and its environmental impacts interpreted. All this documentation fills entire filing cabinets. Much of it will be in computer form, developed and updated by computer-assisted design (CAD) systems. Constructing a physical model of the plant, an essential requirement because two-dimensional diagrams do not provide enough data for effective analysis and decision making, is highly time consuming and labor inten-

Toy Story has attracted a lot of attention as the first computer-generated, full-length, 3-D cartoon. It marks a significant milestone in the evolution of multimedia. To put it in context, though, it was by no means simple multimedia. Its 114,000 frames occupied 600 billion bytes—1,000 hard disk equivalents—and required 800,000 hours of machine processing time to produce. The producer states that, in assembling the largest number of Ph.D.s to work on any film in history. Disney created history. And the firm saved a lot of money as well as producing a film even the snobbiest critics praise. Toy Story cost just $25 million to make, compared with the $40 million for The Lion King. *The team that made it numbered 110, versus* The Lion King's *800.*

sive. A multimedia extension of both CAD and physical modeling is the system marketed by a UK firm, CADCenter, which takes video input from a series of on site cameras and produces a complete 3-D model, using "photogrammetry" techniques, which calculate the exact location of each image and derive from them the precise position and size of each machine, piece of pipe, opening, and the like that is in the field of vision.

The system was developed by University College, London, and illustrates two of the major emerging, if easily overlooked, trends in multimedia: (1) the use of scientific software development theory and tools to create easy-to-use applications that are of value to business, and (2) the increasing readiness, even need, for university researchers to turn those tools into marketed products. The CADCenter product is the result of successful academic research combined with an already-successful commercial company's own software and marketing capabilities to create something many businesses need but do not know about. They do know about or can easily find out about multimedia games, office technology, "edutainment," and CD-ROMs aimed at consumers.

A major opportunity for both research organizations and multimedia services providers and businesses is thus to find out about each other. Scientists look for every opportunity to turn developments in computer technology into useful tools; World Wide Web and Internet browsers were the creation of physicists looking to make the Net more of a community of researchers, for example. They have taken the lead in many areas of 3-D because of the importance of visualization in their work. Well over half the articles and ads in any 1995 issue of *Scientific Computing World* were about visualization tools that can be used with the same standard graphical user interfaces employed by businesses and individuals. Three years ago, comparable publications developed at most 5 percent of their pages to these topics.

See also Virtual Reality

Access Time Access time is the waiting time between a computer instruction's requesting data from a CD-ROM, hard disk, or other device and the data's being located. To that must be added the time to transfer the data. Think of yourself looking up the number of a business contact in your Rolodex. The time to locate the name is the access time, and the time to write down the phone number on a piece of paper is the transfer time. Your Rolodex access time is generally far slower than the transfer rate. That is typically the case with computers. For example, the first CD-ROM drives took almost a second to locate data and then transferred it at 6 printed page equivalents per second (150,000 bits). The newer 4× drives (four times the speed of the original) that are found in most standard multimedia PCs have an access time of a quarter of a second and a transfer rate of 24 page equivalents per second. Go on to the next generation of drives, 6×, and the access time is just 0.15 seconds and the transfer rate, 36 printed page equivalents per second. If you take these figures from an ad, it seems reasonable to conclude that, because the 6× drive's transfer rate is six times that of the basic drive, it will transfer, say, 2 printed book equivalents (15 million bits) of data six times faster. The 6× drive should take a total of 16 seconds; the 4×, 25 seconds; and the base drive, 100 seconds.

No way. Consider two very different combinations of data access amounting to 15 million bits: (1) 10,000 accesses of short items, each of which is 1,500 bits (a paragraph) in size and (2) 5 accesses of items, each of which is 3 million bits (half a book) in size. Here are the time factors in seconds:

EXAMPLE 1 / EXAMPLE 2

	10,000 accesses of 15,000 bits				5 accesses of 3 million bits			
	Access	Transfer	Total	Improvement factor	Access	Transfer	Total	Improvement factor
Original	10,000	100	10,100	—	5	100	105	—
4×	4,000	25	4,025	2.5	2	25	27	3.9
6×	1,500	17	1,517	6.7	0.75	17	18	5.8

The heads that read the data on a disk float above the disk as it rotates. The gap is so tiny that a wisp of smoke would hit it like an avalanche. It's the equivalent of a Boeing 747 flying along at full cruising speed four inches above the ground.

The same total volume of data takes between 105 and 10,100 seconds to access and transfer on the base drive—2 minutes versus almost 3 hours, a hundredfold difference. The 4-times-faster 4× drive is only 2.5 times faster when handling frequent accesses to small data items. The 6× drive takes 40 minutes to process all the short items and just 18 seconds to handle the longer ones. So, the overall difference in performance is 18 seconds to 3 hours for exactly the same number of bits.

There are instructive lessons for managers in this oversimplified example (it doesn't include the effects of software processing time and the exact type of operating system, which can further change the relative performance ratios between the 4× and 6× drives). One lesson may simply be not to believe ads. Just as horsepower figures don't tell you much about a car, neither do figures on the raw speed of hardware. More general lessons are that access time can dramatically affect overall performance and that it is the mix of applications, number of accesses involved, and size of the data items they transfer that determine the overall performance of the computer. This poses many challenges to designers of multimedia systems. How to cut access time for its CD-ROM encyclopedia consumed much of the Microsoft development team's personal lives for a year, for instance, as they probed for ways to save fractions of a second.

You can easily see, from the numbers used in the above example, how a system that performs very quickly in handling some requests can be abominably slow in handling others. CD-ROM is poorly suited to short, bursty data traffic, such as 10,000 accesses of 1,500 bits. Hard disks have a shorter access time and outperform CD-ROM in this area. By contrast, CD-ROM performs relatively well in accessing the lengthy files characteristic of multimedia. That said, it still takes half a minute to access just 5 photographs using a 4× drive. The typical hard disk access time is now around 20 milliseconds, with newer devices offering under 10 milliseconds. Transfer rates are 2 to 3 million bytes per second, half a printed book, around four times faster than even a 6×

CD-ROM drive. The advantage of CD-ROM is simply low-cost storage capacity.

Access time is mostly idle time to a computer, although there are ways to overlap operations so that the machine does not sit totally spinning its electrons. Access time is generated by the simple reality of physical movement. Hard disks, floppy disks, and CD-ROM disks all rotate, just like a compact disc or its predecessor, the rapidly disappearing long-playing record. There is thus a small delay as either the reading part of the drive has to move to the track where the data are located, or as it waits for the section of that track to spin around to it. On a hard disk, the heads have to move, albeit a tiny distance, to read the data.

In many instances, computer access time does not affect your own waiting time, called "response time," the gap between your inputting a request and getting a response. Acceptable response time is 3 to 5 seconds, depending on the application. When it takes you a second or so to absorb information, you won't even notice 100 milliseconds (thousandths of a second) for a single transaction. The problem is that your request may generate many computer disk reads—dozens, hundreds, or thousands—to locate and move needed data. That's why searching for information on a CD-ROM can be so slow. Each individual access and transfer is faster than your awareness of the elapsed time, but they can add up.

Senator Everett Dirksen, a power player for decades in Congress, once commented about the federal budget, "A billion dollars here, a billion there and pretty soon you're talking about real money." The equivalent for access time is "A millisecond here, a millisecond there, and pretty soon you wish you'd never bought this damned computer."

Adobe Systems Adobe Systems is the company that dominates the graphic arts and publishing part of the multimedia software market. Adobe is not as well known as Microsoft, nor as aggressive, but its PostScript print programming language is as

The opinion of a leading 3-D modeler and animator on multimedia skills: "The best people in the multimedia industry are almost all design-centered people. At some of the industrial design schools there's a tremendous amount of care and sensitivity taught, the dedication to doing it right and doing it with the best tools. . . . You've got to keep working on the edge because this stuff runs out of date every six months. . . . Still, you need to crawl before you can walk and you've got to walk before you can run. I think you need to be able to draw before you can start playing around with a Mac. You've got to know what a good line is. I think you've got to know how to do 2-D design on the computer before you can do 3-D design." (Vivid Studios, Careers in Multimedia, *1995)*

much the industry standard for printing and image setting in publishing as Windows is for PCs. Adobe beat off an effort by Microsoft to establish a beachhead in high-end publishing in 1990; in one of its rare defeats, Microsoft withdrew the product from the market within two years.

Adobe's current strength in multimedia is its PhotoShop program, by far the most widely used software for editing images, especially on the Macintosh. It also has a close alliance with Netscape, the hugely successful company in the Internet "browser" market. Netscape itself has become the dominant design for Internet access on PCs. Now that just about anyone, including high schoolers, can create a home page on the World Wide Web using the simple HTML language, more and more people and companies are looking to create less bland-looking Web pages, which include animation, 3-D, high resolution pictures, sound, and video instead of small images and lots of text. Adobe's Acrobat software provides for this as well as including advanced features for storing and indexing multimedia. It faces strong competition in each of its market segments, and its close link to the Mac community in general and to publishing professionals in particular may have left it weakly positioned to capture the far larger PC market or to maintain its strong position in the SOHO market against Windows-based competitors. SOHO stands for "small office, home office," where most Macs are installed; Mac has by far the highest brand loyalty in personal computers.

If you as a manager have heard of, say, Lotus Notes, Microsoft Windows, and WordPerfect but not Adobe's Premiere, PostScript, and Acrobat (or the strong rival to it, MacroMedia's FreeHand), then you may be a little too narrowly focused in your views and knowledge to be able to get the best value out of multimedia in your firm—or for yourself. Until very recently, multimedia was a niche at the high end of the personal computer market and a specialized area in business and professional use of computers of all sizes and types. Adobe in software, Silicon Graphics in hardware and the Apple community in both these areas dominated its evolution. Now, 70 percent of PCs sold to consumers have multi-media capabilities. This is creating a PC-, not a Mac-oriented, mass market in which the software is used by people who are not professionals in SOHO, publishing, or the arts. PhotoShop, Premiere, or Acrobat may be more than they need or know how to use.

Or they may be exactly what your own company needs. If so, it can find people who already know how to use these proven and powerful tools, which will soon be basic ones in business, not just in studios. At present, multimedia software and hardware involve many design compromises in order to provide adequate perform-ance, sound quality, image resolution, size of video picture, num-ber of images per second, and ease of use on standard PCs. The Adobe community is one in which such compromises are not acceptable and where they have not been demanded because the machines they use cost two to three times the standard PC and thus have far more multimedia performance. Within two years, the standard PC will be more powerful and cheaper than those premium machines are now. That means that there will be fewer design compromises and that companies can make better use of Adobe level software and Adobe-level talents in multimedia.

Advertising through Multimedia Multimedia is a natural for advertising—natural images, special effects, animation, 3-D. There are three main areas of current opportunity: CD-ROM, the Internet, and customer point-of-contact use of multimedia.

CD-ROM offers the opportunity to make a sophisticated sales pitch to a potential customer without a sales rep's having to call. Toyota is typical. It offers a free CD-ROM, advertised in maga-zines. These ads in themselves save money. The following is al-most all the text for a one-eighth page black-and-white ad in *Scientific American* (September 1995), which is, of course, much cheaper than a full-page color ad or a four-page insert: "Imagine live footage of every Toyota Car, Truck, SUV and Van in any COLOR or from any ANGLE, right in front of your EYES. With all the information of every brochure right at your fingertips. All in full STEREO." The CD-ROM meets most of Toyota's promises. It takes a few minutes to install and contains a lot of sheer hype before you can get to the content. Like most of today's CD-ROMs, it is slower than it could and should be. You have to sit for several seconds watching the screen change the menu, and you can't quickly cancel and skip over an item. (It is much like being a captive of a television infomercial.)

That said, once you locate the information you want to look at, the CD-ROM is easy to use, instructive, and attractive. One of its most useful features is the ability to rotate the car, which goes well beyond looking at a color photograph. You can also change its color and see it move in video clips. In 1996, GM introduced an on-line equivalent of the Toyota CD-ROM on the Internet. It contained 16,000 pages on GM cars and also includes the rotation of images. The Internet is at present much slower than CD-ROM, if you are using standard dial-up phone lines.

The low cost of reproduction for CD-ROMs, around 60 cents, as well as the growing number of home PCs with drives, makes them almost throwaways; they are regularly given away with magazines that offer demo versions of software, for instance. Until either interactive TV, the Internet, or other on-line information services combine very fast and almost free telecommunications, CD-ROM seems likely to be the main vehicle for advertising that meets the four criteria for effective use of multimedia identified in the Introduction:

1. *Knowledge management.* They provide the storage and retrieval tools to manage large volumes of complex data. The Toyota disk would be a many-hundred-page series of printed brochures that could not be easily explored and assimilated.

2. *Customer interaction.* You can't interact with a TV ad or a brochure. The Toyota CD-ROM is like having a somewhat gabby car salesperson at your shoulder who

gives you answers to your questions and points you to the topics you might want to explore in more depth.

3. *Natural decision input.* Obviously, the value of visual information and motion depends on the specific type of product or service being advertised. It's not surprising that car makers are among the leaders in the use of multimedia for advertising. The more they can show images of the cars, close-ups of features, and the car in motion, the more easily you can visualize the real thing.

4. *Shared understanding.* When you go to the nearest Toyota dealer (identified for you by the disk), you are a more informed buyer than you would have been otherwise. Whatever he or she has to show you, you have already seen. You have a shared context that should make it faster and easier for you to choose and for the sales rep to work with you.

CD-ROM is the primary off-line medium for digital advertising. On-line advertising can reach a wider audience, just as broadcast television reaches more of the population than individual newspapers and magazines. There are many on-line information services, including America Online, CompuServe, and the Microsoft Network, but it is the Internet that is the fastest-growing target for advertising in many forms. Some companies use vivid World Wide Web pages with graphics, video, and music as a sort of giant billboard that will, they hope, immediately attract the attention of the estimated (or, rather, guessed-at) 30 million people who surf the Internet and the hundreds of millions they believe will be doing so within a few years.

Companies that place ads and information on the Internet often pay less attention to how to lead the surfers to them in the first place than to catchy design. The Net is not organized in any way. There are no tidy product or market categories, only sites where pages are joined to each other in a very tenuous way through "hot links," words or phrases that you click on to move to other pages on the relevant topic. There is no comprehensive classified directory. It's very hard to browse the Internet efficiently.

Browsers are also not yet likely to be buyers. Many are "lurkers," who view a site and move on quickly. The only information advertisers get that tells them how successful their ads have been is the number of "hits" on their site. This is the equivalent of a Nielsen rating, which estimates how many television sets were tuned to a particular TV program, without reliably indicating what proportion were actively watching it rather than keeping it on in the background while they ate dinner. Page hits are simply a count of the number of times a single page is accessed. It may not even be read, only skimmed and abandoned. A Web "page" can be as long as a book—it's really a computer file. If a Web page has 10 pages of text and graphics and all ten are retrieved, this counts as ten hits. Yet market researchers point out that the number of hits is irrelevant—the value of hits lies in who (such as a kid playing around on the family computer versus a qualified buyer) retrieves the data and how that retrieval affects the user's awareness, attitude, or behavior. At a meeting of a large bank's top management team, one executive proudly announced that the firm's newly installed Web page was already getting 50 hits a day. He didn't seem to notice that 5 of today's hits had just been made in the demo that preceded his remark.

Web pages contain far less information than CD-ROMs because of the limitations of data transfer by modem. A CD-ROM drive can easily process and send to a PC full motion video, and designers want to include as much movement and color as they can. Internet advertisers are always advised to minimize movement and color. Otherwise, it can take minutes just to reach a single page and hours to transmit the same information that on the Toyota CD-ROM can be zipped through in 20 minutes or so.

All this means that on-line advertising is not a simple electronic extension of broadcast TV, home shopping, the Yellow

Shoppers in New York's Union Square have been dazzled and amazed by the realistic 3-D images of products from Bradlees department store that float above them on the sidewalk outside the shop. The "suspended volumetric displays" look virtually solid. The response of passersby has been so positive that Bradlees was able to sell 3-D "virtual" advertising space to manufacturers. Even if such advertising doesn't sell more goods than does conventional advertising, it grabs much more attention.

Pages, and newspaper ads. The keys to success seem to be (1) "narrowcast"—find ways of getting your message to the specific individuals and communities that are most likely to respond actively to it rather than passively; (2) focus on navigators, not surfers, on the Internet; (3) focus very carefully indeed on using multimedia for communicating information rather than exploiting its striking visual and auditory effects for "eye candy"; and (4) provide more than just a passive reading of what's on the screen; the attraction of the on-line world is interaction and exploration.

See also Business on the Internet; On-Line Shopping Malls

Agent   Agents are smart software routines that are the equivalent of your travel agent, a secretary, or a caterer who carries out tasks on your behalf without tying up your own time or making you wait around. Traditional software requires you to launch a function, typically by clicking on an icon on your PC screen. If it needs to link to another computer to search for data, for instance, it ties up your communication line during the time it is at work.

Agents go their way, leaving you free and your communications link open for you to use in other applications. They exploit well-established software principles that are only beginning to be translated into practical tools (technically, these are called object-oriented design, application program interfaces, remote procedure calls, and client-server computing). They are both a relative novelty now and a guaranteed major line of development for the future.

Examples of real agents rather than just prototypes or computer vendors' demonstrations, are performing a variety of functions:

- *DHL Worldwide Express's* package-tracking service enables customers to check when a package is due by phoning a voice-response system, a computer that queries customers and recognizes what they reply. The voice-response software launches agents that, in a few seconds, filter into the flow of communications traffic and data base inquiries to get the answer. Other agents work all the time in the background, tracking packages and notifying the sender and recipient by fax if the scheduled delivery is delayed.

- *Subscribers to AT&T's PersonaLink* service can select from among agents that filter and route electronic mail, flagging priority messages, responding automatically to certain types of electronic mail with canned messages, or paging them when a stock price drops below a specified level. They may also activate agents to order plane tickets for them, based on such instructions as "Schedule trip to Boston Thursday."

- *An Italian bank* is trying out a system that alerts bank staff when a client exceeds overdraft limits or other requirements and automatically notifies an area manager. Other agents spring into action, searching through relevant records to suggest ways of responding to the problem. If it turns out that the customer whose account is 300,000 lira short of the 800,000-lira check that is being submitted is also the chairman of the bank's best corporate customer and that he or she deposited a 12-million-lira bonus check into his investment account just three hours ago, these electronic equivalents of Santa's helpers may help avoid a very embarrassing situation. Without them, it is almost certain that the customer service rep would not have thought of logging onto the other computer systems that would have alerted him or her to these important facts.

- *Prodigy's Homework Helper* builds a student profile so that agents can automatically gather and present the information he or she needs to complete homework projects.

- *Telecommunications equipment vendors* use agents to help manage the ever-growing complexity of networks, as do IBM and Microsoft (for its Microsoft Network). Agents monitor traffic across the network at key points, taking action to filter out unnecessary messages, fix such problems as files being dumped onto overloaded disks, and report performance and security problems.

Agents are a necessary support for multimedia, in that "simple" computer systems are already far too complex for most people. Agents remove much of the complexity of software use. The entire premise underlying multimedia is that it is *natural* and uses computer power and communications speed to take away all the delays and procedures that get in the way of your natural response to and interaction with what you see and hear.

From the perspective of business managers considering multimedia applications for customer service, marketing, or training, agents are, by definition, a background issue. In the foreground is design of the multimedia application. The staff they will seek to build it will be specialists in the multimedia software package being used to create the video, CD-ROM, or publication, as well as experts in the subject area. This is fully adequate at the tactical level, but it is worth their considering the strategic level, too. This requires building the technical expertise to create the same overall organization and environment we take for granted in PCs. That environment includes help desks, software support, network administration, and data base management, all of which remove—or, perhaps more accurately, try to remove—from users the complexity of PC use.

The multimedia environment adds technical complexity to the already-overcomplex world of PC use and local area networks, to the extent that network managers cannot keep up with the demands of today's relatively slow speeds and simple networks. That is why they are looking to agents as the keys to network manage-

A simple example of an agent is the software that works in the background to correct your spelling mistakes as you type, automatically changing "teh name of the game" to "the name of the game." A more complex one is Computer Associates' personal finance program, where agents monitor your transactions and provide alerts and advice about any patterns or discrepancies in your activities. The technology of agents is in its adolescent stage at best, but there is every reason to be sure that they will be a key feature of multimedia tools.

ment and efficient use of telecommunications resources. Designers of multimedia software are looking to them to take over tedious procedures and to simplify users' tasks. Competitive advantage through networked multimedia almost surely lies in agents for providers of network equipment and services, for designers of multimedia tools and work environments, and also for companies aiming to make multimedia a core element of customer interaction and internal collaboration, coordination, and training.

America Online America Online is one of the most recent commercial providers of on-line information services, mainly for consumers, and to date is the most successful. It has an estimated 6 million subscribers, although the numbers claimed by on-line service providers are rather suspect because they do not distinguish between people who try them out very occasionally and people who make real use of them. Whenever you buy a new PC or a PC trade publication such as *Byte, Windows,* or one of dozens of other weekly and monthly magazines, it is likely that it will include a disk for AOL or one of its competitors with an offer of 10 hours' free use. Anyone who logs on to try out the service is counted as a "subscriber."

Whatever AOL's exact subscriber base, it is clearly in the lead in the consumer market for on-line services. What's special about America Online in comparison with the Internet is that it's where the teenagers and old folks are. The Internet is not representative of the broad population; it is overloaded (often literally as well as figuratively) with students and professors, affluent males and technical professionals. America Online's chat rooms are full of far more diverse users. Several music stars have held their own chat room sessions, attracting hundreds of people who interact with them on-line. Examples of the most popular rooms are Romance Connection, Gay and Lesbian, and the News Room.

As with the other on-line services, AOL offers Internet access, though without the (current) prestige of an Internet address like "Svensen@22kse.unive.edu," in which the "edu" suffix shows you are from an educational institution. For Svensen to send electronic mail to an AOL user, the address will be the recipient's pseudonym, such as Sweetdee@aol.com or even Bigears@aol.com. An Internet address is like a business card; an AOL one, more like a CB radio "handle."

All the on-line services have to deal with the same problem as cable TV—"content." If you have a satellite dish or cable, you have around 100 channels to access. Of course, there aren't 100 channels of programs worth watching; you may be lucky to find 5. Similarly, the problem with on-line information services is what information is worth accessing. AOL provides access to a wide range of business and news publications. Among those that use it as their main or sole on-line carrier are *Atlantic Monthly, Time,* the *Chicago Tribune,* and *Multimedia World.*

The Internet offers just about everything and anything—if you can find it. AOL, Prodigy, and CompuServe provide easy-to-access information, organized in clear categories, but much of it is of marginal value. For example, you can access an electronic version of *People* magazine on AOL, with news items and gossip pages. It will cost you five to ten times as much in phone and usage charges than you pay for a weekly copy of *People,* and the electronic version adds little to it.

In 1995, AOL expanded rapidly, buying companies that provided it with additional content and Internet facilities. In late 1995, it was trading at 70 times its estimated 1996 earnings and was capitalized at more than $4 billion. Its price then began to slip as margins dropped because of accelerating competition from the providers of servies on the Internet and from the Internet itself, which offers free information, whereas America Online's services carry an hourly fee. Content providers like *People* are demanding extra fees, and more and more content is being provided for little, if any, fee over the Internet. The Internet and Microsoft together are setting the competitive context in which on-line services will either extend or lose their identity. Microsoft made an unexpected alliance with AOL in March 1996, with

The president of America Online (AOL) believes that "content is no longer king." Instead, building communities around that content is the key to success. If, as a consumer, you want "information," then log onto CompuServe. Use AOL to hang out and exchange opinions. You might join its Rabbit Chat forum, as one journalist did, thereby saving some newborn rabbits abandoned by their mother, or "Pot Belly Pig Chat" or "Vultures as Pets." It's clear that millions of people are forming electronic communities that could not otherwise have existed.

Microsoft aiming to close off the expansion of its main rival, Netscape.

The future of AOL, like that of other on-line information services, is uncertain. Many commentators see them as a gradually dying species, to be edged out as the Internet becomes easier and easier to access and use. That said, America Online may well evolve into a giant Web site of its own. Ordinary folk *like* AOL, and they can get value out of it through its friendly chat rooms, e-mail, and menus of news, sports, and hobbyist information. They get the Internet too; currently, around half of all Internet access is via one of the three main on-line services, with AOL accounting for one-third of the total. That will certainly change over time, especially after AT&T's February 1996 announcement that it will offer its 80 million long-distance customers low-cost Internet access. AOL is just one of many offering the Internet. Netscape provides the Internet direct. Phone companies offer it as a simple add-on service. On-line services like AOL offer the "free" Internet as an extra, for which they charge by the hour. With a browser like Netscape Navigator, you do not need an on-line service, though you still must subscribe to an Internet service provider to get yourself a home page and Internet address. AOL provides that automatically, with the "@aol.com" that follows your pseudonym.

See also CompuServe; On-Line Information Services; Prodigy

Around half of all Internet access is made through one of the three largest public on-line services—AOL, CompuServe, and Prodigy—with 30 percent on AOL alone. The on-line services are moving rapidly to become not just Internet Web servers but huge Web sites. Others that had intended to be "content" providers independent of the Web are now abandoning those plans.

Animation Animation is one of the most easily assimilated modes of information display. It is remarkably well established, with hand-cranked animation machines dating from the eighteenth century. The multimedia principle is the same now as it was then: flip rapidly through still images, fooling the eye into seeing them as a continuous, moving stream. Animation is thus a natural extension of computer graphics and as such is a low-cost addition to the increasingly powerful hardware and software used for accessing, generating, and editing still images, whereas full-motion digital video involves very different techniques and places far more demands on speed and storage.

Most people associate animation with cartoons. That is obviously one of its main uses, but animation is also a very powerful way to get *ideas* across, sometimes more so than realistic video. It sends a very concentrated message by stripping out detail. It is easily absorbed and is one of the most age-, culture-, and language-independent of all media (as the continued success of Disney's over 50-year-old animated films show). It is easy to assimilate and holds viewers' attention.

It is for this reason that animation is becoming a common, though still controversial tool for presenting evidence to juries, as discussed in an article in *Multimedia World* (July 1994). Courtroom use is typical of the general impacts of animation. Computer reenactments played key roles in the murder conviction of a California pornographer who gunned down his brother; the animation showed how he did so. In several other cases, the jury "witnessed" the crime through animation, long after the victim had been buried. One of animation's special advantages lies in manipulating the rules of space and time. For example, a process that takes years, such as soil erosion or a bridge rusting, can be shown meaningfully in a few seconds. Conversely, the movement of an arm can be slowed down. The space in which an animation takes place can be highlighted, especially through the 3-D tools that are increasingly becoming available on standard multimedia PCs. You can remove background buildings, isolate characters, or freeze the image for several seconds.

The power of multimedia worries some legal experts: "Full-motion video simulations confer pseudomemories on jurors, giving them the feeling that they witnessed the event. Any portrayal of a crime requires making certain assumptions—about where people are standing, their states of mind, whether they're behaving in anger—and those assumptions are missing in animated video." Proponents counter that animation gives juries the vocabulary they need in order to understand often-complicated

"If 12 jurors are given the same description of a complicated event, you can be sure that they'll all have different movies running in their heads. . . . Engineering Animation Inc. produces computer-animated re-creations for courtrooms and television news programs. The cartoons may not accurately depict what happened, but at least everybody gets the same idea." (Wired, September 1995)

evidence. Attorneys like the way it speeds trials and gives a jury a better grasp of facts. "A trial isn't the presentation of the truth, it's a search for the truth. And if animation helps you to see another point of view, it will help people find the truth."

Most courtroom animations in fact look more like video games than videotapes. This is deliberate. Too much realism will get an animation dismissed as inadmissible because it is prejudicial. Animators therefore neutralize grisly details, for instance. Faces do not match that of the accused or the victim. One case was thrown out of court, for example, because the animators put a face on the animated accused that made him look menacing, prejudicing his plea of self-defense.

The era of multimedia evidence has arrived steadily and quietly, but unequivocally. It is becoming part of everyday law. "Everyone understands that a witness may lie. Now we have to educate juries where videotapes, computers and virtual reality may lie." The cost of producing courtroom animations has fallen from around $250,000 in the mid-1980s to $5,000.

Animation software is widely available at very low cost on any PC that meets the minimal hardware requirements for handling multimedia. The software part is now easy, and the hardware part has been so for some time. What is, of course, more difficult is the human part. At one level, anyone can be an animator, for two-dimensional animation at least. But taking advantage of the features of animation software calls for special skills that are not common either in businesses or in schools: the ability to build visual models. Over the past 30 years, business thinking has been geared largely toward analytic models and numbers rather than toward pictures. The business school training of managers is strongly focused in this direction. Managers think in words and numbers. Slides used in management presentations generally make only limited use of color and still graphics, enhancing them but not exploiting the power of animation to communicate.

That calls for multimedia *thinking* rather than just multimedia tools. Just how scarce this skill is in businesses can easily be seen in the poor layout and graphics on many companies' Web pages—and this is one of the most basic semimultimedia applications. One of the key long-term issues for business use of multimedia is attracting people with visual and design skills who are also either experienced with or adept in learning the tools of multimedia. Getting value from the many animation tools widely available at low cost is no longer just a question of technology.

The opportunities of two-dimensional animation for business are substantial. Full-motion video for multimedia marketing or training remains a complex process requiring powerful hardware and plenty of time. By contrast, still images can be easily edited, sound added, and animation then used to provide visual sequencing, interaction, and communication. For many departments that now make effective use of PCs, animation may be the most productive and simple extension into multimedia.

AOL *See* America Online

API API is the abbreviation for "*a*pplication *p*rogram *i*nterface." APIs are one of the key elements of the computer programmer's art. They provide the links from one software application to another, by sending messages in a standardized form, which each software routine can interpret and reply to. For instance, for a spreadsheet to automatically insert a piece of video that provides visual commentary on its figures, the application must pass a message to the video software. APIs are the routines that handle this; they generate the dialogue between the applications.

The message formats must, of course, be standardized so that each software package can work with many others. Ideally, the "many others" would be "any other." but this is not the case. APIs are a relatively recent innovation in commercial use of computers. Leading families of products use their own APIs, with standards only gradually emerging. Thus, for instance, Microsoft's MCI

(Media Control Interface) handles the programming calls for media from Windows-based applications; Microsoft has added a set of APIs for what it terms "digital video device class." This class includes audio, video, and images. The goal in creating and publishing the APIs is to eliminate the need for programmers to write different software for different manufacturers' video boards' software "drivers," for instance.

The entire world of computer software is moving toward objects and APIs. Objects are self-contained "things" that can be shared, combined, and reused in many applications—things like a picture, a phone message, or a routine to calculate a figure, rotate an image, retrieve a data item, display a graph, or even monitor prices of airplane tickets for a few hours and let you know when it finds the best deal (these routines are special objects called "agents"). APIs are the messages that allow objects to be linked together.

Multimedia is fundamentally object-based. "Play me this tune and at the same time display this photograph and then call Jim and tell him this is coming from Peter and record his reply and store it in my Jim file" would be an impossible request to meet in practical terms in the 1980s. Now, a skilled programmer can use objects and APIs, and some software packages handle them automatically. The request is converted to "Send this API message to software A to locate and play the tune. Also send an API to software B to access, convert, and display the photo," and so on. Here, any multimedia item is an object "thing," as is any software routine needed to find or deliver it.

The scope of APIs is growing very rapidly. Since anything can be an object, APIs can be developed for them. Thus, for instance, Microsoft also offers TAPI (Telephony API) that competes with Novell and AT&T's TSAPI. It's working on SAPI (Speech API), which will allow software that handles speech recognition to annotate electronic mail or allow you to talk directly to standard word processing packages.

See also Agent; Object

Apple Apple Computer is the struggling $13 billion company that has always been the leader in personal computers, that created most of the innovations in multimedia that are now routine, that has an almost religiously devoted community of users (myself included), and that still, in the opinion of most expert commentators, may not survive unless it is acquired by a stronger partner. IBM offered to buy Apple, but the firm's chairman rejected the bid as too low. In late 1995, Apple's chief financial officer resigned because he did not believe Apple was viable by itself. Sun Microsystems later met with Apple to hammer out terms for Sun to acquire it; the (rejected) offer was even lower. The business and information technology trade press monitors Apple on an almost-weekly basis, with most, at best, cautiously not too pessimistic. By the time this book appears, Apple may well be a subsidiary of Sony, Motorola, or ABM—any firm but Microsoft.

Apple increasingly looks like the Betamax of the PC field. Betamax was a failure because a technically inferior technology—VHS—became the dominant design in the consumer marketplace. Apple similarly was displaced by the dominant design of Windows but remains a strong force at the high end of the market, though much less so than before. Just about every innovation in multimedia that is now the mainstream on PCs came first on the Mac.

Fewer innovations now come via the Macintosh. Whereas a few years ago the multimedia innovators began by developing their software for the Mac and then added Windows versions, they now naturally begin where the market is. Although many Mac users claim that Apple's computers are far ahead of Windows-based ones, even of Windows 95, in terms of ease of use and reliability, the advantages are smaller than before, and Apple has priced itself out of the main market.

1996 began with yet another Apple confession of problems. Four top executives left the firm. Apple announced in mid-January that it had lost almost $70 million in the last quarter of 1995 and misjudged the Christmas market. Its chairman was forced

Apple's ads show that in 1995 it was rated the leader among computer manufacturers in the following categories: (1) highest customer loyalty, (2) top-selling single brand in the United States, (3) top-selling multimedia machines, (4) top-rated home computers, (5) most reliable PCs, and (6) top computers in education. For almost two decades, Apple has been the innovator in multimedia PC hardware, and the most innovative software multimedia developers built their pros for Apple. That Apple is seen by most experts as unlikely to survive on its own shows the power of the Windows juggernaut.

out, making Apple the first multibillion-dollar firm in which every chairman since its founding has been fired. Apple still has many weapons in its armory as it faces the Intel-Microsoft hordes, although those weapons may be deployed by whomever acquires it. For over a decade, Apple deliberately kept its machines incompatible with Windows. Now, it is easier and cheaper than before to run both Windows and Mac programs on its PowerMac line. For just as long, it blocked any licensing of its designs and software to other manufacturers, trying to prevent the growth of the same "clone" imitators that lost IBM its control of the PC market (Compaq, Dell, Toshiba, Packard Bell, and so on). Now, it has allowed clones to pace price and quality, with Apple learning how to match them. It has a new generation of operating systems and development tools targeted to its stronghold of multimedia thinking and innovation. It has belatedly licensed its PowerPC software to Motorola. Its Pippin technology may be a strong player in the growing market for game machines, low cost Internet "appliances," and personal digital assistants. As one of the most successful venture capitalists in the information technology field comments, Apple still has assets that other businesses would kill for.

This guide was written on a Windows-based laptop computer. I don't remember *ever* using it for more than an hour without saying to myself at some point when wrestling with Windows' quirks, "This would be *so* much easier on a Mac!" I hope that my management guide to business multimedia is hype-free, objective, and dispassionate. This entry is, I also hope, hype-free, but it is both subjective and passionate. In the eternal distinction between heart and mind, Microsoft is mind, and Apple is heart. My mind accepts that I must now use a Windows machine. Apple has been left behind in the laptop market: too slow, too expensive, and lacking such features as the CD-ROM drive that I use more than I do floppy disks.

I'm not a multimedia innovator, expert, or even skilled user. I like books better than CD-ROMs, paper better than screens, and bookstores better than the Internet. But if I'm passionate about

Apple Powerbooks, what about the multimedia innovators, experts, and skilled users who are more likely to be Apple devotees than Windows victims? Whenever you as a business manager are looking for multimedia experience, creativity, and innovation, don't overlook the Mac community as a source of talent.

That talent is conservative as well as innovative. The editor of *Publish* commented (October 1995) about the multimedia PC-Mac debate that

> Those who'd like to see Windows 95 as a "Mac slayer" overlook some of the main reasons designers and publishers use Macs so much more readily than the rest of the computing world—simple inertia and familiarity. For most designers, the Mac is the conservative choice. The design schools where they learned their trade are outfitted with Macs, the studios where they got their first jobs are equipped with Macs, and the design stars they look up to work on Macs. When they choose computers for their own studios, where do you expect them to turn? I've watched designers use Quark/XPress to write form letters and simple lists of names because they're not comfortable with a word processor—these people are not going to switch operating systems lightly. . . . The corporate world made its choice a long time ago and—talk about inertia—have you ever tried to get a corporation to change its mind? The Mac has become a high-end tool for a specialized market and ironically, the Intel/Windows PC has turned out to be the "computer for the rest of them."

Applet   An applet is a small application, a self-contained piece of program code that is like a Lego block. The term has been in use for many years but is now closely associated with a programming language called Java, which is aimed at "network-centric" computing via the Internet. Instead of using a PC with massive operating systems and software applications that may take up half your hard disk storage, the logic is that you work with a low-cost Internet appliance that downloads applets from the network as you need them. Few people use more than a fraction of the features of Windows or of the many word processing, spreadsheet, and data base management packages that work with it. Why not have these stored on a telecommunications network and accessed only if and when you need them?

That question is now dominating the information technology field. Essentially, Microsoft and Intel see the future as one of applications on PCs that access the network for information, communication, and shared resources such as high-speed printers. Sun, Oracle, and many PC, television and game machine makers and software companies see it as one of applets on far simpler Internet appliances. Of course, neither extreme may win out, and both futures may coexist, with neither one having greatly altered current trends in computer usage. Whether that is so or not, applets represent a major innovation, which is especially important for multimedia, in that many people need powerful software routines for handling sound, video, and image only very occasionally. Instead of clogging up your hard disk with hundreds of these, it makes a lot of sense to get them from the network.

Applet is obviously derived from "application," which means a software package that does something specific, such as word processing or desktop publishing. The software trade talks about "apps," especially the "killer app" for which companies continuously search; these are the blockbuster packages that become dominant designs. *Applet* is now part of the trade vocabulary.

See also Java; Network Computer

ASCII   ASCII, standing for "*A*merican *S*tandard *C*ode for *I*nformation *I*nterchange," is the simplest code for digital information and also one of the oldest terms in the vocabulary of information technology. It is the antithesis of multimedia and represents the minimum of monomedia. ASCII was developed at a time when the only type of data handled by business computers was alphanumeric numbers and letters. It provided an almost industrywide convention (IBM ignored the standard-setting group's efforts and implemented its own EBCDIC system) for the characters 0 to 9, *a* to *z*, *A* to *Z*, and such common characters as $, *, and @. Each is assigned a unique value between 0 and 128, which requires 7 binary digits to represent. *X*, for instance is 0010100.

ASCII is too simple to include all the many additional data items needed to handle telecommunications messages, word processing, and graphics. Companies developing software for, say, word processing thus used their own conventions to store formatting (boldface, superscript, spacing, paragraph marks, character size, and so on). As a result, the text of this paragraph, which is in a file produced by Microsoft Word, must be converted to the format of any other word processing software, such as Amipro or WordPerfect, even though it contains only text characters.

Today, ASCII means text that is stripped down to the barest data needed to convey its content. That makes it useless for multimedia or, as one commentator says, useless for business. The main use of ASCII is in simple electronic mail systems. ASCII is a reminder of how difficult it is to establish common standards for media formats. When even text is not standardized, it is hardly surprising that there are so many file formats for graphics, with each one coding the very same information in a slightly different way.

ATM   ATM, which stands for "*a*synchronous *t*ransfer *m*ode," is the emerging base for the telecommunications networks of the late 1990s. Rarely referred to by its cumbersome full name, it is more generally called ATM, which is also, of course, the acronym for "*a*utomated *t*eller *m*achine." It offers step shift, not just incremental, improvements in speed and cost over the transmission services offered by both long distance (wide area networks), regional and local phone companies (metropolitan networks), and local area networking technology (within buildings or campuses). It also makes these very different technologies equivalent in terms of how the designers of the enterprise network can fit the local, regional, and national pieces together. The goal is to create a

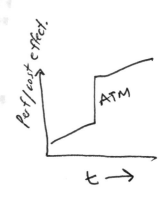

"seamless" business resource like the electrical utility that we take for granted and use on a plug-in-and-go basis. It will be anywhere from 3 to 10 years before companies will have the telecommunications version of the utility, but the basics of the technology are proven, and the pieces are becoming more available and reliable.

ATM is almost surely a key to business multimedia networking, just as CD-ROM is the key to PC multimedia that does not require high-capacity telecommunications links for access to remote information or for data sharing. This is so because (1) ATM provides the raw transmission speed needed for fast and efficient movement of very large video, audio, and image files; and (2) it handles this on an on-demand basis, providing the relevant speed of transmission as needed, when needed, instead of through a fixed cost leasing of high-speed "private" lines.

ATM and a simpler and more widely available technology called "frame relay" also reduce the transmission delays inherent in today's networks, which were built on less reliable technology than is now available. In today's networks, overhead is added as a message moves through the many intermediate devices ("nodes") that route it to its destination, because each node checks for transmission errors. This extra processing time can add up to 100 milliseconds (thousandths of a second) from end to end. This is completely unacceptable for many multimedia applications, making a video transmission like watching a 1920s newsreel. ATM and frame relay do not require complex and time-consuming error checking, instead pumping data through nodes very quickly.

Prior to the emergence of ATM and frame relay, high-speed transmission facilities could be obtained only by large companies leasing circuits from such providers as AT&T, MCI, or comparable international providers. These "private" networks were expensive and "point to point"; that is, they connected two major hubs, such as London and New York. The speeds they offered ranged from "switched 56," two printed page equivalents per second (56 kbps), up to 60 pages (1.54 Mbps "T1"), with faster speeds available but used only for special operations. The upper limit was T4 service, at 40 book equivalents (274 Mbps). ATM offers multiple options on demand, with 25, 45, 155, and 622 Mbps being standard units and 300 book equivalents (2.5 Gbps) practical. In March 1996, three competing firms demonstrated transmission at 1 trillion bits per second. At that speed you can send about 300 years of a daily newspaper every second.

ATM exploits any and every improvement in transmission speeds. It's a technique, not a medium. It works on any type of network. Like so many innovations in the telecommunications field, ATM was grossly overhyped when it first appeared in the early 1990s. Commentators overextrapolated from early successes on small-scale networks and talked as if ATM were an instant opportunity. It's not. Its evolution rests on equipment vendors' making major innovations in products and on telecommunications providers' deciding when to launch services, how to price them, and how to manage them. Building an enterprise's high-speed network pushes the state of the product art in many areas: the switches that manage the flow of traffic, the software that coordinates the ultrahigh-speed traffic, new types of equipment specific to ATM, and the configuring of transmission facilities. There are several interim options for firms to choose from, which provide some, though not all, of the advantages of ATM. These are not described in this Glossary. They include frame relay (wide area networking), SMDS (regional and metropolitan), and CDDI and Fast Ethernet (local area networks).

ATM = technique, not medium

interim

It may thus be a decade before the promise of ATM is fulfilled. Meanwhile, however, companies are rapidly adopting it for applications in which the costs and risks of being on the bleeding edge of technology are more than offset by the payoff of being able to move masses of multimedia data across long distances and multiple locations. Examples are print production, time-dependent high-value financial transactions, film editing and postproduction, videoconferencing, medical imaging, television broadcasting, and seismic analysis. Here are four illustrations of what the pioneers are up to and why:

- *Oil exploration.* It can take up to a year for seismic data collected by oil companies from remote sites (including the middle of oceans and jungles) to be accessible for analysis by scientists, using their computer workstations and PCs. The Aries consortium of computer equipment vendors, telecommunications service providers, and oil firms demonstrated an ATM network in October 1995 that covers 3.5 million square miles and effectively puts the supercomputer on the drill site. It runs at speeds of up to 6 printed book equivalents per second (45 Mbps). The demonstration system linked two AMOCO oil rigs out at sea in the Gulf of Mexico, two U.S. locations, a federal government node in Washington, D.C., and a NASA satellite communications hub. The data gathered at the oil rigs were available immediately. The volume of information is massive. One seismic probe may generate a trillion bits of data—several Library of Congress equivalents. That takes over 60 hours to transmit even with ATM. However, sent in megabit chunks, processing and interpretation can begin within seconds. Here, ATM will certainly have as much impact on oil exploration processes as the other ATM—the automated teller machine—has had on banking processes.

- *Securities trading.* Donaldson, Lufkin and Jenrette (DLJ), the New York brokerage firm, recovered the costs of its installation of ATM in less than 10 months. The firm's Finance Desk has to pay the Federal Reserve Bank fees for what are called "daylight overdrafts." These fees are charged *by the minute* on the firm's inventory of Treasury bills, notes, and bonds. The quicker DLJ can process deals and move them out of the firm, the lower these fees. The high-speed ATM network enables the firm to reindex its ever-changing trading file in 5 instead of 15 minutes and removes all bottlenecks in communication.

In DLJ's business, fast is never fast enough. That's why it replaced its already very fast network, which operated at around 13 book equivalents (100 Mb) with a 100 to 155 Mb ATM system that links its trading desks. One distinctive advantage of the 100 Mb ATM capability over the 100 Mb existing system is that, although the transmission speed is the same, ATM can handle multimedia isochronous video traffic. (*Isochronous* means that the traffic has to be precisely synchronized so that it flows continuously and smoothly.)

- *Publishing.* A Phoenix newspaper has installed ATM to handle the new multimedia nature of publishing, which is becoming more and more interactive and "image-intensive" rather than word-intensive. The new network makes practical such experiments as presentation of up-to-the-minute news over the Internet.

- *Film and TV multimedia.* The Soho area of London has more advanced broadcast postproduction facilities for TV and film companies than any other site in the world. This is where Britain's top video editors, animators, and graphic artists produce what are recognized as among the very best TV commercials anywhere. Most of the firms are too small to afford the $40,000 ATM installation charge plus the cost of monthly service. As a result, British Telecom has piloted a shared ATM network with links to New York and then on to Los Angeles. One of its users commented in late 1995 that it will put couriers out of business and make products "faster, cheaper and of better quality." The network also enables services that are otherwise impractical, including taking output directly from the Silicon Graphics computers that are the multimedia workhorse of Hollywood, thereby cutting out several time-consuming steps that also lose some of the original information. "We will be able to scan clients' film and download it to their computers via ATM. . . . We are working on a development which would allow us to transfer to film in almost real time. So if they send it to us in the evening, we could get it into the lab and they'd have it for viewing in the morning" (a manager at CineSite Europe). One firm's technical director, though, states that the ATM network is still too slow, even though it is around 15 times faster that what he now has available.

The entire telecommunications field is in a frenzy of technical, business, and regulatory innovation that makes the 1980s and 1990s pace of change in the PC industry look like a turtle on Valium. It is also coining a morass of alphabet soup jargon. Of all the terms and trends, though, ATM is one of the most important two or three for every manager to know about.

See also Bandwidth; Latency; Telecommunications Legislation

Audio   Audio is sound. In digital form, it can be stored and accessed as if it were a document. It originates in the everyday world in nondigital form: the low-frequency sound waves of our voice, the much more complex interplay of musical instruments, and the sounds of nature. Audio technology captures these waves and processes them. It can also create digital sounds that it converts so that we hear them as sound waves; a synthesizer can create musical "instruments" that have never physically existed. A standard tape recorder or camcorder captures and stores the waves as waves; it simply creates an analogous copy of the sound—hence the term *analog*. A sound board in a computer captures the waves but must be able to digitize them in real time, as fast as the music is played; the same is required to convert digitized sound for us to hear it.

Audio has long been a component of the multimedia digital toolkit, mainly through the music compact disc technology of which CD-ROM is the direct extension. More recently, digital audio has been incorporated in, first, computer game machines and, now, multimedia PCs. The Internet offers limited digital radio and phone services and primitive digital television. Much of the most imaginative application of digital editing techniques has come from music studios, through the use of electronic synthesizers and imaginative production of TV videos, with MTV establishing a new style and level of quality. Music has been the main driver of multimedia audio.

The telecommunications and storage demands of audio are far less than those of video. The basic tools of digitization have been established for several decades and first used by the public phone system. The sound wave is sampled at a rate of 7,000 times per second for voice phone, for instance; sampling means simply that its characteristics are recorded at this rate instead of the continuous wave being sent. The relative frequency of the sound wave at each sampling moment in time is coded as a number, from 0 to 256, which requires 8 bits—or 1 byte, the basic unit of computer coding—to store the value. This means that a second of digital voice requires two printed page equivalents to code (56,000 bits) to and thus a 56-kbps transmission link to send it.

The higher the rate of sampling per second and the more bits used to code the waveform height, the better the quality of the sound. For CD audio, the sampling rate is 44,100 times per second (technically, the sample is digitized at 44,100 kHz, where kHz stands for kilocycles, which means thousands of cycles per second), and 16 bits are used to code the sample. The human ear can start hearing sounds that are around 20 cycles per second, which comes across as a deep hum, and the upper range is around 20,000 Hz or 20 kHz. Very high-frequency—high-pitch—sound, at 1 million Hz, hits your pain threshold; you can't hear it, but you sure can feel it.

The dynamics of psychoacoustics are complex. Our ears have evolved to localize sound, perceive the frequency of a sound as a particular pitch, convert its level of intensity into loudness, and detect gaps and changes in notes. In many ways, our ears are more

The antecedents of multimedia are the silent slide slow, management presentation graphics and silent movies. Now, multimedia without sound is as unidimensional as the silver screen before the talkies—a great medium but an artificial one.

Voice Example
8 bits to store sound frequency

8 bits × 7000 samples/sec
= 56,000 bps

• Can use > 8 bits to store
• Can sample > 7000 x/sec

CDs ⟹ sample 44 K/sec

sensitive than our eyes. The entire nature of animation and video is to trick the eye into seeing a series of still images as if they were a continuous flow of movement. Our eyes can't process them fast enough to spot the difference. Our ears are less easily fooled and pleased.

This means that in many multimedia applications, the quality of audio is more important to us than that of video. Users of videoconferencing systems frequently report that they can easily put up with slightly fuzzy video images or occasional flicker, but not with "noisy" sound, breakups, hiss, or echoes. Until the availability of the specialized computer chips called "digital signal processors," sound quality for multimedia PCs was mediocre. Game machines like Nintendo and Sega used the MIDI standard ("*mu*sical *i*nstrument *d*igital *i*nterface"), which is an efficient and compact way to store and communicate music but inadequate for video and high-quality playback. You need a MIDI port (physical connection point on your sound card) only if you want to link your PC to an electronic instrument.

It was until recently very difficult to synchronize video and sound tracks in real time. AT&T's Videophone, for instance, suffered from the sounds' arriving a fraction of a second after the picture, making it almost impossible to use in comfort. Although sound and image must work together, as they do with TV, they play a somewhat different role in human communication. We get our sense of apprehension from image and our sense of comprehension more from audio—you often take in the picture without consciously understanding it. The words add the understanding. Try turning the sound on your TV set way down on a news program. You'll struggle to follow it. If, though, you make the picture a little blurred, you will get most of the sense of the program from the sound. That is, you can deduce much of the picture from the sound, but not the other way around.

A sound file on your PC hard disk is just like any other file, such as a word processed document or a digital image of a photograph. Your PC will need a sound card to process it. That card is really a mini-PC in itself, with dozens of electronic components. The dominant design here is the 16-bit Sound Blaster board (the terms *sound board, audio card,* and variants on these are used interchangeably) that was built into well over half of all multimedia PCs sold in 1995. In addition to a sound card, the PC requires speakers and a microphone. Installing all these can be an exercise in saintlike patience, a Swiss watchmaker's precision, and Nobel prizewinner's intelligence in interpreting the manuals, so that more and more multimedia PCs come with everything built in.

Audio files are not as large as those for video, measured in bits per second, but still chew up disk space. A low fidelity mono recording at 11 KHz with 8-bit resolution takes 20 printed page equivalents (660 Kb) per minute of recording; 16-bit sampling at 22 KHz takes four times that and twice that again for stereo sound (two channels instead of the one channel of audio). Data compression reduces this somewhat, but at the cost of loss of quality in most instances. Stereo can be compressed down by a factor of 10. There are a number of different audio file formats. Ones that have the suffix ".MID" (as in JINGLE4.MID) are MIDI files. Those with ".WAV" are Microsoft Sound files and thus the ones you are most likely to find installed on your Windows-based PC. AVI files interweave audio and video; the audio for each video frame is stored next to it in the sequence of data.

Audio on multimedia PCs is a matter of configuring hardware; today's sound cards and other devices provide everything the typical business or consumer user needs. It's a more complex matter to handle audio over multimedia networks. For collaborative work via videoconferencing and for interactive work such as multimedia training, it is vital that all voice transmissions be clear and easily intelligible and that there be no intermittent delays. Complex networks inherently add delays to the transmission of high-speed, high-volume data. This delay is called "latency" and is typically around 100 milliseconds, but it can be much more on a congested network. Studies show   100 milliseconds latency is acceptable to our ears and brains. A 250-millisecond

"It is a whole other level of communication. Sound provides the author a direct line of communication through dialog and narration. It provides them an emotional palette for music and an enriched palette with effects and design elements. Ultimately it broadens the limitations of a computer experience" (interview with a leading sound designer, in Multimedia Demystified*).*

delay leaves speech comprehensible but irritating to listen to. At 600 milliseconds, it becomes incomprehensible. Ensuring quality audio is often a far bigger challenge than handling video. You can test that out by using your camcorder. The video will be far better than the audio.

Adding audio to other digital tools offers many business opportunities. McCaw Cellular's service people troubleshoot phones over the phone by playing audio tones digitally stored on their workstation until the customer recognizes the sound that indicates the problem. They then can provide that customer with information about how to solve it. Voice synthesis is now routine for customer service via push-button phone (getting your credit card balance, for instance). It greatly augments computer software. Cemex, the Mexican company that has been a consistent innovator in the managerial use of computers, uses it to guide new users of systems through tutorials and provide help. A soft-spoken voice explains menus and options, and when you move the cursor to an item on the screen, you get a voice explanation, instead of text.

A number of companies have found that first rate voice with informative still graphic images is as effective for many multimedia training programs on PCs as video, and much cheaper to develop. Video gets most of the attention in discussions of multimedia, mainly because of its importance in entertainment markets, but from a business point of view, audio may be the more effective medium. Pictures plus voice overlay are cheaper and easier to generate, as well as being very effective. PBS used no video whatsoever in delivering its powerful, vivid documentary series on the Civil War. Training programs can do the same.

See also CD; Latency; MIDI; Sound Blaster

Authoring   Authoring is the multimedia equivalent of writing but involves very different processes, skills, and tools. Authoring means structuring an interactive multimedia product. It is more like computer programming than writing and indeed uses many tools that are equivalent to those programmers use in information systems development. Books are linear, in the sense that the author builds a sequence of presentation that adds to readers' interest and knowledge as they proceed. Clarity of structure, avoidance of repetition, and smooth transitions are key to communication of content. An author here moves the book *forward* in a sequence built of relatively long building blocks: chapters and sections within chapters. A book is irritating to read if it is choppy or keeps making references to previous or future pages. The best book is a "page turner." An acceptable one holds your interest, but you may skip a few pages.

By contrast, multimedia is interactive and presents relatively short bursts of information. Rather than start at the beginning and move forward, you may start anywhere and work sideways or backwards and not even know where the pieces fit in sequence. A CD-ROM is irritating if you can't jump around, if the screen is full of too much text that you have to scroll through to read, and if it's too static. A multimedia page turner is thus a boring poor substitute for a book.

These differences mean that multimedia and written books are not equivalent, that each has its advantages, that you can't turn a book straightforwardly into multimedia, and that you can't turn a book author into a multimedia author. It also means that most CD-ROMs are execrable. It's not at all surprising that the reported return rate to stores of purchased CD-ROMs is around 20 percent. My own estimate is that only one-fifth of the more than 100 CD-ROMs I have bought and used in developing this book have any redeeming value. Several of the real duds are electronic versions of excellent paper magazines, which result in lousy electronic magazines jazzed up with pictures. Similarly, most Internet home pages on the World Wide Web are management presentations jazzed up with a flash of color and a few uninteresting graphics.

Many of the worst products come from very large firms with very big budgets. The CD-ROM version of *Time* magazine, given away with many multimedia PCs, is about as useful as a pile of old magazines pawed through while wearing mittens. The graphics are an arbitrary hodgepodge of photos. The CD-ROM *Wheel of Fortune,* my own favorite TV game, is more useful as a coaster than as entertainment, with some of the dumbest possible uses of graphics and sound.

Companies with large budgets and plenty of experience in their markets are coming up with truly bad products that the sponsors authorize for release in the obvious expectation that they will be a hit. These people are not stupid. The problem appears to be that they don't see just how different multimedia design and use is from that for traditional media. Of course, only a fraction of the thousands of published books are more than mediocre, so it's unreasonable to expect that CD-ROMs, interactive training software, and Web pages should all be good. All the same, when firms put their image and reputation on line or spend hundreds of thousands of dollars to develop a multimedia product, they must make sure they meet the highest standards of customer expectations for multimedia, not the standards for an acceptable book.

This means that multimedia authoring is as distinctive a skill as writing books. *Multimedia authoring involves a different way of thinking and a different development process, to produce a different product for a different use by what is often a different type of audience.* With books, the writer does around 10 percent of the work. The typical multimedia author has to do 90 percent in a much more compressed time frame. For instance, the writing of *Every Manager's Guide to Business Processes,* my book that was published as I was finishing the first draft of *Business Multimedia Explained,* took me around eight months of work, averaging 30 hours a week. That draft was reviewed by outside experts. I produced a new version that incorporated (or rejected) what they had to say. From there, the book went into the key process, where the development goes through the exhaustive structuring, cleaning up, compressing, and other improvements that move a book from the writer's very personal creation toward the product that people pick up in a bookstore. My guess is that at least 80 percent of the draft pages bear a stream of editors' red pencil marks. Add to this the generation of diagrams, layout, indexing, and other aspects of production, and it's not surprising that it can take a year or more from finished manuscript to finished product. Production follows writing and is clearly separate from it.

In multimedia authoring, production begins with and is intertwined with the writing, in that right from the start the developer has to address the "multi" aspects of multimedia and make ongoing decisions about how content will be structured and delivered rather than just focus on content. For example, here are a few of the basic questions to ask when choosing an authoring tool:

- Will your application be used only by passive viewers? interactively?

- Who is your audience? the general public? high school students? professionals?

- Do you need linear presentations? menu selection? random-access interactivity? data base capability? hypertext? audio? animation? hard-copy output? touchscreen control? student management?

- What media sources will you use? audio? still images? motion video? animation?

- Will these be clips from existing material, obtained from outside sources? created as part of this development?

- What is the authoring metaphor for this project? hierarchical? slide show? book page? window? timeline? network? icon? (These are terms that multimedia authors use to describe the integrating style of the multimedia material from the user's viewpoint, in terms of what they see and how the interactive dialogue is structured.)

- How is interactivity to be provided? buttons on screen? menus? hypertext? touchscreen?

A 200-page book becomes 700 pages in multimedia form because of the addition of material that would be impossible to provide otherwise. It is likely to be a mediocre book if it is a straight conversion of the written one with the addition of music and video. A first-rate 700-page electronic "book" should be designed for interactivity, which requires an entirely different authoring process.

Software authoring tools help answer all these questions. Typically, they use the answers to guide the author through a sequence of steps that build the material. For example, the IconAuthor software package provides about 50 types of icons from which the author can pick to build a flowchart of the structure of the material before actually developing its content. The icons include such steps as play a transition sound, erase all remaining displays, prompt for an answer to a question on the screen, show animation, pause, pick a video clip, and many others. Some tools amount to a multimedia programming language, and others are scripting languages, media creation systems, storyboards, and presentation systems. There is no standardization of authoring software to date, and no one set of tools has become the dominant design. Leading examples of authoring tools are MacroMedia's Authorware Professional and AimTech's IconAuthor.

Many firms will author their own interactive multimedia product manuals, training materials, customer service kiosks, and interactive marketing and advertising. They face many barriers, all of which are surmountable but need to be anticipated, not backed into when it's too late. They include the cost of acquisition and development of the multimedia itself, production quality, especially audio and video, lack of standardization of software and hardware tools, conformance with copyright laws and rules of intellectual property, and trading off ease of use and power in choice of authoring tools. With all these to deal with, perhaps it's not surprising that the most basic issues of design take second place and that production dominates style. This is the opposite of book writing, where content design takes first place and production is often left, if anything, until too late.

The sheer mechanics of multimedia development lead to the poor-quality products that I have criticized earlier. From my own review of the best multimedia products I have come across, several points seem key to success. The first, and most important, is that these products are truly multimedia in their entire conception. The CD-ROMs that provide interactive versions of *Time, Sports*

Illustrated, and *Wheel of Fortune* are clearly multimedia adaptations of existing media and hence existing presentation structures. They are interactive only in an elementary and limited way. Ones like *Myst, Passage to Vietnam,* and *500 Nations,* to choose just three exemplars, are naturally interactive. In addition, it's obvious that a great deal of thought went into structuring the interaction at the start of the design process.

The good products also seem to balance the multimedia they use. In others, you sense that, say, video has been added only because the author feels that video must be part of any multimedia offering. More generally, most audio seems an add-on and not intrinsic to the design. For example, a visually superb CD-ROM that displays Audubon prints also offers audio clips of bird songs. These don't tie to the visuals at all and are like an electronic appendix. By contrast, *Passage to Vietnam* weaves photographer's comments, sound bites, and video clips into its main sequence of photographs in the same way that the music and atmospheric background sound in *Myst* augment rather than accompany the visuals of the game.

In my own experimentation with four authoring tools, I found them quite easy to use technically. They can be fun, too. It's very enjoyable to see your own animated diagram come to life, or to morph an image. It's not hard, either, to work with short video clips and to insert audio into the sequence. That said, my product was consistently lousy. I found that books and tutorials on how to author multimedia don't help any more than those on how to write a book. All they help with is the mechanics. I sense that what matters most in multimedia authoring is developing the interactive *structure*, not the interactive content, interactive menus, or specific videos, music, displays, and the like.

No book editor can rescue a badly written book with no content, but he or she can help immensely in rescuing a weak structure; that's the case with my own books which tend to lack clear structure. The situation is the opposite with multimedia; no strong or exciting content can rescue a weak structure. The challenge is to balance three types of talent: (1) the ability to design a structure, which is the skill of the computer programmer; (2) the visual skill of the multimedia graphics designer or video producer; and (3) the content skill of the writer. When one of these skills dominates and the others are missing, you won't get the product you hoped for and, quite probably, the authors won't realize what's missing. The probability of your own firms' authoring multimedia products within the next three years is about 95 percent. It will need to locate, encourage, reward, and retain at least a small team of people with this mix of talents.

Bandwidth   Bandwidth is the fundamental measure of the carrying capacity of a telecommunications link. It is often referred to as a "digital pipe." The wider the pipe, the more information that can flow through it. Technically, bandwidth is the range of usable frequencies of an electrical signal, but it is more generally discussed in terms of bits per second.

The evolution of multimedia rests on two enabling technologies: (1) low-cost, very fast hardware that can process and manipulate the huge volume of bits inherent in multimedia images, sound, and video; and (2) low-cost, very fast telecommunications networks that can move them across locations. The first of these has been moving along a growth and innovation path of around 30 percent improvement in price-performance a year, driven by chip technology, industry competition, and price wars; there is literally not a single multimedia application need for computing power, storage size, and speed that cannot be met by today's available commercial products. Some of those products may be expensive in comparison with nonmultimedia PC hardware and software, but they are still far cheaper than the commercial and scientific equivalents that companies routinely bought five years ago.

The second enabling technology—the capacity to move multimedia over telecommunications links—rests on the availability of bandwidth and the cost of bandwidth. Here, progress was stalled for much of the 1970s and 1980s, when the chip revolution was gathering speed. Thus we now don't have the bandwidth we need. The technology is there, but a combination of regulatory blockages and economic factors has limited its rollout into everyday services. This is changing fast. The improvements in telecommunications technology have in the 1990s outpaced those of even the microchip industry. Regulatory and industry barriers are coming down. As a result, it is certain that, five years from now, bandwidth speed and capacity will be as available as computer power, though not perhaps with quite the same 30 percent per year improvement in price performance.

The gaps between what the technology provides and what the customer can get is most apparent in the widely varying levels of telecommunications service to users of the Internet. Individuals dialing up from their homes via the public telephone system typically get a pipe with only enough bandwidth to send or receive information at half a page per second (14.4 kb) and at most one page. At that speed, the Internet is barely usable for interactive multimedia, though fully adequate for electronic mail, searching for text information, or downloading images while you sit and wait a minute or so.

There's no technical reason why the public telephone system should be limited to a one-page-per-second speed for individual users. In the late 1970s, phone companies across the world defined a blueprint for the Integrated Services Digital Network (ISDN) which would make five pages (128 kb) the basic unit of bandwidth for subscribers. ISDN was rolled out very slowly and reluctantly by U.S. public telecommunications providers. The huge capital investment costs of ISDN, fiber optics, and other components of what is so often called the "Information Superhighway" are immense, and telecommunications providers want to preserve existing revenues and minimize risks. That has slowed down the exploitation of the new technologies. Only in the past two years have Internet users been able to get an ISDN line installed in their homes at reasonable cost; it was the Internet that drove

Glasgow, Kentucky, has a population of just 13,000. Its residents, though, enjoy what is almost surely the very best Internet access service available to the public in any city—around 70 times faster than the top speeds available by dialing up via modem and 16 times faster than those available over the more expensive ISDN lines that you can get in some parts of the country. They receive unlimited use for $22 a month. This service is provided by the city's municipally owned electrical utility, which gives every new customer an Internet address. In 1988, the city's managers spent $3 million to install a fiber optics network for its agencies and the utility.

demand here, not the phone companies that drove supply or tried to build demand.

Matters are very different for large organizations; there have been plenty of drivers on both the demand and the supply side. Whereas in 1987 the bandwidth available on the local area networks that are the foundation of internal telecommunications within buildings and departments provided for speeds of up to 2 book equivalents per second (2 to 16 mb), now they routinely offer over 10 book equivalents (100 mb) over fiber optics links. In the 1980s, the workhorse networks that businesses built for wide area communication used what are called T-1 lines at 60-page equivalents per second (1.54 mb). Now, they can obtain a wide range of services with speeds of 3 to 20 book equivalents (25 to 155 Mb) through the emerging transmission facilities called ATM. Universities, engineering and scientific operations, and comparable units with needs for rapid transfer of massive multimedia files can obtain gigabit-speed facilities. The small organization that operates the Yahoo! information retrieval service on the Internet, which is one of most requested sites on the World Wide Web, uses a T-3 link at 6 book equivalents per second (45 mb). When its executives demonstrated Yahoo! to a journalist, Web pages came up instantly—zap, and the screen is full quicker than you can think. Yahoo! users dialing up at half a page per second (14.4 kb) get the same screen in half a minute or more. Those in such small towns as Cadillac, Michigan, can get only one tenth of this speed—a paragraph equivalent per second—through dial-up service (2.4 kb); that means that what takes seconds for the Yahoo! service provider becomes minutes, and minutes become hours, The information is the same in all instances. The Internet is the same. The user bandwidth is totally different.

In early 1996, Congress at last agreed on a long-debated overhaul of telecommunications regulation. The debate was basically about who can provide bandwidth to the home and to businesses, and what they can use that bandwidth for (entertainment, phone service, publishing). From a technical perspective, there's bandwidth everywhere. Now, the Telecommunications Act of 1996, signed into law in February 1996, allows just about anyone to provide it. Coming back to the example of the consumer sitting at home waiting while a video or music clip is downloaded from the Internet, here are practical ways of getting bandwidth, given the changes in regulation:

- *Local phone companies* can use existing "twisted-pair" lines to improve speeds from 1 page to 1 book per second (28.8 kb to 1.54 mb), an improvement of a factor of 50. *ADSL* They want to use this to offer videos on demand.

- *Cable companies* already have high-speed links into the home. They want to add anything that uses bits—phone calls, Internet traffic, home banking, and interactive games. The battle between the cable and phone companies, as well as their cooperation through alliances, mergers, and acquisitions, has been building in the 1990s. Each has bandwidth to spare, and they are now allowed to deploy it anywhere.

- *Local phone companies and long-distance providers* can move into each other's markets, bringing their distinctive strengths and attacking the traditional providers' distinctive weaknesses. The long distance providers bring national coverage and a decade of experience in cutthroat and cut-price competition. It's not yet clear that the local phone companies bring much more than plenty of money and name recognition with customers.

- *Amtrak, oil companies, and electrical utilities* can use their rights of way and lengths of rail, power lines, and oil pipelines to add fiber optics cable (and have been doing so).

These add up to a powerful combination of supply-side drivers. The demand side is there. More than any other factor, regulation has been the blockage, and its elimination makes it certain that these forces will not be blocked.

They soon saw that it could be used to provide phone service and cable TV. Once MCI installed a high-speed link (called a T1) from Glasgow to the nearest Internet connection, not just the city was "wired," but every residence and business now had total multimedia capabilities. Glasgow is an exception, not a typical case, but does illustrate that bandwidth is available. The issue is who provides it and for how much.

The table below summarizes the technical details of the bandwidth market evolution. The figures are in bits per second.

	Public Services	Local Area Networks	Company Networks	International Networks	Nonphone Company Providers
1970s	2.4–9.6 kbps	2 mb	56 kb	2.4–9.6 kb	None permitted
Mid-1980s	9.6	2–16 mb	1.5 mb	9.6 kb	Value-added networks (specially licensed and restricted services)
Now	14.4–28.8 kb 128 kb (ISDN)	100 mb	1.5–45 mb	9.6 to 64 kb	Internet, on-line services, cable TV pilots
2000	28.8 kb routine	100 mb to 2 gb	On demand up to 2 gb	9.6 to 1.5 mb	Anyone

Without bandwidth, multimedia means CD-ROM. With bandwidth, the Internet becomes what it is struggling to be—a universal multimedia infrastructure for anything and everything. Opponents of telecommunications deregulation worry that consumers will be exploited by the giant, lumbering local phone companies who blocked the rollout of ISDN in order to protect their existing revenue base. They expect that the behemoths will slow down the expensive infrastructure investments that digital service demands and also use their market power to reduce competition. They fear that cable TV firms, who have a bad reputation for service, will use their new freedom to build local oligopolies in order to increase prices. Proponents (and I'm one) believe that deregulation will unleash the same wonderful imagination, innovation, entrepreneurship, and price slashing that has marked the nonregulated computer industry.

The evolution of multimedia rests on unleashing the supply of bandwidth. Data communications—electronic mail, electronic financial transactions, standard business transactions, and the like—involve mainly streams of short messages. The difference in bandwidth requirements for digital media is astounding. A complex 3-D image can take over a million times as many bits as a short electronic mail message—100 printed book equivalents (800 Mb)—to transmit in noncompressed form. If you were to send an uncompressed high-resolution image of what's on your computer screen, that could take hours. Full-motion cinema-quality video requires 30 "frames," or images, per second. You could send a 15-minute video clip, but it would take almost two weeks to download over the Internet at half a page per second (14.4 kb). Some universities can download it in around 5 seconds *today.*

Bandwidth is the future of business multimedia. In the 1980s, that future rested on technical innovation. Now it rests on deregulation and industry competition.

BBS Bulletin board systems (BBS) are specialized information subscription services. They are comparable to mom-and-pop stores, with America Online and the Internet as national retailers. BBS is now a somewhat misleading name for these on-line services offered by a vast range of individuals, companies, and public sector organizations that combine provision of information, chat lines, and sales catalogues. They grew up as part of the PC revolution, before the Internet became an easy to use, easy to access communications infrastructure. As such, they relied on dial-up access via modems and the public telephone system. They offered a connection point for PC users to communicate with each other—hence the term Bulletin Board Systems.

Many BBS are now linking to or migrating to the Internet. They represent a grassroots movement within the larger Information Superhighway–Internet–AOL–CompuServe on-line trend. The entry and operating cost to become a sysop ("*system opera-tor,*" BBS jargon for service provider) is low. An eight-line service (allowing a maximum of eight users to dial in at any one time) requires a standard PC with plenty of disk storage and a fast CD-ROM, eight modems, installation of phone lines, and peripherals, all of which can be bought for about $5,000. The operating costs will be mainly for phone lines. All told, the system would

Bulletin board systems offer many low-cost opportunities for firms and individuals who can identify and fill a need, however simple or small. They are cheap to set up and use. An example is Exec-PC, with 20,000 subscribers who send 5,000 messages a day, for an annual fee of $75, which includes 10 hours a week of free time. Exec-PC provides information on what is called "shareware"— software and data files that are paid for through a small and usually voluntary fee. Operated by a husband and wife plus a staff of two, it has grown from 1 phone line in 1982 to 200, and into a nearly $2-million-a-year business.

cost less than $10,000. Sysops typically recoup this by selling memberships for perhaps $40 a year or through access fees.

As with most on-line services, successful BBS are generally narrowcast; that is, they attract a carefully targeted audience with shared interests. It's quite possible that BBS will disappear over time as a distinct business and social niche through being absorbed into the World Wide Web. Whether or not that is so, they illustrate one of the most obvious aspects of emerging on-line business: the opportunity for the smallest of providers to find a niche and enter it at very low cost. The main limitation of BBS is that they cannot easily offer multimedia by the very fact that they use standard low-speed, low-cost phone lines and provide services for anyone with even the cheapest PC and a modem.

With so much press and attention being given to the Internet, it's easy to overlook the prevalence of BBS. There are around 64,000 in the United States, with over 20 million subscribers, and their demographics are broader than those of the Internet to date, which is predominantly male, student, and professional. They are well suited to local needs. A number of city governments, hospitals, and school districts operate them. For many people they are far simpler to use than the Internet or such on-line services as CompuServe, though this is changing as more and more BBS migrate to the Internet and as browser software makes it easier to use the Net.

Here is just a random sample of BBS now in operation:

- *The Well,* set up in 1985 and the home of over 250 ongoing conferences ranging from cooking to virtual reality, The Grateful Dead, and Windows. It has 11,000 subscribers, many of whom are well-known writers and leaders in the information technology field. The cost is $15 a month plus $2.50 an hour usage fee. The Well links to and from the Internet.

- *DCN OnLine* demonstrates computer and telecommunications products offered by Durand

Communications and includes a live chat session where customers discuss technical aspects of the products.

- *The Electronic Trib* is operated by the *Albuquerque Tribune* and includes stories that were not published in the printed newspaper. It also provides local information, such as its Crime Stopper Bulletin and advice from county agencies.

- *DSC* has a live feed from the Internet and operates 7,000 conferences, with a business focus in the daytime and an entertainment focus at night.

- *The Federal Bulletin Board* lets visitors download federal government publications and documents free or for a nominal charge. Some government offices provide their documents only in electronic form through this BBS.

- *Home OnLine* lists properties in the Ohio State area. Users can search by zip code, price, type of dwelling, and so on. It also puts them in touch with agents, builders, and inspectors. Photos of properties may be downloaded using software provided by mail.

- *My Rose Colored Pony* is a free BBS dealing with issues of children's mental health and chronic and terminal illnesses.

The main differences between BBS and the World Wide Web are that the Web is a vast collection of resources to be browsed, whereas BBS are more focused. Users know what's there and can get directly to what they want.

Bitmap   A bitmap is the digital representation of a single display screen—basically a digital snapshot. The number of bits required for the snapshot is a function of the resolution of the screen and the range of colors and hues it provides. The screen is built up by coloring a grid of picture elements—"pixels"—which are phosphorescent dots. A typical screen on a multimedia PC will display

Col
_____
       480

Rows

640

640 rows and 480 columns (shown in ads as 640 × 480) with up to 256 colors that require 8 bits—1 byte—to code per pixel. This means that the bitmap takes up the equivalent of 100 printed page equivalents (307,200 bytes) on your hard disk, where it will be stored as a file with the suffix ".BMP" (or its variant, ".DIB," which stands for "*d*evice-*i*ndependent *b*itmap"). It can be compressed down to around one-third of this, but that's still the equivalent of a book chapter.

A high-resolution screen will have both more pixels and a far wider range of colors. Multimedia generally benefits from the extra capability, which translates into far higher-quality images. For instance, IBM's innovative ThinkPad 755CDV, which costs roughly twice as much as laptops with the same chip but a smaller display and fewer multimedia features, has a resolution of 1,024 × 768 pixels with 16-bit color coding. Here, the bitmap is over 500 page equivalents (1.6 million bytes).

Bitmapped files are efficient and their storage demands manageable in comparison with most of the roughly 30 other most common graphics standards. The icons displayed on your PC screen when you use America Online, Windows, or a screen saver are very likely to be bitmaps. These can be directly matched—mapped—to the screen location, whereas vector graphics files, which contain descriptions of lines, shapes, and area measurements, must be translated into the exact coordinates on the screen. The disadvantage of bitmapped files is that, if you enlarge the image, each individual pixel is enlarged, and the picture loses quality as you begin to see jagged edges. Vector images are composed of mathematical descriptions of, say, a line. When you enlarge the image, the line is stretched without any part of it becoming jagged. Vector images require more storage.

Bits and Bytes   Bits and bytes are the basic measure of size in the information technology field, as basic as feet and inches or pounds and ounces. A bit is the equivalent of an atom, and a byte the equivalent of a molecule. A bit is either a 0 or a 1; all data can be coded as bits. A byte is 8 bits and is information rather than data, in that it signifies a numeric value, character, or code. Consider 00010011. That is the bit representation of the decimal number 200; 01101000 is the representation of 22. The largest number a byte can represent is 256. Thus a byte can represent up to 256 characters, such as @, n, N, or +. Or it can represent 256 different colors, the palette available on standard PCs. It can capture 256 different sound levels. Coding audio, video, and color in more detail than this requires more bytes per item.

Bits and bytes are as basic to computers and telecommunications as horsepower is to cars, but just as knowing the horsepower of a car tells you only a little about its performance, safety, and comfort, bits and bytes are only relative indicators. They are important for understanding multimedia simply because each medium—text, pictures, video, and audio—differs widely in its digital equivalent of horsepower.

One of the most confusing aspects of multimedia is that some figures quote sizes and speeds in bits and others in bytes and others without making it clear which is which. For instance, the amount of information needed to code a multimedia image, such as a photograph or video frame, is generally specified in bits, but the disk space needed to store that same image is indicated in bytes. All telecommunications speeds are defined in bits per second. The size of CPU chips is expressed in bits, but the size of the computer memory with which it works is in bytes. Below is a brief summary of which measure applies to which element of multimedia, with illustrations of *typical* ranges:

Item	Measure	Examples
Computer CPU chips	Bits	The Intel 486 is a 16-bit chip; the Pentium is 32-bit
Size of computer memory	Bytes	A multimedia PC will have from 4 to 32 million bytes (Mb)
Size of hard disk	Bytes	200 Mb to 1.2 Gb (gigabytes, which are billions)

Item	Measure	Examples
Software operating systems	Bits	Windows 3.1 is a 16-bit OS; Windows and Windows 95 are 32-bit
Color coding	Bits	8-bit coding provides for 256 colors;16-bits offer over 65,000; 24-bits offer 16 million
Sound coding	Bits	8-bit equals mono recording; 16-bit equals CD quality
Telecommunications speeds	Bits per second	The typical home PC accesses the Internet at a speed of 14.4 kb (14,400 bits per second) or 28.8 kb; high-speed networks offer anywhere from 64 kb to 2 gb (gigabits)
Still images	Bits	10 kb to 500 kb for simple images 500 kb to 60 Mb for high-resolution photographic images
Video image transmission	Bits	100 kbps for low-quality compressed images 1.5 mbps for $\frac{1}{4}$- or $\frac{1}{2}$-size screen image, medium quality; 6 to 24 Mbps for high quality
File sizes	Bytes	Thousands for most nonmultimedia applications (e.g., word processing, spreadsheets); no upper limit for multimedia

BLOB BLOB stands for "*b*inary *l*arge *o*bject (data) *b*ase" and means essentially a multimedia data file such as a video clip. Items in a nonmultimedia data base—customer information, purchase orders, payroll records, documents, and the like—are relatively small, a few hundred to thousands of bytes. The entire data base may be huge, but each accessible unit is relatively tiny. That's not so for more and more multimedia objects. They chew up gigabytes of data. A BLOB is loosely defined as a 2-gigabyte unit of data, around two-thirds of a movie equivalent. BLOBs must be organized in pieces that can be quickly put together and transmitted from the server computer on which they are stored, across a telecommunications link. Examples of business BLOBs are "compound" documents, which contain text and detailed graphics, geographic maps, parts diagrams and econometric time-series data (the latter is nonmultimedia).

Within the next five years, the variety of data that companies will store on servers and that PCs will access will range from e-mail messages which may be less than 100 bytes (a paragraph of text), to BLOBs. The nature and use of the information will cover just as broad a range.

Boards and Cards   Boards, adapter cards, graphics cards, and PCMCIA cards are all hardware units that contain chips and electronic connectors for PCs. The terms are used somewhat interchangeably. Boards are the bigger of the two types, starting with the motherboard that is the guts of your PC. This has the CPU, internal memory, power supply, buses (connectors), and much else glued onto a fiberglass board. Graphics boards, fax cards, card modems, sound cards, and the like similarly either have chips and connectors glued on a base or are packed into a credit card–sized housing that slides into a connection point on the machine. They typically cost between $300 and $1,000 depending on their function and the complexity and power of the chips they pack.

These add-on units are essential for multimedia. The general-purpose PC is designed for general-purpose applications that involve mainly processing instructions that work with relatively small amounts of data at a time. The cards provide extra storage and a memory/CPU combination designed to optimize performance that meets a specific need. A video card, for instance, can't carry out spreadsheet calculations, but it sure can move video fast. A high-end video card will use 64-bit specialized CPU chips or link together two or three 32-bit ones. It will include software permanently stored on the chips, which handles such needs as setting the rate for "refreshing" the display screen and smoothing the flow of the video to remove flickering. Sound cards will contain similar hardware and software for handling audio, with 16-bit cards being able to sample and convert the sound wave more precisely than cheaper 8-bit ones. They will also synthesize the sounds of specified musical instruments.

Much of the quality of a multimedia system rests on such cards. They can easily double the cost of a PC. The differences

A PC built on yesterday's Intel 486 chip with a 64-bit graphics accelerator board added on will often outperform a more recent and far more powerful Pentium system, which has just a standard accelerator board. This is because our perception of speed rests on the things we actually see. The Pentium may be faster in computation than the 486, but the high-end accelerator updates the display screen faster and provides richer color.

among cards in terms of speed, storage, and functions are very wide and for some multimedia uses there's no point in trying to economize. The terms *board* and *card* suggest simple little systems. If you look at a photograph of a sound card, it looks like the aerial view of a crowded city, with dozens of office buildings (chips), parking lots (connection grids), and smaller buildings visible everywhere. Cards are computers in and of themselves.

In early 1996, several companies began to market a new type of chip with multimedia instructions and features embcddcd in it. These media processors are a natural evolution of existing trends. They will be faster and in the end much cheaper than boards and cards—and much less bulky. It's too early to tell how quickly these will move from the periphery to the center of multimedia and thus from the periphery of the PC itself to its literal center, the motherboard that contains the master hardware. For business managers, the implication of media processors is simply that in forward planning about how to exploit large-scale use of multimedia for, say, training, they should take advantage of today's tools at today's costs in experimenting, building systems for local use, and implementing "production" systems for a small number of users and uses but not be locked into tomorrow's use on the basis of those costs. If your plans for multimedia for training and customer interaction, for instance, are expected to move into full deployment in 1999, get the best advice you can on what the hardware platform of 1999 will be. Don't bet on it being there at the price you need, but be ready to exploit it if it does in fact get delivered. The very strong probability is that in 1998 you will be able to launch the system that in 1997 requires boards and cards, costing today anywhere up to $2,000, on a machine that won't need them, for only around $150 more than the cost of today's PC. If Intel doesn't provide this, Texas Instruments, AMD, or perhaps joint ventures that include IBM, Sony, or Toshiba will do so. The demand is there, the technology is already proven, and the industry knows how to move down the cost curve fast.

By definition, size is a key issue for mobile computing and communication, as it is for consumer electronics and cameras. With disk drives and a mass of specialized chips, even the smallest portable soon becomes a luggable. A consortium of 13 electronics firms is designing a memory card that will contain the equivalent of 45 floppy disks and will be around the size of a postage stamp. This will reduce the size of a laptop computer by one-fourth. One main use will be the exchange of stored data between such devices as cameras, mobile computers, and any other digital device.

See also Media Processors; Pentium; Pentium Power

Bulletin Board System *See* BBS

Bus A bus is a very short set of electrical conductors inside a computer that links component devices. All the slots on a PC into which you can insert adapter cards (for fax modem, software, extra memory, and so on) have a bus connection from the slot to the relevant internal chips on boards inside them. Video and audio hardware boards which handle rapid input, processing, and transfer of signals have buses everywhere.

Buses substantially affect hardware performance because they can easily become a bottleneck in the flow of bits between, say, the CPU and sound cards. Part of the reason for Apple's falling behind Intel-based machines for use in multimedia in the early 1990s reflected its not adopting the PCI bus that is now the standard for personal computers—including the new range of Apple PowerMacs. This moves data from graphics cards into the computer memory at rates three times that of Apple's own NuBus technology. Overall, this leads to around a 25 percent improvement in the performance of graphics software, a significant gain for multimedia professionals. That gain comes at a cost of between $600 and $2,000, though.

Buses are part of the technical expert's domain, not the managerial one. The only issue for managers to keep in mind is that whereas performance of nonmultimedia applications, such as word processing and electronic mail, is most affected by CPU speed and size of memory, multimedia applications are far more dependent on hardware add-ons to the PC, particularly graphics accelerator boards, sound cards, and special-purpose memory chips for video. These are what can turn a $2,000 PC into a $5,000 multimedia machine. Not paying the extra can mean that a fast PC becomes an unacceptably slow multimedia toy.

Business on the Internet   Selling goods and services over the Internet has become a major target of opportunity for more and more businesses. To date, small companies seem to gain the most from access to an on-line community to which they would otherwise never be able to market. Large firms benefit from the Internet mainly as a form of corporate public relations, a source of information about products and services, and an experimental selling vehicle.

Inc. magazine (no. 3, 1995) offers some examples of small companies' Internet experiences, in five categories: downtown storefront, shopping mall, mass marketing, direct marketing, and warehouse.

The *downtown storefront* is where a firm sets up business on the World Wide Web. It creates an electronic storefront that the 30 million or more users of the Internet can check out via their Web browsers. Hello Direct, California (http://www.hello-direct.com), sells telecommunications products. In November 1994, it put its catalogue on the Web and takes orders over an 800-number phone line. Some 4,500 Internet users look at Hello Direct's Web pages every month, leading to 400 e-mail inquiries. The firm estimates it would need to mail out 6,000 to 7,000 paper catalogues to generate this number of responses. The cost to develop and maintain the on-line catalog was around $50,000 over the first 18 months. The firm pays $1,000 a month to a company that manages its on-line operation. Though the resulting sales are small (just 0.25 percent of its $26 million 1994 revenues, around

$65,000), they are 10 percent higher on average than the average print catalogue order of $200.

In an Internet *shopping mall,* the firm does not have its own distinctive address but is part of a "cybermall," a single Web address shared by a number of companies, each with its own home page. The firm *Inc.* cites here did far better than Hello Direct. Hawaii's Best Espresso Co. ran a coffee bean store in Maui, where escalating rents and overhead raised its monthly operating costs to $12,000, on sales of $15,000. The husband and wife team that owns the store spent $1,000 for a local Internet service provider to create a Web home page, with color photographs and descriptions of its premium gourmet beans. For a few hundred dollars a month, it linked the home page to six cybermalls, including Planet Hawaii and Downtown Anywhere.

This on-line store now gets over 1,000 visits a month, which generate $15,000 in sales. The owners closed their physical store in Maui. One of the owners comments, "It's a gas to turn on the computer in the morning and have a couple of hundred dollars of business be there waiting. All we're doing on the Internet is the same as what we did with the shop, except we're open 24 hours a day and we don't have to be there."

With Internet *mass marketing,* a firm uses the Internet to reach the many thousands of "newsgroups"—public electronic bulletin boards used by people who share a common interest, which may be political or social issues, entertainment, a professional focus, or just a shared eccentricity. It can add ads to the bulletin board for almost nothing and reach a wide target market. However, the informal cult of today's Internet is strongly opposed to advertising outside the Web and may rise up in electronic arms to "flame" offenders. Sending out unsolicited e-mail messages to a wide list of people is termed "spamming" and constitutes electronic junk mail. It's dangerous in that it can clog both your own hard disk and the already-jammed Net. MCI will cancel the account of any individual or firm if it receives 75 complaints from other Internet

One filmmaker sees the Internet as a very attractive opportunity to distribute interactive, serialized versions of his products for just 25 cents per selection, but he states that they will be "cool" only if the Internet has a multimegabit digital "pipe" into the home and the user has a far more powerful computer than today's typical multimedia machine, which takes up to 30 minutes to download a 30-second film clip. He dislikes the software that is the base of the World Wide Web, calling it like painting with a brick. "The Internet may be the information superhighway but right now there are a lot of people setting up just lemonade stands."

users about a spam. Offended Net zealots will do their best to overload the server of the offender with a flood of flaming (angry and abusive) messages.

Inc. cites as a successful example of how to advertise without upsetting the Net community a 12-person firm in Delaware called Harvard Business Service, which claims to have doubled its revenues through its ads on the Internet, America Online, and other on-line information services. It is careful to place them only with newsgroups that specifically allow them. HBS, whose sales are around $2 million a year, helps companies incorporate in Delaware and find venture capital. Its staff surfs the Internet looking for groups where it may post, not ads, but offers to answer questions and to "educate" anyone about its services. A typical question will be how to set up a subsidiary in the state. An HBS staff member will answer it *personally*, without making any overt effort to advertise. The head of marketing comments that the firm trolls the Net looking out for newsgroups that are business oriented or entrepreneurial and that are accessible by entrepreneurs across the world. He adds that finding the right ones is very much a matter of trial and error.

Direct marketing on line substitutes bits for paper in mass mailing. The costs of printing, paper, and postage make direct mail a very expensive form of marketing. Response rates of 2 to 4 percent are average for most industries. On-line charges are far smaller, but instead of sending the mail as with paper, firms have to find ways to compel people to request the electronic version.

Mountain Travel-Sobek is an adventure travel company with 40 employees. It gathers information from travel agencies and guides around the world and publishes it in its weekly on-line publication, *Hot News*. The news may include items on how political conditions in Zaire might affect travel itineraries or the impact of weather conditions on animals in the Kasmiri forests. All this is provided as substantive information to any Internet user, together with information on available trips, prices, and discounts. The founder of the $15-million-a-year company asks, "Can you imagine if we tried to mail these every week? I just push the button and *Hot News* goes to everybody."

"Everybody" in this case is about 77,000 people a month. Of these, 1,500 are subscribers who receive the three- to four-page weekly publication in their electronic mailbox. The rest read it on MTS's Internet World Wide Web page for free. In 1995, the firm's business increased by 37 percent, with "a significant portion" coming from the on-line information/marketing publication. The cost of development was estimated by *Inc.* as at least $10,000, perhaps closer to $100,000. It costs only $200 to put together and publish a new weekly edition of *Hot News*.

The fifth category of marketing listed in the article is the *warehouse*, which means being an intermediary between on-line customers and services. An example is a real estate firm in California, Pinel, whose gross sales of real estate grew from $259 million in 1992 to $451 million in 1993 and $690 million in 1994, all in a sluggish local economy. Alain Pinel recognized that real estate agents are basically just a link between home buyers, sellers, builders, and banks. He sees the Internet as a proven and wide-reaching infrastructure that can make the buying and financing of property more efficient for *all* parties. Pinel spent around $2 million to establish electronic mail links to other agents, lenders, title companies, and its own clients. This uses a wide area network set up by Pinel with links to the Internet. Pinel's agents can find out the status of escrow accounts or update the relevant parties with information on the progress of loan proceedings.

The impact of the system has been limited by client awareness and readiness to use the Internet's electronic mail. Even though several of its offices are in the high-tech Silicon Valley, only 20 percent of clients are willing to accept e-mail, and the rest prefer face-to-face meetings, which are essential in any case when signatures are needed for documents. Most real estate agents and many lenders and title companies are not on line and cannot accept electronic mail. Few ancillary real estate service agencies, such as building and termite inspectors, are on line. A senior executive

Popular Internet Web pages generate about 10,000 hits a week from 40 to 50 countries. Few people stay with the site for more than 15 minutes before surfing on. If others find a page interesting, cool (being picked out as a cool site is one of the Internet compliments), or useful, they may hot link it to their own page, the equivalent of word-of-mouth advertising.

at Pinel comments, "We're definitely in a transition period. The learning curve of the general population needs to catch up." He adds that the $2 million investment has been well worth it in terms of improved productivity, streamlined sales processes, increased sales, and better customer service. (Other studies report that typical home buyers make 15 visits before finding the house they decide to purchase and that the use of multimedia cuts this by half.)

It is far too soon for any clear patterns to have emerged from the three years or so during which the World Wide Web has moved the Internet from the backwaters of academic computing to the mainstream of popular culture, and from irrelevance to business to just about every firm's feeling that it must get into this game, even if it does not know quite why or for what specific goals. There are plenty of scattered successes in terms of increased revenues and profits, though most Web pages are little more that electronic corporate PR handouts. To date, there do not appear to have been any striking gains for large businesses; it is smaller firms that gain a leverage.

A 1996 survey by International Data Corporation found that the cost of setting up a commercial Web site on the Internet is four times what companies expect. A small business can set up a simple site for a few thousand dollars, but that is just the equivalent of a Yellow Pages advertisement.

The obvious reason for this is that the Internet reduces the investment for small firms to enter the electronic marketplace. Previously, they needed 800 numbers, expensive leased telecommunications lines, and their own network management capability. Now they can get a presence on the Net for the equivalent of petty cash. They can target smaller and smaller niches profitably and move very quickly. A less obvious reason for the relative successes of small versus large firms is the demographics of Internet users and the more general characteristics of users of on-line services, including America Online and CompuServe. The Internet is totally unrepresentative of the wider population, although over time more and more women, and older and less affluent users are infiltrating the predominantly male academic/student/technical professional Net culture. Today's on-line users appear to be driven by a search for information and services that (1) are a little different, (2) relate to a special community or interest group, and

(3) provide some sort of interactive feature rather than just passive reading of ads and placing of orders. They want to express their own opinions, link up with others for discussion, and gain a sense of personal impact rather than of being just a consumer.

One of the most ambitious larger organizations focusing on the Internet as a new business opportunity is ESPN. Its SportsZone site on the Web attracts 140,000 people a day. It thus has one of the highest advertising rates. It is not expected to make a profit before 1998. It is free to Net users, but charges a fee for the sports junkie who wants premium service and premium information. This challenges the Net ethos of free information freely accessed. One observer comments that "if ESPN can't sell its service, then the prognosis for selling information on the Internet is very poor indeed" (*Fortune*, 4 March, 1996).

ESPN has a highly focused strategy that, if successful, may serve as a blueprint for others and, if a failure, will educate the many firms looking to make money on the Web. The strategy, as reported by *Fortune*, is:

- *Don't rush* to make easy money in the short term. ESPN has enough information, image, and audience of gamblers, college alumni, and others to be able to generate revenues. It has chosen to focus on building a base of subscribers and advertisers.

- *Target* the right customers. Sports and the Internet are a unique demographic match, which advertisers may well pay a premium to reach: 18- to 34-year-old males, the older ones with relatively high incomes. A subset are the "displaced fans," most classically Boston Red Sox fans living in Florida or Knicks true believers off on a business trip in Europe. Around 10 percent of SportsZone users log in from overseas.

- Provide a *superior Net product*. There are now so many Web sites, with so much text, so many graphics, and so little distinction among them. SportsZone was one of the first sites to offer three-dimensional graphics. It mixes the up-to-the-minute information essential for sports with archival information beloved by sports nostalgists. In sports, the most valuable information tends to be either a few hours or more than two weeks old. As *Fortune* points out, most media companies either load this morning's paper or last week's magazine onto the Net, in what is called "Shovelware."

- *Create synergies by leveraging brand names.* ESPN analysts reuse their on-air TV commentaries to create on-line columns. There's plenty of promotion of anything with "ESPN" in it. By contrast, *Sports Illustrated,* about as strong a brand as any in sports, was just a part of the Time Warner Web site until recently.

- *Drive the market.* ESPN is not, unlike most companies, looking to test the temperature in the Web pool. It charges advertisers $100,000 for three months. It charges premium service subscribers a premium monthly fee. The logic is that "it is easier to defend market share than it is to create it."

The final comment, from an ESPN executive, is almost a summary of business on the Internet: "This is still a very young business. We're all building it. Will they come? If people come to the Web, the economics will take care of themselves. If they don't, no economics will matter."

C++ C++ is a computer programming language widely used for developing multimedia and other business applications that depend on very efficient machine performance. Networked multimedia applications push the limits of today's computer and telecommunications speeds and power. The software that manages them must be very efficient in terms of how it exploits hardware capabilities. C++ has emerged as one of the small group of languages that provide that efficiency but also offer features that reduce the programmer's effort and handle many utility tasks. It is terse and efficient in terms of producing "tight" program code that runs quickly, a critical requirement in multimedia. A sample line is

if Ipjfill ->hCurMark = _hCurMark (Ipjfill, ol)

C++ is not for amateurs.

Programming languages fall into three main categories: application generators, higher-level languages, and assembly language. *Application generators* produce machine code—the sequence of instructions the hardware executes—from a description of the application. A spreadsheet package is in effect an application generator. When you click on a cell and type in =SUM(C1:C5)/A29) (which means "Add up the figures in cells C1 to C5 and then divide by the figure in cell A29"), the spreadsheet software interprets the command and generates what is termed "machine-executable code." It won't produce the "tightest" code, because it is a general-purpose piece of software that has to cater to a wide range of possibilities. A skilled programmer could inspect the code and tighten it up, speeding up execution, but this makes no sense. The computer operates faster than you can even read the resulting calculation, and it makes no difference to you if it takes 40 microseconds or 200.

Before the widespread availability of powerful PC-based software, the main business programming tools were *higher-level languages* that translated into computer instructions such detailed statements as IF BALANCE-DUE >= 0.99 PRINT "BALANCE AS OF"; DATE; TOTAL-DUE, ELSE GO TO CTL-CREDIT-ROUTINE. Almost all of what are rather misleadingly called "legacy systems," the firm's workhorse accounting, reporting, payroll, and other systems built up over decades, were originally developed by using a higher-level language such as COBOL or, for engineering applications, FORTRAN. More recently, they will have drawn on data base tools, including the widely used search and reporting language called SQL ("Structured Query Language"). Again, these general-purpose tools sacrifice efficiency of machine code for easier and faster development. The simple line of code shown earlier in this paragraph would take around 80 lines in machine language and the programmer would have to meticulously keep track of where in memory "DATE" and "BALANCE-DUE" are stored. With COBOL, a translator called a compiler assigns machine addresses to such items, without the programmer's having to do anything.

Higher-level languages of this sort are not at all well suited to the development demands of multimedia and client/server computing, the emerging blueprint for networked applications that exploit the combination of powerful PCs (clients) and a mix of small, medium, and large machines (servers) that provide communications, information, and transaction services. Adding just 200 microseconds (millionths of a second) of execution time to a server routine that handles real-time video and has to be run 20,000 times in a minute means a processing delay of 4 seconds. If the video needs to be processed at 15 frames per second to maintain the continuous flow, then this is impossible—the data flows faster than the software can handle it. The programmer may in this situation write code in *assembly language,* which is the closest to the machine code the hardware uses. That takes meticulous precision and lots of time and is practical only for small programs or military and NASA projects with billion-dollar budgets.

Multimedia development tools have to cover the entire range from application generators, whose advantage is that the tool does much of the grunt work but does not produce efficient machine code, to higher-level languages, right down to assembly. Authoring tools are a form of application generator. These are software packages which multimedia developers use to work out the structure of, say, an interactive training program or CD-ROM software dialogue, without having to write program code. Most client-server and multimedia applications require coding, though. Standard higher-level languages can't handle most of this, and assembly is too difficult and time consuming to develop for most applications.

In this context, C++ has emerged as providing a broad range of capabilities that spans application generator to assembly. Most leading multimedia software packages include components written in C++ or languages very similar to it.

C++ is one of the languages that best embodies the most important development in the complex field of software development: objects. *Objects* are self-contained units of code that can be linked together like Lego blocks. The dream of the development field has long been to build up entire libraries of reusable code, rather than craft, by hand, in program after program, software that handles the same functions. The goal has also been to reduce the amount of effort involved in repeating information and procedures. The key concept here is called "object-oriented programming." C++ has emerged over a 15-year period as one of the two main embodiments of object methods. The other is a language called Smalltalk; there are almost-religious arguments among purists about which language is better, with the debate resting on whether or not an object should be permitted "multiple inheritance." Visual Basic, heavily supported by Microsoft, offers a powerful higher-level object-oriented development environment. There are also several variants on C++, some of which will work only in a given hardware and software environment, such as Windows or the UNIX operating system. Microsoft offers its own Visual C++.

Multimedia development essentially requires building, linking, reusing, and combining objects. Objects are thus the basic building blocks of multimedia, and the multimedia object race is on. In mid-1995, Sun Microsystems began licensing its Java language, which is closely related to C++ and offers many improvements on it. Java had already been adopted by Netscape, the market leader in Internet browser software. HotJava, a subset of Java, looks as though it will become the base for the next generation of World Wide Web pages. To date, these have been built through a miniprogramming language called HTML ("*Hypertext Markup Language*"). The pages it creates are static and two-dimensional. HotJava will make them interactive, animated, three-dimensional, and thus truly multimedia. It also provides the first serious threat to Microsoft's dominance of PC applications through its stranglehold on PC operating systems. Java opens up the opportunity to replace much of the complexity of the PC environment and its growing cost; most estimates are that upgrading from Windows 3.1 to Windows 95 adds $1,500 in software and hardware costs, an unacceptable figure for any company that has a thousand PCs in use. If Windows 95 adds such extra costs, what about the Windows version for 1999?

Java represents a new potential direction for networked computing. Software objects, called "applets"—little applications—will be accessed over the network from a stripped-down PC, sometimes called an "Internet appliance," as and when needed. Today, the PC operating system and the applications stored on your hard disk sit there even when their components are never used. For instance, your disk is packed with such items as edlin.exe, for you to edit your autoexec.bat and config.sys files; Pkzip and Unzip, for compressing and decompressing files; Qbasic, for you to write short programs; and hundreds of others. Java would have these become applets on the network, not on your disk.

Together, C++ and Java look like the wave of the very near future. That's a dangerous prediction to make in the volatile world of information technology. Whether it is accurate or not, all large firms must choose the development environment for client-server and multimedia. They are in many ways exactly the same. Both require object methods; multimedia is basically the management and delivery of objects: a video clip, graphic, animation, or interactive dialogue for a training program, or retrieval of information from a CD-ROM. Client-server is the interaction between client systems, usually a PC, which handles front-end functions and servers that provide information, communication, and sharing of resources. Both multimedia and client-server require rapid prototyping of interactive tools, management of the PC screen dialogue and display, management of communication links, incorporation of more and more media types, cross-linking between applications in order to use, say, a graphics object in a word processed document, and so on.

The danger for organizations that lack a clearly defined, business-centered set of policies for managing the enterprise information resource as a key business resource is that development is made on a decentralized, ad hoc basis. That too easily leads to multitechnology chaos, with software systems that cannot share data, multiple networks, and multiple development tools. The firm that has five different electronic mail systems, that cannot combine information from its individual product lines to get a profile of customer usage and profitability across products, or that cannot link its ordering systems to its production systems to its distribution systems to its payments systems competes at a disadvantage today. In many instances, it is paying more to systems integration firms to fit the pieces together than it would have cost to work from a blueprint for integration in the first place.

GAP M3

Multimedia systems development will for many years be more marked by systems disintegration than integration. That is because the tools are relatively new, the hardware, software and telecommunications demands far different than those for traditional business systems, and the pace of change so fast. It makes sense for firms to experiment with the best available authoring tools, desktop publishing and video production software, and video and audio hardware. At some point soon, though, they need to think about how to ensure that the new systems are part of a shared business platform. C++ looks very much like one of the main elements of that platform.

See also Java; Network Computer; Object

Cable TV   There are around 11,000 cable TV providers in the United States, with a total of 60 million subscribers. This amounts to 60 percent of all households. Cable television companies are naturally and aggressively interested in exploiting the opportunities of multimedia, with two main relative advantages over phone

IIK?

companies: the transmission capacity and speed of cable and the potential for cable modems to provide a level of low-cost, high-speed telecommunications for Internet users that no phone company will be able to match for many years.

The 1996 deregulation of telecommunications now allows cable firms to enter the local phone market (and for phone companies to offer TV programming). The type of cable they installed is the coaxial cable you use to link your television to a VCR. It can carry several hundred programs. The newer cable, which can carry up to thousands of programs, video on demand, phone calls, and computer traffic is built on fiber optics. Today, around 18 percent of subscribers receive their programs via fiber optics trunk lines (to the local office, but not directly into the home). The 1995 figures for the five largest firms are: (1) TCI: 11 million total subscribers, 10 percent via fiber; (2) AT&T/Time Warner: 7 million, 42 percent; (3) Comcast: 3 million, 45 percent; (4) Continental: 3 million, 34 percent; and (5) Cox: 2 million, 100 percent.

Even without fiber, coaxial cable is so much faster than today's phone lines that the cable companies have a sizable opportunity to capture the market for high speed two-way communications from the home. No one knows just how big that market will be or how soon it will emerge. They are piloting cable modems, ultrahigh-speed versions of the standard phone modem used to connect to the Internet. The phone companies have equivalent boxes that provide high speeds but nowhere near the speed of cable.

The figures below show the relative time to download a two-hour movie (in uncompressed form) and the competitive state of the technology.

- Today's standard home *phone line* and highest speed modems: 16 days.
- *ISDN,* the digital lines available in most states from the local phone company: 7 days.

- Using *video-on-demand technology* that operates over existing phone lines: 6 hours (called ADSL, this is proven in field trials and is being slowly brought to market by local phone companies, with Bell Atlantic the leader).

- *Cable modems* using existing cable already installed: 54 minutes. (The modems are in sporadic use and the technology proven.)

One more figure is needed to complete the picture. A fiber optics link can transmit a full movie in 3 minutes. Whose fiber will it be? Will the phone companies' ADSL over existing wires be more than enough to meet most needs? It looks like 1997–1998 will be the time when the answers begin to be clear. The cable TV companies have several weaknesses in this competition for dominance in the delivery chain of multimedia entertainment and related consumer information services. These include their generally bad reputation for service and price gouging and their frequently overleveraged balance sheets, which show heavy debt incurred in expanding geographic coverage and investing in facilities. It will be far easier for the regional phone companies to raise large amounts of capital than for most cable firms. A 1995 survey of consumers in the Middle Atlantic region found that 46 percent of subscribers said they would dump their cable company if a comparable service were available from their phone company. Taking them at their word is the basis for the regional Bell firms' many expensive (and, to date, profitless) forays into the cable providers' territory.

The most likely evolution of interactive multimedia into the home is through alliances and mergers between phone and cable companies. Many of these have been proposed, but few have been consummated. There have also been many experimental joint ventures, with not a single major success. Interactive television has largely been a bust so far. Consumers seem happy with their VCRs and movies rented from Blockbuster Video. Meanwhile, the search for a key to multimedia success goes on, with billions being gambled. Some of the largest alliances and their outcomes have been:

- *Bell Atlantic and TCI:* Over $16 billion. The deal fell through.
- *Southwestern Bell and Cox Communications:* $5 billion. Collapsed.
- *Jones and BCE International:* An agreed upon $400 million was renegotiated.
- *BellSouth and QVC:* $500 million, renegotiated.
- *US West and Time Warner:* $2.5 billion.

Just a few of the pilot trials under way in 1995 that linked cable TV and phone companies were Ameritech and Booth Communications (electronic shopping); Ameritech and IT Network (electronic Yellow Pages); AT&T and Paramount (interactive TV); BellSouth, Viacom and AT&T (video on demand); NYNEX and Liberty Cable (video dial tone—video on demand over the phone lines); and US West, AT&T, and TCI (interactive TV).

The failure of cable TV ventures to date and of interactive television pilots may not be the disasters they appear, in that much of the effort has been deliberately exploratory. The goal is to be there when demand for such services takes off, to learn what the many technical problems are and how to solve them, to identify consumer response and nonresponse, and to make sure the firm is not outflanked by others. Common sense says that there will be a large market for interactive information and entertainment services *sometime*. It took the cable industry many years to reach critical mass. It will take them many more to use that critical mass to exploit the digital opportunity. Somewhere out there is a radical innovation that may mark a new forefront, as CNN, MTV, and the Home Shopping Network did with noninteractive, nondigital cable.

Phone companies are moving fast, too. Within three weeks

of the 1996 telecommunications act's being signed by President Clinton, US West, one of the seven regional Bell companies, paid nearly $11 billion to acquire the third-largest cable TV provider, Continental. Prior to that, US West had entered a partnership with Time Warner, the second-largest cable firm. Time Warner had made an offer to buy Turner Broadcasting, which is partly owned by the number one cable company, TCI, and by Continental. US West is suing Time Warner to block its purchase of Turner.

Penetration of cable television varies widely across the world:

Canada	78 percent of households
United States	62
Argentina	54
Sweden	52
Germany	39
Japan	19
France	7
United Kingdom	4

Cable faces competition from a new generation of satellites called direct broadcasting systems (DBS). These transmit programs digitally via satellites 22,000 miles above the earth down to tiny receiver dishes. The satellites have immense capacity and will offer video on demand, as well as extra services. The direct satellite broadcasters sold 900,000 kits in their first nine months of operation, beginning in mid-1994, with a plan to offer interactive services in 1996.

DBS technology has been available only since 1994. The first service, DirectTV, has built a subscriber base of 1.25 million, about one-third of all satellite customers in the United States; AT&T bought a small share of the it in early 1996. MCI and Rupert Murdoch's News Corporation bid $682 million for the last available DBS satellite in early 1996, which MCI will operate. DBS will make it cheap and fast to deliver 150 to 200 channels, which is MCI's plan for going into service in 1997. MCI plans to use the DBS satellite to distribute Microsoft's software at a cost of around

Cable television lines pass by over 90 percent of U.S. homes, of which 60 percent are now cable subscribers. The revenues are relatively small, though: $20 billion versus $200 billion for the phone service industry, whose lines also pass by well over 90 percent of homes. The size of each industry's customer base plus all those lines already in place, make the cable TV and phone companies determined to win in the consumer multimedia market—in partnership or in competition. It is estimated that it will cost $20 billion to convert the coaxial cables now in place across the United States to fiber optics. The comparable figure for rebuilding the phone system is $100 billion.

4 cents, taking under five minutes. Distribution by physical disk-ettes with all the packaging involved costs around $20. A 100-page document will take 15 seconds to transmit. Internet commands could travel over existing phone lines, but large files could be routed over the DBS satellite, cutting hours to minutes.

The difference between DirectTV and the MCI service is that the first is targeting the multimedia home entertainment market, and the latter is focused completely on the business market.

See also Interactive Television

Cache Memory   Cache memory is a high-speed hardware memory store that supplements the computer's larger main mem-ory. It acts as an intermediate storage area for items such as data or program instructions, which are needed often enough that moving them constantly from hard disk slows down performance, but are not used often enough to justify keeping them in main memory, which is the system's most limited resource.

Cache memory and cache disks, which are in essence the same, are tools for overlapping functions and for meeting the speed needs of multimedia, with its floods of bits that must be processed quickly. Cache chips improve hardware performance by 10 to 20 percent, at a cost of under $100.

CD Audio   A compact audio disk can store 75 minutes of music. Because it is stored in digital form, it can be directly processed by a computer, even though the original digital CDs were used only to play back music. Fundamentally, CD audio is the same as CD-ROM in terms of the physical formatting of the disk. CD-ROM is thus built on CD audio. CD plus is built on both of them; it allows a disc to be played for its music on a stereo or Discman or for its videos and interviews with performers on a CD-ROM drive.

CDs are organized in blocks of information rather as a book is organized by pages. The index of a book points you to the right page. The CD's index points you to the right "frame." CD audio can access the music stored on it in frame increments as small as

1/75th of a second. This means that it is easy to extract short clips, store them, and add them to videos or presentations.

See also CD-I; CD Plus; CD-R; CD-ROM; CD Technology; CD-XA

CD-I CD-I (CD interactive) is one of the offshoots of the original CD audio and related CD-ROM technology. It is a format for use on consumer electronics devices that do not require an external computer; the CD-I player plugs into a TV and stereo system. It includes video as well as music. To date, CD-I has had limited success, because of the need to buy the player and the lack of any distinctive advantage over a combination of VCRs, CD-ROMs, and music CDs for entertainment.

See also CD Audio; CD Plus; CD-R; CD-ROM; CD-XA

CD Plus CD plus is a variation on CD-ROM that allows you to play a disc on your CD player to listen to the music or play it on your CD-ROM drive to get the video as well. CD plus, enhanced CD, and CD+ are all the same. The lack of a standardized term hints at the lack of a clear direction for this hybrid technology, which is being driven by the music community. It is in many ways a curious technology, in that it is an effort by the industry to reverse the current momentum of multimedia, which is led by the PC. CD plus aims at making the PC a music entertainment center. It has the strong support of such leading personalities as Peter Gabriel, The Cranberries, and Quincy Jones; of innovators in music looking to be part of the PC future, and of such firms as Sony, which is a PC company in that it makes many hardware elements of personal computers, a game machine company, a software firm, and a music company.

The many skeptics about CD plus see it as an executive from Microsoft, who insisted on anonymity, did: "What this is really about is music companies rehashing and reselling or cross-merchandising other products to the fans. There's a big push to go get some old album, reintroduce it with 'Never-Before-Seen pic-

The Rolling Stones' Stripped, released at the end of 1995, looks like a standard compact disc. If you insert it into your Discman or stereo, it plays 14 Stones oldies. Inserted into a PC CD-ROM drive, though, it adds on-camera interviews with Mick Jagger and Keith Richards, plus a few minutes of music video. It is one of the hundred or so CD plus, or "enhanced" CDs, that appeared on the market in time for Christmas. The 35-disc LaserLight series of classical CDs lets listeners also watch and follow the musical score and see notes and videos about the composer and performers. Supermodels in the Rain Forest *combines on one CD plus the standard multimedia of today's "edutainment": music from such artists as Duran Duran and Soul II Soul, barely clothed females photographed in the tropics of Costa Rica, and a more dignified set of videos, information, and discussions about environmental concerns. Will people really choose to sit down at their PC when they come home and have some interaction with the performers or performance, or do they just want to listen to music? There's a lot of money riding on the question.*

tures.'" The many enthusiasts see it as the next evolution of what has for several decades been the main driver of multimedia—music. Music on CD underlies CD-ROMs on computers. MTV launched the integration of music and video.

From a general business perspective, CD plus may not be of direct relevance to firms except in relation to the advertising and marketing links that have made Michael Jackson as much a corporate voice as a singer. That said, music and multimedia are so intertwined that each affects the other. It is possible that the evolution and impact of CD plus, whether it is a success or a bust, will provide insights into the likely evolution and impact of multimedia in any context.

See also CD Audio, CD-I; CD-R; CD-ROM; CD Technology; CD-XA

CD-R CD-R stands for "*CD* recordable," in contrast to standard CDs, which can only be played, not created or updated. CD-R devices allow you to "master" your own disc. They have been available for several years but at a cost of tens of thousands of dollars and a hundred dollars for the blank discs (once the master disc is created, it costs just a couple of dollars to produce and package copies). In 1997, the costs are as little as one-tenth of those of 1994.

As firms make more and more use of CD-ROM technology to develop training programs, archive information, and distribute software, to name just a few applications, the need for low-cost capabilities for producing CD-ROMs has created a niche opportunity in the market. As a result, the prices of CD-R devices have dropped 50 percent a year for the past five years. In mid-1995, they were widely available for around $2,000, and by early 1996, Hewlett-Packard had introduced a "quad speed" CD-R machine for under $1,000. Quad speed refers to the rate of data transfer, with the original CD-ROM players being single speed. Most are now 4× or even 8× devices, where the × means "times as fast as the single-speed version." Blank discs now cost under $10, much less in volume. This means that CD-R is now cost-effective and practical for individual PC users as well as for companies.

It isn't easy to use, though. Writing a disc means transferring data in a continuous, uninterrupted flow. On the standard double-speed (2×) CD-R writers, that typically takes half an hour. To produce a full CD-ROM disc of 90 printed book equivalents (650 million bytes), you need double that amount of storage on your hard disk—the original data plus the space needed for the formatted data to be sent to the writer. The discs are also more fragile than standard CD-ROMs. The data on a CD-ROM are burned in—the writing component uses lasers to etch pits in the surface. CD-R alters a green dye surface instead. If you use a ballpoint pen to mark a CD-ROM, you will probably not damage it, but you almost surely will damage a CD-R disc. There are wide variations in CD-R features and quality. In tests of different products, the time to produce the CD-R disc ranged from 40 minutes to 2 hours.

In late 1996, CD-R was *almost* ready for everyday use. That means that by 1998 it will be fully ready. Then it will surely be a valuable tool for most individual PC users for the simple reason that it will make it as easy to create and store multimedia files on CD-ROM as it is to save word-processed files today on floppy disk. Today, the demands of multimedia in terms of bits per second of video and audio, or bits per high-resolution photo, are far more than can be met by hard disks, which store typically between one and two CD-ROMs. Imagine being able to routinely create and store your own multimedia files scattered over, say, 50 CD-ROMs that cost only about $3 each (the likely 1997 figure). With that cost and capability, hard disk storage is no longer the main constraint on your use of multimedia. CD-R will still have its limitations. Hard disk is far faster than CD-ROM in data transfer and, just as floppy disks are much slower than hard disk, a CD-R disc is likely to be several times slower than read-only CD-ROMs.

See also CD Audio; CD-I; CD Plus; CD-ROM; CD Technology; CD-XA

CD-ROM Compact disc–read only memory (CD-ROM) storage is one of the foundations of multimedia. Available for around a decade, it is only since late 1993 that CD-ROM drives have become so widespread that they are now a standard feature on PCs—to the extent that around 70 percent of all new PCs sold include them. In 1990, the figure was closer to 0.7 percent.

A CD-ROM disc stores around 100 printed book equivalents (650 million bytes of data). That is a huge amount of storage by any standard. Given that CD-ROM discs now cost under a dollar to duplicate in volume and titles aimed at the consumer market sell for as little as $20 and rarely for more than $100, it means that you can build up an electronic library of 1,000 books for less than the cost of buying a dozen hardbacks. When you buy a $1,500 multimedia PC, you typically get with it 10 to 20 free CD-ROMs. When you buy a $3.95 magazine about PCs, it now comes wrapped in cellophane to hold the free CD-ROM. It is routine for a book on multimedia to contain a CD-ROM on the inside of the back cover.

CD-ROM discs are primarily used for reference (38 percent), games (29 percent), and "edutainment" (25 percent).

CD-ROM speeds are defined by transfer rate and average access time. The transfer rate is the number of bits per second of data moved from the disc to the computer CPU. The original CD-ROM single-speed drives had a transfer rate of 6 printed page equivalents (150,000 bits) per second and an average access time of around 300 ms (milliseconds, or thousandths of a second). Double-speed drives offer twice the transfer rate; 4×-speed ones, four times the basic rate; and the current most widely available devices, the 6× CD-ROM drives, 54 printed page equivalents, with the average access time being twice as fast as for the single-speed drive (145 ms). All CD-ROM drives must slow down to 6 printed page equivalents (150 kb) to play music. That's a limitation created not by technology but by the technical standards agreed on by the two leaders in the manufacturing side of CD technology: Sony and Philips.

How these capabilities translate to what you as a user experience varies widely. A 6× drive may not be faster than a 4× for some types of applications; application speed is strongly affected by how data are organized, as well as the time needed to move the reader head to the right location on the disc. Accessing a color photograph typically takes 25 to 30 seconds on a $4\times$ or $6\times$ drive; this type of application involves transferring a long stream of data in one pass (around 3 printed book equivalents). Here, the faster the transfer rate, the faster the overall performance. Locating every reference to a specific word in an electronic 20-volume encyclopedia held on a single CD-ROM relies more on software speed and access time; very little data are transferred. This application takes around 20 seconds, with speeds varying from 17 to 30 seconds in tests of 30 leading products. Turning a page in electronic books takes around 9 seconds. These speeds are both very fast and very slow, depending on you and your application. Whatever multimedia enthusiasts may claim about electronic books' replacing physical ones, today's drives are far too slow for you to turn the pages of a thriller or skip ahead. If this guide were on a CD-ROM, turning the electronic pages alone would consume 30 minutes. On the other hand, locating every reference to "CD-ROM" in it would take under a minute. Thus you and this physical book are a far more effective combination in the acquisition of information called reading, but you and a CD-ROM are more productive in searching.

There are so many CD-ROMs now on the market that no one of them is typical any more than there is a typical book. The most interesting ones go beyond being just an electronic version of print. A case in point is the CD-ROM created by Britain's Kew Gardens, one of the most comprehensive botanical collections in the world. The Royal Botanical Society's CD-ROM on plant toxins illustrates the main advantages this multimedia offers over alternative tools. The advantages are visualization, interaction, compactness, distribution, and low reproduction cost.

- *Visualization.* The disc, called Plato, contains drawings and color photos of the more than 2,000 known

The basic documentation for an F-18 fighter aircraft is over 300,000 printed pages, and the paper takes up 68 cubic feet of storage. CD-ROM can reduce that to 0.04 cubic feet. In addition, this information is not static but changes frequently. It is far cheaper simply to throw away the old CD-ROM and use a new one. In addition, hypertext links make it easy for users to locate information, clicking on the item they want to find next without having to know exactly where it is located. Most computer software and hardware manufacturers rely on hypertext on CD-ROM to provide customers with technical manuals. Hewlett-Packard estimates that it ships over 8,000 different manuals a year to customers. All of these fit on just a few CD-ROMs.

The cost of producing CD-ROM discs is now so low that they are giveaways with magazines. In quantities of 10,000 or more, the production cost is around 60 cents per disk, or double that for one with a two-color label and jewel case to store it in. For a run of 100 disks, the cost is around $10 each—a $700 mastering charge plus $3 per disk for production.

poisonous plants and others that look very similar and commonly cause false alarms. The data are organized by 208 plant groups. The photos have to be very detailed to highlight the differences among the plants.

- *Interaction.* Used mainly by hospitals, Plato includes software that asks nontechnical questions about the leaves, seeds, roots, stem, and other parts. Artificial intelligence tools choose from 120 questions to identify the most likely plant.

- *Compactness.* The CD-ROM would require around 12 printed pages of text per plant, amounting to 24,000 in total, all of which would be noninteractive and extremely difficult to search through.

- *Distribution.* The first versions of Plato were developed for use by doctors and toxicologists. An educational version is now available for schools, garden centers, and the general public. This is the first time the society has mass marketed a specialized scientific publication.

- *Low reproduction cost.* The cost of printing 24,000 pages of high-quality color photos and text, together with the very limited market that can afford to buy them, would put the price of the book equivalent of the CD-ROM in the thousand dollar plus range. The reproduction cost of the disc is around 60 cents. Packaging adds a dollar or two.

See also Access Time; CD Audio; CD-I; CD Plus; CD-R; CD Technology; CD-XA; Hard Disk

CD Technology   CD—compact disc—is a well-standardized vehicle for storing and accessing huge volumes of information in digital form, by exploiting laser technology. Introduced in the 1970s as the successor to the long-playing record, it has transformed the music industry. Now, the same basic technology and standards—industry agreements on how the information on CDs is organized and formatted—are being extended to provide more and more digital multimedia facilities. CD-ROM was the first of these; though it has been available for a decade, it has reached the mass market in large volumes only since around 1993. CD-ROM includes the playback of music, speech, still images, and video, but not their recording.

There is a bewildering profusion of extensions to CD technology, which aim at increasing storage capacity, letting you create your own discs, combining different media, and extending interactivity. CD-I (for "*i*nteractive") plugs into a TV set. CD-XA (for "*e*xtended *ar*chitecture") makes it practical to interleave several media within the same unit of information. With CD-ROM, the music and video are separate, and the computer's microprocessor can handle only one at a time. The graphics are loaded into memory first and the audio then located. Only then are the graphics displayed as the sound is played back.

As the term *CD-ROM (read-only memory)* indicates, it is a playback medium, as is CD-DA (digital audio), the term now used for the plain old musical CD, to distinguish it from its more recent progeny. Now, devices for writing, not just for playing discs, are becoming widely available, at a cost of under $1,000. This technology is variously termed CD-R (recordable), CD-WORM (write once, read many times), or just CD-WO. There is also Kodak's Photo CD, a format for converting your photos directly to CD-ROM so that you can show them on any device that accepts CD-I discs. Now, DVD (digital video disk) technology is positioning to challenge the earlier CD technologies, offering storage capacities up to 15 times larger than CD-ROMs. CD plus allows a disc to be played on either a compact disc system for the music tracks or on a PC for added multimedia video, interviews, and the like.

All of these are built on the same core technology, which was pioneered by Sony's and Philips's agreement to standardize CDs instead of trying to compete with their own "proprietary" versions, as Sony had tried to with Betamax and Philips, with its laser disc. The standards were published in a book with a red cover. When the two firms agreed on a much-needed standard for CD-ROM, it was published in a book with a yellow cover. That precedent was continued, so CD technology is referred to among experts by the relevant book.

- *Red Book.* The standard for physically formatting all CDs. CD audio is often referred to as Red Book discs.

- *Yellow Book.* CD-ROM, with two levels. Mode 1 is for discs that contain programs and data but do not require full multimedia functionality, and Mode 2 is for true multimedia. CD-XA and Photo CD use Level 2 Yellow Book.

- *Green Book.* An extension of the Yellow Book Mode 2 to operate with Philips's proprietary CD-I (CD interactive) software operating system. That means that any standard PC can play Yellow Book CDs but not Green Book ones.

- *Orange Book.* The standard for erasable CD-MO discs (MO stands for "*m*agneto-*o*ptical"). Orange Book Part I excludes CD-R discs, which are included in Part 2.

- *White Book.* Discs that work with both CD-XA and CD-I. This is the standard for full-motion video CDs.

- *Blue Book.* Mixed-mode CDs—those that can be played on both audio CD players and CD-ROM drives. They combine Red and Yellow Book technology. Implementations include enhanced CD and CD plus.

To add to the confusion, there's also ISO 9600, which makes it possible to play all standard Yellow Book CDs on different software operating systems, and Hybrid Disk, which can be played on both Apple and Intel-based systems. CD/R compounds the complications by using an entirely different way of physically recording data. Instead of burning pits into the substrate layer of the CD, it discolors a spot on a layer of green organic dye.

All the books use the basic original principles of CD-DA: a 1,200-millimeter disk with precisely stated organization of every component. For instance, the inner 6-millimeter space around the 15-millimeter center hole is kept blank and used by the CD player to clamp onto the disc. Next to this is a 4-millimeter volume table of contents. The program data are held on a 33-millimeter spiral that winds roughly 20,000 times around the disc. Data are coded in "pits," which look like tiny bumps to the laser beam scanning the disc, and "lands" the flat surface of the disc. The pits are interpreted as 1s and the absence of a pit, as 0s. The disc is organized in small groups of data called "frames"; these in turn form blocks (CD-DA) or sectors (CD-ROM and CD-I). Those blocks are the smallest units of information that can be addressed and thus located. It is this feature that allows you to select, say, track 16 on a CD and CD-ROM software to locate a specific image or entry in an encyclopedia.

The original developers of the Red Book made some partially arbitrary decisions about size, density, and even how the disc revolves. These constrain future exploitation of the underlying technology, but to diverge from them would be to lose the standardization that has made CD technology so widespread and cost-effective. For example, the choice of what is termed "constant linear velocity" (CLV), instead of an alternative proposal used on hard disk technology, means that there is a longer delay for the laser to locate and position itself above blocks on the outer circumference of the CD than those on the inside. This rotational delay can be as long as one-fifth of a second. A lot of time is chewed up before the laser begins transferring data: synchronization of the clock that controls the timing of the data transfer from the disc, rotational delay, and seek time can add up to a full second. This makes CD technology very slow in comparison with that of hard disk. Its advantage is its massive storage capacity, close to 100 printed book equivalents (650 million bytes) per disc for the basic technology and far more with the coding and storage techniques used by CD-I. It takes 3 to 10 times as many bits to store one minute of stereo on CD-DA compared with CD-I, depending on the desired level of quality.

CD technology is a workhorse of all multimedia and the door that opened multimedia to the mass consumer market. Only CD-ROM and its extensions can today manage the huge volumes of data inherent in multimedia, though there are some quite exotic and promising alternatives emerging fast. The advantage of CD-ROM technology is that it is well-established, familiar and trusted, with millions of devices and billions of disks already in use. As a result, there will be continuing efforts to squeeze the most out of the technology foundations of the Red and Yellow Books. The problem, as always, is that the new will make the old obsolete and thus involve extra hardware or software investment, or that the new will not be adopted because of existing investment in equipment. In late 1995, a miniwar between parties that included Sony, Toshiba, Philips, and many other computer, entertainment, and consumer electronic firms, ended in an agreement on a new standard for high-capacity digital video discs. (This DVD standard, technically called Digital Versatile Disk, is usually referred to more naturally as Video rather than Versatile.) They will cost around $20 per disc and require a device that is expected to cost $500. Will consumers adopt these to replace videotapes and VCRs? There are as many skeptics as believers.

To most managers, the discussion of the technology is of limited relevance or interest. The main points to recognize, though, are that this CD technology is the basic driver of most low-cost use of multimedia, which it is rapidly developing with plenty of room for innovation, and which companies need in order to protect themselves from obsolescence. It is foolish now for a firm's training department not to ensure that any multimedia PC it acquires with a standard CD-ROM drive also supports CD-XA, for instance. CD-ROMs look simple to purchase and use. They are anything but that for business applications. A home PC will use only Yellow Book CD technology. Businesses will need to draw on the entire range of capabilities: Yellow Book for manuals, CD/R for backing up large PC files and for archiving, perhaps White Book for customer service kiosks, and Orange Book for customer records.

See also CD Audio; CD-I; CD Plus; CD-R; CD-ROM; CD-XA

CD-XA "*CD* extended *architecture*" (CD-XA) is a relatively new extension of CD-ROM technology, which interleaves video, audio, graphics, and text in small "packets" within the same file. The major limitation of CD-ROM is that these are stored as separate files; a file can store only one type of media. That means that playback is a two-step process. The nonaudio elements are first read into computer memory and then sent to the hardware, which handles their display as the CD-ROM drive then accesses and plays the audio. All this adds time and increases the needed hardware components.

CD-XA divides up the multimedia flow into small packets that contain all the data for 1/75th of a second's playback. The "streamlining" of the packets is synchronized so that it appears as if all video and audio data are being played simultaneously. This both makes CD-XA discs faster than CD-ROMs and cuts down on the special-purpose computer memory that has to be used in the processing (these are called "cache" and RAM "buffers").

See also CD Audio; CD-I; CD Plus; CD-R; CD-ROM; CD Technology

Censorship Multimedia is powerful. The Internet has made it widely available and easily accessible. A small fraction of that material, however, is raunchy and, in some instances, downright disgusting. This has led to a flurry of censorship. Some governments, most notably Singapore, are determined to control what is created, accessed, and stored by users in their country. Some exercise control across national borders. In December 1995, for example, a German prosecutor informed CompuServe that a number of its newsgroups (electronic discussion groups) violated

French law strongly protects the privacy of public figures. For decades, journalists knew of but did not write about President Mitterand's mistress and illegitimate daughter. They also knew that he had kept secret his long bout with the cancer that killed him. His family prevented the sale of a book by his doctor about his illness, forcing it to be withdrawn from stores.

But the ban applied only to printed copies. The book was already up on the Internet, where the laws of privacy do not apply and are ineffectual anyway. People immediately began downloading the entire book, with over 1,000 calls per hour for weeks. The cybercafe that put the book on the Internet has arranged to move it to an Internet server in the United States if it is prosecuted.

German law. CompuServe immediately cut off the groups, but around the world, not just in Germany, because it had no technical way of blocking access just by German subscribers. It thus imposed on its 4 million subscribers a law designed to protect Bavarian minors. Such laws don't apply to the United States, and any effort to apply them to shops selling pornographic videos in the United States would have been entirely rejected. As many experts pointed out, it was easy to bypass the blockages, but the general principle that foreign governments could force their censorship rules on the rest of the world both set a precedent and raised concerns.

In the United States, the long tradition of freedom of speech embodied in the First Amendment has been zealously adhered to on the Internet. There is a strong community opposed to any regulation and equally strong political groups just as committed to ensuring it. At the moment, the latter are in the lead, having stimulated the passage of a new law that prevents obscene material from being transmitted over telecommunications networks, where it can be accessed by juveniles. That law will be challenged all the way to the Supreme Court, if needed. It puts the onus on the provider of material, rather than on the author. In this case, CompuServe was just a conduit; the items objected to were electronic mail messages generated by on-line discussion groups.

If there is a consensus that the Internet should be censored, the government approach of putting the censorship, fines, and prison sentences at the origination end makes neither technical nor legal sense. Swedes are permitted by law to put cyberporn on a Swedish computer connected to the Internet. A postal inspector in, say, Chicago, has no legal right to prosecute the Swedish originator. Does he or she have a right to prosecute someone in Chicago who downloads the information? If so, then the postal inspector broke the law in going "to" Sweden and sending the "illegal" material along the open Internet lines. The computer in Sweden does not know where a message is coming in from, anyway. CompuServe does know, though, because each server that is an on-ramp to the Net contains basic information about the users who connect to it as an access provider. That would not have made any real difference in blocking the material to which the German prosecutor objected, because experts use the Compu-Serve software to get onto the Net and proceed to bypass Com-puServe from then on.

Censorship, freedom of speech, and government control of the Internet are huge issues that can only grow bigger. They affect businesses, too, which may need their own policy rules about internal censorship. How to enforce such rules is a complex matter in itself, as is the right to do so, but companies need to address the question of just what type of multimedia information they will sanction on their own networks and on their own PCs. Multimedia is very powerful and now very available. There are a lot of people who know how to get it, how to bypass efforts to control it, and where to locate it.

For example, in February 1996, the "McLibel Two" set up a Web site containing 1,700 pages of information about McDon-ald's as a follow-on to a leaflet the pair had distributed, which charged the company with exploiting children, destroying rain forests, and causing cancer and heart disease. McDonald's sued for defamation. The trial began in mid-1994 and was expected to last until 1997. The Net site includes audio clips from witnesses, interviews with the McLibel Two, scientific papers, and transcripts from the case. In addition, the leaflet that led to the suit can be downloaded and printed in 17 languages. To forestall additional legal problems, the site is located on a host computer in the Netherlands, which has far less restrictive libel laws than the UK, where the case was filed.

See also Copyright; Pornography

Client-Server Client-server computing is the emerging main-stream in large organizations' use of information technology. It is a form of what is widely called "distributed computing," in which functions that used to be handled on large central mainframe computers are "distributed" out to departmental ones and to PCs and computer workstations (these are essentially special-purpose PCs with telecommunications built in). Client-server is the extension of distributed computing to place information and processing anywhere in the distributed resource. Clients are generally PCs that handle front-end applications. They link to servers for additional resources, such as information stores, communications management, or processing services. Servers may be souped up PCs, minicomputers, or mainframe host computers.

Client-server is independent of multimedia, but most interactive networked multimedia systems will rely on client-server technology and design. For example, shared CD-ROMs and interactive training videos will be stored on a multimedia server. Pay per view movies offered by cable TV and phone companies will be delivered from a server. Network servers will handle the flow of multimedia data across the network; this will require very fast devices with very large storage. In many ways, the difference between client-server for multimedia versus transactions and nonmultimedia applications is that multimedia adds "very" to the description of any needed element in the technology: fast, large, expensive, reliable, and so on.

Client-server is extraordinarily complex in terms of technical design, needed skills, and efficiency of operation. Multimedia is only gradually being added to leading firms' client-server platforms. Much of it remains on separate technology bases. Most PC use of multimedia today relies on CD-ROMs, which are not stored on a network server but on each PC. Videoconferencing and interactive video for training use telecommunications transmission links which bypass the client-server network resource. As multimedia becomes part of everyday business operations, that will change. Images and videos will be part of customer service data bases and transaction systems, for instance, and PC clients accessing corporate information stored on servers will make no distinction between alphanumeric data, text, image, audio, and video. They will access servers that contain all of these. When this happens, which will surely be no later than 1998 for most large companies, multimedia and client-server become equivalent.

See also Server

Clip Art   *Clip art* is the term used to describe the many photos, cartoons, symbols, and other images, supplied on hard disk and CD-ROM, that you can copy, edit, and insert into presentations or documents. Most clip art is disappointing and little more than simple cartoons, symbols, and schematics. The reason for this is straightforward: storage space. Compressing and storing a line drawing or a low-resolution image of a building, flag, or road sign takes up less than a printed page (10,000 to 20,000 bits). A small photograph with a level of resolution that looks fairly good on a PC screen takes about 4 printed page equivalents. A CD-ROM can hold thousands of these images but less than 100 high-resolution photographic ones.

The main use of clip art is either to make presentations more colorful and visually interesting or to streamline the production of such printed material as brochures and newsletters. It is now very simple to select a piece of clip art from a CD-ROM and insert it in a word processed document. The clip art can be enlarged, the colors changed, or a small part selected. You can select, for instance, a clip art photo of a beach with palm trees, insert a scanned-in photo of your product, and then add advertising text to the resulting image. One museum offers a delightful range of clip art that shows old versions of modern appliances and equipment, so that you can place in the background of a graphics presentation of your firm's new PC or office furniture a photo of the office of yesterday.

The key feature of clip art is simplicity of access—just clip it and use it. It is a small part of multimedia, but an important one in that the old world of text produced by word-processing packages (their very name shows their limitation) is being rapidly replaced by a hybrid combination of easy-to-generate text and easy-to-generate images.

Clip art really isn't art, but it's certainly clip—point your mouse to it and copy it at once. It has to meet three main needs: (1) it's royalty free, meaning that you can use it without breaching copyright; (2) it doesn't take up too much storage, encouraging the provision of cartoons, symbols, line diagrams, and very small photographs; and (3) it offers visuals that add something extra to a brochure, presentation, or newsletter. In fact, $9.95 buys you a CD-ROM containing 2,200 low-resolution photos, of which at least half meet these criteria.

How would you like to be the well-known photographer who used to make two-thirds of his income from selling "stock" photos to companies for use in presentations and brochures? or the photo library whose entire business was selling images for the same purpose? The photographer's firm went bankrupt in 1994. It couldn't make money out of taking photographs.

Codec A codec is a coder/decoder that processes nondigital data to convert it to and from digital form and to compress and uncompress it. (It is also sometimes referred to as standing for "*compressor/decompressor*," which is technically incorrect but an understandable neologism.) Codec is a computer equivalent of a modem (modems include codec chips). It converts a sound wave signal such as the spoken voice or a more complex video signal, such as that produced by a camera in, say, a videoconferencing room, into digital bit form to transmit it. A codec at the other end converts it back from digital to analog form. Here, the device begins with a medium that is not digital, not in a form that allows it to be manipulated, stored, and transmitted over a telecommunications link at very fast rates. It is the best of both worlds: the analog world of our senses augmented by the processing and communications power of digital information technology. In short, codecs make networked-based multimedia possible.

A modem does the reverse of a codec and gets the lesser of both worlds. It takes bits that could be transmitted at rates of millions (book equivalents) or even billions of bits per second (movie equivalents) and converts them to a wave form that can be sent at just thousands (a few pages). Tricks of the technology trade have increased those thousands from around 1 to just under 30, but that's it. Phone modems can't process media that involve book equivalents of bits to represent the data—high-quality images, CD-quality music, and TV-quality video—and are limited by the analog lines that make modems necessary. Thus modems process fast data in a slow way, and a computer generates many bits that then get transmitted by electronic carrier pigeon. Codecs process very fast data in a fast way. They still have to address the same basic issue: how to transmit data on lines that cannot keep up with the flow of the traffic.

A codec reduces the traffic size without losing the information it contains. It takes many bits in and sends many fewer out. For example, current codecs can take in a full motion video signal that takes just over 1 book equivalent (9 million bits) per second to represent and accurately transmit and can compress it so that what is actually sent is only 16 page equivalents (384 kbps) per second, a ratio of 230:1. Some codecs operate at output rates of 4 page equivalents (112 kbps), a compression ratio of 800:1.

Of course, it's easy to compress a picture in terms of bits if you are willing to lose some of the information it contains. Your fax machine does that. If you fax a color photograph, it is sent in blurry black and white. This type of compression is called "lossy," contrasted with "lossless" compression. To get lossless compression, you need an ultraexpensive digital fax machine, which codes the colors pixel by pixel—digital dot by dot—and then sends the data over a high-speed digital line. In a way, the fax machine accomplishes the same thing as a codec: it converts all the information into the format that fits into the available transmission capacity.

Codecs get pretty close to capturing most of the original data, unlike the fax machine. A top quality video requires around 200,000 pixels per image, or frame, to reproduce perfectly, and the TV screen must be refreshed 30 times per second for our eyes to see it as flicker-free and continuous. Each of the pixels takes a byte to represent its color. $200,000 \times 8 \times 30$ amounts to 48 million bits—over 6 printed book equivalents for just 1 second of information. That's beyond the capabilities of today's standard technology. The best available codecs provide 175,000 pixels at around 20 frames per second (fps). Others degrade the quality of the video, providing 5, 10, or 15 fps. In general, people notice the loss of clarity at around 16 to 18 fps. Some codecs address this through data and motion compensation techniques—fast electronic touch-ups.

Codecs are key to multimedia, in that data compression is so central to its progress today. The newest codecs are built on specialized computer chips called digital signal processors, sales of which increased from about 100,000 in 1991 to an estimated 1.5 million in 1995. The relevance of codecs to today's business use of multimedia is mainly in the area of interactive videoconferencing. Codecs reduce the cost of the telecommunications lines needed to ensure acceptable-quality video. Companies have for a long time been able to get good quality transmission at a high price. Now, codecs allow them to range widely over the quality-price trade-offs or to get more quality for the same price. Companies obviously must pay extra for the codec equipment but in doing so reduce the monthly rental charge for the lines they lease.

See also Data Compression; Digital Signal Processors; Modem

Color Color and multimedia go together. The old world of computers was one of black-and-white displays, such as airline reservation terminals and reports printed in black on (mainly) white paper. The PC introduced colors to the display. Initially, color printers were very expensive, but prices dropped quickly from over $20,000 to $200 or less. CD-ROM has made high-quality color photographs and video routine features of PCs. It is estimated that over 80 percent of PC users are now working with color screens.

All color is not created equal in the multimedia world, unfortunately, making it difficult in many instances to match the color you see on your display with the color you see when you print it on paper. Displays and printers handle color entirely differently. Displays—monitors and built-in screens on a PC—shoot electron guns at phosphors (from which the term *phosphorescent* comes) attached at the rear of the screen. These phosphors come in three colors—red, green, and blue (hence the frequent references to RGB in discussions of multimedia color). By varying the intensity of each electron gun and exactly which phosphor it hits, the standard PC can create any color (up to 16.7 million, though most standard PC displays are limited to a selection, or "palette," of 256 within an application).

Printers use ink to reflect light off paper (they are designed for white paper), mixing four colors: cyan, magenta, yellow, and black. Displays and printers are really speaking two different

What we all learned in elementary school about colors being composed of three primary colors—red, blue, and yellow—is true for digital color as well, except that here they are red, green, and blue (or, more precisely, magenta, green, and cyan). The difference is that paints use subtractive color mixing and computer screens use additive mixing. When paints are added to a white paper background, each blocks a particular type of light. Blue, for languages to each other. This poses ongoing difficulties in applications that require high quality color printing. Color matching is an art form.

Top-end computer graphics tools use 24-bit color: three 8-bit specifications that provide 256 shades of each of the three RGB color guns. That gives a total of 256 $\times$ 256 $\times$ 256 combinations. This adds up to the 16.7 million possible colors mentioned earlier. That may sound like overkill, but a single leaf may have hundreds of thousands of subtle shades of green. Storing 24-bit color graphics images consumes large amounts of storage—around 30 printed page equivalents (900 kb) on a typical PC screen's display. That takes time to transfer from disk to screen. For this reason, 24-bit color is not used for multimedia presentations that require a fast pace, real-time animation, or quick visual response. Multimedia is a constant trade-off between speed, resolution, and cost. Managers need to think about the trade-offs and not look just at the specifications for a given system. Vendor ads and expert professionals will tend to highlight the resolution, which amounts to quality, or the speed, which translates to cost. Today, everyday business use of multimedia is likely to favor the best combination of speed and cost, at the expense of resolution.

CompuServe CompuServe is one of the longest-established on-line information service providers in the United States, together with Prodigy, the oldest, and America Online, the newest and most successful. CompuServe's strongest feature is its wide range of special interest groups (SIGs), which people use to find technical and specialist information and expertise. It also accesses a fairly strong base of business and technical information sources. It has taken decades for CompuServe to reach critical mass, and even now it is only marginally profitable. It has around 4 million subscribers, 1 million fewer than America Online's total.

Its historical weaknesses are highly relevant to on-line multimedia: slow transmission of graphics, clumsy user interfaces, complex navigation, and high cost. The improvements have been

instance, blocks red light. Yellow blocks blue, so that mixing yellow and blue blocks the two, leaving us seeing only the green light. Computer screens add color to a black screen. Red, green, and blue together mix all three colors, giving us white.

One 1995 survey of on-line services summarized CompuServe as "boring" and mainly for "multinational types, nerdies and microserfs." That means it's content driven, whereas America Online is "for all of us," chat driven. The world of networked multimedia is increasingly one in which firms position to be content providers/ owners (CompuServe), communication providers/owners (AOL), or information monopolists (Dow Jones).

substantial in the past year, such that CompuServe now matches its competitors, including America Online, and surpasses them in terms of the business information it provides.

See also America Online; On-Line Information Services; Prodigy

Computer-Telephony Integration   Computer-telephony integration (CTI) is the incorporation in computers (PCs and servers) of the telephone-based capabilities that have until now been features of phone companies' large "switches." Just about any phone feature you can think of that requires you to dial a phone number is becoming a software feature of PCs, and just about every telephone hardware system is becoming an add-in board for PCs. CTI makes phone call services just another standard medium.

Here are a few examples of CTI:

- *Visual voice mail.* This lets users scan their voice mail messages on their PC, with each one identified by caller name and number, so that they can go directly to the most important ones, instead of having to listen to them in order. These, faxes, and electronic mail messages can also be organized in a "universal in-box" and broadcast over a LAN, so they can be shared.

- *Visual telephony control.* Users can set up conferences from the PC, transfer calls, and record conversations.

- *Automated "screen pops."* As calls come in from, say, customers, the caller identification code automatically opens specified records, such as account status and history.

- *Automated call handling.* Automated attendant, interactive voice response, pager notification, and many other features.

The breakthrough in CTI has been the development of standardized telephone application program interfaces, called TAPI

90 percent of course registrations made at Aloha State in Hawaii are now made by a phone call that links into a set of three top end PC server machines, each of which runs 24 software applications that handle the calls, access data bases, and registers students for courses. This is an extremely complex application. It's not like using a push button phone to get your credit card balance. The system has to manage the telephone interface, interact with a host mainframe, and manage an interactive dialogue with the student, and TSAPI. APIs are messages that allow two entirely different pieces of software to work together. TAPI stands for "*telephony API*" and is Microsoft's contribution. TSAPI is Novell's and AT&T's, and requires use of a Novell-based local area network; it stands for "*telephony services API.*" Software developers can use APIs to include telephone features and commands in, say, a customer service or even word processing application. The phone system becomes just like a printer or floppy disk as far as the application is concerned. Voice becomes just another type of multimedia data. TAPI is designed for PCs, and TSAPI is aimed at call centers.

In parallel with developments in CTI software, innovations in telephony boards are taking place rapidly. Basically, you can put a small phone exchange in a PC for $200 to $1,000. The boards include CD-ROM and CD-audio links, voice mail, voice synthesizers, microphones, fax on demand, and high-speed modems.

Given the importance of phones to large and small businesses, the opportunities CTI opens up for cost savings, customer service, and internal coordination are almost unlimited. A simple example of how CTI and PC can work together is an insurance company's claims department. A customer phoning in gets a recorded message that says, after the "thank you for calling" introduction, "Press 1 to access our fax data base of claims forms, 2 for information on your claim," and so on. The CTI system can page specific people and move priority messages into the universal in-box. This fairly routine level of customer service can be extended to internal staff, so that, for instance, they can phone the human resources department to get forms, information on benefits, job openings, and the like, and even initiate transactions. All incoming faxes are automatically filed and routed electronically, and outgoing ones are handled by the PC, reducing paper clutter. Copies of forms are extracted from a fax data base on a server and filled out by the PC software application. They are then automatically sent. Customer voice mail descriptions of problems or needs are appended to relevant documents so that the techni-

addressing issues of course availability, time conflicts, prerequisites, auditing, and many others. And it's the computer-telephony integration that makes it work. The software needs to keep all 24 software applications open at the same time and be able to link the same phone call to any or all of them as needed. That would be completely impossible without CTI and the multimedia programming tools that support it—all new to the systems development field.

cian hears them explain matters in their own words. Calls can be automatically recorded and indexed, an important need in many financial service applications—for instance, to keep a precise logging of orders to brokers.

CTI may soon be one of the fastest-moving, highest-payoff applications of multimedia. It brings phones into the mainstream of computers, thus meshing two of the main productivity and service tools of modern business.

See also API

Consumer Electronics   Until 1994, consumer electronics and personal computers were fairly separate industries. They are converging rapidly now because of multimedia. Game machines, TVs, music CD players, cameras, and tape recorders, the staples of consumer electronics, are being challenged by personal computers. The new models of game machines launched in mid-1995 are more powerful in terms of raw CPU speed than most PCs. They have posed a threat to the home PC market for priority on the consumer budget. The Sega Saturn and Sony Playstation offer a wider variety of games, with more special effects than most personal computers and at one-fifth to one-tenth of the price.

Sony's chairman sees changes in technology as rearing a new generation of "digital dream kids." He describes Sony's founder as a Walkman kid and himself as a CD kid. He is entirely revamping the company to address the wants of the digital dream kids, creating two new information technology companies focused on multimedia, making alliances with Intel and Japan's Oki Electric to develop new semiconductors, and

The convergence of computers and consumer electronics is accelerating. Apple's new technology, Pippin, is as much suited to games as to Internet networked computing, personal digital assistants, or home computers; it was introduced onto the market by the Japanese company who gave the world the Mighty Morphin Power Rangers. The PC offers better TV for some applications than standard TV sets, but TV sets may become the electronic appliance of the future that contains basic software and hardware functions and accesses others, as needed, over the Internet. CDs (consumer electronics) can be played on stereos but not on CD-ROM drivers (PCs) unless extra software is purchased, just as CD-ROM can't be played on stereos. CD Plus combines them, so that the same disk on a stereo plays music and on a PC shows videos and interviews. Camcorders connect to PCs. The PC is a device not just for recording and playing back audio, but also for editing it. Digital cameras link to PCs. All in all, multimedia represents a convergence of all the technologies, industries, and devices relevant to audio, video, image, and computing.

All this turns previously divergent industries upside down. Microsoft's biggest competition could become Internet appliances connected to TVs. TV's biggest competitor could become the PC. Game machines could become Internet access devices. And the phone could be in the PC.

Sony illustrates both this convergence of consumer electronics and the computer industry and the relative weakness of companies like itself that have hitherto driven the individual media in the multimedia market. Sony's strengths have been its "pocketability," packaging more and more power and features into devices you can carry. Sony's Walkman and its wide variety of cassette recorders, portable TVs, and the like are examples. In the early 1980s, it made a major foray into the microcomputer market but failed badly. For the next 10 years, it had no need for expertise in and products based on digital technology. Now it urgently does. It is not unthinkable that Sony, once one of the half-dozen strongest companies in the world, will, in the phrase of the *Financial Times* (18 January 1996) be "relegated to the annals of 20th century Japanese legends."

One major competitive advantage of consumer electronics firms is their skill in manufacturing. They are able to produce at low price, in huge volume, and with superb quality. By contrast, personal computers too often suffer from manufacturing defects. As price wars erode margins, some manufacturers cut corners on details like keyboards. If a PC stays on the retailer's shelf more than 23 days, according to an industry survey, the profit is gone. Of the $89 Microsoft charged when it introduced Windows 95, only $3 goes to the retailer and $1 to distributors. Microsoft gets the remaining $85.

Consumer electronics firms know how to make money on small margins. They are already leaders in the provision of TVs

setting up two new corporate laboratories dedicated to R&D in telecommunications, multimedia hardware, and software. Sony, the pacesetter in consumer electronics for well over 40 years, has seen its sales stagnate, with less than 10 percent total growth since 1991 and profits falling every year since then, with a loss in 1995. During this period, PCs have captured much of the game market and are the new base for multimedia. Sony wants to get that base back.

and game machines. Many of them are well established in multimedia through stereos and cameras. More and more of these devices are digital and include powerful chips. Consider the set-top boxes used in pilots of interactive television. Thomson, the firm that sells around 80 percent of all cable and satellite descramblers for TVs, was one of the half-dozen firms placing billion dollar orders in Europe in early 1996 for huge volumes of set-top boxes. The ones it commissioned are more powerful than many PCs, with eight megabytes of memory, the new Motorola PowerPC chip, and an MPEG-2 data compression chip built into them. They have a built-in slow modem, obviously intended to make them Internet "appliances," too. This is equivalent to a full desktop PC and more powerful than the specifications the Multimedia Product Council laid out in its MPC3 recommendations for multimedia hardware. This is just one instance of a consumer electronics firm moving into the core of what is essentially the PC field. Sony has entirely reorganized itself to emphasize digital multimedia and semiconductor research and manufacturing.

See also CD-ROM; Consumer versus Business Use of Multimedia; Interactive Television; MPC; Network Computer

Consumer versus Business Use of Multimedia   The consumer market for PCs has always lagged the business market in terms of technology and use. It amounted to just $11 billion in 1995 versus over $80 billion for the corporate market, a ratio of 1:7. In 1985, the gap had been well over 1:100. Up until early 1995, the typical office PC was faster and had larger memory and storage than the typical home machine, ran more and more sophisticated software, and linked to networks and servers instead of being primarily a standalone device.

That has changed very quickly, with the 1994 Christmas season as a watershed. It was then that the long time promise of a CD-ROM on every PC began to come true; now, over 70 percent of home PCs are sold with the basic components of multimedia hardware built in—a sound card, video card, CD-ROM, and speakers. By contrast, most PCs in business still lack any of these. Only a fraction of laptop computers have a CD-ROM built in; the premium price of such machines is at present too high to make it practical for companies to purchase them in thousands of units.

It was in 1995 that the Internet became a consumer resource, mainly through such on-line services as America Online and CompuServe. These began to flood the consumer market with disks offering around 10 hours of free usage. They now provide simple access to the Internet. Internet browser software is being given away free with PCs or sold for less than $50. The best-known such products are Netscape Navigator and Mosaic. Microsoft Windows 95, the operating system targeted to consumers, not only includes many multimedia features but also comes with free (to date) access to and use of Microsoft Network, an equivalent of America Online with links to the Internet like those offered by AOL and the other main on-line services. When Microsoft radically revamped its entire business strategy to embrace the Internet, not compete with it, it soon thereafter announced alliances with around 30 phone service providers, consumer electronics firms, and computer manufacturers, with the explicit aim of dominating the consumer multimedia market.

Business followed, rather than led, the march onto the Internet, which built critical mass as more and more individuals found it useful for electronic mail, still by far its largest use. In 1995, Microsoft replaced its earlier operating system, Windows 3.11, with Windows 95, targeted mainly to consumers. Many companies decided to wait rather than to adopt it immediately, because of the expense and the inevitable number of bugs a complex new piece of software would contain.

Together, technology cost improvements and industry factors have increased the supply of multimedia capabilities in the consumer market far faster than in the business market. Consumers have benefited from PC price wars. They can buy a fully multimedia PC for $1,200 and get onto the Internet in 15 minutes. It's tougher for businesses to exploit the same forces. For in-

In mid-1995, 70 percent of new PC purchases for use in the home were for multimedia machines. The figure for large firms was under 10 percent, and for small businesses most estimates were less than 5 percent. Business is now lagging behind your teenager in simple multimedia use.

stance, installing Windows 95 on PCs requires upgrading hardware and storage in order to operate efficiently in a networked environment; the cost is estimated to be around $1,500 per machine. For a company that has 5,000 PCs in use, that's $7.5 million. *PC Laptop* magazine's choice of the best portables of the year (January 1996) shows the premium for networked multimedia machines. It picked IBM's ThinkPad 755CD as the "notebook that everybody wants." With its built-in CD-ROM, stereo sound, and telecommunications, "the 755CD has it all. . . . It satisfies just about every need a user might have in a portable computer."

PC Laptop's choice of value portable, the Winbook XP5, has basically the same hardware capabilities as the ThinkPad except for the multimedia features. It cost, in January 1996, $3,000. The IBM 755CD cost over $6,000. Is the difference worth paying? For a sales rep, an executive, or a consultant buying a single machine, the answer is probably yes. For a company looking to replace 100 laptops, maybe. For the company with 10,000 PCs, the entry price to the world of multimedia as an everyday part of business operations is $20 million before any discount for volume purchases (the $2,000 premium per machine for built-in multimedia).

1997 sees the use of multimedia as a relatively routine element of home PCs, albeit mainly for playing CD-ROMs and surfing the Internet, and a relatively exceptional element of business PCs. For business managers this raises the issue of how to ensure that the price differential of multimedia *machines* doesn't block experimentation, piloting, and targeted use of multimedia *applications*. CD-ROMs on multimedia PCs are the consumer option of choice. The business option is more likely to be networked multimedia, with servers providing the software and information resources on which existing PCs can draw.

See also Consumer Electronics

Content Providers　Content providers are the firms in the media and multimedia industry that aim at making their competitive differentiation the nature of the digital bits they offer, rather than buying or delivering someone else's bits. Those bits may be news, films, data bases, or libraries. The contrast to being a content provider is to be the service access provider that delivers that content; phone companies and cable TV firms are examples.

The multimedia industry competition is basically one among content providers, access providers, and total providers (of both content *and* access). The access providers have an advantage of what the cable TV business terms "point of presence"; their phones, cable descrambler boxes, and on-line information service software given away in magazines already lend them a presence in your home. They can charge content providers a fee for being part of what is offered at that point of presence, or they can pay a fee to them for the right to offer their content. Phone companies want the content of movies for videos on demand. Cable TV firms constantly add new channels to their basic, premium, and add-on packages. The Internet can be thought of as in itself a contentless vehicle for accessing content. As its points of presence grow, content providers rush to ensure they are on the menu of options.

Content providers have largely had an edge over access providers, for two reasons: (1) until recently, there wasn't much access, so that content owners could insist that access come via their own telecommunications facilities; and (2) there is now so much access and such a shortage of content that every provider is looking for it. Entire cable TV channels like Discovery and Arts and Entertainment (A&E) were built on buying content at low cost from Britain's BBC. When Turner Broadcasting, the owner of CNN, bought MGM's film library, it was to provide content for its new TNT channel.

Multimedia demands masses and masses of content for news, entertainment, education, television programming, publishing, on-line data bases, CD-ROMs, World Wide Web sites, games, and many other applications. Billions of dollars are being gambled on each of these and many other alliances, acquisitions, and joint ventures. A lot of that money will be wasted, and in many areas, innovators are learning as they go. For all the profusion of CD-ROMs, for instance, literally only a handful make money. The old phrase in the media industry, that "content is king," seems even more accurate in the multimedia industries.

It is worthwhile for managers to spend a little time with their planners and staff thinking through their own opportunities as content providers and their strategies for identifying the multimedia content they want to access as organizations. In financial services, there is a flood of new offerings in the form of multimedia news packaging, for instance, which illustrates both parts of this—supply and use. One of the players offering news is Reuters. Reuters's dominance of the foreign exchange and international information market is so strong that it constitutes an electronic franchise and an electronic brand. But this was a by-product of its news service, which was little more than a skunkworks, led by an internal heretic and resisted by many of its managers.

Reuters used the information it gathered to become a new type of content provider. Its clients now have to judge whether they want to move into the multimedia content that Reuters, Bloomberg, Murdoch, CNN, and others are delivering or planning to deliver. Many trading companies and banks are poorly prepared to exploit the resources, in terms of assessing their value, upgrading their telecommunications networks and PC base, and developing policies. One banker voiced ambivalence about the applicability of the offerings, such as being able to view interviews with CEOs on a PC. That was very much the attitude taken by bankers in the 1970s about Reuters.

To date, multimedia has been driven most by improvements in access rather than by content. That is already shifting, though, especially as there are more and more access providers. Managers now will benefit from taking inventories of their own content resources and asking what value these may have as a product; the cost of entry to being a content provider on the Internet is very low. International data, industry information, technical data, even historical corporate data all may have commercial value. Managers certainly need to make inventories of content offerings and not be locked into their standard information systems and services. The opportunity of multimedia is knowledge management. Access is now easy. The issue is access to what?

Copyright Multimedia strains the letter and the law of copyright, to the extent that it is not at all clear that it can be enforced or even effectively adapted to address a world where laws are accidentally bypassed every day and where no one can be sure of whether they even apply. Consider the following routine use of a PC to produce, say, a newsletter. You find an attractive magazine photograph of a child on the beach. You scan it into your PC desktop publishing software and crop the image to select just the child's stretched-out hand. You edit the new image, altering the color and tone and adding a texture that makes it look embossed. You place the hand, which looks entirely different from that in the original photograph, in a picture you have created entirely from scratch. It seems reasonable for you to feel you have created something original. However, you are in violation of copyright on three counts. You violated the photographer's reproduction right by scanning the photo, his or her modification right by altering it, and the distribution right by selling the altered photograph as part of your newsletter. Technically, you need a license from the owner of the copyright. This is the case even when your multimedia work is not shown or marketed in any public domain—an in-house training program, for instance. If you scanned photos of, say, a famous athlete for your own private use, that may not constitute the "fair use" that copyright law allows, because you have violated the copyright holder's reproduction right. Adding even two seconds of music recorded from a song and using your software to change the pitch and instrumentation violates modification rights.

One myth about copyrights is that the law applies only to material that has a copyright notice on it, with the well-known © symbol. Since 1989, that is no longer required. Paraphrasing an

How to protect intellectual property in an era when information is accessed, moved, changed, and used in ways that are impractical to track and impossible to control is one of the most complex issues facing multimedia. The main community of Internet users and multimedia experimenters is generally resistant to any idea of regulation of information use. They can, though, protect their protective rights against overt copying of their works. Time Warner had to pay $2.2 million in damages in 1992 for using a short clip from the Beatles' "Yellow Submarine" on a *videocassette. The distinctive feature of multimedia is that it changes the underlying work. Using a MIDI synthesizer, you yourself could turn "Yellow Submarine" into a new tune or edit a family photograph to include a cropped section from a copyrighted photo and then change its colors and focus. You've still breached copyright, but who could tell?*

author's words instead of using them verbatim may call for a license just as does making a hand-drawn copy of, say, Mickey Mouse from a photograph. (Disney once sued a day care center where teachers had painted murals of its cartoon characters on the walls of the school.)

All this means that just about anyone with a scanner, most people using the Internet, and everyone whose hard disk holds a gigabyte of graphics, video, and audio are inadvertently violating copyright laws and that copyright owners could never track down those violations, especially when the original has been altered or an extract has been made from it.

The process of licensing and assigning rights to use multimedia products is just as complex and full of ambiguities and deviations from commonsense expectations. For instance, a publishing agreement must clearly state the platform for which you are granting distribution rights, including operating systems, home consoles, and game machines. A license should consider the implications of distribution by CD-ROM versus over a network. The Internet adds issues of legal jurisdiction. What copyrights and licenses apply when the information is on a server in, say, Amsterdam and is accessed from San Antonio?

As is so often the case with a new technology, the law cannot easily keep up with the new realities. Many people believe that copyright law will be effectively dead within a few years except for blatant pirating of an entire work. It is so easy to copy multimedia material, modify it, and distribute it that traditional protections are close to worthless.

Costs of Multimedia Development　The costs of developing a multimedia application obviously vary widely, depending on content, quality, length, and the specific type and variety of media employed. Creating an interactive training program that uses specially shot full-motion video is much more costly than one that uses simple animation, for instance. The following figures from published case studies can provide a base for your own firm's planning.

Wilson Learning Laboratory estimates that it costs $150,000 to develop a two- to four-hour interactive multimedia system. The cost breakdown is:

Design, research, and writing	12%
Video and audio production	56
Graphics and text	6
Programming	9
Project management	8
Mastering and copying disks	11

Andersen Consulting's estimate for half a day of multimedia-based instruction is:

Design and development	$150,000
Administration and management	36,000
Subcontracting	80,000
Miscellaneous	11,500
Total	$277,500

The cost per finished minute for this is:

Low	$1000–1500
Medium	$1500–2200
High	Over $2200

The new tools of multimedia available on PCs should reduce this cost, and using them in house may be a good reason and incentive for companies, especially in generating training materials. They will then need to recruit people with the same skills to which outside studios have access.

An award-winning and business generating electronic catalogue produced for a furniture maker has 5 gigabytes of graphics files—7 to 15 hard disks, or 8 CD-ROMs. Animating the character around which the system is built required one person to draw over 1,600 frames by hand. The designers conclude that there is no easy way to predict in advance costs and effort for any innovative multimedia venture. Companies that are developing multimedia-rich World Wide Web sites are often surprised by the jump in cost over that for producing the fairly static ones that crowd the Net. Whereas anyone can knock off a simple Web page using the HTML tool, a scanner, and a music synthesizer program, it costs $100,000 to $1 million for even a fairly small-scale corporate site that will attract potential customers.

CTI   CTI stands for "*computer-telephony integration*," the merging of telephone features into the hardware and software of PCs and the "servers" that provide information and communication services to networked PCs. Many observers of the multimedia field who have the best track record on interpreting trends see CTI as a "killer application," cyberspeak for an area of technical development that users race to adopt and that becomes a springboard for a continuing flow of innovations. Given the pivotal role of the telephone in just about every area of business and the near-pivotal role of PCs in many areas, there are many potential business opportunities from putting the phone system in the PC so that it can directly work with word processing software, turn electronic mail into multimedia mail, and automatically connect customers' phone calls to data base inquiries and answers.

See also Computer-Telephony Integration

Data Compression   Data compression is the technique of reducing the data needed to code information in digital form by analyzing and stripping out redundant elements or summarizing items in a way that allows them to be reconstituted later. A real estate ad that reads "2 bdrms, a/c, $860/mth inc. uty" compresses "2 bedrooms, air conditioning, $860 a month including utilities" from 63 characters and spaces to 30. The compression is "lossless," meaning that, when you decompress it from the shorthand of the advertisement back to its full meaning, no data are lost. "Lossy" compression would be like substituting a sketch of the house for a high-resolution photo. You can't convert the sketch back into a photo; too much detail would be lost.

Data compression is like a court stenographer who substitutes short symbols for the full spoken testimony of a witness, then hands it over to a typist who knows the conventions of stenography and transcribes it to produce a text version. The typist would not be able to keep up with the witness's speech. He or she cannot process it in "real time." The stenographer is an encoder and the typist a decoder in this example. The symbols handed over from the encoder to the decoder are a shortened version of what was said, but they can be easily converted back to the original. Obviously, something gets lost en route: voice tone, pitch, and facial gestures, for instance. Data compression techniques for multimedia aim at capturing as much of the original digital data as possible and transmitting or storing them as quickly and cheaply as practical. That obviously involves many trade-offs. A photographer needs far more accurate representation of digital images than does someone using photos as clip art for a management presentation on overheads. An L.A. film company that is sending postproduction images to editors in London will need to send the uncompressed material or lossless compressed image files. The latter may require a supercomputer to compress the data and take several hours to compress a minute of the original. Today's low-cost color printers produce acceptable copies of compressed photographs sent over the Internet, but there's no point in sending them high-resolution uncompressed ones, because they can't capture the detail accurately enough to produce a better reproduction.

Compression of still images is now routine. Until very recently, video compression involved many compromises because of the massive volume of bits involved. The screen size was reduced to about one-quarter of the original broadcast size, and the number of frames per second was cut in half. (At 30 frames, or images, per second, your eye sees a continuous flow of full-motion video; television and film provide this. At 15 fps, you are aware of occasional jerkiness.) Software tools then compress the data by a factor of between 4:1 to 10:1. In 1995, a dominant design called

Compressing two-hour long movies requires a supercomputer, not a PC, and can take 120 seconds to squeeze down a single second. Without data compression, there would be no multimedia. One commentator expresses the problem as how to take a Niagara Falls flow of digital data, such as a video, and "somehow" funnel it down a soda straw to get a Niagara at the other end.

MPEG-2 (Motion Pictures Expert Group), which resolves just about all the problems of data compression, arose. It extended the MPEG-1 standard that provided compression ratios of 6:1 for full-motion, reduced-display video, but required massive (in other words, expensive) computer time. MPEG-2 delivers up to 200:1 compression, with compromises on size and speed. It can take up to 500 seconds to compress a single second of video, though. In early 1996, the committee drawn from across the computer, tele-communications, and consumer electronics industries developing MPEG standards was close to completing MPEG-4, which is aimed at compressing any type of media for transmission over telecommunications links with very low bandwidth, such as today's phone lines.

Data compression is a whole subject in itself and obviously very important in just about every area of multimedia. Apart from the obvious need to reduce storage demands and telecommunications transmission time, MPEG-2 data compression makes it practical to edit video through PCs, to add "drag-and-drop" video clips to presentations, insert video into electronic mail, enable television quality videoconferencing, and greatly improve CD-ROM videos.

See also Codec; Digital Signal Processor; MPEG

Data Storage   Data storage devices are the physical media that store the data that turn into the video, text, graphics, and sound that are the natural media of our senses. The main impact of multimedia on computers is to greatly increase the amount of data storage they must have. There are three basic measures of the value for money provided by different types of data storage: how much data the device can store, how much it costs per million bytes of storage, and how fast the data can be accessed and transferred to the computer. Multimedia chews up storage to the extent that the fastest low-cost medium of hard disk, the work-horse component of your PC, cannot meet the need for size. This

The Duchess of Windsor's famous comment that you can never be too thin or too rich can be extended to "or have too much data storage on your PC."

favors use of the slower but far cheaper CD-ROM. Where fast access is essential, the trade-offs between capacity, cost, and access time favor chip-based devices such as flash memory cards, which are around 20 times as fast as hard disks and 20 times as costly per unit of storage.

The most common storage devices are floppy disks and hard disks. Floppy disks are now mainly used to store the software programs you install when you buy a printer, operating system such as Windows 95, or word processing package, or to back up your files.

Hard disks are the everyday mechanism for storing just about everything you need to have directly accessible from your PC, such as your operating system, application software, data files, electronic mail messages, and those elements of multimedia that can fit on the hard disk without overloading it. Hard disks are very fast, but they cannot match CD-ROM in terms of low-cost storage of large volumes of multimedia information. They are also temperamental and, though very reliable, are the component of your PC not only most likely to "crash" but also the one where a crash has most devastating impact.

The figures below show the relative performance factors of different storage media, as of late 1996. By the time you read this book, they will almost certainly all have changed to be bigger, cheaper, and faster, but it's unlikely that the *relative* differences will have shifted.

Medium	Capability (Mb)	Cost per Mb	Access speed (ms)
Floppy disk	1.4–2.8	$0.70	2,000
Floptical	20	1.00	1,000
Hard drive	40–900	1.00–4.50	10–20
Cartridge	44/88	1.00–1.40	15–30
CD-ROM	650	0.003	300
Magneto-optical	650	.25	90

Medium	Capability (Mb)	Cost per Mb	Access speed (ms)
CD-WORM	300–650	.15	1,200
DAT	1,300	.01	long and variable
Flash memory card	20	30.00	1

See also Access Time; CD-ROM; Disk

Data Transfer Rate   Data transfer rate defines the speed in bits per second at which information is moved by a piece of multimedia hardware. It is one of the basic measures of performance of such devices as CD-ROMs, audio cards, and video cards that transfer digitally coded multimedia information from, within, and to a computer. A single speed CD-ROM transfers data at the rate of 6 printed page equivalents per second (150 kb) and a 6× (six times single speed) at 36 pages (900 kb). That's awfully slow but not as slow as a floppy disk. Your PC hard disk is far faster than CD-ROM, transferring data at rates of around 1 to 5 printed books per second (1 to 5 megabytes).

When you work with some data item only occasionally, or when it's one with which you need to think while you work, you will accept slow transfer rates. Thus you can expect to sit for a minute or so while the new software application you are installing on your hard disk drive is transferred from a floppy disk.

See also Access Time

Desktop Video   Desktop video is the capture, editing, and playback of what we routinely see in the nondigital world of television and film. It is the enabling element of multimedia in two ways: (1) its cost and quality define the practical limit of widespread application of multimedia tools, and (2) it is by far its most processor-intensive component. The cost of top-quality video with sound has been very high to date, requiring either specialized supercomputers or high-end PCs/workstations, such as the Silicon Graphics machines that are the tools of Hollywood special effects in films such as *Jurassic Park* and *Forrest Gump*. As *Video Magazine* commented (January 1996), PC video capabilities have been very limited but full of promise for the near future. "This time last year, multimedia was the Next Big Thing. Jerky postage stamp–sized windows were the standard bearers of a new digital information age. 'Look,' they said, pointing to a blurry Intel logo lurching across the page. 'Look not at what your average PC can do now, but at what it will be able to do in a year's time.'" The next year saw PC video much further on but still limited in comparison with the machines multimedia professionals could use and afford.

The improvements are so continuous and rapid that it's difficult at any point in time to calibrate just what measures to use to capture the status of desktop video for routine business, rather than top-level professional, use. There are more first-rate tools available, but they need careful configuring of hardware and software, with sound and video boards, memory size, displays, printers, and scanners all affecting performance. The technical minutiae of video demand very substantial expertise and experience: RAM transfers, disk defragging, matting lens flare, key and infrastructure-frame compression, and hundreds of others.

Basically, though, just about every element needed for producing VHS-quality short videos is in place. As always with multimedia, the main issue is the dramatic increases in power, speed, and storage capacity needed to get extra quality of output. For instance, to produce a 3-minute promotional clip generally requires capturing 15 to 20 minutes of footage for editing. That takes up around 700 printed book equivalents (700 MB) for VHS quality. Going to Super-VHS doubles this. Betacam quality requires six times VHS level—1.5 movies' equivalent (4.5 GB).

Editing tools on PCs are top rate. One commentator states that, with Adobe's Premiere software, your wildest visual perversions become reality. Once video footage is on disk, you can do anything with it: warp, mix layers of images, add multiple tracks of audio, crunch, crease, distort, ripple, pointilize, emboss, and zigzag. It's now routine to film a subject against a solid blue backdrop and then drop in a weather map, image of a room, or outside scenery to fill the background. This is called "blue-screen" work. The problem is capturing, transferring, and storing all the on-line digital bits. A general principle is an obvious one: the better the quality of the source material, the better the finished product. All in all, desktop video is getting close to broadcast quality at a high but manageable cost and is at VHS level for a reasonable cost.

A representative example of desktop video production that gives a flavor of the steps involved is a five-minute video that presents a company's new product. It includes footage from interviews with executives, some straightforward animation, titles, and voiceovers. The software used was Adobe's Premiere, for capturing and editing video footage; Adobe's PhotoShop to handle titles; plus four other packages to (1) improve low-quality sound and add voiceovers, (2) insert music, (3) render animations, and (4) add special effects. That's typical: the system is built around a few proven and widely used general-purpose packages— in this case Adobe's dominant designs, Premiere and PhotoShop, with other software chosen to address more specialized needs.

The steps involved in generating the video are:

1. *Capturing.* A VHS-quality camera or, preferably, a Betacam professional-level camera is used here. These are nondigital, so that the footage is digitized and compressed by the Premiere software via a hardware video board add-on to the PC. There are hours of often-frustrating preparation. The PC hard disk needs to be tidied up—"defragged"—and organized to minimize video frames' being dropped while the disk's read/write heads search for space and can't keep up with the video. Lighting is critically important; the most widely used data compression hardware and software have trouble with film that has large patches of black

and white, for instance. Premiere is used to tidy up the footage before editing, trimming unneeded footage, adjusting colors and contrast, and the like.

2. *Titles.* It's easy to generate flashy and vivid titles that include still frames from the video, text and extracts from still images. The most time-consuming element here and in the video as a whole is generating transitions. A half-second fade takes up to 30 seconds to calculate on a Pentium 90 PC, and a more complex special effect that warps or distorts the title image may take 10 minutes.

3. *Transitions.* These include fades, very short clips from another 20-minute video, and slowdown and freezing of images.

4. *Animations.* The special-purpose software used for this facilitates entering drawings and adding 3-D, texture, rotation, and so on.

5. *Voice.* Although digitized audio is simple to edit, it's hard to get the tone and echo of live footage, so special-purpose software is used. Voices recorded directly into a mike sound flat and tinny, so voice "reverb" is added.

6. *Music.* It's easy to add CD-quality short clips and mix them in with voice and sound from the video footage.

See also Adobe

Device Driver A device driver is the software that provides the computer's operating system with the information it needs to cooperate with a hardware device, such as a printer, camera, or scanner. This software comes with the device and must be installed before you can use it. If you try to use a friend's device without the driver installed on your machine, it won't work. Your PC's operating system, which can run all your software, can't control a device such as a sound card. This is why, whenever you buy a piece of hardware to add to your computer, you must install driver software.

That software stays in computer memory whenever your PC is running. When it detects a command directed to the device with which it is associated, such as a sound card or printer, it activates instructions that control the flow of data and instructions between the computer application and the device.

Multimedia and device drivers go together in that, whenever you add multimedia capabilities to a PC, you're likely to add a sound card, new printer, video accelerator card, scanner, or some other hardware add-on. Your computer's operating system must incorporate these into its set of master procedures for running software and hardware. If anything goes wrong, you need to understand the details of the operating system to sort things out, because the malfunction means that there's a literal disconnect between the software operating system and the physical device.

In the consumer marketplace, this disconnect is more than just a problem. Large firms can afford technical support groups to handle the details of installation and troubleshooting. Consumers return the device for a refund from the store where they bought it. Microsoft, the generator of most of the problems, in that its Windows operating system determines whether an installed device driver works, has moved to be the solution. Its MCI ("*m*ultimedia *c*ontrol *i*nterface") and Plug and Play features aim at removing the need for PC users to do anything other than plug in the device. The operating system sends a signal to identify it from a list of manufacturers' products that are in its data base as Plug and Play devices. As is so often the case with Microsoft, this works well but not always, so that installing multimedia hardware remains an often-frustrating chore.

See also Installation of Multimedia Devices

Digital Cameras A digital camera is one that takes photographs not on film but on computer disks or in computer memory. No development is needed; you can take the disk out of the camera and insert it into your PC's floppy disk drive (cameras targeted at the consumer market) or connect the camera to a computer to edit the stored images.

There are three types of digital camera: field, studio, and PC.

- *Field cameras* in the $10,000 to $30,000 price range are computers in themselves and the main area of competition and innovation, with vendors of traditional cameras like Nikon, Canon, and Kodak among the leaders. They store the photographic images on PC cards, the credit card–sized software and data devices that can be slotted into a PC.

- *Studio cameras* ($5,000 to $40,000) are linked to a computer, which handles processing. They are unsuited to taking pictures of moving objects and require a strong, continuous light source. Their advantage is that they produce images of very high resolution. The resulting files may be as large as 100 printed book equivalents (100 million bytes), which means that only 4 to 10 can be stored on your hard disk for processing. That level of detail produces images that can be used even on billboards.

- *PC cameras* (as low as $150 and well under $1,000) take pictures that are good enough for displaying on a PC screen but are, not surprisingly, far from matching what you get from taking your roll of film to a store for development. The Canon QV-10 camera, for instance, sells for around $700 and stores up to 98 images, which can be immediately downloaded onto hard disk. A rule of thumb with PC cameras is that they are adequate for producing 5-by-7-inch prints, but not yet for 8-by-10-inch ones.

Today, digital cameras require many design compromises, which result in poorer-quality photos than you can get from a

"We found ourselves continuously amazed at what we could do with digital cameras. On the other hand, we found the cameras a continual source of frustration and disappointment. . . . We had mixed feelings about all three [field cameras] —they seemed awesome one moment and awful the next." (from MacUser *magazine's review of digital cameras, November 1995)*

comparable nondigital camera. Building up the digital picture pixel by pixel—in picture element dots—requires either exposure times measured in minutes or less resolution (fewer pixels and less precise detailing of the image). Many can't handle conventional photographers' studio lighting, which relies on very short and intense flashes of strong light. The images invariably need correction and touching up through the ubiquitous Adobe Systems software.

It is obviously very attractive to be able to take your own photographs and immediately be able to start editing them, check out the results on the spot so that you can immediately take other photos as needed, and insert them in brochures, training materials, and articles. There is plenty of excellent software available for doing all this, as you will see if you go into any large PC store and look at the demo machines on display. Insurance and real estate agents can buy a digital camera for as little as $500 to use the images in claims processing (insurance) or brochures and customer service (real estate). The photo quality matches that of a Polaroid camera, which is good enough for their needs.

That's not good enough for other uses, of course. The quality of multimedia output depends very heavily on the quality of its input. To date, that quality comes from film. The resulting image can then be processed by the software, but at present all the digital cameras on the market are suited to particular types of image, setting, and use.

Digital Pen   A digital pen is a penlike device that attaches to a computer and allows its user to write directly on the machine's display screen. Digital pens are used mainly with wireless computers to enter information on forms. Parking meter attendants use them to issue tickets, and warehouse workers use them to record inventory transactions, for instance. Until they can recognize handwriting quickly and accurately, however, pens will not replace keyboards as the main input mechanism for computers.

See also Pen Computing

Digital Signal Processors A digital signal processors is a type of computer chip specifically designed to handle the translation between noncomputer and computer media. Noncomputer media consist of signals in the form of sound waves and visual images that must be rapidly converted to digital format to be used in a multimedia system. This requires extra chips in the computer, whose CPU and main memory can process only digital information. The conversion has to be done in real time; that is, the digital output must keep pace with the analog input and compress it rapidly. DSPs do this by using complex mathematical procedures called algorithms and by sampling the input signal at a given rate per second. Although the principles underlying the algorithms are well established, each vendor implements them differently, and there are wide variations in the quality and accuracy of the digitized output. The chips are relatively expensive but greatly affect multimedia performance, so that cutting corners is a false economy.

There are around 30 vendors competing to provide multimedia DSPs. Prices are dropping 50 percent every 18 months. One of the main uses of DSPs is in telephony boards, the increasingly powerful hardware that puts the equivalent of a fully automated telephone exchange in a PC or on a local area network. This computer-telephony integration (CTI) is perhaps the area of business multimedia with most immediate and highest payoff.

See also Codec; Computer-Telephony Integration; Data Compression

Digital Video Disc Digital video discs are a high density version of the 4.7 inch compact disc that plays up to 75 minutes of music but lacks the storage capacity to play back movies. In late 1995, the two main competing consortia, Time Warner and Toshiba on one side and Philips and Sony on the other, agreed to a compromise single standard for digital video disc, rather than go through a VHS-versus-Betamax fight, which one of them would surely lose. Both innovations promise storage capacities that are

CD-ROMs are based on a technical design that is well over a decade old; they represent the past, even though it is only in the last two years that they have become widely used. Meanwhile, the technology moves forward. Digital video discs can store up to 15 times as much data as a standard CD-ROM and provide better video quality than standard videotapes. Their design makes it practical to issue a movie where you choose the language of the soundtrack.

12 to 15 times that of CD-ROMs. That is enough to hold two full-length movies, with a choice of a dozen languages for subtitles if it is a foreign film. Both parties' products rely on a new data compression standard, MPEG-2.

Will DVD replace CD-ROM and be the "killer application" technology of 1997, when a flood of machines will have arrived on the market, or will consumers stick with the tried and true and also be unwilling to spend $200 to 500 for yet another electronic appliance? Opinions range from those who believe CD-ROM is dead to those who see the combination of CD-ROM and VHS tapes as so well established and adequate to most peoples' entertainment needs that DVD will face the same troubles as laser discs in reaching critical mass. Little is predictable in the multimedia market, except that we need more data storage capacity. Even DVD may be seen as too little within a few years.

See also CD Technology; MPEG

Digitization   Digitization is the process of converting a photograph, sound clip, video, phone call, piece of handwriting, or any other type of information from its original form to the 0–1 digital code of computers and modern telecommunications. The principle is essentially the same for all media: (1) a choice is made about the degree of accuracy of detail required in the representation, generally termed "resolution"; (2) the input is analyzed and converted to a number that represents its color, sound level, intensity, and the like (called "sampling"); (3) the stream of digital numbers is compressed, using complex mathematical procedures; and (4) the resulting digital output is transferred to the computer or hardware storage.

Digitization takes up processing time; the more accurate the resolution, the more the amount of sampling that is needed. This generates more digital bits, which increases demands for processing power and speed and telecommunications transmission speed. Capturing video and sound at the highest level of resolution and outputting it without compression is impractical; it requires supercomputers and ultrahigh-speed fiber optics telecommunications links. Specialized applications, such as teleradiology (digitization of X rays and MRI scans) or seismic analysis, get close to full reproduction, but multimedia in general requires many compromises. For instance, a scanner will digitize a photograph or article at a level of resolution that may range from a few hundred dots per inch up to several thousand. A sound card may sample an audio signal at a speed that produces tinny AM radio sound or CD-quality stereo. Color may be represented by just an 8-bit number, which is only enough for 256 different colors; 16 bits, which allows over 65,000; 24 bits; or even 32 bits, which increases the range to billions. Each increment, from 8 to 16 to 24 to 32, increases the amount of digital data proportionately. Your computer display may have a maximum resolution of 640 pixels per row and 480 per column, or it may be a high-resolution screen with $1,280 \times 1,024$.

Every increase in level of resolution multiplies the data needed, which can grow huge. Consider the difference between a very basic computer, whose screen displays images of 320×200 pixels in 256 colors, versus a standard laptop of today, with a display of 640×480 and 16-bit color (65 thousand different colors) and a top-of-the-line workstation used by a Hollywood film maker, with a $1,280 \times 1,024$ display and 24-bit color (16.7 million). The number of bits needed to scan in, say, a photograph for the two are:

- *Basic machine:* $320 \times 200 \times 8 = 512,000$ bits
- *Laptop:* $640 \times 480 \times 16 = 4,915,200$ bits (9.6 times larger)
- *Workstation:* $1,280 \times 1,024 \times 24 = 31,457,280$ (6.4 times larger than for the laptop and 61.4 times larger than the old machine)

And this is just for a single screen image! To get full motion, television-quality video means moving 30 "frames" per second. Multiply the 31.5 million bits per screen by 30 and you get close to a billion bits a second. That's not possible except on highly specialized, government-funded "gigabit" networks.

Data compression is what makes the possible practical. There are many techniques and standards, specialized chips, software, and mathematical procedures that achieve it. Digitization is the basis of multimedia, and data compression, the basis for cost-efficient multimedia. Data compression through hardware rather than software is the basis for speedy digitization. Any computer function is by definition faster if it can be carried out by a hardware chip than if it requires software instructions, simply because the software has to be processed by a hardware chip anyway.

See also Data Compression; MPEG

Disk   Disks are the devices that store computer data. They fall into two categories and three distinct types of media. The categories are off-line and on-line, and the media are floppy disks, hard disks, and optical disks (CD-ROMs are a type of optical disk). They all share the same basic features:

- Data on them are organized in small units that are indexed so that they can be directly retrieved; this is called "random access." It contrasts with a videotape, where you cannot go directly from, say, frame 102 to frame 453 but must first move past 103, 104, 105, and so on.

- The disks rotate inside a drive; the time it takes to locate a data item depends largely on the waiting or "access" time for the reading head of the drive to be positioned over it.

- They vary in storage capacity, measured in bytes. The basic determinant of capacity is how many bits can be packed into a given space and still be recognized by the reading head; this is termed "density." The floppy disks you use in your personal computer will be labeled as "high density," "double density," and the like.

The aim with disk technology is to pack as much storage as possible into a given size—that is, to increase density; reduce access time through faster rotation, more reading heads, or reduction in the distance the head is above the disk surface; and speed up transfer time, the time it takes to move the data item from the disk to the computer memory where it is used. In addition, of course, the goal is to do all this for less cost. Each disk medium has a different balance between storage, speed, and cost. Multimedia pushes the limits on demands for storage and speed and thus generally involves a higher cost.

On-line disk storage is, by definition, immediately accessible on demand by programs. Off-line disks have to be inserted into the disk or CD-ROM drive, the hardware device that handles location of, access to, and transfer of data. All PCs now have a built in on-line hard disk drive that stores the software programs and files routinely needed in its operations. They equally routinely use off-line floppy disks for installing new programs and off-line CD-ROMs that contain a multimedia mix of games, reference books, manuals, photos, and videos. The distinction between on-line and off-line is really between often needed and only occasionally needed data. It makes no sense to waste expensive and limited on-line storage on files you access once a year. Equally, it makes no sense to have to load your word processing software from an off-line floppy disk every time you want to run it.

Floppy disks are the main form of cheap and simple off-line storage, although they are being replaced more and more by off-line CD-ROMs. Just about every PC has a floppy disk drive that does not use disks that flop. The term comes from the old 5.25-inch and 7-inch ones that flop, bend, dangle, and fold. These have been replaced by 3.5-inch disks that typically hold around 1.5 printed book equivalents (1.5 million bytes of data), enough to store a new piece of software on 1 to 5 of them and a new operating system on 10 to 25. Floppies are convenient, cheap, robust, portable, and reliable.

And short on space. CD-ROMs hold far more data. One disc

is equivalent to about 400 floppies, and the cost of creating and reproducing them is dropping so rapidly that they are given away with most PC magazines. The floppy is not yet an endangered species, but it is at best a vestige of the past. Floppy disk drives remain essential for off-line storage simply because CD-ROM drives are not yet a feature of every PC. That's why in 1994, of the 180 million units of disk storage devices sold in the United States, 45 percent were floppies.

Of the units sold then, 41 percent were hard disk drives, which are the workhorse of the present. They offer the best combination of price, performance, and capacity, although they are not the best option on any single one of these measures. Multimedia demands such huge storage capacities that hard disks that hold around 500 printed book equivalents (500 megabytes) are soon overloaded. Manufacturers are raising the limits of storage from megabytes to gigabytes, with 2 and 4 gigabytes offered on top end multimedia PCs. A gigabtye is equivalent to 1,000 printed books.

The hard disks linked to host computers that handle such transactions as airline reservations and ATM deposits and withdrawals, or to the servers that store shared software and data resources, routinely have gigabytes of disk storage. They will be complexes of drives, multiple arrays of disks organized to maximize speed of updating and retrieval and to minimize data losses from crashes. RAID ("redundant array of independent disks") is a key technology here, which is becoming the base for networked multimedia.

Optical disks, which today amount to 11 percent of the market (this figure includes CD-ROMs), are the inevitable successor to hard disks in the long term. They are termed "optical" storage because they use the technology of light beams and lasers instead of magnetic recording. Optical disks are inherently more reliable than the 40-year-old magnetic disk media simply because the hardware that reads the data does not include moving parts that have to be positioned a tiny fraction of a millimeter over the tracks on a fast spinning disk. Just about every PC user has had a hard disk crash, and manuals are full of warnings about backing up your files. Optical disk drives do not crash in the same way or at the same frequency. They vary widely in storage capacity, with 4 gigabytes typical for PCs and hundreds of gigabytes—the equivalent of 100 or more hard disks—provided on complexes of "juke box" optical devices on telecommunications networks. Emerging developments in CD technology are packing more and more storage onto disks. Digital video discs, for instance, each hold around 12 CD-ROMs. The main blockage to adoption of any new disk storage technology is investment in existing technology. So unless the new is compatible with the old, even a step shift in performance may not be enough to justify changing systems.

The storage demands of multimedia are immense, to the degree that hard disks cannot possibly match the need. There are only two practical ways to resolve the problem: install high-capacity off-line optical storage on the PC, or install on-line massive-capacity servers on the network. Networking is about sharing scarce resources. It used to be that computer power was scarce; hence, computer terminals linked to mainframe machines. Now, of course, it's computer power that's cheap. Mass multimedia storage isn't. Thus, for example, multimedia servers can handle terabytes—trillions of bytes—of data; a terabyte is a million printed book equivalents. Some of the objects it stores may in themselves be several gigabytes—1,000 printed book equivalents. An hour of compressed video takes close to a gigabyte of storage.

It's now rather misleading to call a company's data center "the computer room," because the computer gets smaller and smaller and cheaper and cheaper. It's really a disk farm where the acreage gets larger and larger.

See also Access Time; CD-ROM; Data Transfer Rate; RAID

Disk Mastering   Disk mastering is the creation of the master disk that will be copied many times. It's part of the jargon of the multimedia trade and usually refers to a CD-ROM. The disk is created by using authoring software. It costs around $1,000 to create a master disk plus 100 copies.

Dithering　Dithering is a trick of the multimedia trade that fools the eye into seeing an image as composed of more colors than it actually contains by using patterns of different-colored screen pixels to create blended colors. When two pixels of different colors are very close together, our brains average them together into a single color. A 50 percent blend of red and yellow dots is thus perceived as orange. Dithering is a feature provided on most multimedia video editing software as a sort of electronic paint-brush feature. It is also used on systems that have fewer than the optimum number of colors available. In multimedia graphics, it is employed to fill in an area with gradations so that the color transition looks smooth instead of stark.

DSP　*See* Digital Signal Processor

Education　Education and multimedia are a natural fit. The chairman of NEC comments about the role of the teacher in his company's Global College, an international community of students and teachers linked by computers: "The excitement of NEC's Global College is that it will allow an educator to establish contact with anyone who has access to a terminal, and to provide that student with a full range of cultural data. . . . With the student virtually swimming in a sea of input, the teacher becomes a guide to vivid new experiences and discoveries. This strikes me as an ideal mode of education" (NEC brochure).

This ideal is, of course, what dedicated and skilled teachers have always tried to do. Enthusiasts of multimedia in education and related edutainment sometimes talk as if they will make teachers obsolete. They thereby trivialize the wider issues of motivation, interaction, social space, personality, individual cognitive differences, and the like that make education far more than just the absorption of information. One of the leading pioneers in multimedia, Steve Jobs, is very pessimistic that technology will have more than a useful minor impact on classroom learning, seeing the politics of teacher unions and the role of parents as far more dominant in their impacts. As the force behind the Apple Macintosh, developer of one of the first high-end multimedia machines, and most recently the entrepreneur/manager behind the tools that created the first computer-animated movie, *Toy Story,* Jobs might be expected to be a multimedia zealot, of which there are many. It's an open question whether multimedia will transform the classroom or just jazz it up.

There are, of course, thousands of examples of successful individual applications of multimedia in school and business classrooms. There appear to be some common patterns underlying their effectiveness. Most obviously, multimedia greatly augments learning where visualization is of central importance. It adds simulation capabilities that cannot otherwise be equaled in the classroom; examples include medicine, engineering, science, and geography. A noted example of this, used in more and more medical schools, is A.D.A.M. (*"Animated Dissection of Anatomy for Medicine"*). This is one of the most successful uses of multimedia for a combination of medical education and interaction between physician and patient. Users can display every structure of the body and peel back successive layers of tissue, practice surgical procedures via animated scalpel, and explain the details of a proposed operation to a patient. The CD-ROM cost $5 million to develop over a three-year period. It sells for $295, with an advanced version priced at $2,295. It contains a data base of over 3,500 detailed color illustrations plus 20,000 anatomical structures. It includes video clips showing surgical procedures, quizzes, interactive textbooks, lecture notes, animations, and self-paced training modules. In working with patients, the physician can choose the sex and race of the body to be displayed. Users can record their own surgical procedures through A.D.A.M. and save them for later playback.

The inventor of A.D.A.M. is a professional medical illustrator who graduated from medical school and then built his company to be the number one provider of courtroom exhibits used by lawyers in personal injury cases. He observed how often doctors were sued by patients on the grounds that, had they known beforehand what was going to happen to them in surgery, they would have probably not have undergone it (or signed the in-formed consent form legally required for the surgeon to go ahead). Doctors obviously weren't communicating clearly. He got the idea for a tool that visually simulated the surgery from a medical encyclopedia that included a series of five to six overlaid transparencies that allowed the reader to peel away each layer of tissue. His primary target for the system was physicians, but when he looked to raise seed money, it was medical schools that were the most supportive and responsive. Now, A.D.A.M. is close to being a required tool in medical training. It is also one that is easy to use at many levels, from the layperson interested in self-learn-ing, to nursing colleges that issue associate degrees, to all levels of medical school, and to physicians working with patients.

The size of the education textbook market is huge. Texas alone recently spent $100 million on a single reading program. Only in 1992 were schools in California permitted to spend textbook funds on nonprinted materials such as CD-ROMs.

The general lesson here is that good multimedia simulations are useful in many contexts, by the very fact that they are imme-diately communicative (otherwise they don't meet the criteria of "good" and "simulation"). Their multimedia nature removes the need for a classroom teacher in the direct use of the tool, but that's not at all the same as removing the need for a classroom teacher in the full learning process. It also illustrates what may well be an important longer-term opportunity: the cross-linking of education and business. A.D.A.M. meets the four main impacts of multimedia that I identified in the Introduction to this guide. They apply to its use in and outside school:

1. *Knowledge management.* Acquisition of information as part of basic learning (school and individual at home), use of knowledge (physician-patient), or simulation (all of these).

2. *Customer interaction.* With the student as "customer," there is obviously an augmentation outside the classroom that adds to the interaction with the teacher in the classroom. That's one reason why medical school professors were so enthusiastic about A.D.A.M.

3. *Natural decision input.* Visualization is fundamental to the learning process here and to the individual self-learner, as well as to the teacher-student and patient-physician relationship.

4. *Shared understanding.* Simulation and visualization as the base for the teacher-student and patient-physician dialogue.

This example suggests that the simulation and visualization capabilities of multimedia are generic to the learning and inter-action opportunity, regardless of context. That in itself may break down the distinction between school and business. A.D.A.M. is both a learning tool in school and a decision and communication tool in business. An engineering simulation may serve the same role.

Another emerging common pattern among successful uses of multimedia in education is its impact on learning in specific types of subject matter. In ones where the fundamental issue is internalization of information in one's own head rather than through discussion and interaction, the effectiveness of multimedia seems to depend on the motivation of the individual. That is especially so in learning mathematics. A number of studies suggest that here multimedia does improve the rate of progress, understanding, and application of students who are already well motivated, but has minimal impact on those of others. For this reason, many CD-ROMs aim at motivating students through making learning fun. This "edutainment" philosophy underlies much of children's television, the literal analog of digital multimedia, in such programs as *Sesame Street* and *Where in the World Is Carmen Sandiego?*

Educationally, the 5 percent of our population that is dyslexic or has learning disabilities is disenfranchised from much of the mainstream of political and social life, as are the more than 30 million who do not speak English in the home. The U.S. Department of Education reported in late 1993 that half the nation's almost 200 million adults are functionally illiterate (in terms of carrying out simple everyday functions). Just under half of young adults can locate information in a news article or reference book.

Much of multimedia education/edutainment aims at stimulating interest, through either exciting and well-presented visual and auditory information, via CD-ROM and/or the Internet, or through communication over the Internet. Examples of the latter include:

- The *Antarctic expedition,* which provided ongoing reports, images, commentary and discussion to and among schools across the world over the Internet.

- *Sweden Post's World Wide Web site,* which enables schools both to access extracts from this week's news in multimedia form and to compete in a weekly on-line quiz. Around 400 schools routinely enter the competition.

- *Multimedia research projects* are now routine in schools at every level, from second grade up. These encourage the cross-curriculum, creative, cooperative group work that has always been a feature of school projects, adding richer information and communication resources for participants. Instead of cutting articles out of magazines, students have the Internet world to surf.

- *Museum kiosks.* One indicator that multimedia may be edging toward a significant enhancement of learning is the great success of so many of the multimedia kiosks that museums are installing. Informal reports show that they are very popular with children, who come back to them often. Here, the education combines individual and group, as it is typically a cluster of kids working with the kiosks.

Education is now as fundamental to business as to schools. Multimedia may help both benefit from each other's tools. Business certainly needs plenty of education tools. Given the growing evidence in business training that multimedia halves learning time and increases retention by an extra half, many of those tools must be multimedia. The number of hours of formal training offered to employees by companies in 1992 is estimated to be close to 130 million. This adds up to the equivalent of 13 Harvards. The increase is greater than that in the total enrollment of college students between 1980 and 1990.

See also Training

Edutainment   Edutainment means education in the form of entertainment, as well as entertainment that is educational. PBS's *Sesame Street* and *Where in the World Is Carmen Sandiego?* are television examples. Many CD-ROMs and computer games are targeted to edutainment; multimedia encyclopedias like Microsoft's Encarta add animations, quizzes and cute characters to liven them up. The edutainment combination highlights the strong focus in the multimedia field on education and training, its underlying philosophy of making information vivid and immediately communicative, and its reliance on interaction father than passive viewing. By far the most widespread success, perhaps even the only widespread success, in truly interactive multimedia is games. Most of that success has come from companies' like Sony and Sega making superb hardware and many software providers' developing the games for those machines. The PC industry is racing to make its hardware as popular a game machine as a computer. Edutainment is basically a PC-based field, information centered but gamelike.

Entertainment   Entertainment is one of the wellsprings of multimedia; the others are information technology, education, and publishing. The multimedia "industry" is a confluence, conflict, convergence, and collaboration involving them all—if you're in one of these, you're in the others or soon will be. Entertainment will drive much of multimedia expenditures, if not sales and innovation, because that's where the proven demand is: games, films, television, and many elements of publishing. That means that any new mass markets in multimedia will depend on entertainment. Thus Bell Atlantic (telecommunications) tried to acquire TCI (cable TV) and is a pioneer in video on-demand enter-

The Boeing 777, brought into service in mid-1995, has more lines of computer code aboard than any other airliner. Fully 40 percent of that code manages in-flight entertainment. Of the 1,880 microprocessors on board, 1,700 run interactive games, videos, and seat phones.

The United States is an entertainment economy. In 1993, 12 percent of all new jobs created in the United States were in entertainment and recreation. In 1994, 20 percent of all discretionary income went to entertainment. The world is a tourism economy. The largest single industry globally, it amounts to $4 trillion a year. Both tourism and entertainment are natural and eager users of multimedia.

tainment. Microsoft (information technology) has many joint ventures with companies such as NBC (television) and MCI (telecommunications) and is a leader in multimedia CD-ROM publishing of encyclopedias, art gallery and museum guides, flight and driver simulations, and games. Disney bought ABC. Intel (information technology) has an alliance with CNN (television). And so on.

Because of the prominence of entertainment in multimedia to date, it's easy to associate it mainly with games and video entertainment. Many of the most visible players are mainly in the entertainment field: Disney, Viacom (owner of Blockbuster Video), TCI, Time Warner, and Steven Spielberg, for instance.

A subset of entertainment that is playing a strong role in the convergence of the wellspring industries of multimedia is TV news. News ranks last in the four categories of TV programming, as rated by consumers, behind entertainment, sports, and children's programming. Yet just about every player in and on the fringe of the multimedia industry is rushing into it. Disney/ABC plans a 24-hour channel for late 1996. Others with similar ventures include NBC/Microsoft, Fox, CBS, CNNfn, and cable consortia.

News is low tech. It doesn't need high-resolution displays or multimedia beyond decent graphics, short video and audio clips, and text. The goal appears to be to use news to establish business brands and to ensure home access to multimedia. That's why Microsoft is a leading player in several of the ventures. Just as essentially unbranded local cable companies rely on such names as HBO, ESPN, and CNN, many multimedia firms see news as their entry brand for a time when a small number of Internet service providers dominates the market, together with a larger but still small number of interactive TV service providers. Interestingly, it was news that drove the emergence of the first mass market in multimedia: broadcast television.

Evidence   One of the longer-term and rapidly emerging social impacts of multimedia is the disappearance of documented reality. Given a digital photo, document, video, or audio, you have no way of knowing if it has been edited or is an artificial creation. There are services available that will take family photos and edit out the ex-husband or wife. You can "grab" a frame of CNN news on the fly and insert yourself, so that you now have a picture of yourself shaking hands with Michael Jordan or Boris Yeltsin. Your handwriting can be digitally generated from samples you provide, to the extent that even words you never used can be created in your exact hand. One of the explicit goals of the most advanced multimedia workers is to create virtual realities that fool your senses in thinking they *are* reality.

Multimedia is essentially about making digital information of any sort natural and thus, to some extent, deceptive. Videos deceive our eyes by moving single images so fast that they appear to be in full motion. Virtual reality aims at fooling our senses of location, touch, and movement. Desktop publishing and image processing tools can fool us into believing a picture is "real."

Even handwriting is no longer always real. You may at some time have received a "personal" mailing from the Democratic National Committee chairman, Senator Christopher Dodd. The label will be "handwritten," right down to its having a scratched-out mark where the Senator made a mistake on your street number. He has initialed that part of the mailing label that permits the package shipping company to deliver the package even if you are not at home. Of course, the handwriting is just a $2,000 software package's recreation of his handwriting.

It will be several years before all this affects everyday life, but it's coming. Meanwhile, businesses need to start thinking hard about what "documentation" means in their own everyday operations and how they will authenticate multimedia records. Plenty of work is going on in research labs, computer companies, universities, and other organizations to address these issues: techniques for placing invisible marks on multimedia data that indicate if any part of it has been changed, for instance.

Reportedly at the urging of an editor, writers for one of the most widely read magazines in the world removed a few "irrelevant" details of the background of a news photo. Is this a breach of ethics that alters evidence or just a routine element of what multimedia makes practical and sensible?

Fax Fax machines are now almost as common as telephones. By contrast, electronic mail is nowhere near as common as PCs. Fax may be the technology of yesterday, but the machines are so easy and cheap to use that they may still be the preferred tool of tomorrow. They are currently nondigital; that is, they make a copy of the original by simply reproducing the shades of dark and light. They also rely on slow analog phone lines. Increasingly, fax is being built into personal computers, so that you can directly send a word processed document, add a spreadsheet, or automatically send faxes to multiple recipients. PCs and network servers are adding more and more phone and fax capabilities, called computer-telephony integration (CTI).

The fax machine was invented and patented in 1843. The French emperor Napoleon III used it during the Franco-Prussian war.

At some point, there will be a shift from analog black-and-white fax sent to fax machines to digital color electronic mail sent to a PC. Fax doesn't offer multimedia. Meanwhile, it will remain a simple, low cost, and convenient means of basic communication of black-and-white documents.

File Format A multimedia file, such as an image or music clip, will be created by a software application. That application will identify its format exactly, by adding a suffix. Thus, for instance, a file created by a program that synthesizes music using the MIDI interface (a standard for producing musical instrument sounds) stores them as, for instance, CLIPOBOE.MID. Other software programs recognize the format from the suffix and either carry on, if it is a format it can handle; convert it to another format; or scream, "File format incompatibility" or some such message.

The most popular graphics file formats—or at least the ones most widely used—are .TIFF, .JPG, and .GIF. TIFF stands for "*tagged image file format*," which means a file with descriptors of the shapes and lines it contains. .JPG and .GIF, formats are widely used on the World Wide Web. You have also .BMP, .WMF, .GIF, .CGM, and DVI formats .a9 and .a16 to draw on—among others. Each format will reflect either a particular software family or an industry standard. BMP files, for instance, are bitmaps of a screen display. They contain the detailed pixels—picture elements, the dots of color that make up what you see. WINLOGO.BMP stores the Windows logo that appears when you start up Windows 95. BMP files are independent of any one vendor. By contrast, .WAV files are Microsoft's own wave sound file format, though many other software developers support it.

Naturally, all these file formats lead to many differences in quality of image, storage demands, and which software packages can handle which files. Never buy a software graphics package that doesn't support at least 15 different file formats. Never buy a video or audio software package without asking a technical specialist in multimedia what range of commonly used file formats it can handle.

Frame A frame is a single complete display on a screen or in a video camera. Flicker-free, full-motion video is generated by changing frames at a typical rate of 30 frames per second. That is the speed at which movies have operated for a century; at that frame rate, the human brain sees the display as a continuous flow. At slower rates, the brain is not so fooled, and the viewer is aware of the flickering as frames change.

Video is thus really fast photographs. Many of the tricks of the multimedia trade manipulate individual frames and then move them to create an illusion. You can buy software for a few hundred dollars that turns a frog into a prince, for instance. The beginning and end images are matched through other tricks of the trade, and the frog image is slightly changed one frame at a time. A few thousand frames later, running them together looks like a continuous flow; this is called "morphing"—perhaps it should be called "schwarzeneggering," because it's what creates many of the special effects in the Terminator films. Animation similarly changes a frame to move an arm, stretch a line, and the like. The computational demands for animated or morphed video can be immense, because so many frames have to be manipulated. Every single one-thirtieth of a second of top-quality video is a separate frame that has to be individually generated. Think of an animated 3-D movie like *Toy Story*. Its 114,000 frames took 800,000 hours to process on very fast machines. That's around half a day per frame and 80 hours per finished second of film.

See also Frame Rate

Frame Grabber Frame grabbers are analogous to electronic photographers waiting to snap a racehorse as it gallops past. Sometimes called "video capture boards," they sample (a technical term for interpreting) a single frame of video and convert it to a computer graphics file that can be stored, transmitted, and processed. The sampling and conversion process determines the quality of the resulting image. The term *grabber* accurately captures the problem. The frame has to be caught on the fly and processed before the next one arrives, which for the full-motion video of films, VCRs, and camcorders is 30 frames per second. Hardware boards handle the conversion.

Frame Rate Frame rates are fundamentally a matter of how to fool the human eye. Think of a movie as a set of photographs each of which slightly changes the one before. Send these at 30 per second, and the human eye sees a movie. Send them at less than 10 per second, and the eye sees a set of photographs being presented one at a time.

Here are the impacts of different frame rates on human perception

- *Less than 10:* No perception of motion.
- *12 to 15:* Jerky movement.
- *30:* TV news and soap operas
- *60 to 75:* The level of image that TV ads for TV sets tell you that you will get on the TV that the ads are pushing, a level that is much better than what that TV will really give you. Technically, all this is called HDTV—"*high-resolution digital television*."

- *90:* The limit of human perception.
- *1,000:* Scientific video quality.

Because of the heavy demands that video places on computer storage, telecommunications transmission, and processing speed and power, the full-screen, 30-fps rate is rarely a practical option. Instead, a window is opened up on the PC display screen which is only one-quarter or one-half of full size, and the frame rate is set to 15 fps.

Graphics Accelerator Graphics accelerators (or graphics cards) are special-purpose chips mounted on a board that plugs into a PC. They speed up the rate at which the PC display screen is "refreshed"—redrawn after some operation that changes what is on it. They are essential for multimedia. Redrawing a 640 × 480-pixel screen that uses 24-bit color means moving 7 million bits, printed book equivalent.

Graphics accelerators are like a small add-on computer. They have enough memory inside them to process the image without drawing on the central processing unit. Their performance varies by about the same as cars' does. You would never go out and buy a "car" without considering fuel consumption, acceleration, number of cylinders, brakes, and the like. Graphics boards are the cars of multimedia traffic, perhaps even the airplanes. They are complex, and you as an individual need to choose them as carefully as you would choose a car. Multimedia professionals need to choose them as carefully as companies choose a corporate jet.

Hard Drive Hard disk drives are the on-line storage units in a PC that feed the programs that run on it with data and also contain its library of programs. Think of the CPU as a greedy monster demanding "Gimmee! Gimmee the first word in the document named JPL.DOC! Gimmee the next number in the spreadsheet . . . the next bit of this video!"

On-line means "Gimmee at once!" Off-line means "Go fetch"

—go fetch the floppy disk that contains the file you want to update or the CD-ROM that contains *Myst* (the beautiful and engrossing game that is most distinctive in its entire lack of violence) or the entire directory of phone listings in the United States. Hard disks are the on-line, high-volume storage device of computers. On the larger mainframe computers that handle transactions such as airline reservations or ATM cash withdrawals or the file servers that store the data bases that departmental PCs access, the equivalent of hard disks are DASD ("*direct access storage devices*"), RAID ("*redundant arrays of inexpensive disk*"), floptical (floppy optical disk)—all just types of disks.

Multimedia takes up space—more space than most PC users can afford to give up on their on-line hard disk. Hard drives thus are mainly used to store software, including the operating system that runs software applications and frequently used files.

See also Disk Storage; RAID

Not 10 years ago, HDTV was seen as the next Japanese threat that would tighten their stranglehold on the world's consumer markets. Now, they are seen as having fallen between the wrong technologies. The analog-based systems they developed were the last, best implementation of an obsolescent mode of transmission. In speaking before an FCC commission in 1991, a top CBS executive stated

HDTV   HDTV stands for "*high-definition TV.*" In the mid-1980s, it was a very hot topic; now it's just a small subset of moves toward digital TV. HDTV is simply a bigger and better picture. The underlying long-term goal was and still is a giant screen just a few inches thick which produces a flicker-free display of exquisitely accurate color, in fine detail. This was a very ambitious goal when television makers began their work on HDTV in the early 1980s. That was the era of analog television with no multimedia technology to draw on. Analog signals are ones in which the camera, transmission system, and television set all work with light and sound in a continuous electrical wave that mimics the light and sound waves of what we see and hear in the real world. Digital TV turns these into something we would never recognize, a flow of 0s and 1s that represent instead of mimic the original. Television industry thinking was so dominated by analog thinking that a CBS executive stated to a congressional committee as late as 1991 that digital television was an impossibility because "it defies the laws of physics."

The American Electronics Association (AEA) sounded the alarm bells about the perceived coming Japanese triumph in HDTV in 1988. It forecast a "continued declining world market share" in computer manufacturing, PCs, and semiconductors, followed by losses in telecommunications and "other strategically critical industries." All of this would lead to the erosion and the eventual loss of a U.S. manufacturing base and in the end the United States' loss of position as a major world power. The Japanese did get there first, as the AEA feared, but in the first three years of HDTV set production, total sales were under 25,000.

The TV standard now in use in the United States is called NTSC (its main European equivalent is PAL). This was defined in 1941 and specified a frame rate of 30 frames per second (individual pictures sent at 30 times per second blur together to give the perception of a continuous stream of movement), 525 scanning lines, and an "aspect ratio' of 4:3 (width versus height of the picture). The likely standard for HDTV will be 30 fps, 1,025 scan lines, and a 16:9 aspect ratio. Like CD-ROM, it will be fully digital, whereas the Japanese implementation was analog, now a dead end. CD-ROM quality is roughly that of a 16 mm camcorder video. HDTV will be that of a 35 mm cinema movie. There will be a direct conflict between CD technology and HDTV, with CD having the edge in terms of consumer acceptance, cost of devices and availability, and digital HDTV, a potential edge in perform-ance. The storage demands of HDTV far outstrip the capacities of the most advanced CD technology of today. The Quad-CD format, in widespread use today, can hold four times as much as a standard CD-ROM, around 100 minutes of VHS quality video. HDTV would require a fourfold increase over Quad-CD.

that digital television was impossible because it defied the laws of physics. The transmitters that handle analog broadcasting are all scheduled to be switched off by 2010. Another CBS executive said in 1994 that "2010 is just around the corner."

Home Page   A home page is a kind of billboard on the World Wide Web, the fastest-growing component of the Internet. Any-one or any business can set up a Web site and "author" a home page. The term is a little misleading, because a home page can be as many pages or computer screens and as long and large as you wish.

The home page is stored on an Internet node that is its home site. That node is a server computer with a unique Internet address. A typical address is http://www./mcewans.co.uk/football. This address indicates that the site is to be handled in the communication language and formats of the hypertext transfer protocol (http), is a Web site (www), and that it is part of the Internet node registered by McEwans, a maker of fine English beer. (If the address began with "ftp" instead of "http", the request would be for this communication to be handled via the Internet file transfer protocol.) That node is used by a commercial organization (co.) in Britain (uk). The page is one of several on the node and addresses soccer (football). There are a number of variants on these basic addresses (the international "co" versus "com" in the United States, for commercial organizations, for instance), but the logic is simply to provide the information needed to uniquely identify an Internet service, its type, and where it is located.

Because of the limited transmission speeds available to Web users who access it over the public phone system, the generally accepted rules of thumb for creating Web pages are the very opposite of what they will be when these limitations are removed. The experts' recommendations for businesses' advertising, informing, or selling on the Web are: (1) scan photos in at the lowest acceptable level of resolution (turn a high-quality photo into a small image that is a little better than a color photo in a newspaper); (2) begin your page display either with text or by very quickly loading nonphoto, low-quality graphics so that people have something to read while the graphics are being downloaded; (3) use HTML to create a two-dimensional page that has no animation, 3-D, or video; and (4) consider offering a nongraphics page for the millions of users who have access only to very slow phone lines and modems or whose computer operating system cannot handle graphics.

For corporations creating their own intranets (Web sites accessed only by their own staff over high-speed network links), the recommendations are exactly the opposite: (1) use informative and attention-grabbing high-quality images; (2) minimize text; (3) use VRML, HotJava, and other emerging tools to provide 3-D and animation; and (4) use all the media of multimedia.

The future growth of the Internet rests on how quickly the majority of business and consumer users get the high-speed, low-cost communication links that are fully practical today but not yet fully available. How a business exploits the opportunities of the Internet for knowledge management, customer interaction, natural decision input, and shared understanding rests on its assumptions about when this will occur. If you're a pessimist, your strategy will make only limited use of multimedia. If you're an optimist, your Internet strategy will be *completely* multimedia.

My own judgment—which has no more weight than that of any other qualified business and information technology researcher, consultant, or writer—is that the optimists are the true realists in this context. There is an immense demand for multimedia on the Internet. That's proven by the growth of Internet radio, the almost infinite demand for pornographic images, the success of Internet music, and the downloading of film clips, games, and the like, despite the many limitations of today's tools and telecommunications. The enthusiasm of 1995 became the frustration of 1996 for many casual Web surfers who see its value and interest but also its slowness. The Web tools of 1995, though, also became the multimedia development tools of 1996. This combination of existing demand, frustration and tools is complemented by the ever-improving price performance of telecommunications transmission. That seems almost certain to break the bandwidth constraint on the Internet as a multimedia and business resource.

See also Internet; World Wide Web

Home Shopping   Home shopping is a term applied mainly to buying goods advertised on TV programs dedicated to displaying and selling goods, but the concept is now a more general one, covering catalogue purchases and large-scale shopping over the Internet and interactive television. There have been many scattered pilots and small-scale successes in on-line home shopping, but many uncertainties remain about the evolution of what many commentators feel is a major multimedia opportunity.

Home shopping TV programs generate $3 billion in sales—quite substantial for a relatively new industry with a limited number of major players but less than 1 percent of all retail sales. Catalogue sales are far greater, at $50 billion. Interactive TV would combine the two via multimedia, and many companies are awaiting signs of such a breakthrough service.

It is not yet at all clear that people are willing to pay to use interactive, set-top television boxes, what benefits they get from on-line shopping versus the already-convenient media of catalogues and telephones, and exactly what will lead people to make purchases over the Internet, which users see at present as a channel for information gathering more than for actually buying products. Of 23,000 Internet users surveyed in early 1996, the fraction gathering information about a topic and those who actually purchased a product over the Internet were:

- Music: 35 percent looked, 11 percent bought
- Movies and video: 42 percent and 5 percent
- Hardware: 70 percent and 16 percent
- Vacations: 42 percent and 10 percent

That says there's a 50–50 chance that someone will even look at your advertisement/offer and a 1 in 10 chance he or she will ever make a purchase of your or a competing product.

Returns of goods bought from home, through either catalogues or TV programs, are at least double those bought in stores. The richer visual information that multimedia provides may change that, though. The costs of developing World Wide Web sites have been low (that's one of its attractions), but the need to differentiate the firm's offering from the 100,000 or so other commercial Web pages is dramatically increasing them. Benetton's and General Motors' sites, which were set up in 1996, are examples. They contain around 200 separate pages, with rich multimedia features for customer interaction, information searching, and communication with the company. These are million-dollar investments, not the $5,000 to $50,000 that make the Net a profitable opportunity for small firms that benefit from small revenues.

It's easy for enthusiasts of new tools to forget how well many of the existing ones work. That applies to fax, paper, pens, and catalogues versus electronic mail, screens, keyboards, and on-line shopping. The same is true for television viewing. Given extra choices, people seem pretty happy with the ones they have, especially scheduled programming. Less then 30 percent of cable TV subscribers have *ever* ordered a pay-per-view movie, even though doing so takes just a phone call. Between 1983 and 1989, 9 out every 10 interactive TV ventures were abandoned. The predictions made when they were launched held that they would generate $8 to $10 billion in profits. The recorded *losses* were over a billion dollars.

Security is widely regarded as the single key issue. Even people who routinely give their credit numbers over the phone or write them on postcards to renew magazine subscriptions are worried to use the Internet, with all its actual, potential, and reputed hackers, for financial transactions. Security is now very high. Cellular phone fraud is 30 times greater than Internet credit fraud. A flood of tools has been developed within the past year that make the Internet not totally secure but secure enough. "Secure enough" here means enough to reduce the risks to buyer and seller to the same level that is routine for electronic funds transfers, ATM transactions, and physical credit card use. The real issue, though, is one of *consumers'* being comfortable enough. The general consensus is that only when they are fully comfortable will home shopping take off.

For home shopping via the Internet, America Online, electronic kiosks, or interactive TV to fly, multimedia will be key for the obvious reason that it is the basis for showing goods, marketing them, attracting customer interest, and answering queries.

See also Business on the Internet, Security

60 percent of the managers of Internet host computers use Macintoshes as their personal machine (Forbes ASAP, 26 February 1996); 56 percent of those hosts are Sun machines. Microsoft has just a 4 percent share of the Internet server operating system market. IBM retains a dominant share of the host computers that handle business transaction processing. The Internet and multimedia are restoring much of the position IBM lost to PCs. Its strengths have always been handling complex systems. The multimedia networks and the many hosts on them are immensely complex.

Host   A host computer is one that is accessed by guests; that is, it provides services and information for a wide range of devices that link to it via telecommunications. Originally, "host" meant big, centralized mainframe computer. For instance, ATMs access a host to update banking transaction records. Those hosts are complexes of massive and typical IBM systems that handle hundreds of transactions a second. The leading airline reservation system hosts, such as those used by American Airlines' Sabre and United's Apollo handle up to 2,000 transactions a second. In today's ethos of small-is-beautiful and smaller-is-beautiful-and-also-portable, the mainframe is seen as the edifice of the past. *Host* is perhaps a better term for any computer that must provide service to masses of clients.

Networked multimedia demands very powerful hosts. The Internet does, too. The multimedia Internet will need hosts that make the distinction between mainframe, minicomputer, and micro increasingly meaningless. The hosts determine the performance of the overall system.

HotJava   HotJava is an Internet browser that runs applications written in the Java programming language and also accesses the home pages that are the core of the World Wide Web. Today, these pages are largely static and make only limited use of multimedia. The development tool for these is called HTML ("*Hy-pertext Markup Language*"). HotJava is aimed at more than just extending HTML (it is fully compatible with HTML-based pages). Java "applets" add full multimedia to the Web.

Java was developed by Sun Microsystems, the leading firm manufacturing the powerful workstations that use the UNIX operating system. UNIX underlies the original design and use of many Internet services and offers many technical advantages over the Microsoft operating systems that now dominate personal computers: DOS and the Windows series. It is built around entirely different computer chips than are PCs, which use Intel processors.

Sun and its many supporters, which include other hardware and software leaders, are using Java to attack and even replace the dominant Microsoft-Intel model of ever-faster PC hardware and ever more complex software operating systems as the basis for computing. Its model is one of simple appliances' accessing complex software over the Internet, termed "network-centric computing." HotJava is a key part of this strategy, as it is the World Wide Web that constitutes both the network and the centric part of the phrase. One of Sun's key allies is Netscape, the company that dominates Web browsers by having the same market share that Microsoft has in PCs, but a far larger share of the corporate market for Internet software on network servers. HotJava browsers greatly extend the features available to developers of Web pages. For example, they can download a Java application and run it directly in part of the Web window. It is in many ways the first World Wide Web operating system, whereas HTML was its first publishing system, and the browsers based on it were its first search systems.

See also Java, Network Computer

HTML   *See* Hypertext Markup Language

http://www   Http://www is the standard prefix for the Internet address of a World Wide Web home page. It indicates a request that this transaction be handled through the standard Internet "*hypertext transfer protocol*" (http) and that it is to be processed on a World Wide Web (www) site.

Hypermedia   Hypermedia is an extension of the more well-established term *hypertext*. Both words refer to the technique that is fundamental to multimedia information on the World Wide Web and CD-ROMs. Individual words and phrases, sometimes called "hot links," are cross-linked to other pieces of information. This is the feature that makes CD-ROM encyclopedias and reference

Drexel University in Philadelphia has for almost a decade required students to own a Macintosh computer. One of the by-products of this rule has been the development of the Drexel Disk, a hypermedia disk which is both a guide map of the university and a source of detailed information about it. Thus, for instance, the map shows the location of Building 53, which houses the campus repair facility for computers. The student can click on it to display the layout of the building, get information on service hours, read room numbers, and so on. When you play the CD-ROM game Myst, you click on maps, boxes, switches, books, and many other objects to explore which may take you into hidden rooms or open up secret locations. All this is done through hypermedia links.

manuals so much more useful in searching for information than paper books.

See also Hypertext; Hypertext Markup Language

Hypertext   Hypertext is a philosophy of information organization and use first implemented in the 1970s. According to this philosophy, you should be pointed from one piece of information to other relevant information and be able to jump directly to it without knowing where or in what form it is stored. Hypertext builds links between text materials, as the term indicates. Hypermedia extends this concept to the linking of text to photographs, videos, sound, and other media. The terms *hypertext* and *hypermedia* are essentially equivalent now, however.

Hypertext is fundamental to making information interactive rather than passive. It is the basis of the World Wide Web. Web pages are electronic documents enhanced with codes, or "tags," that provide the information needed to navigate through the Internet to locate related information. An example might be a document containing the following text:

> Morgan, Inc., builds <u>statistical multiplexers</u> for use in high-speed networks. Its sales in 1995 were $135 million, an increase of 25%. Its 1995 Annual Report was issued in May. Morgan's main product is its MI-650/G, designed for <u>ATM</u> and <u>frame relay.</u>

Hypertext links documents to each other. Clicking on the highlighted words or pictures in one document pulls up other documents, which provide additional information. These may in turn link to others. (The text may be underlined or blocked out in a color that highlights it.) In this example, clicking on "<u>ATM</u>" will pull up technical information on asynchronous transfer mode, the emerging mainstream of ultrahigh-speed telecommunications transmission, which may in turn show hypertext links to articles on, say, telecommunications industry news reports and product surveys.

Hypertext is thus a form of electronic cross-referencing, which can, if well designed, make an encyclopedia, manual, or magazine article more immediately informative, encourage browsing, and make the plain linear text nonlinear and interactive. Put more negatively, for many of us it can make simple text cluttered and discourage careful structuring, attention to writing style, and even basic syntax. For this reason, it underlies an ongoing debate about the future of reading. For hypertext does have a "hyper" element. It encourages the writing of short blocks of text and hence brief lines of thought, with the reader having no overall picture of the whole. You have to keep jumping around, not knowing what you will find or even what else exists at the other end of the hypertext links. Multimedia tricks dominate content. The editor of *Wired* magazine, by far the most influential and widely read periodical in the multimedia field, proudly told a group of publishers in 1995 that its "distinctive look of maimed photography and fluorescent hues" reflected the fact that "I sometimes have to sacrifice readability when I'm pushing the edge of design" (*Utne Reader,* September 1995). This is typical of much of the most innovative work in the basics of multimedia; form dominates content. My strong recommendation for business managers is to ignore the form and think of how the tools that create it can enhance content of interest to them for knowledge management, customer interaction, natural decision input, and shared understanding. The issue here is the difference in focus between how it looks and what one can do with it.

Some of the best-established and most useful applications of hypertext are those in which both the information needed and the natural mode of organization and access fit the hyper approach. On-line help manuals and electronic catalogues are examples. Hypertext offers a form of enhanced browsing. J. Nielsen, an expert in hypertext, has defined Nielsen's law of manuals, analogous to the famous Murphy's Law that "if anything can go wrong, it will." His first law states that users don't read manuals, period. The second states that, when a user does want to read a manual anyway, he or she is in big trouble. Because of the first law, people can't find the manual when they need it because it is sure to be lost. My own corollary to this law is that, if you don't understand the system, you won't find the manual useful, and, if you do, then you don't need it. When the manual for a package like Microsoft Word is over 800 pages long and the index alone takes up almost 50 pages, hypertext is the obvious means to make the content accessible and meaningfully organized.

On-line manuals have become standard for computer software. The manual can be found immediately, and if you are in trouble, you have it at hand. You never have to read it all; hypertext links guide you around it. Without hypertext, manuals are often pretty useless as a vehicle for learning a new system. An IBM study found that business professionals rate them second worst out of 12 methods for initially learning a computer system. Many car companies supply instructions to mechanics in hypertext form, mainly on CD-ROM. There are so many different combinations of models and parts that sorting through the volumes of paper is far less efficient, effective, and productive than compressing them on a single disk and letting the PC do the work of sorting through the pages to zero in on the right ones. In 1993, sales of CD-ROM encyclopedias passed those of printed ones. Now that multimedia PCs are becoming both widespread and inexpensive, they are killing off printed manuals in the same way and for the same reasons. Accountants, lawyers, programmers, and engineers are the professionals most able to take advantage of this trend, which can only be accelerated by the availability of hardware and software tools for even the smallest business to create its own master CD-ROM and copy it for $5 or less.

Price Waterhouse estimates that 30 percent of the time spent on an accounting audit, which can take teams of 100, cost millions, and last six months, goes to producing, cross-referencing, and reviewing "Audit Working Papers." Hypertext systems, not yet widely in use in auditing but growing in availability, make it straightforward to track figures from a financial statement back to the original documents that generated them.

See also Intranet; World Wide Web

Hypertext Markup Language Hypertext Markup Language (HTML) is a free software capability included in most Internet browser software, such as Netscape and those provided by America Online, CompuServe, and other services. It allows relatively fast and simple design of home pages on the World Wide Web. It is to date the most widely used tool for this, but its limitations make it difficult to differentiate your own page from the millions of others on the Web. It does not offer the features of emerging tools like HotJava and VRML (virtual reality modeling language), which add animation, 3-D, virtual reality, and improved graphics, video and audio.

HTML is in effect the native language of the Web. The others build on it and extend it. HTML is designed to run on any computer, but how the results appear may differ a little depending on the receiving machine's hardware and software operating system, in terms of fonts, color, and graphics quality. It consists of descriptions—HTML "tags" to show that this is a heading, to include a picture here, to show this text, to make this next word a hypertext link, and other features. Nonprogrammers can generally create a basic Web page in under a day.

HTML embodies the principles of hypertext, as its name indicates. Hypertext links one document to another. With HTML, you indicate, for instance, that the underlined words on the following sentence are hypertext links: "You can check our conference schedule, register your name on our mailing list, or get information about our sister organizations." When readers of the Web page click on "our sister organizations", for instance, they get information on the company's European and Asian associates. Clicking on a hypertext link on that page may link them to, say, the Web page for the Japanese operation. That may link back to the original page. Of course, the designer of the HTML page description must specify the Web address of the sites to link to. A hypertext link may also be a photo, phrase, or any other object on the display.

The main limitation of HTML is implicit in part of its name—hyper*text*. It isn't hyper*multimedia,* but it has in itself generated a huge demand for multimedia, which is increasingly being met by Java and VRML. HTML has guaranteed its own obsolescence. It's still a work of genius, not just talent. The World Wide Web, a product of other genius, made possible the transformation of the Internet from an academic and technical specialty to a literally universal communication tool. HTML democratized the Web by making it practical for anyone to have a public presence on it.

That means that a bright student with design flair, a small business with something to sell, and a large company with news can all use the Net as peers. HTML may also make them look equivalent. Differentiation of message and appearance increasingly means going beyond the basics of HTML. That said, many extensions to HTML are being developed, and any new tools, including Java, must be compatible with HTML, which is as much the underlying basis of the World Wide Web as MS.DOS is of personal computers.

See also HotJava; Java

IETF   *See* Internet Engineering Task Force

Image Processing   Image processing is the capturing and management of images, mainly documents and photos. The principal tools for this are scanners that digitize the document; software that indexes and retrieves all or part of the image, edits it, and manages image data bases; and, more than anything else, the organizational disciplines for streamlining paper-dominated workflows. The range of capabilities and costs is immense, going from the excellent $300 scanners that input documents and photographs at different levels of resolution up to the complexes of hardware and software that manage entire document workflows. The latter are tools widely used by organizations whose customer service, costs, and efficiency depend on how well they process document-based transactions. Obvious instances are insurance firms and state government agencies. The impact of image processing in government is shown by the reductions in the time it takes to obtain copies of such documents as land registrations and marriage certificates. These take up to a week to retrieve manually, but 15 minutes from request to printout using image processing. The pioneer in image processing, USAA, used it to create by far the highest level of customer service in the insurance industry. A single phone call to its 800 number accesses a service agent who can bring up on the screen every document and computer record relating to the customer, including handwritten letters. It burns incoming correspondence once it has been scanned and indexed.

Image processing evolved well before multimedia. Its technology is an extension of photocopying and data base management, with the scanner the direct equivalent of the copier. The software that manages the images is key. For many multimedia applications, the software is secondary to the scanner in that, for instance, someone using desktop publishing to create a brochure has at most a few hundred images to work with. These will be stored on the PC's on-line hard disk or off-line floppy disks. Libraries of images will be available on CD-ROMs. Matters are very different for an insurance company, which will have millions of images that must be comprehensively indexed and organized; accessed by many users in many locations; transmitted accurately, securely, and quickly; and updated frequently. The scanner is just the input device here.

There's really no difference in concept between image processing and multimedia image use. The term *image processing* applies to situations in which the main work need is to improve a business process, such as insurance claims processing, document administration, and customer service. The term *multimedia* applies more to situations in which the need is to work directly with images and to edit and include them in a training program or marketing brochure.

See also Scanner

Information Superhighway The Information Superhighway was a rallying cry generated in the early 1990s by a combination of advocates for a national telecommunications infrastructure funded by the federal government. That superhighway was to pull together all the many individual networks that provided research and technical information across the country's labs, universities, and research centers; ensure that all schools had access to low-cost or free telecommunications; and bring some coherence to the mass of separate commercial network services.

In 1990, when momentum was building for coordinated action in national telecommunications, the Internet was almost entirely inhabited by academics and researchers. Although its use was growing rapidly, it was complex and cumbersome and required specialized knowledge and expertise. The World Wide Web did not yet exist, nor did the Web browsers that make it easy to navigate. The leading on-line information services were marginal, not central, to telecommunications use. The leader, America Online, had under a million subscribers. It was extremely difficult for individuals to obtain high speed communication lines, such as ISDN (integrated services digital network), which is close to five times as fast as the highest speeds now available over standard phone lines. Those speeds are almost three times faster than the standard of 1990.

Deregulation of the long distance phone industry had led to price-slashing competition but also to fragmentation in telecommunications. The separation of deregulated long-distance and still-regulated local phone service added to the fragmentation. In the late 1980s, proponents of a national infrastructure contrasted the situation in the United States with that in France, where the Minitel system had generated a huge base of services. Minitel was in retrospect a sort of mini-Internet. It was set up explicitly to encourage use of telecommunications by individuals, public associations, and small businesses. The government sponsored the development of computer terminals for use in making telephone directory inquiries, instead of calling an operator. The terminals were simple and robust—they were tested by hitting them with a mallet. The Minitel platform generated many innovations and very much paralleled the course of the Internet. Instead of Web pages, Minitel presented simple "videotext" screens, which looked clunky by PC standards, and menus of options. Minitel was the first true success in consumer and small business use of data communications, albeit at a huge subsidized cost. It was as naturally part of the French tradition of strong central direction (*dirigiste*) as the Internet today reflects the American preference for relying on market forces and letting luck play a part.

What a difference the last six years have made! In 1990, it looked as if the government would need to play a central role in ensuring the building of infrastructures for the Information Superhighway. Then-Senator Gore led the way, with initiatives leading to the NII (National Information Infrastructure) legislation Several phone companies planned to implement Minitel. Even in 1993, not much had changed, so that there remained a need for guiding direction if there was to be any true national infrastructure. Then, of course, the Internet became that infrastructure, but a worldwide one. The government funding of, first, the ARPANET and then NSFNET, two base components of what became the Internet, showed the value of central direction. Luck played its part in the invention of the Web by a British scientist working at a high-energy physics lab and in the invention of the Mosaic Internet browser by a small team of graduate students at another scientific lab at the University of Illinois. Market forces contributed in many ways, especially the entrepreneurship of the Mosaic team, which ended up leaving the university and setting up the two competing firms, Netscape and Spyglass, that are now the leaders in Internet browser software. When Netscape went public in 1994 with tiny sales and zero profits, it raised over $2 billion in a day.

In the new context, much of the Information Superhighway debate looks less and less relevant as the market and luck continue. There is no longer any need for a Minitel-like national strategy. The Internet has been privatized so that the government no longer pays for it. Telecommunications is now entirely deregulated, through the 1996 federal bill that allows multiple players to exploit the existing nationwide infrastructures of the phone system and cable TV. We don't really even need the term *Information Superhighway*. Many experts have in any case long disliked the term for the hype that too often goes with it.

What's most useful for managers to keep in mind when they hear about anything to do with the future of telecommunications and computing is simply that the next five years will be at least as packed with change as the last five have been and that most of what happened in those years was largely unpredicted. It was the product of turmoil and experimentation rather than formal planning. The big schemes of the 1970s and 1980s that were loudly and dogmatically trumpeted as the wave of the future have largely been overtaken by forces that in many instances did not exist then. Thus, for instance, the grand plans of ISDN, HDTV, and OSI, the universal blueprint for integrating everything, have moved from committees designing them to lead change to their being left behind change. Dominant designs emerge from a mix of customer choice, vendor need, and market innovation far more than from committees, with few exceptions.

Infrared Connections   Infrared devices substitute light signals in the infrared spectrum for wires. They are in limited use today for connecting PCs to local area networks, printers, and other peripheral devices, but the systems are not standardized and are mostly of interest to large organizations that have to avoid cabling because they are located in buildings that are of such historical value that zoning regulations prohibit drilling through the walls.

They are also used in companies where desks and groups are moved around a lot to meet seasonal and peak work demands. Because it can take weeks to rewire a desk to a LAN, infrared links save money and time.

Now, a consortium that includes Hewlett-Packard, IBM, Sharp, and others is looking to standardize infrared controls for PCs and peripherals. Standardization will, if effective, open up a huge market and in doing so immediately reduce costs by facilitating volume production. The IrDA standard enables two devices to transfer data between them at 115,000 bits per second, which is about the same as PC users get on an office network. (IrDA stands for "*Infrared Data* Association"; the mixing of upper and lower case is a growing trend in the field). The devices must be directly facing each other with no objects in the way. Some types of lighting can affect the transfer of data. Windows 95 includes support for infrared control and Hewlett-Packard already markets IrDA-compatible printers.

IrDA is part of the growing innovations in wireless communications, not all yet successful or widely adopted, which include cellular phone, digital broadcast satellite, and personal digital assistants. All have their own special features and limitations, and pose their own regulatory and technical problems. Infrared controls can operate only over very short line-of-sight distances, and their speed is very limited. They will be of most value in sending data to printers. They will not dramatically open up multimedia opportunities, but they will make the use of PCs just a little easier.

Wireless infrared is not the only proposed innovation in linking to computers. A California company announced in late 1995 that it would be shipping PCs that are operated by thought control via biofeedback to a tiny sensor that fits over your finger. Now *that* would dramatically change the use of PCs. The announcement has been received with, shall we say, a little skepticism. But as Arthur Clarke, the prescient science fiction writer, commented decades ago, in any society advanced technology is indistinguishable from magic. We've seen enough such magic in

A PC industry vendor association is moving rapidly to let you operate a PC in the same way you use a TV or VCR, by pointing an infrared "zapper" and clicking. This could mean "an end to fumbling around with masses of cables and the disappearance of the rat's nest of wires at the back of your computer" (Computer Buyer, October 1995).

the field—fiber optics, chips, and 3-D ads floating above the sidewalk outside a department store—that biofeedback may be a practical line of future development. It shares a concern that IrDA addresses: wireless links instead of cables, keyboards, and rats' nests. The telecommunications field talks about the main problem being "the last mile": the slow link from the fast fiber network to your house. In the PC area, the problem now is the last 10 feet from the PC to the printer, or from you to the PC. The infrared mouse, infrared pen, and infrared bar code scanner are already routinely available.

Inkjet Printers   Multimedia makes color printers absolutely essential. Until very recently, they were also very expensive and far slower than black-and-white printers, for the obvious reason that the picture has to be built up pixel by pixel. There are two main types of color printer technology, laser and inkjet, both of which provide practical products that are affordable and offer good-quality output. Inkjet printers are the cheaper option, but their limitations are substantial. They use color cartridges which contain three colors of ink to blow a fine spray of ink onto the paper, mixing them to provide a wide range of colors, tints, and hues. A cartridge typically costs around $20 and lasts for up to 300 sheets, depending on "coverage" of colored versus blank areas of the output. Because normal paper absorbs some of the ink, special paper is preferable to cheap paper, which adds to the operating cost. Inkjet printers are also slow. It can take up to eight minutes to produce a full color transparency and two minutes to produce a graph for a brochure or report.

Rather than use a low cost inkjet printer directly attached to a PC, most companies rely on a higher-speed laser printer which is shared by many PCs through a local area network. Laser printers can store the digital image of the full page and do not have to rebuild it for multiple copies. With most inkjet printers, it takes as long to print the second and third copies as the first. That said, for low volume uses, inkjet technology has made color as affordable as black and white.

Installation of Multimedia Devices Multimedia is a set of hardware technologies as well as a set of media and set of software tools. The pace of change leads to many differences in the hardware, and the wide range of prices and capabilities means that there are few standard hardware configurations. There are even wider variations in types of use, development skills and experience, and size of pocketbook.

As a result, the most distinctive—and most scary—feature of multimedia is selection and installation of hardware components. *PC World*'s list of 10 installation tips for adding multimedia to a PC (September 1995) reads very much like a list of 10 reasons either to have nothing to do with multimedia or to have someone else do it for you—or to buy an Apple, where the disadvantage of limited variety and often slightly higher prices is offset by the huge reduction in the infinite variety of ways things can go wrong that marks today's multimedia systems. The tips are, with my own comments added:

1. Before you buy a multimedia upgrade kit, make sure your PC has an available drive bay. Otherwise, you have to remove your floppy disk drive to install the CD-ROM drive. (*Comment:* This is why a Phillips screwdriver is the foundation of multimedia.)

2. Check what kind of interface the CD-ROM kit has. You may have to buy a SCSI adapter, which requires an ISA slot. (SCSI is pronounced "scuzzy," as it deserves. It's one example of the reality that PCs are not in the computer business but the cable business, with the PC the loss leader for the cables and adapters.)

3. Make sure you are familiar, for example, with which IRQ addresses your fax modem uses, so that you can avoid any IRQ conflicts with the CD-ROM drive or

"At the rear of the drive you will find two SCSI ports allowing you to daisy chain multiple devices. You will also find the SCSI ID number switch which is required. . . . The two ports are SCSI 2 affairs which means that for many of you with SCSI cards which have the larger 50-way connectors you will need to invest in either an adapter or a SCSI 1 to SCCI 2 cable. The manual was fairly good but could have been more detailed on explanations about SCSI IDs and terminators. This is where most users have the majority of problems." (Description of a CD-ROM drive, whose ad for this very machine claims that it virtually installs itself—"even better, our interface kits not only come with SimpleStart software, they actually turn 'Plug and Play' into a reality.")

sound board. Also map out your DMA channels. (These are the *basics* of the hardware, not the fancy stuff!)

4. Check out the vendor's technical support hours for phone assistance (you'll need it).

5. Have a Phillips screwdriver and small flashlight handy. Keep the PC manual by your side because you may have to locate a diagram of the motherboard. (Step 5 already, and you have yet to install anything.)

6. Unplug the power cord and any peripherals. Touch any unpainted metal surface on the PC to discharge any static electricity through your finger, not through your CD-ROM drive. (Do you really think you'll remember which cable goes back where?)

7. Connect the CD-ROM drive ribbon (a tiny cable, with the only extra feature being extra fragility). Check for and set the CD-ROM drive master-slave jumper. The space behind a drive bay may be cramped. (It will be.)

8. Install the CD-ROM drive first. (There's *more?*)

9. Don't be afraid to give the sound board a good shove; otherwise, it won't snap into place. Don't push too hard, though, or you'll damage the board. (What's the fine line between a good shove and a push that's too hard?)

10. Above all, keep a detailed diary of the installation. That way, you can more easily backtrack to solve a system conflict and communicate with the vendor's technical support phone service more easily. (So that's why the support phone lines are always so busy.)

The issue of *PC World* in which the list appears contains 410 pages. Not one of the hundreds of ads says anything like "Free Phillips screwdriver for your everyday use. Free hundred hours of telephone chat with our expert who'll help you work out what's happened. Free installation diary." Instead, they are full of talk about more "expandability and upgradability than anyone else," "favorite options" (including a SCSI controller chip), and "many other affordable upgrades and options available. Call for details!" One more piece of affordable upgrade and you'll be a nervous wreck.

Intel Intel is one of the most extraordinary companies in the history of business and a driving force in the PC industry, far more so than Microsoft, which depends on Intel more than Intel depends on it. Intel has paced PC hardware. Microsoft drove the software that used it. Together, they led the movement of PCs—first, across the office landscape and then into the school, home, briefcase, and even hotel room. Now, both of them, individually rather than cooperatively, are targeting multimedia as their next source of growth.

Intel built its success on three main principles, as well as on plenty of technical and managerial savvy: (1) massive and effective investment in R&D; (2) commitment to a smooth transition from each generation of CPU computer chips; and (3) rapid introduction of each new generation of chip, even though the previous one may still be a best-seller. Intel's core business is obviously chips, but in recent years it has become a dominant force in producing the main component of a PC, the motherboard that houses the CPU and main memory plus all the other hardware needed for the basic PC. That means that it is both a supplier to and a competitor of such companies as Compaq, in that Compaq buys Intel Pentium chips and Intel sells motherboards to many of its rivals in PC hardware.

The Intel chips and all PC motherboards today are not built around hardware specifically designed for multimedia. Multimedia is added on through special-purpose boards and adapters, such as a graphics accelerator, sound card, or video board. That's changing fast, and the next generation of Intel chips will be packed with multimedia facilities. Intel's most recent ads stress this. They review the company's development of "native signal

The pace of change in the semiconductor manufacturing industry and Intel's even-faster pace of business success are illustrated by the fall in Intel's stock price when it announced disappointing results for the fourth quarter of 1995. Revenues increased only 41 percent over the previous year, and profits grew only 56 percent.

processor" chips. These operate with the nondigital native signals of sound and vision. They are an extension of digital signal processors, codecs, and related hardware which mediate between the digital and nondigital world.

Intel's first major chip was the 30XX series. This led to the 30286, 30386, and 40486, now called just a 486. The last of these is still used in many PCs, especially laptops; it provides fully enough power to handle most applications, including multimedia. It is the successor to the 486, the Pentium, that really opened up multimedia. (This was scheduled to be named the 586, but litigation blocked the use of what a rival claimed as a generic nonproprietary label.) Every new chip has shown the validity of the great insight of Intel's cofounder, Gordon Moore—that the most basic trends in the computer industry ensured a doubling of chip performance for a given cost every 18 months, driven by miniaturization and manufacturing production yields. Moore's law has held up for almost three decades. There are some experts who believe that we are close to the physical limits of silicon chip–based technology and that within 20 years we will see a slowing of the pace of innovation, because there is a limit to how small the lines etched on chips can be drawn and because of the escalating cost of the manufacturing plant and equipment needed. Even if that's so, there are several generations of Intel chips on the horizon that will soon make today's speed blazers look slow.

The main threat to Intel and even more to Microsoft is coming from something entirely new: a frontal challenge to the basic concepts of personal computers. The evolution of the "Wintel" path (Windows plus Intel) has been to use ever-more-powerful chips to drive ever-more-powerful software. Wintel concentrates computing on the desktop, with telecommunications a secondary element. (Microsoft was late in recognizing the importance to the business use of PCs of "enterprise" telecommunications, losing that growing market to Novell and others.)

Sun Microsystems has from its inception taken an entirely

different view, one that now may seem obvious: the network is the driver of computing as well as communication. This "network-centric" philosophy was independent of the Internet, but the Net's explosive growth in reach and scale created a massive opportunity for Sun, largely through sheer bad and good luck. The bad luck was a failed project to build a prototype device that would control all household appliances, including TV sets. When Sun failed to win a much-needed contract to develop the set-top boxes for Time Warner's interactive television trials, it scrapped the company that had been set up to license and develop systems using the new programming language the Sun team had created. This marked a major breakthrough in the entire computing field. Building on a language called C++, one of the main tools for building networked applications, it created the Java programming language, which amounts to (1) a better C++; (2) a fully object-oriented development tool (objects are self-contained, reusable pieces of software code; object tools are viewed as the key to future software quality and productivity); (3) secure code that can be protected against software "viruses," the perennial threat from saboteurs and mischief makers; and (4) a software environment that amounts to what the information technology field desperately needs—an operating system that can run on any computer.

In 1994, Sun thus had a magnificent product looking for a market that had failed to materialize. The good luck was the World Wide Web. It established network-centric computing as the next mainstream. More importantly, because the Internet's telecommunications protocols allow any computer of any type to communicate with any other computer, Sun now had the market, a machine-independent operating system and telecommunications infrastructure, and a powerful development tool.

The key use of all these will be to try to change the direction of computing from power and complexity in PC chips and software to simplicity of hardware and applications. A host of companies are racing to build what are called "network computers," "Lite computers," and "Internet appliances," among other terms.

These will be stripped-down devices in terms of memory requirements, disk storage, and cost; the target price for the machines already developed but not yet mass-marketed is $500. Should they become the preferred machines of consumers, schools, travelers, and businesses buying computers in huge volumes, then Wintel loses its primacy. Intel thus has much at stake. Its executives largely belittle Lite computers as depending on the widespread provision of very fast telecommunications links at very low cost. The new tools request small Java applications—"applets"—from the network as needed. Today, it takes around 15 times as long to process a networked applet as it does to run a C++ application on a Wintel machine.

My own view is that Java *will* redefine the basics of competition in the computer field, over time. And that time is likely to be 4 years from now, not 10. Meanwhile, Intel will continue its dominance of the established PC market, where it has 85 percent market share. It will almost surely dominate the multimedia hardware market; there's no reason to believe that this superb R&D machine will lose its edge.

See also Digital Signal Processor; Java; Media Processor; Operating System; Pentium

Interactive Television   Interactive television combines the existing reach and multimedia capabilities of TVs with the interactive features of telephones. Your TV zapper becomes a limited PC keyboard. It also becomes indistinguishable from your home PC and home phone. The set-top box with which the zapper communicates is literally a special-purpose PC. The billion-dollar order placed by one European firm in 1996 was for a device that has as much memory as a midrange multimedia PC, includes the latest in data compression technology, has a modem for communicating with the Internet, and runs on the same CPU chip as the latest Apple computer. This machine "intelligence" turns the television into an interactive system.

The question is: What type of interaction? There are plenty

of candidates—most obviously, interactive shopping for goods and financial services, multiplayer games over a network, gambling, on-demand entertainment, access to information, and voting in public referenda or, more prosaically, expressing your opinion of what play a football coach should call next. All of these have been piloted. All of them are the subject of ongoing trials. There is an old saying that Brazil is the country of the future— and always will be. That saying may also apply to interactive television, which has been a promise for well over the 20 years of trials that begin with expansive hopes and claims about its potential and end with just a few hundred or few thousand subscribers making about as much use of it as you make of the advanced programming buttons on your VCR. Just as the VCR is a device that we use almost entirely for playing videotapes and occasionally recording TV programs, a TV set is something we switch on to watch TV. To date, nothing has changed that. It may be years before viewers start using it to control their own programming. Here are extracts from two articles in *Time* magazine about interactive TV, published just over one year apart:

> The brave new world that futurists have been predicting for decades is not years away but months. By this time next year, vast new video services will be available, at a price, to millions of Americans in all fifty states. (12 April 1993)

> The faith [about interactive TV] is being sorely tested. It is here that the rhetoric about the information highway comes face to face with the realities of engineering. (23 May 1994)

In other words, the state of interactive TV in 1994 was no further advanced than in 1993. It was no further advanced in 1996, either. Time Warner's much-heralded but so far disappointing trial of interactive television in Orlando, Florida, attracted just 4,000 subscribers. The cost of the special set is $5,000.

Change is well underway in the relationship between viewers and their television sets, though. The main difference is the range of choice. Instead of being limited to the three main networks—

Television is a young medium. The first black-and-white broadcasts began in 1941. Color TV sets became widely available only in the 1960s. Cable TV took off in the 1980s. Off the roughly 40 channels that are now part of standard cable packages, the household names, such as CNN, HBO, and ESPN, were founded in the 1970s. In that context, the wildest promises of interactive TV via the merging of telecommunications, computing, and cable are as much an evolution in an always rapidly evolving field as is a "high tech" revolution.

CBS, NBC, and ABC—viewers in most of the country have the choice of many cable and satellite channels, plus Blockbuster video and pay-per-view. In other countries, most of the government-controlled or -influenced TV services are losing ground to newly licensed cable companies, with a virtually infinite demand for U.S. entertainment. Broadcast TV is vulnerable to PCs. "A battle is shaping up for America's eyeball. Television growth trajectory is over. . . . The average American watches 55 hours a week of television. . . . In the future there is simply less time spent watching broadcast television. There are other screens to sit in front of" (*Forbes,* 25 September 1995). In 1994, sales of PCs were 25 million, with over half to consumers, mostly in the age range 25 to 39, the primary target for advertisers. Interactive video games amount to a $10 billion business. On-line information services have around 7 million subscribers. In 1995, for the first time ever, more PCs were sold than TVs.

Hence the expensive and sustained investment in interactive TV. The leading investors include media megafirms like Time Warner, phone companies like Bell Atlantic, and many others inside and outside the TV establishment. The CEO of Bell Atlantic Video Service believes that it will be able to take the roughly $25 a month that people pay for cable TV and command a further $35 for such services as video on demand and directories. Advertising revenues will reduce this by $12. Bell Atlantic aimed at getting 22,000 subscribers by the end of 1996. The CEO thinks it will take at least four years for interactive TV services to make a profit.

Interactivity Interactivity is the degree to which the user and the system influence each other's requests and responses. Most multimedia experts view interaction as the primary purpose of what they do. Interaction is a two-way process. Many systems are one-way, with either the computer or the human giving orders to be obeyed. An ATM is an example. The machine instructs you to insert your card and key in your password. You instruct it to process your cash withdrawal. Technically, this is interactive computing, but it is very limited and inflexible. Many computerized training programs and CD-ROMs are, too. How to design for interactivity is perhaps *the* skill of the multimedia developer.

The special promise of multimedia is interaction, instead of passive viewing of one-way transmission of information, education, or entertainment. One expert summarizes two-way versus one-way communication as the difference between a conversation and a lecture. Interactivity—a medium's inherent degree of interaction—determines how new and broad a perspective that medium provides on peoples' access to an audience, to technology, to a community, to entertainment, to education, and to information. Historically, computers have restricted interaction in that the human had to accommodate to the machine—the "do not bend, spindle, fold, or mutilate" era followed by the era of enigmatic messages about "Host dead" (an old Internet response to a remote computer's being out of service), "Unidentified UUO at User Loc E88078," "Floating divide underflow," and "Invalid input, please try again."

Today, the primary goals of the innovators in information technology are fourfold and interrelated:

1. *Make computers easy to use,* first through graphical user interfaces (GUIs), then through Internet browsers, and now through multimedia.

2. *Facilitate interaction,* first through menus of options, then through communication over networks (electronic mail, videoconferencing), and now through trials of interactive television, wider use of the Internet, authoring of CD-ROMs, and development of training programs and "edutainment."

3. *Exploit the opportunity of the Internet,* first through the World Wide Web and now through intranets, the combination of easy to use Web browsers, the Internet's communications capabilities, and secure Web

"It's awfully hard to be pious about the printed word when the National Enquirer uses the same medium as Shakespeare. Brilliance has always coexisted quite comfortably with trash in any medium, and the same is already true of interactive media. There are plenty of bad titles out there, and the unfortunate pioneers who are buying them find they're chock full of gratuitous button-blinking, disco music and flashing video. A good interactive title chooses the best information from all of the media at its disposal and combines them into something indefinable and powerful" (Utne Reader, *January/ February 1993*).

computer servers accessible only from within a company.

4. *Add multimedia,* first through off-line CD-ROM; then through networked graphics, video, and audio that don't overload the network delivering them; and very soon, through multimedia via the high-speed transmission links that are technologically proven and sure to be made more widely available over the next few years.

Interactivity puts the person in command of the computer, instead of the other way around. That means that many of the uses of interactive multimedia will be unpredictable. New tools create new uses. One example comes from the most interactive technology we all routinely use—the telephone, which is just an empty pipe. When the Eskimos in remote northern Canada first got satellite telephone communications in the 1970s, it seemed just common sense that they would use it to talk to each other. Instead, they started doing something new: calling Seattle to check the markets for seal meat and negotiating their own deals instead of relying on intermediaries. The imaginative use of cellular phones and pagers by drug dealers is a similar instance of how changes in interactivity lead to innovation that is outside the control or often the forecast of the provider of the tools that enable it.

See also Authoring; Business on the Internet; Interactive Television

"Here is interactive design in a nutshell. Nobody wants to read a manual. Nobody wants to wait. Everybody wants to be in control!" (The creator of Broderbund's Living Books CD-ROM series)

International Multimedia The technology of multimedia is available worldwide, but there are two key differences across nations: the cost of telecommunications and government restrictions on the use of the Internet. The price of the same volume of annual domestic phone calls varies from under $500 in Scandinavia, to $800 in the United States, to $1,400 in Italy, and $1,900 in

Portugal. For business communications, the gaps are even larger, as the following figures from INTUG show:

Price per Year	Domestic Telephone Price	Price for the Same Mix of Business-Leased Lines
Australia	$1,189	1,032
Canada	1,256	1,478
France	856	708
Germany	988	501
Italy	1,481	512
Japan	963	814
Spain	1,418	1,353
Sweden	497	266
United Kingdom	816	438
United States	827	500

These price differences reflect monopoly and competition rather than supplier costs, which are obviously very much the same for all the providers that use the same technology. Sweden and the United Kingdom show the impacts of opening up their telecommunications markets. Canada and Germany, which were both bastions of protectionism in telecommunications until the mid-1990s, show the impacts of the reverse policy. France shows how superb technology can compensate for almost obsessive opposition to deregulation.

Telecommunications prices will have a profound effect on multimedia in both the consumer and the business markets. On-line information services are far more expensive to operate and access in Canada than in Sweden, for instance. Corporate network costs in Japan are double those in the United Kingdom; that's one reason why, in the late 1980s, over 40 of the 50 largest Japanese multinational firms had their global telecommunications systems located in London, not Tokyo. Most importantly, the international differences in cost and availability of services are even higher for the ultrafast transmission services essential for enterprisewide business multimedia, such as digital videoconferencing; use of three-dimensional video graphics in engineering, pharmaceutical research, or manufacturing; or interactive networked training.

The costs of accessing the Internet do not vary as widely across nations. What does vary internationally is the availability of sites through which to access it and government willingness to allow those sites to exist and operate without interference and censorship. The Internet is profoundly democratic and even libertarian (with some elements of anarchism). Essentially, any organizations or individuals can join the Internet and have their own site on it. Thus Greenpeace and neo-Nazi parties both have their Web pages. During the French nuclear tests in the Pacific, journalists were "hitting" Greenpeace's pages at the rate of over 50 per minute to get up-to-the-second news not blocked by censorship and not filtered or delayed by wire services.

Many governments insist on blocking, filtering, and delaying traffic on the Net, though. They are concerned with stemming the free flow of information that created the spiritual foundation of the Internet, to the extent that its strongest enthusiasts resist any efforts to control it, including restrictions on pornography. The practical reality is that its size, complexity, openness, span of operation and breadth of information resources make it now impossible for any government organization to get in the way of its use by anyone.

That won't stop governments from trying. The simplest way to block the flow of information is to block use of the Internet itself. Even universities may not be permitted to use the Internet in countries ruled by religious fundamentalists, including Saudi Arabia as well as Iran and Algeria; by autocracies that manage news (China); and by regimes that use military control and fear as the main forces of stability. Their fears are often more about the disturbing impacts of sexual material and discussion than political concerns. Singapore is the most aggressive in this regard among nations with advanced economies and advanced telecommunications. It has been a paternalistic society since its creation.

It's been an information technology economy, too, with its use of electronic data interchange the main reason it moved from the tenth to the busiest port in the world. It encourages use of business telecommunications and discourages use of the Internet.

The state of a nation's economic and telecommunications infrastructures obviously affects its ability to use the Internet. Some 90 percent of all Internet host sites are in the 25 countries that comprise the OECD (Organization for Economic Cooperation and Development), with 60 percent in the United States. Some 96 percent of on-line data bases are in North America, Western Europe, and the most developed nations in the Asia-Pacific region. As of late 1995, there was not a single Internet host in any of the 49 least developed nations of the world. Mongolia's installation of a satellite dish for Internet communication in early 1996 was world news.

Many less-developed nations see the Internet as a major opportunity to stem the brain drain of emigrating academics and scientists. Estonia, for instance, has twice as many Internet connections as Denmark, which has five times its population; this is part of a sustained initiative to ensure that Estonia's scientists and engineers are in the mainstream of their fields. The growth in connections in Eastern Europe between 1991 and 1993 was from 68 to 792 (the comparative growth figure for Asia is from 133 to 626), with the increase fueled by scientists' eagerness to collaborate with their Western peers. By mid-1996, there were over 1 million sites accessible from Eastern Europe, up from 100,000 in late 1995.

International uses of the Internet for multimedia will be very limited in most countries because of the cost and slowness of accessing video, graphics, 3-D, and the like. That's a temporary situation for developed countries that have low-cost, technologically advanced telecommunications. Competition, deregulation, technology, and alliances among the most aggressive international service providers are so rapidly driving down prices that *The Economist* argues that developed nations are moving toward "tariff-free" service, in which the cost of tracking usage and billing customers is greater than the cost of operating the service. That said, a widely quoted figure is that 60 percent of the world population has never made a phone call in their lives.

One of the most positive stories about international use of the Internet, instead of negative efforts to block it, comes from Peru. According to official statistics, about half the Peruvian population lives below the poverty level, yet it was the third-fastest-growing Internet nation in the world in 1995, with sites increasing from 171 at the beginning of the year to 1,200 by midyear. One reason for the growth is the policy of the network provider, a consortium of academic and nongovernmental organizations, to provide free usage to around 95 percent of users. The head of the Peruvian Scientific Network comments that his organization believes it has a social responsibility to address such issues as poverty but that development also entails staking a place the future. It views itself as giving Peruvians a tool with which they can generate wealth. The religious fundamentalists and Peru's Scientific Network share the same belief that the Internet is more than just a net. It changes things. If you want to block change, block the Internet. If you want to encourage change, open up access to the Net.

Internet The Internet is not a network but a network of networks and the vehicle by which computers of any type can communicate with other computers of any type for the sharing of information and communication. That means that it can grow, if not forever, then at least for as long as the computers on it can send and receive messages to and from each other. The Internet evolved from the interlinking of a number of large networks originally funded by U.S. government agencies. These formed what is termed a backbone, analogous to the spinal system of the human body. More and more other networks were linked to the "backbone. "They all had their own nodes, computers that stored information that could be accessed via the backbone by any computer that in turn was linked to a node on this growing "network of networks." The great—almost magical—achievement of the many people and institutions who evolved it was to enable any type of computer to link to any other anywhere on the Net regardless of its make, the type of operating system it used, or its location. They accomplished this at a time when the mainstream of business telecommunications was built on and constrained by myriad entirely different communications protocols and standards. Computer manufacturers like IBM and Digital Equipment had their own proprietary systems that could not connect to each other. Telephony and data communications were separate technologies, professions, and suppliers.

The Internet was made practical by a very pragmatic approach to telecommunications called TCP/IP, which ignored many of the issues of efficiency and security central to business telecommunications and telephone service providers. TCP/IP simply got the message to its destination as best it could. This meant an immediate dropping of the barriers to entry for organizations to add nodes to the Net. By 1993, when the tools that opened up the World Wide Web became available, the Internet was a disorganized and rapidly expanding community.

That community had to be very computer-savvy to use the Net. It was the individual and collaborative efforts of graduate students, computer science professors, and scientific researchers that evolved its many tools. The software that provided the information and communication services enabled by the Net was built pragmatically in the same way and by many of the same people who evolved TCP/IP. These were based (as is TCP/IP) on an entirely different technology base from the business mainstream. Personal computers in the home made little use of telecommunications; in 1994, only 10 percent had modems. Business PCs were largely limited to access to company networks. Around 90 percent of all PCs used either the DOS, Windows, or Macintosh operating system. Around 90 percent of the business computers that handled transactions and stored information were built wholly or partly on IBM systems and standards.

The explosion of Internet use in the early 1990s was a surprise to everyone except a tiny band of true believers. Two excellent books on multimedia published in 1994 are typical. One has no references to the Internet whatsoever, and the other has two paragraphs on it.

The Internet software environment was built around UNIX, the very specialized operating system favored by academics, scientists, and engineering specialists. The distinguishing feature of UNIX and UNIX-based applications was that, if you knew what you were doing, you could make the machine do almost anything and that, if you didn't understand UNIX, you would be hard pressed to get it to do anything. Thus, prior to the Web, using the Internet meant memorizing many obscure acronyms and wrestling with conventions for entering commands. (On the Web, you still see the vestiges of the UNIX tradition in such commands as http://www.wadewin.com/jsoft.html).

By 1990, the Internet was expanding widely, partly because the United States had no national infrastructure for the use of PCs to access information and communicate with each other. France had its Minitel system, a low-cost and heavily subsidized network sponsored by the French government to broaden the use of computers across its society. The United States had a morass of regional phone companies, company "private" networks, and competing information service providers, such as CompuServe, the fledgling America Online, MCI Mail, and expensive specialized business services.

The situation can be summarized as follows: the Internet provided the infrastructure but required specialized knowledge. Businesses owned their own infrastructures, which required specialized hardware and software. A wide range of telecommunications service providers offered access to communications, but only within narrow ranges in terms of cost, reach, and information. The Internet had it all. Just about any service the others provided could be routed through the Internet. If only the Internet could be easily used by ordinary people. The World Wide Web came out of nowhere to begin to make it so. As with so many of the innovations on the Internet, it was the initiative of a small group of very computer-savvy researchers—in this case, physicists at CERN, the leading European high energy research lab—whose main quest is the search for the Higgs boson, the postulated smallest building block of matter. It is both ironic and typical that one of the most practical and down-to-earth innovations in modern society came from the genius of someone involved in the most impractical of research. The drive for knowledge is what has made the Internet so important to the dreamers. The Web was invented to make it easy for researchers to share information. Together with the essentially free worldwide e-mail provided by the Internet, the Web fueled the growth of the Net in the 1990–1994 period. What made 1994–1995 years of explosive growth was the development of Internet browsers, again an innovation by scientific researchers at the University of Illinois's center for supercomputing studies. They saw a need to hide the arcane UNIX-based commands needed to access the Net. Their first product, called Mosaic, was given away free, and then began the growth in numbers of Internet users of several hundred percent per year, with no slowing in sight. The team that built Mosaic split up, giving the rights to the name to the people who formed the Spyglass company. The other group built Netscape, which accounts for 70 percent of all browser use.

All this occurred during the first half of the 1990s. In that period, there was limited consumer use of such on-line services as America Online and Prodigy, so that it was only in 1995 that they rushed to add Internet access. Microsoft totally missed the boat here. When it launched its Microsoft Network, it was clear that Bill Gates thought he could make it a counter to the Internet. Microsoft was taken by surprise both by the success of Netscape and by the extent to which the Internet became the driver of PC software innovations, not the other way around

The use and impact of the Internet is close to impossible to describe, and there are many myths, misconceptions, and even some misinformation about it. It is as much linked to political views, attitudes toward business and government, and the demographics of computer users as to its relatively clumsy technology. For some people it's magic. For others, it's overhyped. For all the 1995 articles about businesses not surviving until the year

Liechtenstein is the smallest nation in the world in terms of land mass. It may be the one that makes most money per capita from the Internet. In late 1995, it launched its Interlotto lottery, with a million dollar jackpot for correctly picking six numbers between 1 and 40. It's probably legal. No one knows, because nothing like the Internet has ever existed, and gambling laws never envisaged it.

2000 unless they are on the Internet, we are now seeing articles about its limitations and disappointments. Its growth has outpaced its technology base. TCP/IP was not designed to provide security; the basic philosophy of the Net community is open communication and sharing of information. The demand for multimedia such as Internet radio, phone, videoconferencing, and video strains the capacity of the Net, the server computers that manage traffic and access data, and the number of addresses the system can handle. Lack of widely available, low-cost telecommunications adds to the traffic jams. The Internet is always close to saturation.

The demographics of the Internet community in late 1995 also show just how specialized it is and how unrepresentative of the population at large.

- *Age:* Under 21, 6 percent; 21 to 30, 56 percent; 31 to 50, 36 percent; over 50, 2 percent.

- *Sex:* 95 percent male (1996 figures show this dropping to 70 percent).

- *Location:* North America, 68 percent; Europe, 28 percent; students and faculty, 44 percent; businesses, 3 percent.

- *Hours of use:* 21 to 50 hours per week, 60 percent.

Until 1995, the U.S. government sponsored the Internet and funded it, with voluntary organizations and universities coordinating but not controlling its activities. New users could register their sites on the Internet for free. The Internet Engineering Task Force (IETF) provided technical leadership and still does. However, the government no longer pays for the Net. There's a fee for registration now, paid to the company given the contract for handling this key function. The physical operations of the "backbone" network are another contracted service. The IETF has initiated the Next Generation Internet Protocol (IPng) and has been using the Mbone (Multicast Backbone), a broadcasting capability—technically called "multicasting"—for which there is huge pent-up demand. Visa and MasterCard have cooperated to resolve the factor that most constrains the use of the Internet for business transactions: security in handling credit card payments.

The technology of the Internet is unstable, with most of it reflecting the original conception of the Net and 1970s designs. That is changing rapidly, with Sun Microsystems' state-of-the-art Java programming language as far-reaching in its implications as Mosaic for use of the Web and even more far-reaching for development of computer applications and their delivery over the Net, rather than via PCs. Investors have been very willing to buy the stocks of Internet start-up firms and of multimedia companies whose revenues will grow with the Net. The volatility of these stocks is very high, so that there is some possibility investors will be scared off in coming years, but the most likely scenarios are more technical and business innovation being backed by more stock market capital.

There remain many real concerns that the Internet backbone, the communication links that all users share, will crumble as the volume of traffic grows. Every commentator sees that growth as being driven by multimedia. The developer of Netscape comments that one of the most exciting developments underway is the use of ultrahigh-speed cable modems to access the Net. This "will really open up the floodgates on what you can do interactively." But those floodgates may drown the network with calls for audio and video. Now that the Internet is not funded by the government, many experts believe that its pricing structures must change, both to ensure efficient use and to fund the investment in new infrastructures.

See also Business on the Internet; Internet Advertising; World Wide Web

Internet Address An Internet address is the equivalent of a phone number that contains all the information needed to locate a person and a computer. They are lengthy, and many are impossible to remember. Understanding their structure may make them a little easier to handle, though.

It's close to impossible to come up with any fictional service on the Web that is more weird than many that are on it already. How about the Swedish cursing tutorial, with audio that enunciates the bad words very carefully, because in the author's view, "cursing with a heavy accent is often perceived as mildly ridiculous."

It's fairly obvious who owns the Internet name ibm.com (IBM), and you could probably guess that Clorox owns liquidplumr.com but how about diarrhea.com or hotdogconstructionco.com? These have been registered by Procter & Gamble and Kraft, which owns the Oscar Meyer brand. P&G has also registered pimples.com, headache.com, dandruff.com, and underarm.com. Kraft has velveeta.com and saladdressing.com among many others. P&G and Kraft have exclusive world rights to these addresses, as has the journalist who registered mcdonalds.com as a prank (McDonald's sued him). Internet addresses are becoming brands in themselves. Only one of the many companies in the world named Ace can get the electronic Internet brand. Who should have it?

All Internet personal addresses used for electronic mail include the name of a server, shown by an @ symbol. This part of the address indicates the location of the computer that coordinates your e-mail communications and storage. Technically, it is called the domain of the Internet. If you think of the Internet as a world, then the domain is a unique part of that world. To the left of the @ symbol is your name within that domain, and to the right is your specific location. Thus the Internet e-mail address for Janet Gibson, who works in the marketing department of a British company called Telestyle, might be Jgibson@telestyle-mktg.co.uk This means that her computer is registered on Internet directories as "telestyle"; "co" shows that it is a company. Each country has a two-character code (my own address at the University of Stockholm was keen@dsv.su.se where "se" indicates Sweden and "su" indicates a university site).

The U.S. convention for Internet addresses is:

- "edu" for an educational institution.
- "com" for a company.
- "gov" for government.
- "mill" for military.
- "org" for a noncompany organization. Greenpeace is located on the Internet at greenpeace.org

Alas, there are always variations on any IT "standard." In the United States, academic institutions are "edu" and in the United Kingdom they are "ac" and companies are "co." U.S. addresses omit the country.

There is a distinct though rapidly fading status symbol in having an "edu" rather than a "com" address. Some Internet purists have an attitude opposed to the Internet's purity be sullied by commercialism. That attitude is a major factor in the many debates about whether or not there is a need for more security, or more restriction on publishing and accessing pornography.

Very roughly, "edu" addresses favor minimizing any efforts to restrict, oversee, or even charge for Internet resources, whereas "com" sees such efforts as essential for the Internet to become a business as well as an academic infrastructure. The debate is no minor matter. In many ways, its outcome may determine the future of the Internet, and both parties have very powerful arguments on their side.

Requests for Internet services, such as the World Wide Web file transfer protocol, require a fuller address, which indicates, first, the Internet protocol to be used in transmitting the information involved, then the service, and then the address of the domain. The most common type of such a unique resource locator (URL) is the http://www. that typically precedes World Wide Web requests (the www is optional), such as http://www.net scape.com, the URL for accessing Netscape's home page. It may be followed by additional information about directories of files and formats that uniquely identify the information to be retrieved and transmitted, so that it is displayed correctly in the user's screen. URLs can become very complex and lengthy. Here's one for accessing an anatomical demonstration over the Web, which is stored on a government agency's server:

> http://www.acl.lanl.government/~rdaniel/classesJDK/Pick
> Test2.html

The information separated by the / and the ~ is the equivalent of filing cabinets, folders, and individual pages within them.

See also World Wide Web

Internet Advertising Advertising a company's services on the Internet costs around $1,000 a month for a leased high-speed telecommunications line plus the costs of the server and development of the home page, administration, and operations. That translates to around 3 to 5 cents per potential 1,000 readers per month, assuming there are 30 million on the Net (a figure that may or may not be accurate—literally, no one knows).

Compare this with the cost to reach a thousand users through traditional advertising media:

	Cost	Cost per 1,000 Potential Audience per Month
Leading daytime TV soap opera	$45,000 for 30 seconds	$20
Prime time local TV show	6,000 for 30 seconds	43
Radio ad, drive time	285 for 60 seconds	15
Rush Limbaugh program	475 for 60 seconds	20
New York Times	440 per column inch	50
People magazine	83,000 for a page	24
TV Guide	59,000 for 1/2 page	8
Direct mail	330	330

Source: Canter and Siegel, *How to Make a Fortune on the Information Superhighway.*

Internet Engineering Task Force   The Internet Engineering Task Force (IETF) is a voluntary group with no formal or legal authority, which aims at coordinating what may turn out to be the uncoordinatable. The Internet was never really designed, but grew all by itself. It often seems and may well be out of control. The IETF consists of the best and the brightest technical experts from universities, professional societies, and companies who address the truly big issues about the Internet backbone, the shared network across which all Net users transmit their requests and services. The members have no formal authority but are advisers to the organizations operating the backbone.

The main issues the IETF has addressed in recent years are improving the transmission efficiency of the Internet in handling multimedia, especially phone, radio, and video; and extending the scale of broadcasting capabilities of what is called the Mbone (multicasting backbone), which is used by the IETF itself to hold its 3-day, 8-hour-a-day meetings.

See also Mbone

Internet Phone   Internet phone service is a low-cost, still somewhat primitive, recent addition to the Internet's range of features. Telephone calls have not to date been part of multimedia. They are absolutely key to business and everyday life, and more and more linked to computers, literally and figuratively. When you use a touch-tone phone to check your credit card balance, for instance, the phone is in effect a keyboard and output display (the output is synthesized speech). PCs and telephony are rapidly converging, with chips that can be added to the PC to turn into it a phone switch. That said, phones are phones. They are not associated with graphics, video, and images. Efforts over the past 30 years to introduce videophones have been a bust.

That is likely to change within the next few years. The same transmission links that carry voice calls already carry Internet traffic. Now, the Internet can carry voice traffic. *Business Week* (8 January 1996) accurately summarizes the product: "the Internet can transmit speech cheaply, but not in a satisfying or easy way. Right now, an Internet voice call has little of the tone or intimacy of a regular phone call." The key phrase is "right now."

Right now, you need to configure your PC with odds and ends of standard multimedia hardware, including a microphone, and special software. The software simply uses your PC sound card to convert the microphone analog voice signals into digital form and the reverse, just as it handles music clips that are transmitted across the Net. The traffic is broken up into individual "packets," which may be routed through the network along different paths and reassembled at the receiving end. The phone system uses an entirely different mode of transmission, called circuit switching, in which a circuit is established and held open so that the traffic flows continuously. If you put the phone down and don't speak for 20 seconds, the channel remains open but idle. Packet switch-

"For now, Internet telephony reminds me of the dancing elephant in a circus: One is more impressed that it can dance at all than with the dance itself. But at this stage, teaching the elephant new dances is really what it's all about" (Business Week, 8 January 1995).

ing, the base for the Internet and many other networks used by hordes of devices at the same time, pumps traffic through by filling up the transmission links rather like an assembly line. It is this that makes Internet phone calls choppy, loses parts of words, and introduces pauses. In addition, the traffic flow is one way only. On a phone line, you hear the person at the other end even while you yourself are talking. On the Net, you must take turns. The two of you must also be using the same software.

Internet phone calls may turn out to be an eccentricity or a specialized niche service. However, they do open up interesting possibilities. Already, for instance, they are being used to enhance games played over the Net by people who may be continents apart. It might be used to augment customer service applications or networked training programs. Synchronizing the person to person interaction provided by phones with the richness of multimedia is an intriguing opportunity.

Internet Services The Internet provides several categories of service, with just two—the World Wide Web and electronic mail—dominating both volume of traffic on the Net and public awareness of its capabilities. The Internet does not in itself provide any information, software programs, news, libraries, or any other resource. It only links users to providers of these resources. There are three main modes of linkage, ranging from simply linking to a computer (remote connections) to doing really useful things through it.

The leading players in PCs and Internet services are moving fast to add the missing multimedia tools. Microsoft is developing its Internet Studio technology for use by publishers and other content providers on the Microsoft Network. Netscape is working with Adobe and Macromedia, the two leaders in multimedia software, to integrate their products into its Internet Web

1. *Remote connections.* The Internet is best (and most often) described as a "network of networks," a growing complex of computers across the world, with no structure, extremely limited management and oversight, and very few controls. The core of the Internet, which reflects its origins as a tool for researchers to communicate with computers and with each other is "remote log-in" from any computer on

the Net to any computer for which the user has access privileges. The program for handling this is called Telnet. The user establishes the link by typing "telnet" at the system prompt, then entering "open" and the Internet address of the remote computer to access.

2. *Transferring files.* The main uses of the Internet when it was primarily a researcher's tool were electronic mail and transferring data files from one university computer to another. The FTP service handles file transfers. It is invoked by typing "ftp" and then interacting with the arcane language of the original software operating system on which the Internet was based.

3. *On-line news.* Usenet provides discussion facilities among groups set up with such names as alt.sex.something or alt.politics.somethingelse This is the core of the Net as a political and social force.

Navigational aids, generally termed "browsers," are what makes the Internet easier and easier to use. They disguise the complexity and chaos of the Net and also provide a graphical user interface instead of the command-driven interface.

Intranet *Intranet,* a term that began appearing in the press in late 1995, is a World Wide Web Internet site that uses standard browser software plus standard Web home pages but limits access to within an organization. Intranets are rapidly becoming the network equivalent of the PC explosion in the late 1980s. They solve many of the toughest technical and development problems firms have faced in building information systems over the past four decades. They also have many advantages over public sites in that companies can afford high-speed telecommunications links and can thus exploit the full multimedia opportunities of the Net. In contrast, when they create sites for public access to, say, information about the company and its products, they must avoid com-

browser software. Sun Microsystems' announcement of its Java programming language makes multimedia the sure norm, not the occasional exception, for World Wide Web pages on the Internet.

In the 1980s, an estimated 28,000 for-profit on-line electronic libraries were formed, most of which offer their services via the Internet. One commentator describes this business as one in which 50 million people across the world rent 100 gigabytes of data weekly for $2 to $3 per person per week.

plex graphics, video, and audio because these take a very long time to transmit via today's phone lines and modems.

The Web provides a marvelous architecture for developing small-scale transaction processing services and any size of information access system. First, almost all companies have bought an Internet browser such as Netscape Navigator. Browsers provide an easy to use interface to the Net, which requires no training, is consistent, and combines the visual cues and displays of Windows and Apple Macintosh GUIs—"graphical *user* interfaces." But simple Web applications are far easier to build using the Web's HTML language than by programming with Windows application development tools. The invention of the Java programming language extends HTML to accommodate more complex application needs, which include multimedia. Administering and supporting such Web applications is less complex and expensive than supporting other networks. Finally and most importantly for large organizations, whereas applications have historically been developed for a given technology environment, such as, say, IBM's AS/400 series, Windows 3.11, UNIX, Novell-based networks, Apple PCs and networks, and hundreds of other combinations, the telecommunications of the Net allow any computer to link to any other computer, regardless of brand, and the Web allows any computer to access any page on the Web that it is authorized to use. That gives information systems organizations what they have dreamed of for decades: a platform-independent development base. Building cross-platform applications is at best time-consuming and at worst a nightmare that has cost firms dearly, with many major projects abandoned.

Intranets will not soon, if at all, replace large-scale transaction processing systems. These need telecommunications and computer hardware and software that meet their specific performance and security demands. But that in no way limits intranets to small systems, only that they are not well suited to ones that need instant processing and instant information. One information system specialist who works for Eli Lilly, the pharmaceutical firm, built a system that links 3,000 of the firms' PCs and workstations for a cost of $80,000. He had been struck by just how many different information sources and types could be accessed over the Web and saw the opportunity to bring Lilly's many scattered data bases into the same environment and interface. Previously, selecting sites for clinical trials across 120 countries meant masses of people going through masses of fragmented and scattered data bases of regulatory information, schedules, statistics, and drug submission documents. The intranet allows all these separate data bases to appear as one, via Web pages. Building them in a common data base environment would be totally impractical because they are on a wide range of technical platforms. The payoff has been huge, reducing time, improving coordination, and transforming project management.

The *Business Week* article (26 February 1996) that describes the Lilly intranet gives other examples. Cap Gemini Sogeti, the large international software company, built a system for coordinating projects that has helped halve schedules and speeded up the preparation of sales bids by making all relevant information accessible through a browser, with hypertext links making search easy and helpful. Federal Express has installed Web browsers for use by all its 30,000 employees, which give them access to all internal information resources. This was promoted by the success of its public access Web site which lets customers track their own packages without custom software Fedex has long provided to corporate clients. Ford's intranet was used to coordinate its design centers across the world in the development of the 1996 Taurus. Most of the examples *Business Week* cites are for project coordination and information.

Intranets are also, though, widely used for administrative systems. A large engineering firm, which spent six months trying to implement a time sheet submission and reporting system, abandoned the project. In just two weeks, it built a Web-based system that linked to its administrative data base management software complex. Previously, it was impractical to link all PCs to the data

The Economist estimates (15 January 1996) that companies' installation of servers for Intranets is rapidly overtaking those for the Internet. According to a December 1995 survey by Forrester Research, 22 percent of the Fortune 100 firms are already using an intranet. Some 70 percent of Netscape's sales of its market leading Internet browsers are for use on companies' internal networks. Almost half of expenditures on Internet servers are for intranets.

bases, because there were too many different platforms to which software would need to be "ported." It is impossible to overstate the value of the Web's cross-platform capabilities. It liberates information systems development.

The key component of intranets is the firewall security software and hardware that blocks outside access to the site and the information on it. Security is the weak link in the Internet and one that has to date limited its use for business transactions. Even though security is much improved now, the problem firms will always have to deal with is the widespread knowledge of skilled technical specialists about the technical innards of the Net; too many of them know how to bypass its protections.

There are excellent tools besides those of intranets for coordinating teams streamlining workflows and accessing information. Lotus Notes, for instance, provides a vast range of features for just about every aspect of "groupware." The attraction of the Web is its simplicity of use. It's easier to learn than Notes, which has recently added Internet links, so that firms can have the best of both tools.

All this is not just a matter of formatting Web pages. There are some specialized tools needed for intranet systems development and some specialized jargon, too. Languages like Perl for scripting, hand coding in C or C++, cookies, server holding states, and CGI scripts are examples.

See also HTML; Java; World Wide Web

ISDN   Integrated Services Digital Network (ISDN) is the telecommunications blueprint developed in the 1970s in Europe that was intended to be the base for the public data networks (PDNs) of the next century. PDNs are the computer equivalent of the public voice phone system. The links are "end-to-end" digital. For a variety of reasons, mainly relating to local phone companies' concerns about recovering the investment needed for ISDN, the United States has lagged behind other countries in the deployment of ISDN, the only area of telecommunications where it has not been a leader. In Sweden, for example, it is routine for a household to be able to obtain ISDN lines that are three times faster than those offered in the United States. And ten times easier to get installed; it is only very recently that the phone companies have geared up to provide ISDN as part of its standard services.

They are becoming much more responsive because ISDN is a missing building block in consumer and small business use of on-line multimedia. They are limited to transmission speeds of 1 printed page equivalent (28.8 thousand bits) per second, far too slow and a major and growing source of frustration. The half-page equivalent (14.4 Kb) speed that most PCs use to download information from such services as Prodigy and the Internet is routinely described in pejorative terms by writers in the PC trade press— "like swimming through molasses," for instance. For business users, this is generally not a problem, as their PCs are likely to be directly linked into a local area network, a high-speed digital transmission system that does not require a modem. On-line information will be provided to them through a server, a special-purpose, ultrafast PC-like machine that serves up information on demand. Multimedia servers are one of the fastest growing IT markets.

ISDN is now available in 70 percent of locations in the United States. Demand for installation in homes grew 97 percent in 1994, two to three times the rate of the previous three years. BellSouth reported that demand doubled in 1995. The California growth rate was 200 percent. Equipment costs halved in 1995 as well, and total installation costs are now in the range of $70 to $500, with usage costs around twice that for standard service. Several providers offer unlimited service for $50 to $70 a month.

It's the Internet that has awakened ISDN from its nearly 20-year market slumber. Although they amount to only 10 percent of the population, Internet users are affluent (it's no surprise that

The costs of ISDN vary widely across the country. Bell Atlantic's are toward the low end. They are around $40 for installing the new line, $300 to $500 for purchase of the ISDN terminal adapter, the device needed to link your phone line and PC, and a basic usage fee of around $30 a month. Since ISDN is used mainly to access on-line information services, users tend to stay on line for several hours at a time. Phone companies thus prefer to charge by the minute, as with long-distance calls. Most state regulators are pushing for a flat monthly rate. In 1994, the total number of ISDN lines in place in the United States was just 125,000.

California leads nearly every aspect of ISDN demand and supply) and they typically spend many hours a week on it. ISDN cuts the time to download multimedia by a factor of five to ten. The growing use of ISDN in itself creates growing use of ISDN through the resulting cuts in prices, through creation of the missing critical mass in the marketplace for equipment, and so on.

Java Java is a software tool created by one of the technical leaders in the information technology field, Sun Microsystems. A subset of Java, HotJava makes the World Wide Web fully multimedia. It corresponds to the well-established HTML (Hypertext Markup Language) that firms and individuals routinely use to generate their home pages on the World Wide Web. HTML is simple but limited. In about half an hour, you can build a page that has the following common features: (1) some eye-catching graphic such as a company logo or small photograph of you or your product (it has to be small because of the time involved in downloading graphic images from the net to a PC—if the image is too good, it takes too much time and your target recipient is irritated or has canceled the transfer); (2) text with "hot links," words and phrases that, when the PC mouse moves to and clicks on them, use the hypertext concept of information organization to link to other relevant documents on the Internet; and (3) plenty of documents and images worth linking to, such as product information, contacts, reports, and forms for ordering goods and services.

HTML is limited in its multimedia capabilities. HotJava is not. It is thus rapidly becoming a differentiator among the millions of Web pages which all look very much the same and are very much multimedia in spirit but limited in making use of it. HotJava offers better sound, better graphics, better software support, and overall better exploitation of the Internet opportunity. It also offers something much more far-reaching in its implications: the potential end of the dominance of personal computers as the main vehicle for using the Internet and multimedia resources. The PC is where all the resources you need or may need for an application are stored. It has three main elements: its hardware, its operating system, and the software you use for "applications" such as word processing or graphics. As the range and complexity of PC uses have expanded, so, too, have these three resources. The Microsoft DOS operating system of 1991, which fit on 1 to 3 floppy disks and took up a few megabytes of hard disk storage, now occupies hundreds of megabytes and requires 20 disks. Your word processing software is packed with features you rarely if ever use, but may someday need (hyphenation, formatting algebraic formulae, and printing out your report in any one of a hundred fonts, for instance). You have probably never used well over two-thirds of the software on your hard disk. But you need it there just in case, and, anyway, the providers of the software, such as Microsoft, put it there regardless. Similarly, if you want to use multimedia, you must generally add something to your PC: a sound and video board or a software package, for instance, adding to cost and complexity.

Java signals the emergence of a very different approach to computer use: the stripping away of features stored permanently on the PC in favor of features that are provided as needed through the Internet. Low-cost information appliances can be and are being designed specifically for Internet use via Java. If small and fast software programs can be sent quickly from the Internet to your information appliance, a screen and very simple processor might replace a $1,000 to $4,000 PC with a $500 appliance, opening up home computing to children who may have access to a PC at school but not at home, to kiosks in small stores, and to a whole new mass market. It may also allow large businesses to reduce their costs by allowing them to install more and lower cost machines in more places across the organization that rely on Internet access; these would complement, not replace, PCs that require more functionality and are not Internet-bound.

The official release data for Sun Microsystems' Java software was January 12, 1996. Well before then, 14 of the largest 20 computer hardware and software companies had already signed up for licenses, at $125,000 and up. In March 1996, it released a $100 package targeted at the estimated 300,000 programmers who build applications to run under the Windows operating system. One respected commentator summarizes the implications of Java for Sun as "Java doesn't have to make money for Sun. They just have to break Microsoft's business model."

Java is the first programming language designed to run on a telecommunications network. It generates applets (little applications), which may be spreadsheets, a spelling checker, routines to play a video, games, or data base management tools. There are around 500 Java applications already in place.

An early and successful use of Java is ESPNet SportZone, an Internet site owned jointly by ESPN and one of the cofounders of Microsoft, who is no longer with the company but has several billion dollars of stock gains from it. Subscribers to SportZone download scores of games, images, and video and sound clips. Java is used to update scores on your screen without the full screen's having to be refreshed. The firm plans to add play-by-play broadcasting, again via Java.

Java emerged from prototype use only late in 1995, and it is not yet fully proven in the broader marketplace. Here are some proposed and emerging applications:

- *The Interactive Shopping Network,* which has around 15,000 subscribers, is using Java to build a capability for holding live, interactive auctions on the Net. When it has an odd lot of products or a small quantity of fast-moving items, such as software or office furniture, subscribers will bid against each other for them on line. Its preliminary system can handle 250 simultaneous bidders, with an animated, speaking, on-screen auctioneer.

- *The Internet computer,* being implemented by Oracle and Sun for release sometime in 1997: these will be Internet appliances with around 1 megabyte of memory (versus 4 to 16 needed on today's multimedia PCs) and costing around $500. Oracle demonstrated its device in early 1996. It works.

The sound of "applets" conjures up an image of itsy-bitsy chunks of baby code. But Java is a real programming language that requires skilled programmers. To give the flavor of an applet, here are a few of the over 50 lines of Java code for an applet that randomly changes the colors in a piece of text displayed on the screen:

```
    Thread painter = null
    String text = null
    int delay = 2000;
public void init () (
    text = getAttribute ("text")
```

The end of the applet is exactly as shown below:

```
    public void run () (
            while (painter!=null)
            (           // repaint every delay milliseconds
                    painter.sleep(delay) ;
            )
        )
    )
```

JPEG   The Joint Photographics Expert Group (JPEG) is a well-established standard for compressing the storage size of still images. It takes 3 to 8 seconds to compress the roughly 90 printed page equivalents of data that comprise a professional quality photograph (2.5 Mb). The compression can be as high as 20:1 before the quality of the decompressed image is visibly degraded.

The advantages of reduced storage and transmission time that this compression provides is offset by a reduction in image quality. JPEG is a type of "lossy" (as opposed to "lossless") compression. Lossy compression loses some of the information in the original image. When the image is decompressed, that information cannot be recovered. Studies of human perception show that humans notice changes in brightness (luminance) more than they notice changes in color (chrominance). In compressing an image, JPEG therefore eliminates more chrominance than luminance. A trained eye can see the difference, but displayed on a PC screen, JPEG images look fine.

Jukebox Jukeboxes are optical storage versions of the music jukeboxes in bars and diners where you insert a few quarters to select a record to play. They are used on multimedia networks to store images and, increasingly, on CD-ROMs that are accessed from PCs and workstations. This is often more cost-effective than upgrading those machines with their own CD-ROM drives.

Kiosk Kiosks are multimedia PCs placed in public places, stores, buildings, hospitals, and many other locations. Florsheim, the shoe retailer, reports that sales per store employee went up 20 percent when it introduced kiosks in 550 stores, starting in 1985. The firm's research showed that 35 percent of shoppers walk out without buying anything because they cannot get the size of shoe they want. Its Express Shopper lets customers choose from an electronic catalogue of over 400 styles in 24,000 combinations of size and width. They can see the shoes and order them at the kiosk. Some 30 percent of Florsheim's business is now handled through these new outlets, with the cancellation and return rate being only around 1 percent.

Multimedia kiosks seem most successful for companies that specialize in a narrow range of products and services. A Danish chain of real estate agents increased its market share from 15 to 23 percent directly through kiosks. The average number of houses that customers view before they find the one they want has been halved.

There are many other examples of successful use of kiosks. Earlier ones that were scattered around airports and hotel lobbies were of limited value for several reasons: lack of multimedia restricted them to slow and static information, they lacked speed, they provided very limited information, and they rarely included transaction processing capabilities. All that has changed. Here are typical applications:

- *AT&T's Galileo* kiosk is used at telecommunications trade shows to inform potential customers about ISDN. Its sales reps had been encountering many difficulties in getting their technical message across to the "demand driver type" of business executive who rushes around the exhibits. They needed a way to communicate complex technical material easily and quickly. The multimedia system does that. Instead of throwing information and ideas at people, whether or not they are interested, the attractively packaged interactive Galileo lets them ask their own questions and guide themselves. Galileo cost $30,000 to develop. The hardware costs $2,500. Apart from more effective communication, there are direct savings. Staffing per exhibit booth has been cut from a average of three people to just one.

- *Consumers' Catalog Showroom* stores report a 50 percent increase in accessories purchased with an item like a camera, as a result of installing kiosks. The system allows people to locate specific products by name, shows pictures and videos, and identifies alternatives. When the sale is made, it suggests add-on accessories, such as film, tripods, and filters to go with the camera.

- *Daewoo* saves 5 percent of the price of a car by direct selling, through not having to pay a commission. It has set up concessions in UK stores where customers use a multimedia kiosk to customize their own car, selecting such options as trim, upholstery, and extra equipment. The sales are small, but the investment is still profitable.

In 1994, a riot broke out in Vancouver, Canada, following a Stanley Cup hockey game. The police subpoenaed copies of TV news tapes and used them to develop multimedia kiosks placed in busy locations in the city. Citizens were asked to stop by the kiosks and spend a few minutes to scan several displays of digitized faces, looking for anyone they knew. The police report "a high success rate" in identifying and prosecuting rioters. In the South African election that ended the many decades of apartheid, multimedia ballot boxes played an important role in enfranchising people who would otherwise be unable to vote because of illiteracy.

Knowbot Knowbots are the knowledgeable equivalent of robots. Robots are machines that automate physical work. Knowbots automate knowledge work. They are closely related to agents, self-contained software objects that, for instance, wander around networks looking for the best fare for a specific flight or, in

Microsoft Word 7.0, misspelled words as I enter them on the keyboard.

See also Agent

Laser Disc   Laser discs are an antecedent of CD-ROMs which were developed by Philips. They have not found the mass market Philips expected and remain very much a niche product. The use analog, not digital, recording. They provide excellent-quality video, with a resolution that is around 40 percent more detailed than television broadcasts. That makes them useful for training programs and films, where they provide much higher quality than VHS recordings. Their main niche is for karaoke machines, one of the most pervasive social exports across the world.

Latency   *Latency* is the term used to describe the delay created by intermediate devices as a message moves through a network. It has been aptly described as the silent killer of multimedia networking. To use the most widely accepted metaphor for telecommunications, however fast the transmission speed of an electronic highway, it has toll booths and on-ramps. These are the computer "nodes" that handle the routing of traffic, security, accounting, conversion of messages from one transmission protocol to another, and many other functions. The most basic such combination of computer and communications is the phone system; the local phone exchange, central offices by which your call is moved across country, and the local exchange at the receiving end all add some delay. In a complex business network, a flow of data communications bits may move through hundreds of such nodes, with the total end-to-end latency adding up along the way. (The adoption of the term *latency* seems to reflect its meaning of "the message is there but it'll arrive any time soon"—it's latent, but not visible or having an actual effect.)

For many applications, latency isn't much of a problem (on phone calls, for instance, you rarely notice it), but for multimedia it can be *the* problem. The greater the distance between, say, two teams of engineers working interactively by video, the greater the likely value of multimedia in that interaction. They can talk to each other over a videoconferencing link, share graphical simulations, including image and video. They can work productively and effectively with one group in Germany, another in California, and a third in Brazil. The catch is that all the media they use are time-sensitive but the distances—or rather the nodes along the distances—create latency.

Interactive multimedia collaboration means real-time transmission and real-time response. Processing the multimedia data may demand faster-than-real-time capabilities. Today's business networks were not designed for this, and many aspects of interactive multimedia strain the limits of today's best-practice technology (as opposed to today's best prototype or lab technology). Surveys show, for instance, that routers on local area networks, the key device for managing the flow of traffic from different types of PCs and across different types of LANs, may deliver messages at only 60 to 80 percent of the rated network transmission speed. In other words, though traffic on the highway is moving at 70 mph, the average speed for the whole journey is only 42 mph.

In many instances, such latency does not matter to the user, who may not even notice it. In sending or accessing electronic mail messages, for instance, you can tolerate a few seconds' delay. On transatlantic phone calls, the latency created by the call going up to a satellite 22,800 miles above the earth and back is noticeable, but acceptable; it amounts to 250 ms (one-quarter of a second). Say, though, the call is broken up into two-second units and each one of those has 250 ms of latency. Even though the speech comes through clearly, it is hard to follow it and very frustrating to listen to.

Video is created, transmitted, and organized in very small chunks called "frames." Adding latency is exactly like slowing down a camera. The image becomes flickery and then unwatchable. Here is the impact of latency on the human eye's perception of a video, depending on the speed with which the frames arrive. Television, cinema, and VHS videotapes display 30 frames per second. If the images come through at 10 frames per second, the eye does not see any motion, just a series of snapshots. At 12 to 15, the video looks jerky (this is the standard of most low-end PCs and video games). At 60 to 75 fps (frames per second), the reception is superb; this is the level offered by high-definition digital TV. The limit of human perception is around 90 fps. The best scientific images, including X rays, MRI scans, and astronomical data, may be transmitted at rates as high as 1,000 fps.

Video and audio place different demands on human perceptions. We have more tolerance for jerky images than jittery speech or jerky music. Once a voice transmission begins, it needs to continue without being interrupted or broken up. Consider a phone call, for instance. If the latency is 50 milliseconds or less (50 thousandths of a second), the human ear and mind can't tell it's there. At 600 ms, the speech loses coherence (the drunk slowly explaining the mismeaning of life). For interactive speech and video, network designers typically aim for under 100 ms latency. The best codecs (coder/decoder chips that convert video signals to and from digital form and compress their raw size) create around 30 ms of latency through this processing. Many generate 100 ms.

Most business networks have been built to provide response times—the delay the user sees—of 2 to 5 *seconds*. With multimedia, the user won't see or hear anything if that is the latency. Ways around this are to (1) limit interactive multimedia to local area networks and thus reduce the number of nodes through which the transmission must flow, (2) compress and reduce the data; (3) use "dedicated" links for the interactive application, such as for videoconferencing; or (4) invest in the emerging new generation of telecommunications transmission services called ATM and multimedia network superservers (high-speed nodes). But all of these require a basic rethinking about and redesign of the enterprise network. Even though there are relatively few uses of interactive multimedia across large organizations today, they will surely grow, especially as companies simultaneously emphasize decentralization, global operations, teams, collaboration, and groupware and as they wrestle with the growing need for flexibility, speed, and cross-functional collaboration. Most of them are planning today to use high-speed wide area (as contrasted with local area) networks for transmitting images, for videoconferencing, and for adding more and more interactive uses of multimedia in marketing (including via the Internet), and for training.

Most traffic on their WANs today is conventional transaction processing, electronic mail, communications between local area networks, and access to standard remote data bases. A 1993 survey of Fortune 1000 companies showed the following:

	Firms Currently Using WAN for This	Intended 1998 Users
Videoconferencing	18%	56%
Image processing	16	72
Multimedia traffic	12	64

The expected growth may turn out to be greater than the fairly expansive predictions made here, which look for an increase of 3 to 6 percent. In 1993, there was very little multimedia traffic on WANs because there was very little on PCs or LANs. The predictions in this survey were thus made well before the explosion of multimedia technology that has occurred since then and before the shift of multimedia from being out on the fringe to being in the center. The Internet is fundamentally multimedia in every way, with that fundamental feature being blocked only by the limitation of modems for accessing the Net over standard phone lines.

If you track the growth of non-WAN uses of multimedia since then—CD-ROM, Internet, desktop videoconferencing, kiosks, and video—and assume that WAN growth lags these by two years and grows at half their rate, then the 1993 survey looks conservative. To exploit the opportunity, there's not much time left for business executives and telecommunications planners to get moving on the new generation of WAN designs.

Latency is the silent killer of multimedia networks. Not many business people have ever thought about it. Not many network professionals in traditional WANs know much about it. Multimedia specialists who either have little knowledge of large business telecommunications or work only on PC applications may not know or care about it. There's a big competitive advantage to the organizations that move now to bring all these people together for enterprise multimedia networking.

See also Access Time; ATM; Codec; Frame Rate; ISDN; Local Area Network

Local Area Networks   Local area networks (LANs) are one of the two main building blocks of a firm's telecommunications infrastructure; the other is wide area networks. LANs connect devices locally; that is, within short distances. Over the past 10 years, LANs have been the most innovative element of telecommunications, in terms of technology, competition, and capacity. Only in the mid-1990s has wide area networking begun to match LANs in these three areas.

The typical LAN has around 20 users, and the typical bandwidth is enough to transmit $\frac{1}{4}$ to $1\frac{1}{2}$ printed book equivalents per second (2 to 10 Mbps). This means that, when the network is fully active and all its users are sending and receiving messages, and accessing data from servers, each of them has just 20 printed page equivalents (0.5 Mb) of bandwidth available. That's plenty of capacity for nonmultimedia traffic. Adding multimedia to them can quickly degrade performance, but there are plenty of proven high-speed LAN technologies and products on the market, so that together with data compression, LANs based on 100 Mbps speed (around 12 printed book equivalents) meet most multimedia needs that do not go outside the department, building, or campus the LAN connects.

One example of how multimedia and local area networks are coming together in this way is CNN at Work, the joint venture between Intel and CNN to deliver CNN's TV programs over companies' LANs. The normal broadcast analog (nondigital) signal is received via satellite by a small "dish" (called a VSAT—"*very small aperture terminal*"). This costs under $3,000. The VSAT connects to the LAN. Intel's special-purpose chip technology digitizes the signal and converts it to the most common LAN protocol, called Ethernet, compressing it. The CNN newscast is now just another type of corporate data. It can be received by a PC, displayed in a small window on the screen, and stored on the PC's hard disk. One feature of CNN at Work is that PC users can include key words, such as a company name, currency, or a senator's name. If the digital program includes mention of this alerting tag, the segment is automatically stored on the PC disk.

CNN at Work solves one of the main problems in networked multimedia on LANs: congestion on the network. The transmission is compressed down to around 5 percent of the transmission capacity of Ethernet. Fiber optics will greatly increase the bandwidth available on LANs. The technology is proven and becoming more and more cost-effective. Whereas installing fiber over long distances is expensive and complex, using it on LANs is a routine exercise. The main reason companies have not rushed from cable to fiber is that the many improvements in telecommunications transmission over the past few years have provided enough capacity over the cables already installed to meet the needs of non-multimedia traffic, most obviously electronic mail and access to figures in data bases. That saves them having to invest in the adapters that connect devices to the fiber net, which can be quite expensive for networks that have thousands of PCs and printers on the LAN.

Today, the situation in telecommunications is two sets of extremes: plenty of speed on LANs at low cost but an equal dearth of speed on the public phone system. This means that, if firms are building World Wide Web pages for access by customers, they

Fortune 1000 companies have, on average, 250 sites, most of which will have at least one local area network. Each LAN will have 21 users. When every single PC on a LAN is using a CD-ROM drive, there is no telecommunications traffic on it. If just 6 of them are running interactive digital video (for videoconferencing, for instance), it will be totally congested. High-bandwidth interactive networked multimedia requires a major redesign of the standard business LANs.

can't add too much multimedia that takes a boringly long time to download. When they are using the Web for internal use only, on what are termed "intranets," there are no real boundaries. There is generally plenty of basic speed on the wide area corporate network; firms can now rent it on demand. However, that speed is too often slowed down by the servers that move large multimedia through many nodes, so that it will be a few years before performance on the WAN matches that on LANs. But that's not the case with LANs, which have everything now needed for local networked multimedia. On the very near horizon is the much-heralded ATM technology, already in use but needing some tweaks and bedding down before it is more widely deployed. ATM, which stands for "*a*synchronous *t*ransfer *m*ode," offers bandwidth on demand, at speeds up to many megabits. It's the blueprint for the networks of the late 1990s and beyond. It works with both local and wide area networks.

See also ATM; Intranet, Latency

The high-speed lines that carry the bulk of Internet traffic are the equivalent of interstate highways. Using the Mbone protocol that enables transmission of video and CD-quality audio over the Internet, this is enough for a maximum of 100 simultaneous real-time video sessions.

Mbone   The Mbone is the broadcasting service of the Internet, which reserves part of its capacity for its use. It stands for Multicast Backbone. The Internet World Radio Network broadcasts over the Mbone 24 hours a day into 20 countries. The IETF (Internet Engineering Task Force) holds its quarterly meetings through worldwide videoconferencing using the Mbone. The three-day meetings last 8 hours a day. The Mbone has even been used to broadcast a Rolling Stones concert.

The capacity currently available for such broadcasting is very limited, and, as always with the Internet, there are few mechanisms for coordination, scheduling, and pricing. This is sure to change simply because there is so much interest in and demand for broadcasting, for videoconferencing, radio, concerts, films, and the like.

MCI Driver   MCI driver stands for "*m*ultimedia *c*ommunication *i*nterface" driver and is a software toolkit created in 1990 by

Microsoft and other vendors of multimedia products for programs to control such time-based devices as CD-ROM drives. These have to be carefully synchronized. MCI makes it simple for an application developer to control, for instance, sound volume on screen as a music clip is played, or to program a video to play when a button on the screen is clicked on. It provides all the commands needed to drive standard audio, video, CD-ROM, and tape functions. It is a dominant design which is almost part of the Windows operating system family with which it is designed to work.

The information technology field is fast running out of acronyms. MCI is also, of course, the name of the company in the long-distance telephone industry that is a strong second to AT&T. Similarly, ATM stands for both "*a*utomated *t*eller *m*achine" (banking) and "*a*synchronous *t*ransfer *m*ode," a set of transmission technology and services. So someday we may well see an ad in a telecommunications publication that Megabank, Inc., announced today that it is implementing ATM on its ATM network, with MCI offering the telecommunications links to the machines that have adopted MCI.

Media Processor Media processor is the provisional term for a new type of computer chip specifically designed to handle multimedia. At present, the special-purpose multimedia needs for power, speed, and storage are met by expansion boards and cards, so called because they are a flat piece of, typically, fiberglass onto which is glued a mass of chips and connectors. Media processors will be an integral component of PC innards, working alongside the CPU. The initial versions of these chips are priced between $80 and $150, much less than the cost of the assembly of add-on components in a board.

Multimedia processor chips need to include in their hardware and in the software permanently stored on them the seven basic functions of multimedia processing: video, audio, fax/modem,

"The multimedia PC of today resembles Frankenstein's monster, and it performs just about as well. . . . a multimedia PC is one with a CD-ROM and a hodgepodge of separate add-in cards and various chips that work poorly

with each other to offer limited capabilities." (the CEO of the manufacturer of Mpact, an early multimedia processor)

telephony, two-dimensional graphics, three-dimensional graphics, and videoconferencing.

MPs are an outgrowth of the digital signal processor chips that translate analog signals, such as sound and TV, to digital signals and the reverse. Texas Instruments' media processor is in fact two DSPs on the same chip.

See also Boards and Cards; Digital Signal Processor

Megahertz Megahertz is the most basic measure of both the speed and the information-carrying capacity of hardware and telecommunications. It is the information technology equivalent of horsepower, an indicator of relative power. Megahertz is an electrical signal's cycles per second in millions. Kilohertz is thousands of cycles per second; megahertz, millions; and gigahertz, billions. It's a term like amps or watts which precisely describes a key element of computer chip power (Pentium blazer 200 MHz versus low end 75 MHz), music quality (CD-quality stereo audio at 44.1 KHz versus voice mono at 8 KHz), and wireless telecommunications frequency bands, for instance. You'll see such figures everywhere in ads and discussions of telecommunications. Whether or not this is helpful to most managers is for them to decide. The most useful information these figures provide is just relative ratings. With PCs, the higher the hertz, the shorter the gap between the start and the end of the cycle. For recording, the higher the hertz, the more samples per second and the better the audio quality. With telecommunications, the higher the hertz, the shorter the wavelength and the more tightly focused the signal, plus the more bits transmitted per second.

Microsoft Microsoft dominates the field of personal computers to the same extent IBM once dominated mainframe computers. It now plans to dominate multimedia, by making acquisitions and deals. That's about all that needs to be said.

It's impossible not to respect Microsoft's strengths, which will make it a formidable competitor in any market it targets. But it also faces substantial threats. The main three threats are the Internet, Java, and network computers. The intersection of these three forces puts Microsoft in a reactive stance for the first time in its history. Many other items in this Glossary discuss these and related terms. One point worth highlighting for business managers unfamiliar with the information technology industry is the extent to which Microsoft and Bill Gates seem to generate personal dislike among competitors and customers. There's a real edge in many of the relationships top executives in such firms as Novell, Netscape, Oracle, Sun, and others have with the place. Customers reliant on Microsoft see it as arrogant, even more than IBM was when it ruled the market like Microsoft does now. The information technology press largely admires, respects, and dislikes the firm. It does not have the best of reputations among small companies that supply it.

Microsoft's reputation is primarily for its operating systems, DOS and the Windows family, including 3.1, 3.11, Windows for Workgroups, NT, and 95. There are many experts who criticize all of these for their cumbersome size and complexity, unreliability, or late delivery. I strongly share those views. What constantly strikes me is that what Microsoft is really best at is application software and, above all, multimedia application software. In any given area—spreadsheets (Excel), word processing (Word), graphics presentations (PowerPoint), CD-ROM encyclopedias (Encarta), desktop publishing (Publisher), or multimedia development tools (Visual Basic), it's very rare for Microsoft's product not to have some little extra grace or style. There's a design integrity and a clarity of basic structure that reflect the company's fundamental strength far more than the evolution of the 1970s QDOS that Bill Gates bought (not built). QDOS stood for "quick and dirty operating system." Windows might now stand for slow and difficult disk storage swallower. Many of the attacks on Fortress Gates come from leaders who believe that the complexity of Windows can be

"The Internet makes everything different. You can make any claim you want, however bizarre or ludicrous, that would ordinarily be laughed off the stage, and if you add the mantra 'on the Internet' at the end. . . . You can morph yourself from a typical media clown into a visionary, a prophet, a guru. Nobody pauses to say, 'Huh?'" (Bill Gates in Forbes ASAP, *26 February 1996)*

replaced by the simplicity of networked computing, where the Internet feeds applets written in Java by downloading them as needed over the Internet.

See also Adobe; Apple; Internet; Java; Network Computer; Sun Microsystems; World Wide Web

Microsoft Network Microsoft Network (MSN), is Microsoft's move into on-line information services as part of its aggressive targeting of every area of the consumer personal computer market. This puts it in direct competition with existing services like CompuServe and Prodigy, both of which immediately cut their prices when the venture was announced. The success of Netscape and the growth of the Internet have led to major changes in Microsoft's original strategy for MSN, whose own growth has been stalled because of this. In December 1995, Bill Gates announced a major commitment to the Internet, even making deals with the companies he is competing against who are betting their futures on the Net—most obviously Sun, whose Java programming language offers a frontal challenge to the Windows-Intel conception of PCs as the core of computing, and Netscape, whose Navigator browser has about the same market share of Internet users as Windows does of PC users. Microsoft even made a deal with America Online, one of the primary original targets of MSN.

MSN is included in the Windows 95 software that was launched with the fanfare of a major new movie and was in itself a media event. This is the first PC operating system with built-in access to the Internet and with powerful features hidden from the user, which make communication efficient and fast. Microsoft currently charges for MSN, but its stated goal is to eliminate this once the publishers and advertisers who pay to put their information and services on the network make it self-financing for Microsoft.

Microsoft's strategy rests on its prediction that there will be 100 million PCs in use across the world by the year 2000 and that half of those will be in the home. In July 1995 Bill Gates commented that the most important use of PCs in the future will be for communication. What he was implying, of course, is that he wants that most important use to be communication via Microsoft Network. He added that the real opportunity revealed by the Internet is that on-line communities grow up on it (as they do on America Online, a favorite hangout for many teenagers and people interested in sharing interests, hobbies, and political views). Microsoft's strategy is to build a community of Windows users. Part of the stated goal is to make MSN the best community on the Net and the easiest one to log onto and use.

MSN is far more tailored to multimedia than is the Internet, with sound and animation built into each publisher's and advertiser's offering, which is not automatic with home pages on the Internet. Most media technology today is broadcast-oriented and may come at a high price in terms of phone time to download graphics, animation, and interactive video to the PC. Developments are underway that will mesh Microsoft's software tools, such as Word and Excel, its word processing and spreadsheet software, with standard Internet tools. Users will be able to save a Word document as an HTML Internet file.

It may be some time before the success or failure of MSN becomes apparent. Microsoft's December 1995 shift in strategy to make MSN an Internet gateway seems to mean the end of its plans to be a content carrier. It is phasing down the existing providers and not adding new ones. Even if it sticks to the original strategy, one problem may be that publishers and advertisers will be unwilling to pay fees to access a relatively small group of MSN subscribers when they can set up a Web site on the Internet that anyone can access, including those subscribers. Microsoft is not charging any fees to publishers until it has an active subscriber base of 500,000. Unless there is a rich base of material and offers available only on MSN, there is little reason to join up. However, if it is free, because it is very easy to use and included with Windows 95, there is a strong possibility of its gaining a critical mass.

The single key advantage Microsoft has over other providers of on-line information services is that Microsoft Network is preinstalled—"bundled" with its Windows 95 operating system, of which it sold around 10 million copies within a few weeks of its launch. Notorious for its aggressive, challenging, even harassing, of competitors and widely accused of predatory pricing, marketing, and coercion of suppliers, Microsoft's move led the chairs of the three leading on-line providers, Prodigy, America Online, and CompuServe, who are aggressive in their competition with each other, to write an open letter to Bill Gates, which concludes, "Do the right thing for the industry and millions of consumers. Unbundle Microsoft Network from Windows 95."

Almost by definition, if MSN does reach critical mass, it will become a dominant design. But the Internet is already the dominant design. Microsoft's new strategy adds Internet access to just about every single tool it offers. A valuable by-product of this will be the acceleration of Microsoft's already-fast pace in multimedia. Microsoft has no choice here. To fend off Java, it must make its announced, but not fully ready Internet Studio (originally named Blackbird) even more multimedia than Java, its Internet browser even more so than Navigator, and so on versus all the many firms with strong products and reputations, such as Adobe (another target of Internet Studio).

The growth of intranets—Internet-based applications which can be accessed only from within the firm—offers Microsoft the opportunity to extend its strengths in the business market. It is aiming at displacing Netscape as the provider of server software and at displacing IBM's Lotus Notes as the basis for what is termed "groupware," software for streamlining and coordinating work-flow. If it can establish Internet plus multimedia across its many applications and development tools, it may be able to recapture the momentum it is in serious danger of losing. The key here is that intranets require servers, the computer nodes that handle the flow of data and communication, that link to traditional information systems and other resources. They will use such network operating systems software as Novell's NetWare, IBM's OS/2, and Windows NT. Although Netscape is building a strong presence on these servers for the Web part of the complex link of systems and services, Microsoft offers "industrial-strength" enterprise communications capabilities. So, too, does IBM, which tends to be overlooked in the popular press discussion of networked multimedia.

See also Intranet; Java; Network Appliance; On-Line Information Services

MIDI The *M*usical *I*nstrument *D*igital *I*nterface (MIDI) is a standard for coding music in digital form in an accurate enough reproduction to allow low-cost personal computers to include it in their hardware and software capabilities. It is a compromise between the storage needed to capture music at the ultrahigh-fidelity level musicians demand on the one hand and the costs of storage and devices for data transfer on the other hand. A MIDI file typically requires just 8 printed page equivalents (25 K bytes) for a minute of fairly high quality music. Comparable digital music tools require 40 times this.

MIDI has its own special quirks. The sound of an oboe on an audio compact disc is virtually the same on any CD player, but a MIDI music file can sound like a clarinet on one music synthesizer and a kazoo on another. MIDI music sounds different on each different sound card and is far below CD audio quality. It is one of the primary tools of musicians, however, because of the compact way in which it represents music, the far higher quality and versatility of the professional synthesizers they use, and the power and versatility of the sequencer programs that manipulate digital music in many ways. MIDI provides more music per byte than the CD and acoustic wave audio of PCs, requiring just a kilobyte to code an instrumental passage, where CDs and PCs need a megabyte. MIDI is thus a predominant tool for music composition and production, and CD, far more a tool for its storage and playback.

Modem   Modem, or "*mo*dulator/*dem*odulator," is the hardware device that modulates a digital 0–1 pulse of information to the analog wave form of the electrical signal that carries that information over phone lines. A modem at the receiving end demodulates it.

For multimedia, the modem is the system component that most constrains overall performance. A CD-ROM transfers information at a minimum rate of 150 Kb (thousands of bits per second); the 4× drives have a transfer rate of 600 (double speed, quad speed, 4×, and 6× are industry terms that refer to the multiple of the basic speed). The two main speeds most used on today's modems are 14.4 and 28.8 Kb (1,000 bits per second: $\frac{1}{2}$ to

1 printed page equivalent). There are no developments underway to go much beyond 28.8 Kb, because this speed pushes the practical upper limit of the analog transmission phone lines in place. (Data compression can increase the effective transmission rate, though.) Far greater speeds are available on digital transmission links; these do not require modems, by the very fact that they *are* digital. (They do need an ISDN adapter, which is often called an ISDN modem, even though it's not.) That said, there are many ongoing innovations in modems, which remain the base for home computer use and for use of laptop computers by professionals and businesspeople when they are on the road. DSV modems allow simultaneous transmission of voice and data. This is expected to be widely used for on-line shopping.

One major area of development is cable modems. These convert an analog coaxial cable signal to and from a digital signal, exactly as with an analog phone line. The transfer rate of a cable line is several hundred times faster than phone lines. Cable modems make it practical for in-line information service providers such as America Online and Prodigy to use existing cable television links to greatly improve the speed at which they transfer data to home PCs. Intel's CablePort modem offers speeds of up to 27 book equivalents (27 MB) for downloading (from the host computer to the PC) and 3 page equivalents (96 Kbps) for uploading (PC to host).

Cable modems are currently both expensive (around $500) and based on proprietary (vendor-specific) systems rather than open standards (industry specifications for how different vendors' components can be designed for compatibility). It is not at all clear whether or not they will generate substantial new business for cable operators or if ISDN will gradually, well over 10 years after its introduction, become the main mode of high speed delivery of on-line services. Multimedia demands far faster speeds than the 28.8 kb limit of modem-based services. Demand for multimedia CD-ROM, interactive games, and video-based information may create supply of cable modems. Or demand for cable modems may create supply of multimedia services.

Monitor   Monitors are the unit of a PC that displays information on a screen. Whereas word processing, spreadsheets, and view-graph presentations do not require high-resolution displays, multimedia invariably does, making the choice of monitor an important (and expensive) decision. The typical laptop or desktop computer has a built-in display with a resolution of 640 × 480 pixels. The display will measure between 10 (laptop) and 14 inches (desktop) diagonally (the same way 22- and 31-inch television screens are measured). It will use one of several hardware techniques for managing the display, such as active matrix and dual scan, which vary in their power demands, speed of refreshing the image, and clarity.

These displays lack the crispness, speed, and size of more powerful monitors. The difference between a laptop's display and that of a high-end monitor is like that between a newspaper photograph and one taken by a portrait photographer. A 17-inch monitor displays 30 to 50 percent more information than does the standard 14-inch desktop screen and typically has 1,024 × 768 pixels.

Resolution is not the only measure of monitor quality. The screen needs to be constantly refreshed as the displayed information changes. The faster this is done, the more flicker free it will be. The refresh rate is measured in MHz, with 70 MHz typical. The dot pitch determines the sharpness of the image, rather than its detail (which depends on the number of pixels). The dot pitch is the distance between pixels; the smaller, the better the image, all other things being equal. On a 17-inch screen, 28 millimeters is typical.

Even for word processing, a 17-inch monitor is far more productive than a 14-inch screen, in terms of reduced eye strain, ease of location of items, and simply a better sense of comfort

Innovation in display technology lags well behind other areas of the information technology field. This is reflected in the relative cost per extra inch of screen size. A 14-inch monitor can cost as little as $220 (mid-1996). A 17-inch version is around $700, and a 21-inch, about $1,700—8 times as much as the 14-inch. The quality of display is determined largely by the number of picture elements, or pixels. Today's very best monitors display 4 million pixels on their *screens. To get 35mm film quality requires 16 million. Experimental machines have achieved 8 million. They require many microcomputers running in parallel to process the huge volumes of data involved and to synchronize its transmission and display.*

and well-being. For multimedia, a large monitor is generally essential. Multimedia applications manipulate and display far more information faster than standard uses of PCs. Photographs and videos that are stored in digital form lose their clarity and beauty when displayed on small, low resolution screens. There is growing evidence that large screens are important for worker health, too. A 1992 survey of optometrists reports that 14 percent of all eye examinations were prompted by symptoms of eye strain associated with working at computer screens.

Monitors add expense to the purchase of PC hardware, of course. The 17-inch versions cost between $600 and $1,200, and 21-inch models, $1,400 to $2,500.

See also Color

Morphing   To morph is to combine completely separate images so that they flow together "seamlessly." Morphing is used widely in films. Classic morphing is the way Arnold Schwarzenegger becomes the Terminator in *Terminator II* or Jim Carrey's rubbery body stretches and bends in *The Mask*. In one of Michael Jackson's music videos, 13 boys and girls of different ethnic backgrounds and races were morphed into one another in a segment that lasted over a minute. Morphing is an example of how multimedia technology goes beyond what can be done with the original non-digital medium. It allows you to see things you never saw before.

Hollywood uses morphing for special effects. Businesses will take advantage of it for their TV ads and perhaps in multimedia electronic catalogs. It will also be used in particular types of multimedia training materials.

One very effective use of morphing is that employed by the National Center for Missing and Endangered Children, an agency that helps locate missing children—runaways, those who have been abducted by a parent in a contested divorce case, and others. When one parent successfully takes away a child from the other, it may take years before they are located. By that time, of course, pictures of the then-little four-year-old may give no indication of what the twelve-year-old looks like. The agency uses photographs of the *parents* to "age" the child and produce a photo of what he or she is likely to look like. This use of multimedia creates an artificial reality that is close to the true reality that agency workers need. In one instance, a father took his two-year-old son out of the country. The mother provided family photos which were used to generate an "age progression" of the boy five years later. Posters displaying the updated picture were distributed widely, including to passport offices. When the father returned to Florida to renew his and the boy's passport, the child's face was recognized. The progression was so convincing that the FBI reportedly asked where the NCMEC had gotten Julian's picture.

Morphing offers more than turning a human hunk into the Terminator.

Mosaic   Mosaic is an Internet browser that was once *the* browser. It was designed by a small team of mainly graduate students at the supercomputer research center at the University of Illinois. The invention of the World Wide Web by Tim Berners-Lee, another scientist in another research lab, had fueled immense growth of the useful tools of the Internet. The Mosaic team designed something to make the Web more usable.

The Mosaic developers split up, with one group granted the licensing rights by the university and creating the firm Spyglass and the other, which became Netscape, developing its own browser. A few billions of dollars later, and with many more Internet browsers on the market, the two companies are thriving, with Netscape to date pulling fast and far ahead of everyone else. Spyglass, though, has been more profitable. Its strategy is not to sell directly to the public but to license its product to companies that want to include a browser in their own products; examples are on-line information services. Microsoft is attacking Netscape mainly through its own Microsoft Internet Explorer. It argues that browsers are easily copied and is racing to copy the leaders.

See also HotJava; Netscape; Spyglass

MPC The Multimedia PC Marketing Council, an association of multimedia hardware and software vendors, defined in 1991 a recommended list of *minimum* hardware requirements for multimedia. Its concern was that PC buyers would greatly underestimate the degree of additional speed, power, and storage needed to run multimedia applications compared with what they were used to on desktop PCs. It defined specifications that PC vendors could use to display in ads stating that their products meet the MPC standard.

The 1991 MPC specification was criticized at the time as not being adequately powerful to meet the demands multimedia places on machines, and a new one, MPC2, was defined in 1993. MPC does not carry any real weight in the marketplace, but the differences between MPC1 and MPC2 very clearly illustrate just how quickly the minimum requirement for multimedia changed over a two-year period, to the extent that MPC1 looks quaint and archaic now, just as MPC2 will soon be. Although MPC2 is an acceptable minimum for simple multimedia, such as using CD-ROM, it is already being overtaken by the intense competition in the PC consumer and business marketplace. Machines that exactly meet the MPC2 requirement are close to being toys. In 1993, they would have been high-end machines.

The figures below show the MPC requirements plus those for a typical business system. There are wide variations in products, but these examples capture the pace of change since 1991 (MPC1), 1993 (MPC2), and early 1996 (MPC3).

	MPC1	MPC2	MPC3	Typical Business System ($4,000)
Memory	2 MB RAM	4 MB	8 MB	16 MB
CPU	16 MHz 30386	25 MHz 486SX	75 MHz Pentium	120 MHz Pentium
Hard disk	30 Mb	160 Mb	540 MB	1,200 MB
CD-ROM	150 Kb/sec	300 Kb/sec	600 Kb/sec	600–900 Kb/sec

	MPC1	MPC2	MPC3	Typical Business System ($4,000)
CD-ROM seek time	less than 1 sec	0.4 sec	0.25 sec	.15 sec
Video display	640 × 480 pixels 16 colors	640 × 480	640 × 480	1,280 × 1,024
Sound	8-bit digital	16-bit	16-bit	16-bit

Do these differences really matter? Is it necessary to buy extra memory, speed, and storage and to keep upgrading or replacing systems? Almost surely. Multimedia is made practical only because of parallel, rapid developments in all these areas. As this author can testify, using multimedia on a machine with the capabilities of the typical consumer-oriented system shown above is an irritating process. Yes, the CD-ROM is fast enough for casual browsing and game playing, and, yes, the system can edit photographs and videos reasonably quickly, but any professional user needs so much more—and can get it.

A third standard, MPC3, was issued in mid-1995. If taken seriously, it would make immediately obsolete the entire worldwide installed base of the PCs that met the MPC-2 specification, because it reads, "System Hardware, Minimum Requirements—Processor: 75 Mhz Pentium." This is the first time MPC has specified a product, rather than a capability that can be provided by many vendors' products. The main reason the council made this rather arbitrary specification is that there are no established measures of multimedia hardware performance. Traditional measures of computer performance include mips (millions of instructions per second), Whetstones (speed in handling complex number crunching), and WinMarks (performance in handling office software such as word processing and spreadsheets). Game designers use a range of measures, such as speed of handling transfers of blocks of graphics and millions of pixels rendered on the screen per second.

The MPC in effect concluded that there is as yet no way of

specifying the required performance characteristics of the most basic component of a multimedia system, so, as one member of the council commented, it endorsed what was going to happen anyway, even though a fast 486 processor with added special-purpose digital signal processing chips designed for multimedia outperforms a Pentium-based system in many multimedia applications.

The evolution and almost immediate obsolescence of MPC specifications is in many ways a warning: the technology of multimedia will be in constant flux, and changes in hardware demands are unlikely to slow down.

MPEG   MPEG is a standardized routine for both encoding and decoding full-motion video. This may be done through MPEG hardware add-ons to multimedia PCs, through less expensive but slower software, or through a combination of the two. MPEG is the most widely adopted standard for coding digital information and compressing it to reduce wasted storage space. The Motion Pictures Expert Group, which defined it, is a committee of the International Standards Organization (ISO). ISO plays a major role in developing and publishing standards in the computer and telecommunications field which ensure that devices made by different vendors work together reliably and accurately. MPEG is one such standard, produced by 70 companies working cooperatively as an ISO committee. (Its activities cover many other areas, including certification of quality, electrical devices, and building components.) The companies included Sony, Philips, IBM, PVC, and Apple, vendors with a mutual interest in creating a common format for digital video and avoiding reliance on "proprietary" systems, those that are vendor-specific. Sony's experiences with Betamax, its standard that lost out to VHS, was one factor leading the firms to work together before the new digital technologies spawned a mass of incompatible systems.

MPEG is fairly certain to become the worldwide standard for cable TV compact disc, high-definition television, and direct satellite broadcast. It is an algorithm (mathematical formula) for compressing digital video signals in order to reduce the amount of information to be processed, transmitted, and stored. Data compression is essential to making video manageable. Without it, today's hard disks would be completely unable to store more than a few minutes of video.

The MPEG-1 standard was defined in 1991, and MPEG-2 was completed in 1995. MPEG-1 is designed for limited bandwidth (and hence limited-quality) transmission, such as CD-ROM on a PC. MPEG-2 provides broadcast-TV-level quality and beyond, including HDTV (high-definition TV). Whereas the cinema-quality video that we all want to have on our PCs displays 30 frames or images per second, fooling the eye into seeing continuous, flicker-free motion, software-implemented MPEG-1 displays 24 fps and reduces the images to 325×240 pixels, which is under one-third the size of the typical multimedia PC's screen, with AM radio-level sound. (The image can be expanded to fill the screen through tricks of the multimedia trade that fill in the missing dots, losing some quality.) On a Windows 95-based PC with a 100 Mhz Pentium chip CPU, around 90 percent of the machine's resources are needed to decode the MPEG video. Adding a hardware board that costs over half the price of the PC cuts that to 10 percent, provides a much better image at 30 fps, and provides CD audio quality.

The same standard thus provides very different levels of quality, which is not at all atypical in multimedia. This is apparent in comparing the first PC products offering MPEG-2, targeted to the 1995 Christmas season market. The Windows 95 software-based implementation served up what one commentator summarized as murky movies. IBM's Aptiva used a mix of hardware and software to provide a significant improvement, but at the cost of tying up the PC's processing resources. Compaq took the high road of full hardware decoding.

The MPEG standard-setting process continues at a fast rate. A planned MPEG-3 standard has been bypassed by technology.

The MPEG-4 standard was completed in mid-1996. This compresses video images very tightly, so that they require far less time to transmit over a telecommunications link in comparison with MPEG-2 traffic. Mobile phones will then be able to handle video, for face-to-face conversations. MPEG-4 will begin the extension of multimedia into the field—any field. Likely applications are sending video images from accident scenes to police stations and hospitals, transmitting images for equipment trouble shooting and problem diagnosis, and perhaps catalogue information. More importantly, MPEG-4 will help reduce the traffic jams on the Internet by slimming image and video files.

MPEG-2 looks like it will be the dominant design for video on PCs, and soon just about every ad for multimedia PCs will announce it. There are many variants in how it has been implemented in hardware and software, because a standard defines the "what" but not the "how" of some capability or procedure. MPEG is almost a summary of multimedia today; it addresses its largest challenge—how to provide high-quality video at low storage and transmission cost—uses the main multimedia solution of data compression, and is implemented by manufacturers in many different ways, at many different costs.

MPEG-1 reduced the time needed to send and the storage needed to hold a 90-minute studio-quality video from 243 Mbps (million bits per second) and 160 Gb (billion bytes) to 6 Mbps and 3.6 Gb. I haven't quoted these figures in printed book equivalents because they amount to libraries. All you need to know to see that they are humongous is that a printed book is just 7.5 million bits or approximately 1 million bytes; it is the degree of compression that is so impressive and liberating for multimedia of every type. The MPEG-1 compression is adequate to provide VHS-quality video but not the quality needed for transmission for cable, satellite, and broadcast TV. MPEG-2 provides for this. MPEG-4 will provide for digital HDTV (high-definition television).

See also Data Compression; High-Definition Television

Multimedia Development Multimedia development involves a complex mix of talents rarely found in a single individual. At one level, it is an artistic exercise in design and production, demanding flexibility and careful attention to imaginative display of content. At another level, it is a disciplined application of the structured skills of computer programmers and information systems developers, requiring careful attention to testing, documentation, and scheduling, and imaginative exploitation of an ever-changing technology. At yet another level, it is a highly professional teasing out of content experts' experience and knowledge of the material. It also demands instructional, editorial, or publishing expertise. Put another way, you may need to bring together an art history major, teacher, C++ programmer, video editor, digital musician, CD-ROM technology expert, data base expert, and a few others. What's very apparent from many CD-ROM products is that too often either the skills or leadership are overbalanced in one direction. Programmers' efforts at Web pages are overstructured and dull. Artistic CD-ROMs won't install and are poorly structured, more hyper than media. English majors' on-line manuals and references look like books put on the screen. And so on. It's hard to ensure that a brilliant, strong-willed, and highly analytical multimedia programmer doesn't dominate the brilliant, strong-willed, and highly intuitive content expert.

A book on the development of Microsoft's multimedia edutainment "explorapedia" CD-ROM, *Sendak, I Sing The Body Electric,* spends over 300 pages tracking the project and its personalities. It is too long to hold most managers' interest, but it's well worth skimming through to get a flavor of what's involved in developing what is both an artistic expression and a technical artifact. Above all, what the book makes clear is the vital role of the producer/project manager. That has always been true for information systems development and for book publishers and film directors, but generally they are the design leaders, too. In many multimedia projects, they are more like the film producer: the enabler of designers, the coordinator of talent, the good guy–bad guy supervisor, the negotiator, and the ever-needed still center of what easily becomes a storm.

The stages in a multimedia development project fall into two distinct types of activity, which require a complex collaborative process and blending of skills in content and technical creation.

	Content	Technical
Pre-production	Design concept Storyboarding Scheduling, budgeting Client contracting Staffing and talent pool contracting	Project planning Technology and tools selection Analysis and design
Production	Authoring Gathering images, audio, and video Shooting and recording live video	Programming Unit testing Integration testing
Postproduction	Mixing and editing Finished art and graphics Final audio lay-in	System testing, user acceptance, and feedback testing
Product to market	Master version Distribution Marketing, support	Backup, storage

Multimedia Industry   The multimedia "industry" is an almost-unbounded battleground where companies from many previously well-defined and well-bounded individual industries look to leverage their particular strengths and their original industry's home base to gain a foothold in someone else's territory. The main competitors to date include computer hardware manufacturers, software, broadcast, cable television, entertainment companies, long-distance phone companies, local phone companies, consumer electronics firms, game software producers, publishers, on-line information services, and Internet players.

The *media industry* is the term newspapers use to describe the businesses that make their money from traditional media, print (newspapers, magazines), television (network TV, cable), and films. It's just about impossible to describe the multimedia industry in such a tidy form. There are many players in many industries looking to make, or break, so many deals. In its October 1995 issue, *Vanity Fair* listed the 50 people who "wield influence and billions in the information age." That list provides as good a map as any of the multimedia industry. It will be out of date when this book appears, of course, but that in of itself is of interest. Which companies in this jostling for position will still be on the list in 1997, and which new ones will emerge?

These are the companies and personalities that are driving the multimedia era. Every business manager ought to think through what their plans and success imply for their own firm, in terms of signaling market opportunities and directions, affecting their own businesses, creating demand, or changing the rules of competition. The top 10 on the list are shown below, with my own assessment of their implications for every manager's business.

1. *Rupert Murdoch, News Corporation.* Owner of over 130 newspapers, 24 magazines, many TV stations, the Fox network, plus a new cable network, a major book publishing company, TV and movie studios, and an Internet service owned jointly with MCI, the long-distance phone service provider. Murdoch has always been a risk taker, time and again entering ventures that commentators describe with "This time, he's gone too far and really will go broke." They then turn out to be trailblazing successes. Fox, now the third largest broadcast network, displacing ABC; Sky TV, which has festooned European houses with two-foot wide satellite dishes; and, perhaps most successful of all for the long term, his Star satellite TV network, which covers all the fastest-growing economies of Asia.

Murdoch is very much a traditionalist in his choice of media and a nontraditionalist in his strategies. His most recent ventures target several areas: the business market, satellite distribution of news, software (including Microsoft's) and any communications medium of interest to businesses, and wireless communications.

2. *Bill Gates, Microsoft.* "For all intents and purposes, the entire computer industry." Microsoft's Windows had 80 percent of the worldwide PC business and consumer market even before the release in August 1995 of Windows 95. Gates has targeted multimedia as the company's future in the consumer market; the main innovations in Windows 95 are its implementation of Plug and Play—being able to add such devices as CD-ROM drives, scanners, and printers without having to go through tedious and complex loading of software—and the addition of features specifically for multimedia applications. Microsoft came late into the CD-ROM encyclopedia and education market, but its entries have been outstanding; the main examples are its Encarta encyclopedia and multimedia guide to the National Gallery of Art.

Bill Gates has had an outstanding sense of market direction up to the point where he and his advisers badly misread the implications of the Internet. Microsoft's main rival, Apple, has had the technology vision but a dreadful market sense. Apple has always been committed to multimedia, starting with desktop publishing and moving to provide tools, first for the professional graphics designer and then for the video producer. Gates is moving quickly to lead the consumer multimedia market, repositioning Microsoft across the board to repair its Internet omissions.

The worldwide media industry was estimated to be around $1.3 trillion in 1992. Telecommunications amounted to another $1.2 trillion. Consumer electronics was $1 trillion. The total U.S. economy was around $6 trillion.

3. *Michael Eisner, Disney.* Even though the leader of the world's most dominant entertainment company has a low opinion of the frenzy of alliances and mergers in the components of the emerging multimedia industry, he believes that "In the end, it doesn't matter whether it comes in by cable, telephone lines, computer or satellite. Everyone's going to have to deal with Disney." In buying ABC, Disney positioned itself even more strongly in multimedia. It has always been a "content provider," in the jargon of the media business; now it is an "access provider," too.

4. *Sumner Redstone, Viacom.* Viacom owns Paramount, MTV, and Simon & Schuster, the book publisher most publicly and aggressively looking at multimedia as its future. Viacom has built up content, content, and content.

5. *John Malone, TCI.* "The de facto founder of the cable TV industry" and the maker of deals across the multimedia landscape, including with Microsoft. Malone is betting on cable in the battle of cable versus phone company for the information delivery links to the consumer home. The 1996 telecommunications deregulation of cable and telecommunications is very likely to put TCI in a very strong position. TCI came very close to merging with Bell Atlantic, the local phone service provider that aims to be the leader in video on demand over phone lines and in interactive television. It may still go broke, though.

6. *Gerald Levin, Time Warner.* The world's second-largest media and entertainment company, behind Disney, Time Warner is in every "content" market. Levin believes that cable TV companies will win out over phone companies and sees them becoming the one-stop supplier of banking, shopping, data

communications, entertainment, phone service—the full digital mall. (When this book was written, his position atop this complex company with a history of Byzantine management clashes and palace coups looked fragile. Time Warner's debt of $16 billion makes the pole very wobbly.)

7. *Andy Grove, Intel.* Intel has moved in parallel with Microsoft and has the same 80 percent market share worldwide. It seems very likely that this tacit partnership will diverge somewhat as Intel looks to break away from its products' capabilities being underexploited because of the limits of today's software. Chip technology improves by a factor of at least 30 percent a year, however measured. Improvement in operating systems and application software is evolutionary and, at most, half that rate. Intel sees multimedia and telecommunications hardware as the growth opportunity of the coming century and will move toward the software providers who best support and enhance the power of chip technology.

8. *Steven Spielberg.* The first film producer to exploit the new multimedia technology for animation and special effects, in *Jurassic Park,* following in a tradition begun by George Lucas in *Star Wars.* Spielberg has made multimedia basic to film production.

9. *David Geffen, music.* Geffen is one of the few on the *Vanity Fair* list who is not looking outside his industry home base, Hollywood, although he has made deals with computer and TV companies. He is a partner with Steven Spielberg and Bill Gates in the DreamWorks venture.

10. *Robert Allen, long-distance phone service.* Allen is chairman of AT&T and most noted for a pretty disastrous

"The lords of entertainment, information and technology have continued to stake their billions—on brands, on distribution technology, on software, and on thin air." (Vanity Fair, September 1995)

acquisition of NCR in the early 1990s and more recently for the much-praised breakup of AT&T into separate businesses, selling off NCR and carrying out a massive layoff of staff.

Several points emerge from the full list of 50. One is how many of the firms are close to a market that temperamentally, intellectually, and attitudinally many business managers are not: teenagers. Another is that many of the companies were founded less than 20 years ago and already constitute a new establishment.

It's pretty well known what these (so far) successful high-risk rollers see as the future. Almost all are aiming at a combination of markets, filling gaps through acquisitions and alliances (and not backing away from a few double-crosses as pragmatism and opportunism move them). The prime targets are entertainment, with news and sports as parallel drivers. News services help establish brands and presence, especially within businesses. That's why Microsoft has made deals with NBC and others; CNN, Bloomberg, Reuters, and many others have set up business news channels; and Murdoch has bought rights to just about every sports broadcast he can, including pricing those for the NFL away from CBS, revolutionizing the structure of rugby and monopolizing cricket. Phone and cable television companies cannot afford not to be positioned as strong players in each other's markets; whoever owns the consumer's preferred multimedia delivery route into the home owns the growth opportunity. Traditional content providers have to ensure that their products are not made obsolescent by multimedia. That, of course, is why so many publishers are racing into CD-ROMs.

Meanwhile, a whole new community of start up firms with many nonwhite, nonmale, nonestablishment risk takers is emerging. New York's Silicon Alley and London's Soho are where the artists with technical skills are piggybacking on digital video and entertainment tools and services in the way that many scientists piggybacked on the Internet to create such firms as Netscape and

Spyglass. One reason for every manager to learn about multimedia is simply because that's where the business will be for decades. The earlier personal computer revolution was small scale in comparison with the combination of entertainment and phones.

See also Cable Television; Entertainment; Publishing

Multimedia Market   The sheer scale of the potential multimedia market is as immense as the ambitions of those spending billions to capture a share of it. Obviously, many of those billions will be wasted as the future turns out not be what was predicted. Interactive television has already devoured huge resources, still with no evidence of consumer demand. On-line information services are indeed growing rapidly, but it has taken decades for them to reach critical mass, and they have been overtaken by Internet. But there is a bright rainbow and there are pots of gold at its end for being there when demand takes off, as it surely will within five years.

Various surveys estimate the approximate size of the consumer markets that are seen as the main target of opportunity for multimedia at the following (1994 estimates):

- Catalogue shopping: $51 billion.
- Broadcast advertising: $27 billion.
- Home video: $12 billion.
- Information services: $9 billion.
- Records, tapes, and CDs: $8 billion.
- Movie theaters: $5 billion.
- Video games: $5 billion.
- Cable advertising: $2 billion.
- Value-added telecommunications networks: $2 billion.
- Electronic messaging: $1 billion.
- Videoconferencing: $0.2 billion.

Given that a billion dollars is just $4 per capita and under $10 per household, most of these markets are both small and will boom if only a fraction of the multimedia markets reach $50 per household.

The market for high-speed telecommunications for multimedia applications is very large and very differentiated. Here are estimates of the various physical locations where the communications links will open up the multimedia opportunity:

	Number (in thousands)	Obvious Opportunities
Owned homes	58,000	Games, entertainment, interactive TV
Apartment rentals	33,000	Games, entertainment, interactive TV
Retail outlets	20,000	Kiosks, Internet, 3-D ads
Factories	371	Virtual reality and 3-D simulations, multimedia training
Day care centers	249	Edutainment
Medical practices	225	Telemedicine, kiosks, virtual reality
K–12 schools	110	Education, edutainment
Dental practices	105	Simulation
Pharmacies	60	Kiosks
Libraries	29	Everything informational
Colleges and universities	28	Videoconferencing, information, interactive learning
University-associated research labs	13	Simulation, virtual reality
Commercial research labs	11	Simulation, virtual reality
Hospitals	6	Kiosks, 3-D simulation

These figures don't include offices, banks, customer service centers, airports, and many other locations.

National Information Infrastructure   The National Information Infrastructure (NII) is the blueprint first presented under the aegis of Vice President Albert Gore as the basis for a digital telecommunications line into every household in the United States that can be used for interactive applications. The NII is the intended practical embodiment of the much-overused phrase "Information Superhighway." The starting point is to ensure that there are, first, links to all schools, clinics, libraries, and hospitals and then to extend the infrastructure to the home, with phone companies, cable television providers, and many others competing to capture either what link goes into the home or what entertainment, shopping and banking services, on-line information, and publications get delivered.

The NII initiative has generated some studies, policies, and appointments, but it has been overtaken by two powerful forces, the Internet as the de facto world communication infrastructure and complete deregulation of telecommunications. The market is driving the infrastructure now.

See also Information Superhighway

Netscape   Netscape is the most widely used software for accessing and navigating the Internet and for hiding its complexity and morass of codes and conventions behind a simple-to-use interface. Many investors are quite literally betting on its becoming a dominant design for business and consumer interactions with the Net. When the company went public in 1995, it was a small firm with sales of almost zero in 1994 and no profits up until then. Its stock issue raised over $2 billion. At one point on the day of issue, its shares were selling at twice the launch price. Since then, the price has gone way up and way down and way up again.

The reason for the launch success was that Netscape had already become the leading software browser for the Internet. It has grown in both popularity and features since then and looks like it will be the dominant design for Internet use for at least the next five years. (The key here is "looks like"—in 1991, no one would have predicted Netscape's rise, because there was nothing to rise from or to, with the Internet largely confined to university use. Netscape was a surprise and there are sure to be future surprises out in the software world.)

Netscape may or may not turn out to be the Microsoft of the Internet. It deserves to be, in that every move it has made to date has combined technical innovation, product innovation, and improved ease of use. Its strategy has been to give away its browser or to sell at rock bottom prices in order to build market share and then make money from software it sells to companies for use on their Web servers, the computers that are the home for Home pages. Some 70 percent of its sales are now to companies. It's a little like giving away books in order to own the library management market. Netscape is also benefiting from the rapid move of companies toward using browsers and Web servers to create intranets, Web sites that can be accessed only from within the company. Intranets solve many historical problems of developing easy-to-use information systems, integrating data resources scattered across many locations and building applications that are "platform-independent"; that is, that will run on computers that use different hardware, operating systems and networks.

As Netscape has evolved its Navigator product, it has moved well beyond being a browser. It's really an Internet operating system and the base for telecommunications-centered applications just as, and equivalent in impact to, Microsoft Windows as an Intel chip operating system and the base for personal computer–centered applications. Netscape is thus the focus for many efforts to exploit the Internet as a multimedia and business resource, including ensuring security for financial transactions made over it and efforts to displace the Wintel (Windows and Intel) hold on the direction of the marketplace.

Netscape's perceived vulnerability, often loudly highlighted by Wintel executives, is that browsers are relatively easy to build and that Microsoft's plan to offer Internet features free of charge in all its well-established operating systems software, its Microsoft

Network and its application software will give it a massive edge in the long run. In addition, it is more strongly positioned on the server computers that are the main building blocks of corporate networks, though Netscape is rapidly building its presence here. Microsoft is targeting its Windows NT product to corporate networks and its Microsoft Internet Explorer to the overall Internet market, consumer and business.

Netscape's strengths create Microsoft's new vulnerability. They include Navigator's already being by far the dominant design on the Internet, which is the dominant design for the use of computers and communications; having plenty of allies moving to cut off Microsoft, especially Sun Microsystems, whose Java programming language offers a serious threat to PCs as the basis for computer use; and its product being based on a technical design that is as elegant as Windows is clumsy and cumbersome.

Java is the multimedia network programming language. It's already in Netscape Navigator. Microsoft has licensed Java—"just another programming language" according to Bill Gates, but will also compete with it. Gates comments that Microsoft's browser market share is just about zero "but that will improve." Will Windows become just a PC operating system that is mainly of importance for handling all the chores for the real network operating system, Navigator, or will Microsoft erode Netscape's advantage by embedding Internet features in everything it offers?

See also Intranet; Java; Network Computer; Web Browser; World Wide Web

Network Computers Network computers, "Lite computers," and Internet appliances are an entirely new thrust in the combination of computer hardware and telecommunications. This trend moves in a direction opposite to PCs, by minimizing the software needed to access information on the Internet or to run software programs and hence directly reducing the hardware power—and cost—required to run that software efficiently. PCs rely on increasingly complex software that directly adds to their cost by adding to the hardware and disk storage needed for efficient operations. Windows 95, for instance, requires around 4 to 8 times as much computer memory as a 1991 machine configured for multimedia, and 20 or more times the disk storage, to run efficiently. It needs raw CPU power that is hundreds of times faster. Surfing the Internet is now done on $2,000 multimedia machines that are very complex to learn and run. Only a fraction of the operating system is needed for the functions most people run. Although more and more individuals access the Internet, they largely do it at work, where the powerful PC is.

Network computers are the priority target of opportunity for a wide range of hardware and software companies, Internet service and software providers, and consumer electronics firms. They aim at providing simple and low cost machines in the $500 price range that meet the needs of most users. It's very unclear how successful they will be, but there are powerful arguments to support their becoming a new mainstream in consumer use of the Internet and of standard applications like word processing. There are equally powerful arguments in support of PCs now being unstoppable. In mid-1995, PCs did indeed look unassailable as the gateway into the Internet, the base for educational and consumer use of home computers, and the victorious domain of Intel in hardware and Microsoft in software. Over a very short period of time, the business press began to publish a number of thoughtful articles describing the move by such companies as Sun Microsystems, Philips, Sony, Apple, Thomson Consumer Electronics (the leading maker of TVs and VCRs in North America), and others to change this. Each builds on its own strengths but shares a single assumption: the Internet is driving PC use, not the other way round. They want to build an Internet appliance. They want to let the network handle the software, not the PC operating system.

Sun Microsystems is one of the leaders in the new direction away from the PC to the network. In the late 1980s, Sun coined the phrase "The network is the computer" to capture its distinc-

"Make sure that the Encarta program is looking for the compact disk on the correct drive. Check that ENCARTA.INI file in the WINDOWS directory. The section called (94Options) should have an entry called 'BookPath.' The path should be set to the \encycl95\ directory on the drive that your CD-ROM appears as." (extract from the manual for Microsoft's CD-ROM encyclopedia)

tive strategy, which has been to build high performance computer workstations designed for a telecommunications network environment where, over time, low cost transmission and high bandwidth would make telecommunications power as cheap and available as computer chip power has been for a decade. In 1995, it released its Java software, a new programming language for developing network-based software. Instead of the software needed to handle the accessing, processing, and display of, say, a high-resolution image residing in the PC, a Java-based $500 box gets the software from the network for the few seconds it is needed.

Oracle, one of the leaders in data base management software, joined with Sun. Its chief executive, not noted for lack of certainty and aggression, has stated many times that the PC is "a ridiculously over-engineered device—a mainframe on the desktop." Oracle and Sun announced that they will have Internet appliances on the market in 1997 which will be targeted at the Internet. Netscape, the leader in Internet software has from the start been committed to Java. The software on the appliances will be limited to very simple standard functions, such as basic word processing. More complex functions will be handled through "applets," baby applications provided over the Net. These will do just one thing well. If you need a spelling checker, for instance, click on the relevant icon and down it comes. You don't tie up space on your hard disk with a permanent copy, nor do your PC's Windows operating system and word processing software incur overhead in incorporating it.

"Make sure the power cord is plugged in." (a Sharp VCR manual, on how to deal with a videotape that won't play)

Philips's approach is similar to Sun's and Oracle's. In October, 1995, its CD-Online subsidiary began marketing a $150 Internet starter kit, which provides the modem, cables, and software to turn a Philips CD-i player (interactive CD-ROM) into a Web browser that uses a standard TV. Thomson Consumer Electronics, a firm with a million households using its remote controls and on screen menus for satellite TV programs, is adding Internet modems. An executive commented that "we think about what 100 million households really want. We aim for the lowest product cost and the easiest interface," which, of course, is dirt cheap TVs and zappers. Apple introduced a Pippin machine in 1996 that plugs into a television, following its relaunch of its personal digital assistant computer, Newton. Both of these run scaled-down software and scaled-up Internet features. Sony and the Japanese firm that makes the 3DO game machine have both set up Internet subsidiaries. The distinguishing features of Sony, 3DO, Philips, and Thomson is that, though they may not understand software and PCs well, they certainly understand consumer electronics, consumers, and how to make money on very tiny margins through volume, manufacturing, and marketing. This is muscle—technical, marketing, financial, and development muscle.

The single factor most key to the success of networked computers in this context is bandwidth—high-speed telecommunications into the home, whether via satellite, cable, or phone. Without that, the cost and slowness of today's phone lines means that the PC, not the network, must do the work. Sun's "the network is the computer" was explicitly a belief that just as computing power has become almost free, so, too, would telecommunications. It has become just that, but it will take billions of dollars and decades before the new technology is fully deployed. That is why Andy Grove, the head of Intel, calls the idea of high-speed bandwidth into every home "a fantasy" and why Microsoft dismisses its potential new rivals because "anything that happens in a box on your desk is always going to be faster than something that happens down a wire."

No one knows where the Lite machine approach will lead. Commentators expect coexistence with PCs rather than defeat of or by them. A senior manager at a leading market research firm, IDC, points to the large consumer market that does not yet have any Internet device and adds that banks, among others, will give them away: sign up for home banking and you get the Internet box for nothing. "Once that happens, it becomes a completely

Sony's PlayStation sells for $299. If you add a standard 14-inch monitor display to that, the price is still below $500, the target for all the players racing to offer the Internet appliance as the displacer of "Wintel," the standard Microsoft Windows–Intel combination that is the foundation of personal computers.

According to the head of Oracle, the large data base management system provider, the personal computer is a "ridiculously overengineered device—a mainframe on the desk."

different PC industry. If I were Compaq, IBM or Dell, I'd be thinking hard about that" (*Business Week,* 13 November 1995).

The largest and single most important impact of Internet appliances may and should be to bring Internet access into the homes of children whose parents cannot afford a multimedia PC, even at $1,200. It is widely agreed that PC skills are now important for learning and for preparation for college and career. It's equally widely agreed that the Internet is a superb resource for learning. In that case, making it practical for parents to buy an Internet appliance for the same cost as a color TV ought in itself to be a reason to encourage this new direction.

Large companies are likely adopters of network computers, because they already have the high-speed telecommunications links in place that are essential to "network-centric" computing and are facing higher and higher costs for PC support and administration. There is also both strong support for Java in most companies and a widespread dislike of Microsoft among many of the most innovative information systems developers. By the time this book appears, at least the following network appliances will be on the market: Oracle's system, demonstrated in Japan in 1996; Apple's Pippin, being positioned initially as a game machine by the Japanese company that gave the world the Mighty Morphin Power Rangers; and a number of interactive set-top boxes that are powerful PCs in themselves. Thomson, the company that makes most of the cable and satellite television descramblers, is just one of the firms that have independently placed billion-dollar orders for a million such boxes; they include a modem, obviously for Internet access.

This is going to be fun. Here is the Microsoft-versus-the-world battle, or is it Microsoft versus the Internet?

See also Java; Microsoft; Netscape; World Wide Web

Newspaper   Newspapers are user-friendly, portable personal information assistants that sell for a fraction of what they cost to produce. They are also easy to browse and tear out articles from, recyclable, and great for lighting fires. They have crosswords, film listings, and comics. This makes them multifunctional.

They are not multimedia, though. Every feature they provide is, over time, one that networks can provide more of. The on-line version of *USA Today* can be kept more up to date than the daily printed paper. The *London Times* can be accessed from anywhere in the world, whereas at best even in the United States you will find yesterday's edition, and then only at major international airports and major hotels. Old issues of the *Wall Street Journal* can be searched to find information. The advertisements that on-line newspapers can offer include video, graphics and audio, not static, poor resolution photos. Newspaper readership is dropping even without on-line competition. Around half of people under 20 do not read one. CNN is the news source of record, more than the *New York Times*.

Most major newspaper firms are moving on-line if only to test the waters or ensure that they are not left behind. They can get royalties from such information services as America Online and are experimenting with how to get subscription fees from Internet users, with no success to date. The *Washington Post* has designed its own distinctive on-line version called Digital Ink; distinctive doesn't mean worth paying for. The biggest single problems for newspaper publishers are that users of the Internet get so much free that they don't see why they should pay a subscription fee for an on-line paper that offers less in many ways than a 35 cent physical one. Without subscription fees, papers must make their money the way they always have, through advertising, but companies don't yet see what they get from ads on the Internet.

Future success of multimedia means the slow death of traditional newspapers. The success of the Internet as a multimedia network means a fast death. The advantages listed at the start of this Glossary entry will remain formidable, but it seems almost certain that the newspaper industry as a whole will become more and more marginal in the same way that national television

The Sunday edition of the New York Times *contains around 400 pages, of which 26 percent is editorial text; 11 percent, editorial illustrations; 40 percent, display ads; and 22 percent, text ads. The total digital equivalent of this is 3.2 megabytes of editorial text, 77 Mb of illustrations, 102 Mb of display ads, and 2.8 Mb of text ads.*

network news has been marginalized by CNN, local news programs, and specialized financial, sports, and entertainment news services.

See also Advertising on the Internet; Publisher

Object   Objects are self-contained units of computer data or code that can be linked together. This may sound trivial, but making object-oriented tools work has been for two decades the driving force of innovation in the information technology field. The underlying principles are well established: to transform the development and use of IT by moving away from computer programs, which have to be specified in meticulous detail with all the information and procedures included inside them, toward less distinction between programs and data. Objects are reusable units which make programs and data equivalent, and data mean any type of multimedia. Objects contain everything they need to "know" to carry out their task; this is called "encapsulation." They also "know" where they fit in a hierarchy of classes; this is called "inheritance." When an object called "car" is defined as part of the class called "vehicles," it inherits knowledge that, as a vehicle, it has a speed and wheels. The object called "move" can be given a message to "move car at a speed of 25 mph," for instance. Obviously, it's all more complex than "see Spot run" (an object message in itself)—objects enable you to insert a picture, edit a photograph, and click on a button for help. Application developers build new objects and link to existing ones through message formats that have an arcane language of their own, including object link embedding. Object-oriented development tools include specialized programming languages, with names like C++, Visual Basic, and Java. Object data bases store multimedia "things"—a video clip, a document, a frame of animation. Prior to the object era, applications had to be handcrafted, and you needed separate program code to display or reduce the size of an image versus doing the same with a paragraph of text. The tools of object-oriented development are in widespread use, but they are still rapidly evolving. We are still a long way from the application-as-assembly-of-Lego-blocks that is their goal. Developers still have to hand craft code so that users of the application can move the cursor, click, "drop and drag," and play with multimedia animations, videos, and the like.

Objects are the future of software and the result of now-rapid progress after many years of research, slow embodiment of that learning in practical tools, and slower relearning of the art to shift to the new style of system development. At present, though, there is little standardization among software developers and providers of leading software packages and operating systems. There are four main standards. Until they converge, objects will not be able to link to each other without consideration of the details of their software; achieving this linkage is the entire aim of object-based development methods. The four that must and surely will over time come to some degree of "interoperability" are:

1. *DCE (Distributed Computing Environment)*. DCE is a vendor-independent standard created by the Open Software Foundation and is well established among vendors offering products that run on all the main computer operating systems.

2. *CORBA (Common Object Request Broker Architecture)* is another vendor-independent standard that goes beyond what DCE offers in terms of how objects talk to objects and in how they are built. (DCE is not as purist in its conformance with the main principles of object-oriented methods.)

3. *OpenDoc* is yet another venture by a consortium that includes most of Microsoft's main rivals, such as IBM, Apple, Lotus, Novell, and Adobe. It is based on IBM's implementation of objects.

4. Microsoft has its own *OLE (Object Linking and Embedding)* and other developments underway.

The last item is, as so often in computing today, the key one. Microsoft goes its own way while others try to preempt it while at the same time having to conform to the Microsoft standard. OLE is in place and dominates business software development for PCs. Thousands of software application vendors are implementing their products in OLE and may be reluctant or unable to duplicate their work to support the other standards. Most leading vendors provide connectivity between CORBA and OLE.

At one level, object standard jostling is of minimal concern to most business managers. PC software users already benefit greatly from today's object tools. Being able to move files on an Apple from one folder to another, throw them into the trash, and move icons all over the screen comes from Apple's early leadership in objects, a leadership that helped make them the foundation of modern computing. In Microsoft's suite of software packages called Office, it is objects that allow you to insert a paragraph of text from Word into a PowerPoint graphics presentation, and the reverse.

The reasons for business managers to be aware of the importance of objects is twofold: (1) the tools of object thinking, design, and programming are the core of tomorrow's business applications and the only hope for attaining the dramatic improvements in speed and quality of software development that have been lacking for 30 years now, a lack that impedes effective use of ever-improving hardware and software operating system capabilities; and (2) multimedia is object-based; images, videos, sound clips, animation, and the like are objects. Thus using objects in customer service, marketing, transaction, and training systems means designing software through object tools. In both of these instances, companies need the tools and the skills. It's worth asking what your own firm's plans, expertise, and needs are here.

Shown below are just a few of the information-rich corporate systems needed *today* but largely excluded from the firm's non-multimedia, nonobject information technology base. On the left of the list are the computer data elements that are generally in that base, and on the right are the missing multimedia components that are now just as practical to include as an integral part of the knowledge base. They are equivalent to each other in terms of ease of access, retrieval, and display. They are not add-ons or different data but together build a shared resource; only object methods make it practical to build and integrate them all.

Today's Data Elements	Multimedia Needs
Designs and engineering diagrams created using CAD/CAM systems	Voice annotations, video simulation, simulation
Product information and specifications	Animation and video
Marketing data and documentation	Images, videos, sound clips, animation, 3-D
Customer data	Recordings of customer interviews, photos, authorized signatures
Word-processed requirement statements for design of information systems and design of products and services	Interviews with potential users, simulations, animation of work flows, samples of documents
Customer satisfaction and quality ratings	Recorded interviews, animated reports and statistics
On-line manuals	Interactive video, image, sound, search
Electronic mail	Voice annotation, video clips, pictures inserted into the mail
Financial data and reports	Animation, voice comments, publicity pictures, ads, video or audio clips from senior management
Insurance claims data	Photographs of goods

If all of these can be organized as self-contained objects, and messages passed from word processing software through what are termed "*a*pplication *p*rogram *i*nterfaces" (API) and "*r*emote *p*rocedure *c*alls" (RPC), and if those APIs, objects, and RPCs are organized in a standardized manner so that they can be used by designers of entirely different software packages (Lotus, Microsoft, Adobe), then they can be combined on an as-needed basis. These are all big "ifs," but this is the evolving mainstream of software engineering, and progress is, if not as rapid as needed, ongoing and sustained.

Object Linking and Embedding Object Linking and Embedding is Microsoft's set of software principles and tools to make it easy to move objects (things) between applications. It isn't something that you ever need to know about. That's what makes it both important and key to PC multimedia. Developers of software applications use it and related tools to build the links that let you, for instance, "drag and drop" an audio clip into a word-processed document or insert a picture in a spreadsheet.

On-Line Information Services On-line information services allow PC users to dial a local phone number through a modem that connects them to a variety of information resources, electronic mail and related communications services, interactive interest groups, the Internet, ads, and shopping catalogues. The three main on-line providers for consumers are Prodigy, CompuServe, and America Online (AOL), with the Microsoft Network introduced in 1995 in direct competition with them. There are many other, more specialized business and communications services, such as Dow Jones, Financial Times, Delphi (for business news and search of publications), Lexis (legal data bases), and Nexis (news).

The basics of all these services are the same:

- *PC software* that manages all communications and downloading of information. This software is easy to use and menu-based; that is, you select from a menu of options by clicking on the relevant "icon"—a small picture.

It's taken a long time for on-line information service providers to build their subscriber base. In 1993, there were around 4 million users generating revenues of $530 million. In the same year, sales of home video games were $12 billion. By 1996, the 4 million users had doubled, but the Internet had at least 20 million users.

- *Dial-up access* by most subscribers to a local phone number via a PC modem. The speeds are slow by computer telecommunications standards, typically (1/2 to 1 printed page equivalent per second (14.4 to 28.8 kbps), the practical upper limit on today's nondigital phone lines.

- *"Content,"* the term for all the stuff people can get access to: data bases, games, catalogues, pictures, news items, magazines, guides to films and restaurants.

- *Internet connections,* with the service increasingly becoming a giant Internet site.

The entire emerging multimedia industry is a scramble by network providers to ensure content and vice versa. The on-line services run the risk of being caught in the middle, with the Internet displacing them in terms of both access and content; that is, more and more people will link to the Net directly, and more and more companies and individuals will put their content on the Net. A plurality though not majority of industry experts see AOL and others on a gentle slide to oblivion. That may be so, but they do have a number of strengths, including coherence versus the beguiling and bewildering chaos of the Internet, marketing skills versus the Net's antimarketing roots, and customer help lines. They also seem to have strong customer loyalty. They may well become rather like the television industry, with CompuServe and Prodigy analogous to NBC, CBS, and ABC, and AOL the upstart equivalent of Fox. The Internet is then the cable industry. It's worth keeping in mind that even though the major broadcasters are losing viewers, the hit programs, like *NYPD, ER,* and *Friends,* are all on their channels.

A comparison of on-line services published in *PC Magazine* in October 1995 rated America Online the overall best. Here is a summary of the services it listed. Although the figures have changed somewhat, the picture is still broadly the same a year later.

John Burks, author of Where the Wild Things Are, *provides a cautionary note about the age of on-line information, everywhere for everyone. Too much data is nothing new, and chaos—the distinguishing feature of the Internet—has a bad reputation as an organizer. Time magazine, for instance, was founded explicitly to collect, sort and package "too much information" for people who lacked the time to edit it for themselves. Without guidance, we get lost, on-line or off-line. "If you're confused now, just wait until you have a thousand times more information available, a thousand times faster. Without guidance, such as that provided by an editorial staff and the magazine it produces, we may simply end up with a thousand more ways to be even more confused."*

	America Online	CompuServe	Delphi	Genie	Microsoft Network	Prodigy
Number of "points of presence"	166	420	0.01	600+	n/a	325
Percentage of these with access via:						
ISDN (64 kbps)	0.00	0.00	0.00	0.00	All	4
28.8 kbps	All	16	0.00	0.00	All	10
14.4 kbps	All	300	All	All	All	All
Leased line connection option?	No	Yes	No	Yes	No	Yes
TCP/IP direct connection option?	No	Yes	Boston	Yes	Yes	No
Internet features:						
Archie and FTP (search and retrieve files from anywhere on Net)	Yes	Yes	Yes	Yes	Yes	Yes
Telnet/login (Internet core telecommunications)	No	Yes	Yes	Y/N	No	No
Gopher/Veronica (search engines)	Yes	Yes	Yes	Gopher	Yes	Yes
Web	Yes	Yes	Text only	Text only	Yes	Yes
Web page construction/hosting	Yes	Yes	Yes	No	No	Yes
Fees:						
Basic monthly fee and number of hours included in price	$9.95 (5)	$9.95 (5)	$20 (20)	$8.95 (4)	$19.95 (20)	$9.95 (5)
Monthly Internet fee (20 hours)	$54.20	$24.95	$20.00	$83.50	$19.95	$30.00

On-Line Shopping Mall   On-line shopping malls are marketplaces that display goods and services on a network, provide information interactively, and process orders. There are two main contenders for the potential new mass marketplace this will surely create: the Internet and interactive TV. Although progress to date for both of these has been fragmented and very limited, it seems close to certain that each will eventually achieve the same success as catalogue retailing and TV home shopping. That won't challenge the broad base of retailing—Wal-Mart and Victoria's Secret will still be there—but it will erode the weak players little by little. That's already happening, in that the time we all spend trolling physical malls is around 40 percent less than a decade ago. However, physical shopping is still the norm. In 1995, U.S. retail sales were over $1.5 trillion. On-line sales were around $250 million. Companies that advertised their products on the Internet found that, although thousands of people may have accessed their Web page for information, follow-on sales were insignificant.

There *are* successes, however. For instance, IndustryNet On-line Marketplace acts as a link between 3,000 suppliers of technical and engineering products and services and over 100,000 buyers. Its 1994 sales were $10 million. These tripled in 1995. Those of Virtual Vineyards, which offers carefully selected wines accompanied by a moderated on-line forum, wine glossary, and question-and-answer facility, doubled every month from its launch in early 1995. Other malls whose sales seem likely to reach critical mass include Dealernet, which matches buyer to seller for cars and parts, the Online Computer Market, and Bibliobytes, for book lovers.

Generally, on-line selling and marketing call for a shift in thinking, not the creation of electronic ads. An example of such a shift is Onsale, a company that combines auctions with home shopping. Its founder claims that, within three months of starting up on the Internet, Onsale had cracked the key to making money on the Internet, selling over 100 Apple Macintosh machines in one day, for instance. Onsale explicitly targets the main affluent community of the Internet: "high-income males in technical professions." It offers tickets to Tom Petty concerts and posters from James Bond films along with Macs. It sells goods through a Dutch auction. Identical items—such as Macs—go on sale simultaneously. The lowest successful bid for one of them becomes the price for all of them. Goods are then marked down until all are sold. There is thus some skill involved in bidding and in timing bids. Bidders are informed by electronic mail if their offer is topped. The initials, city, and state of the current highest bidder are displayed with the item for sale. Onsale's CEO sees as the key to its success the creation of a sense of community as a form of entertainment, which he uses to sell goods.

There are no reliable figures on on-line sales revenues. The ten largest mail order retailers in 1995 were:

	Sales in Billions	Category
J. C. Penney	$3.8	General
Dell	3.4	Computer
Gateway 2000	2.6	Computer
DEC Direct	2.0	Computer
Spiegel	1.7	General
Fingerhut	1.7	General
Land's End	1.0	Apparel
IBM	1.0	Computer
L. L. Bean	.8	Apparel
Micro Warehouse	.8	Computer

These are small fry compared with the top ten retailers overall. Multiply their sales by 20 to get the Wal-Marts and the Sears. One feature of the mail order successes that is relevant to multimedia used for customer interaction is the profusion of computer firms, such as Dell and Gateway.

Operating System   Operating systems (OS) determine a computer's capabilities: the type and size of programs it can run, the amount of memory space it can directly reference and use, and how well it exploits the performance of the central processing unit hardware that it runs on. The bulk of today's PC applications, such as word processing, run under 16-bit OS, but these are already obsolescent. The most recent evolution of personal computers, which began in the 1970s with the Apple II and early IBM PCs, involved 32-bit operating systems (OS). They provide a massive increase in capability, which both opens up new multimedia applications and makes existing ones run faster; 32-bit operating systems and multimedia are essentially equivalent in this regard.

An 8-bit operating system works with 8 bits of information at a time, a 16-bit works with 16, a 32-bit with 32, and so on—64-bit operating systems will be in wide use by 1998. There's a direct relationship here with how many bits the hardware central processing can handle at a time. The operating system can't work with more bits at once than the CPU works with. The new generation of standard CPU chips are 32-bit ones. Each new generation also adds innovations in how the chips function, so that the 32-bit Pentium, for instance, is very different in every way from its predecessor, the 32-bit 486 CPU. The progress from 8 to 16 to 32 bits is not just a matter of doubling the speed of the system, size of programs that can run under the operating system, or efficiency. The relationship is closer to squaring raw hardware capability than doubling it in many instances.

For example, because 8 bits can represent numbers up to 256 (2^8), that's the largest single number an 8-bit CPU can deal with in one instruction cycle. (Program instructions and the data needed to carry them out flow through the CPU a cycle at a time, with each cycle like the tick of a clock. The figure you see in computer ads that state that the vendor's machine uses an Intel 40486/50 MHz chip means it is a 16-bit chip whose cycle clock runs at 50 million electrical cycles per second. A Pentium 150 Mhz chip is a 32-bit CPU whose cycle is 150 million "ticks" per second.) The 16-bit chips can directly handle numbers up to 65,536 (2^{16}), and 32-bit ones, over 4 billion (2^{32}). An 8-bit system can directly represent only 256 colors and shades or the pitch of a voice or note of music, but 32 bits is enough to represent more than the entire palette of observable hues and shades. Today's top-of-the-line systems use 24 bits, allowing for 16.77 million distinct colors. An 8-bit CPU could not handle 24-bit color representations, nor could it handle 16-bit digital coding of video and audio. In addition, it would not process data fast enough to meet the computational needs of the programs that manage color, video, and audio, except at the level found in such 8-bit game machines as Nintendo's delightful Game Boy.

32-bit chips differ from 16-bit ones primarily in their impact on multimedia. If all you use a PC for is word processing and spreadsheets, there's not too much you will gain from the extra size and speed. A 16-bit machine is fully adequate for handling text, numbers, and color graphics (you have 65,000 colors available), and the speed of your application depends mainly on how fast you type and think, which is much slower than the computer can process those inputs. You want faster disk drives more than faster computation.

If, though, you wish to use your PC for interactive desktop videoconferencing, access to CD-ROM reference manuals and interactive training modules, or desktop publishing using high-quality photographic images, then moving from a 16-bit to a 32-bit operating system on a 32-bit machine is like going from a Game Boy to a PC. This is not the same as just moving from a machine with a 16-bit CPU to one with 32 bits. The operating system has to be specifically designed to exploit the extra capabilities. That involves years of software development. It's why Microsoft has so aggressively marketed, first, its Windows NT and, most recently, Windows 95.

Most PCs currently use 16-bit operating systems, but 32-bit systems are coming into widespread use. Windows 95 uses 32 bits (although its initial version still contained computer code designed to run on 16-bit hardware CPUs). Windows NT, the operating system targeted to businesses, is a 32-bit OS. IBM's OS/2, the loser in the battle for the mass market desktop won by Microsoft's Windows series of products, has been for several years building a strong niche in such areas as banking, where its 32-bit capabilities provide the industrial-strength robustness and reliability needed to handle very complex transaction processing. High-performance workstations like those offered by Sun Microsystems are 32-bit hardware and software. Now, the race is on for

64-bit operating systems, with Digital Equipment showing in its ads all the other companies that in late 1995 were prototyping or announcing future 64-bit products; DEC had it then, of course.

It is CPU technology that paces the basics of computer performance. *Operating systems pace how well that performance can be translated into practical tools; their development lags that of chips and almost certainly always will.* Chip technology is driven by research, engineering, and manufacturing. (The main obstacle to innovation is now the huge capital investment needed to launch a new generation of chips. A manufacturing plant costs well over $1 billion to build. Motorola's next plant is budgeted at $2.4 billion.)

Once a chip gets into production, the provider benefits from economies of scale and from routinization of manufacturing. Software development, by contrast, remains very much a labor-intensive craft, with if anything diseconomies of scale; small teams outperform large ones. Brilliant project managers who can coordinate, cajole, crisis-manage, and motivate teams of teams may grow old quickly but can mesh the efforts of these special and often eccentric talents. Average project managers with large teams of average talents are likely to end up with inadequate products delivered late, if at all.

Operating systems development demands the very best talents. All large scale software development is complex, with cost and budget overruns more frequent than not. The development of an entirely new operating system such as Windows NT, the dominant design for business use of PCs, and Windows 95, the most probable dominant design for home use, is the most complex and costly. It involves focused, intricate, even quirky, thinking; meticulous attention to tiny details of logic; almost nonstop resolution of a host of design problems; understanding of the human context of the system's use; and, above all, coordination of the many elements of the development project, which will involve up to hundreds of teams, so that all the individual pieces fit together.

Because exactly how people use their PC varies as widely as

The power of chips and software come together to provide the new base for multimedia PCs through 32-bit chips and 32-bit operating systems. They are not fully in step, though. When Intel brought its Pentium Power CPU chip to market towards the end of 1995, Microsoft's Windows 95 operating system had already been launched (August 1995). Intel had assumed that Windows 95 would be a true 32-bit system, but parts of the program code are written for a 16-bit CPU, negating the extra capabilities of the Pentium Power. As a result, it will be mid-1997 before the new chip will appear in consumer PCs. Businesses are already using 32-bit operating systems, such as Windows NT and IBM's OS/2 so that they will quickly see benefits from Pentium Power.

how they spend the rest of their day, and because they will also choose from a wide range of software, printers, hardware, CD-ROM drives, and communications tools to install on it, it is impossible for the developers of an operating system to test every possible combination of inputs and interactions among these many hardware and software elements, all of which have to work together perfectly, speedily and in precise synchronization. The process of testing a new operating system thus typically takes far more time and effort than its design and programming. Microsoft gave away or sold at a token price many thousands of the "beta" version of Windows 95 (*beta testing* is the industry term for testing a product in real use after alpha testing has identified and removed as many glitches as the developers can locate), so that those users could surface the thousands of tiny details that reveal problems. That process took well over a year to complete. When released onto the market, thousands more problems cropped up within the first months; that is typical for any new operating system.

Both business and consumer users of a new operating system will have files, programs, and equipment that they are unwilling, or simply cannot afford, to throw away or convert to the new environment. For that reason, Microsoft, for instance, has to ensure that Windows NT and 95 are "backward compatible"; that, say, its existing versions of Word, Excel, and PowerPoint, designed for a 16-bit environment, still work on the new 32-bit OS. It must also collaborate closely with competitors that have a large PC customer base, to provide them with the information they must have both to enhance their products and again to ensure backward compatibility; the user community demands this and will not switch to a new OS unless it can be sure its existing investment in software is preserved.

All this involves many technical compromises, and the emerging operating system will not fully exploit the advantages of the new generation chips around which it is built. It makes the choice, implementation, and support of an operating system, and the timing of the move to upgrade from one to the next generation, the most important strategic information technology decision in any organization with a large investment in existing systems. Many firms that wrestled with the move from the now venerable DOS to Windows were cautious about moving on to the far more complex Windows NT. Many individuals knowledgeable about PCs resisted Microsoft's advertising campaign that urged all PC owners to rush to install Windows 95 the day it came out, because they wanted to wait until it is stable. Many people who did install either of the two main series of PC 32-bit operating systems, IBM's OS/2 and OS/2 Warp, and Windows NT and 95, were astonished by the dozens of floppy disks needed to load it and the amount of time it took. DOS was originally on a single disk.

The shift in any large organization to a new generation of OS in a networked environment is fraught with technical challenges and pitfalls. It's worth keeping in mind that, even as Windows 95 arrived, DOS is still the workhorse on which it is built, with many of the limitations of DOS remaining a constraint on basic design features.

Paper Paper very often determines the quality of graphics, more so than the computer that creates them in some instances.

Most personal computers are used primarily to author paper. Whether it's a word processor, a page layout program, a spreadsheet, a financial analysis program, a graphics program, or a presentation package, people are primarily generating the same media that society has used for hundreds of years. They're really composing pages on their computers and printing pages on their printer. People do not use computers effectively to communicate. They use fax machines. They use telephones to communicate. They use mail systems to communicate very simple, technically oriented messages. But when it comes to really fulfilling the requirements of systematically moving away from a paper-based to a computer-based information flow, computers

The invention of the printing press is popularly believed to have been a key event in history, which created the concept of media. In fact, it had only limited impact for a century. The real breakthrough was the invention of paper-making machines. Gutenberg's printer was the equivalent of the computer, and paper makers were the equivalent of PCs, democratizing print.

The "paperless" office and word processing increased, not decreased, the use of paper, as it became easy to make a few changes to a document and print out a new copy, always working from a "clean" version. Paper consumption in the United States grew by 50 percent between 1980 and 1993.

In the same manner, multimedia both replaces paper and makes paper even more important.

have failed miserably. (John Warnock, president of Adobe, in a company brochure)

That may be an overstatement, but it highlights one of the main limitations of many World Wide Web pages, CD-ROMs, and supposedly interactive training programs—they are really just electronic versions of paper. If it looks like paper, reads like paper, is mainly text on the screen with a few pictures, is just a passive catalogue or corporate PR handout, and adds nothing paper doesn't offer, why bother? Managers should keep this in mind when they review multimedia ideas and samples. Fundamentally, what makes multimedia effective in knowledge management, customer interaction, natural decision input, and shared understanding is its interactive nature.

See also Interactivity

Pen Computing Pen computing is an as-yet relatively immature technology that does, though, have many specialized uses. Instead of a keyboard or mouse, you communicate with the computer by writing with a pen-like device whose electronic "ink" is a wireless signal that activates the phosphors (from which the term *phosphorescent* comes) on the display screen when you put pressure on that screen. At its simplest level, pen computing records what you write. When UPS delivers a package to you, you sign for it on the screen of a "palmtop" portable computer. The $25 parking ticket neatly tucked under your windshield wipers is likely to have been generated by the friendly public servant's writing it on a similar device, which prints it out—and now has a record that can be entered into the city's main computer system, so that you will now be a permanent part of its revenue-seeking activities until you pay up. Here, the pen is used to make ticks on an electronic form or to add the signature of a parking meter attendant.

The far more complex level of pen computing has seen rapid progress but still leaves an immense gap between promise and performance, expectations and delivery. This involves a computer recognizing handwriting and converting it to printed characters. As a writer, I'd love to be able to use the medium most natural to me, my handwriting, and the tool I most prefer, a heavy, felt-tipped Waterman pen. I wish I could use an electronic pen. Unfortunately, even the best handwriting recognition hardware and software is very limited. You need to write slowly and carefully. If I have trouble at times recognizing my own handwriting, a computer is definitely going to have fits. The early personal digital assistants that incorporated pen input had comic fits. Apple's Newton became the butt of jokes and, worse, of Gary Trudeau in his Doonesbury cartoons. "Happy Birthday" could come out as "Ribby 81dittydap," "Burpy Bistdog," or the like. In fact, however, the performance of Newton, once "trained" in your handwriting, was pretty good—well, prilly goop.

There are many areas of everyday life in which handwriting is a key enabler or blockage of knowledge management and shared understanding. Think back to when you were in high school or college. Would you rather Professor Drone write equations in his chalked scrawl on the blackboard and you try to interpret and copy down the scrawl, or that he or she write in electronic ink on a screen, with the software converting it to a legible display?

This level of capability is coming, though not soon. Handwriting recognition rests on the same principles of all multimedia: digitization and pixels. That's why it is sure to come. It rests on very complex software; that's why it won't come soon. What you "write" on the screen switches pixels on; that means the message is then in digital form. The software trick is to work out where each character begins and ends; with cursive writing, this can be extremely hard. (This is why some of the form-based pen systems are effective and efficient; they require you to keep each character separate and placed in a box on the form.) The software then needs to "pattern-match" the character, estimating whether it is most likely an m, w, or n, for instance. This is not a routine matter and has occupied many of the top researchers in computer science and artificial intelligence for decades. The best systems now have a success rate of over 95 percent.

Pentium   The Pentium is Intel's 1995 premium computer chip, followed quickly by 1996's premium Pentium Power. The next generation of Intel innovations is close to introduction. Pentium is the successor to the 486 chip that is the CPU of standard PCs. What is distinctive about the Pentium is not just the extra speed and power it offers—those are routine features of any new generation of chip—but Intel's strategy in developing, introducing, and superseding it all within a two-year period. More than any other company in history, Intel thrives on not making anywhere near the money it could on its products, but instead deliberately making them obsolete as fast as it can, letting customers and competitors know what its next pinnacle is. The Pentium is already being replaced by the Pentium Power, originally named the P6. The Pentium Power's successor is well into the development process.

The Pentium is thus part of the long evolution of Intel products. It is, though, in some ways the end of Intel's main path of innovation in that it is the last chip that does not *include in the chip itself* hardware instructions *specifically* designed for multimedia. Every new Intel chip now has more impact on multimedia than on more standard applications such as word processing and spreadsheets. Whereas Pentium and its forebears handled multimedia through add-on "boards" and "cards," such as graphics accelerators, sound boards, and video cards, its progeny will handle multimedia faster and cheaper in the CPU.

Intel will face competitors targeting the multimedia opportunity, too. They mimic the Pentium (copying it is illegal). NexGen announced a chip in late 1995 that dedicates 300,000 of its 6 million transistors to multimedia, roughly one-fifth of the surface of the die. It includes 10 to 20 multimedia instructions for handling data compression, "motion estimation," and pixel manipulation. NexGen has been acquired by AMD, Intel's main competitor, one that has made Intel's life a little more stressful but has not as yet threatened its success.

The Pentium cost around $1.5 billion to get into production, with the three-year design costs adding up to $200 million. Each Pentium production plant costs $1 to $1.5 billion with equipment adding up to half of this. The plants have a life of just two years; after that, the equipment is out of date and must be replaced. To recover the cost of investment, plants must be run 24 hours a day, every day of the year. The average cost to produce a Pentium chip is $50, of which only $10 is for chemicals, labor, and materials; the rest is engineering, design, and amortization of capital equipment. The $50 chip sells for an average of $300, with prices going up to $500 for the fastest chips, which are more expensive to produce.

What does this mean for business managers who never see the chips that drive the PCs their firms use? It's an alerting signal that the pace of change in the general-purpose chips that have driven innovation in the use of PCs will be matched or exceeded in multimedia hardware.

See also Intel; Pentium Power

Pentium Power The Pentium Power computer chip is the most recent (but in no way the last) of Intel's microcomputer chips which are the hardware core of PCs (the operating system is the software core). These chips comprise the central processing unit that determines the basic performance of a system. The Pentium Power is explicitly designed for the emerging world of multimedia and is a 32-bit chip.

The relative speed of the latest generations of chips is indicated by its clock speed, measured in megahertz. Technically, this means the cycles per second of the electrical signal that drives it. Basically, the chip processes its instructions and transfers data a cycle at a time, like a pianist playing notes to the tick of a metronome. The Pentium and its successors are designed to get ahead of the beat and process instructions in parallel, so that megahertz

The Pentium Power is the first general purpose chip designed to handle multimedia, including continuous speech recognition, 3-D graphics, and full-screen video.

is the horsepower of a car; it tells you raw engine power, but not road performance. Thus, a low end Pentium runs at 75 MHz; 486 chips, the predecessors to the Pentium, offered reasonable multimedia performance at 50 MHz.

The Pentium Power came on the market in the same year the Pentium was first becoming widely available on PCs, with articles in early 1996 raving about the new "blazing," "screaming," and "power-driving" 133 MHz Pentium-based machines. The Pentium Power makes those look slow. Intel's ads compare it with the Pentium, using a widely used industry benchmark called SPECint92. A 110 MHz Pentium scores 122 on the scale, a 120 MHz Pentium 140 and the Pentium Power, over 200. The specific applications Intel highlights for the Pentium Power are 3-D image processing and rendering, real-time speech recognition, smooth-motion software-only videoconferencing, and advanced multimedia digital sound capability. It signals its aggressive shift from its main market stronghold of PCs into the business world of servers by also highlighting as priority applications sophisticated financial modeling, intensive transaction processing, and extensive multi-dimensional databases.

Intel's advertising now mildly states that servers, workstations, and PCs based on the Pentium Power "are now being developed" and *designed from the ground up,* instead of with its earlier line of 386, 46, and Pentium chips each fitting in to the existing PC hardware architecture. This means that Intel is moving from computing to multimedia as its base.

See also Intel; Media Processor; Network Computer

Photo CD   Photo CD is a product announced by Kodak in 1992 that offered consumers the opportunity to bring their family photographs into a store and have them copied onto CD-ROMs, so that they could be displayed on TVs. The idea was not successful. What was a consumer bust did, though, become a hit with professionals in the graphic arts communities, especially European newspapers. It provided a tool that solved several of their biggest "prepress" problems, by making scanning and image storage and retrieval less expensive and less cumbersome. In early 1995, Kodak shifted its company direction and provided a new focus for its somewhat floundering innovation, announcing that it would offer a royalty-free license for ImagePac, the image format used on Photo CDs (there is a one time charge of $1,000). Kodak's aim is to establish Photo CD as the standard for displaying images on PC screens, rather than the original target of TV screens.

Photo CD has been successfully used in businesses from its inception. When Perko, Inc., a Florida manufacturer of marine products, wanted to create a catalogue with more than 800 full-color images, it aimed at keeping the cost the same as its old two-color catalogue. Using a Photo CD service cost Perko $8 per scan of a photo negative, versus $40 to $60 per scan for the drum scanners that are the base of the publishing industry (drum scanners work on exactly the same principle as photocopying machines, with the image being transferred to a rotating drum). This saved Perko $50,000 and produced a far better-quality image, as well as archiving the images on CD-ROM. Organizations that want such archives are using Photo CD. Harvard University, for instance, carried out a major project in 1995 that required imaging over 100,000 posters. Now that the cost of devices for creating CD-ROMs from original images has dropped to under $2,000, from $250,000 four years ago, individual authors are using the Photo CD software and CD-R hardware (CD-R stands for "*CD recorder*" and contrasts with CD-ROM, which is "*CD read-only memory*"). For instance, the publisher of *Passage to Vietnam* relied on it to scan and organize the hundreds of thousands of photos he and a team of 70 photographers shot on location in Vietnam.

Although professionals agree that the quality of Photo CD is not as high as that produced by the best drum scanners, neither is the price, which is seven to ten times lower for color that is good enough for most needs. As the price of CD-R drops, as it will because it exploits the same 30 to 40 percent annual improve-

Kodak's Photo CD standard is a bridge from the world of film to that of digital processing. If just 1 percent of the photos processed each year were to be transferred to CD-ROM, they would fill up 5 million disks. That adds up to a lot of film for Kodak—and a lot of disks for Kodak, too.

ment in chip technology as the rest of the information technology industry, the differential will grow. In addition, low-price software will open up the market to just about everyone who has a multimedia PC. Adobe, whose software dominates the graphic arts field, is working closely with Kodak to support Photo CD. It takes around eight hours to "burn" 100 high-resolution images onto a disc using CD-R. The resulting photos have far less degradation in color and clarity than those stored on hard disk (which mainly use the data compression standard called JPEG to store them in TIFF files—these are the ones on your PC with the file name suffix .TIF).

While it is not at all certain that Photo CD will become the dominant design Kodak is hoping for, the odds are good. What this means for business multimedia is that it is now time to add to PC applications the same attention to quality of image that word processing has enabled in quality of text. Graphic arts are now moving from the professional to anyone, with the investment cost for training materials, marketing brochures, internal manuals, and reports being around $4,000 for extra PC hardware, the same for a high quality laser printer, $1,000 for software, and a less tangible cost for finding, growing, and keeping a PC-savvy employee with a good eye.

Photographs   Multimedia photographs are ones that are stored in digital form; that is, they are composed of discrete tiny dots of color, each stored as a number representing the exact shade. This is literally in contrast to the continuous chemical surface of standard photographs. This means that, although digital photos are of high enough quality for display on computer screens, use in CD-ROMs, training materials, and desktop published reports, they are inferior to the best nondigital professional ones. In addition, the storage and transmission demands lead to many compromises in quality, by reducing the resolution of the digital image in terms of the number of dots per inch of the camera input, scanned image, screen display, or printed copy (the devices

"What has happened over the years is that photographers have become technicians. They used to be the creative force in the industry; people would come up to them as if they were gods and ask them 'We want you to come up with an idea.' Photographers have become documenters of a client's image and have lost much of their creative control. They've given it away. The Macintosh will allow them to get the control back, if they choose to take it. . . . Multimedia will be very different from traditional photography because the

handling the photo may not be able to provide high resolution in any case). There are many aspects of light, exposure, smoothness of texture, and color accuracy that make a Hasselblad and Nikon in the hands of a pro a far superior photo.

This difference in quality is typical of multimedia. Analog television is far better than today's digital video. The advantage of digital multimedia is in the editing, storage, manipulation, repackaging, and other uses of the stored image. In addition, in many instances, the customer can't tell the difference in quality or doesn't care. Thus, for example, a VHS tape played on your VCR is far inferior to a broadcast analog television signal.

See also Copyright

Pixel A pixel is a picture element, one of the tiny dots that form a display on a computer screen. A typical screen is composed of 640 rows and 480 columns of pixels. Each pixel contains a given amount of red, green and blue. A black pixel has none of these, whereas a white one has the maximum amount of each color. The smaller the size of each pixel and the more pixels per row and column, the higher the resolution of the display—and the greater the amount of storage required. The pixel color is represented as a number. The more bits that are used to code it, the more colors that can be represented: 8-bit color provides 256 different hues, 24-bit color provides billions. Here are the raw numbers of bits required for two displays:

- A laptop computer screen with 8-bit color: $640 \times 480 \times 8 = 2.46$ million.
- A high-resolution monitor used for professional multimedia development: $1,024 \times 768 \times 24 = 18.9$ million.

The difference is a factor of eight—just for a PC screen. (The difference is reduced through data compression.)

See also Monitor

traditional photographer will become a production house. . . . The photographer has a better eye. The photographer has been working with light and understands depth and shadow and concept and texture much better than a technician who sits at a machine. The photographer has never been able to control these tools until now." (an interview with a top photographer, in Multimedia Demystified)

Plug and Play is high on Microsoft's agenda because it is now the most visible remaining difference between an Apple Macintosh and a PC. It has always been easy to add scanners, printers, and multimedia hardware devices to a Mac. It has always been hard to do so with a PC.

Plug and Play   Plug and Play is Microsoft's implementation of one of the most urgently needed features of operating systems: the ability of the software to recognize exactly which devices, such as printers, CD-ROM drives, and video cards, are attached to the PC it operates on.

The first implementation of Plug and Play is Microsoft's Windows 95. Microsoft is the originator of the term. The operating system accesses a data base of information on 1,600 devices that need to be plugged into a PC in order for it to play them. The system automatically detects a new device connected to the PC. It then sends a message to the device (if, of course, it is switched on), requesting its unique manufacturer's identification number. It looks up the number in its data base and sets up the data needed to register as being part of the PC user's systems. It then loads the software "drivers" without which the operating system cannot interact with the device.

Device drivers are the curse of PCs that belie promises of user friendliness. Plug and Play is needed and overdue.

See also Device Driver; Installation of Multimedia Devices

Multimedia is obviously being driven by many nonbusiness forces. A senior executive in a European media company told Communications Week *in September 1995 that "The first wave of real multimedia will be come from three areas—sex, games, and sex games." A member of the Internet Engineering Task Force adds that you need 3 to 5 gbps (billions of bits per second) to perform*

Pornography   Just as one of the main social impacts of VCRs was to make blue movies respectable among people who would never dream of going to see one in a cinema, pornography has been one of the growth areas of multimedia, especially over the Internet. Four of the ten most widely read on-line newsgroups on the Internet network news, according to a survey made at the end of 1994, are about sex. The disproportionate number of regular Internet users who are young male college students may explain much of this. On-line pornography is as sure to find a market as pornographic videos have in rental stores. Still, although blue movies dominated early sales of home videotapes, it's Disney animation films that now command the market.

Cyberporn is causing both debate, conflict, and legislation. A minor German official pressured CompuServe to block discussion groups where sexual material was involved—blocking it across the world, not just for German users—to protect Bavarian minors. Congress added to the Telecommunications Act of 1996 a requirement that all television sets sold in the future include the V-chip that parents can program to block violent and obscene material. Wild claims are made and largely refuted about the scale of and ease of access to obscene pictures and discussion groups. Women face electronic harassment on the Internet.

Prodigy Prodigy is the most consumer-oriented of the four main on-line commercial information services (the others being CompuServe, America Online, and Delphi). It has around 2.7 million subscribers, many of whom make only limited use of it or just try it out for the month of free use that it offers through disks given away with PCs and magazines. Its screens are full of ads and "come-on" offers. It has a wide range of services, including many targeted at children, electronic mail, and excellent sports coverage. There is an hourly surcharge for many of its premium items, including stock market reports and interactive games.

Publishing Publishing is obviously an industry that will at some point be transformed by multimedia. The only question is whether that point will be 5 years from now, 10, or 30. Most publishers of newspapers, books, and magazines seem to believe that little will happen over the next 5 years that will substantially affect the sales and profits of their existing products, but that the changes will be substantial within 10 years. Meanwhile, they are positioning, experimenting, and to some extent complaining. They complain frequently about efforts to change legislation that limits the rights of telephone companies to enter or create electronic publishing markets.

Businesses everywhere have an interest in the pace and direction of multimedia publishing, for the obvious reason that they advertise widely in magazines and newspapers and on television. Is it worth their while now? When will it be, and why? The biggest single difficulty in predicting the take-off of on-line multimedia

reasonable sex over the Internet, meaning that this is the telecommunications bandwidth needed for full tactile body suits and virtual reality helmets; that 28.8 kbps (thousands of bits per second) is the fastest speed obtainable over standard phone lines through a modem; and that the best digital links into the home provide no more than 128 kbps.

"All successful media go through a pornography phase on their way to success. It happened with films, it happened with audio, and everybody knows the story about videotape. The good news is, we passed through it pretty quickly. People seem to be curious about pornography but there's a high novelty factor. They tire of it really fast. The industry leaves it behind and becomes genteel and respectable." (Paul Saffo, Institute for the Future)

publishing is the same as for all such services on the Internet: the volume of use of a free service provides no indication of volume of use for a paid service. For instance, the following two success suggests a strong market for on-line newspapers.

Britain's *Daily Telegraph* publishes its *Electronic Telegraph* on the Internet and claims to be the most visited Web site in Europe. It has 90,000 registered readers, around 12,000 of whom access a total of 100,000 pages of text a day. Some 65 percent of the readers are in the UK, and half are between 20 and 35; 30 percent are over 35. Advertisers such as United Airlines and leading banks are beginning to pay to place multimedia ads in the electronic newspaper. Surveys show that the readers do not object to ads being placed in the pages they read, provided they are not obtrusive and are relevant to the article. Most on-line newspaper editors shorten the length of articles for on-line versus print delivery, believing that readers will not spend time moving through a long document. The *Electronic Telegraph's* surveys show that readers prefer longer articles and more in-depth information.

The *Electronic Telegraph* is not profitable, even with the advertising, because it is free to readers. The *Telegraph* will charge for the newspaper and other services derived from it, such as news clipping or access to archives, once it feels it will be able to keep its readers in doing so, but has no idea when this may be.

What can publishers conclude from such an example? That there is a solid base of readers for such newspapers, which will grow as more and more of the wider population get on-line through PCs, the Internet, interactive TV, and the like, that ads are acceptable to them and that they are real readers, not browsers? Perhaps, but the readership is not representative of readers of the *Daily Telegraph* or any UK newspaper. *Telegraph* readers are largely middle-aged and middle- and upper-income people who read it mainly for its strongly conservative political and social views. The on-line readers are mainly young professionals and academics. Readers of the paper newspaper accept ads everywhere because they are easy to skip, search for, or just glance at. The on-line ads have a cost even when they are free: the time cost of their being downloaded to your PC. This can take minutes, so obviously you will not tolerate the same degree of ads littering every page that you take for granted in a printed newspaper. Finally, the Internet user's preference for longer articles and in-depth information may really be the student's wish for help in homework; the free electronic newspaper is then just another useful free information data base on the Internet.

On the other hand, the 35 percent of readers outside the UK may constitute a real opportunity for the electronic paper. They are mainly in the United States, which is not surprising given that close to 70 percent of all Internet users are located in North America (1996), but they are also widespread in Canada, Scandinavia, the Netherlands, and Germany, locations with many British expatriates. Perhaps these are the target readers for pay-for-service. As a British expat, when I am in the UK, I never buy the *Daily Telegraph,* which I view as among the most boring papers anywhere, but I avidly use the Internet to get really important news from my home in the United States, such as the cricket scores of test matches between England and the West Indies.

Obviously, I am not representative of either *Telegraph* readers or Internet users. That's the point. The distinctive feature of most successful on-line electronic services—advertising, newspapers, bulletin boards—is that they are narrowcast, rather than broadcast, and highly individualized. Instead of companies broadcasting their services out to locate a mass market, they must attract individuals who will seek out the exact community or service they want. If you look at America Online's chat groups, you may be amused by many of their names and topics, but they do show that there are many people who have found and joined them. The fragmented successes of companies doing business on the Internet similarly show this individuation. In this emerging age of new electronic markets, there may be very few mass markets but an almost infinite range of small micromarkets, and thus few mass publications but many specialized ones.

The book industry is larger in sales than the entire TV and film industries and makes its profits without reliance on advertising revenues.

Pricing is perhaps the single key issue for publishers moving into the inevitable on-line future. *USA Today* announced in April 1995 that it would charge $12.95 a month for software and access to its on-line newspaper, allowing three hours of usage for this fee. In August, with only 1,000 subscribers, it phased out the software and abandoned charging anything for access to its Web site. One general lesson supported by this example is that consumers will rarely pay a fee to access a Web site. *USA Today* has 75 employees working full time to maintain the site and over 200 "stringers" who file special reports and update it with hot on-line information. How, then, can such a firm recover its costs? Many companies, including *USA Today,* believe that eventually people will be willing to pay by "micropayment," five cents or even a tiny fraction of a cent automatically billed to them. Today, there is no proven readiness of people to use such a system, and no mechanisms for handling charges and payments. Consequently, as one expert summarizes, publishers make money on the Web in three ways: advertising, advertising, and advertising. The most popular sites, such as ESPN's SportsZone and Playboy's site, are able to command monthly fees from advertisers of up to $30,000 for a small button on their page that links to the advertiser's site. Although many publishers' sites contain ads from many companies, it's not at all clear whether they are getting the free months of use demanded before advertisers make a commitment to this new medium or if the quoted rates are being heavily discounted in practice. A *Playboy* vice president commented in February 1996 that anyone who says they are doing significant business on the Web is lying.

Advertisers report that, in the words of a Chrysler executive, everything they knew about advertising is "out of the window," and they have had to throw out all traditional thinking and start from scratch. The fundamental base for advertising has long been to base prices on how many people will see the ad. This is calculated in cost per mil (thousand, not million), abbreviated to CPM. For a network television show, the CPM would be around $5, and

$40 for a magazine. The CPM for popular Web sites is around $75, if the prices listed are actually charged.

Most companies have found that this is both far too expensive and ineffective. They are in effect paying a lot of money to hand out electronic brochures. As *Wired* summarized the situation in February 1996, "Marketers are not on the Web for exposure, but results." The Web cannot yet match established media for mass exposure. Its potential value is in a site delivering a fully qualified sales lead or customer. The comparison here is with direct mail, where advertisers pay a lot of money to get lists of people who match the profile they seek. Thus more and more companies are learning how to build such profiles on line. *Wired* describes a firm that provides a customized on-line news service. Subscribers pay $3 to $6 a month for the service to extract information from 600 weekly and daily publications; they specify what topics they are interested in by filling out an electronic form. It's that form that is the basis for advertisers' interest. They can target their advertising to the 50,000 subscribers, whose subscription fees amount to just one-third of the revenues; ads generate the rest. The advertisers sponsor individual news sections. Silicon Graphics, for instance, sponsors the section that gives news about the Web (Web servers are one of its key markets). Subscribers see only the ads that relate to their individual profile of interests. The news service is struggling to work out how to price the ads but is making a good profit in the meanwhile.

The Internet is anonymous. You can be whoever you want on it—changing your gender is a popular phenomenon in the world of Net sexual discussion groups—or not tell anyone anything about yourself. When you make one of the estimated 4 million daily "hits" on the SportsZone site, you could be a 12-year-old boy in Seattle, a 50-year-old woman in Italy, a casual browser, a gambler, or a Celtics fan. The art form in advertising is to get you to say who you are in the terms the advertiser is interested in. A car company executive comments that "if you tell me your minivan is five years old, I want to get an attractive lease rate to you immediately." For you to tell him this, there has to be some value for yourself. Many companies are offering "cookies," such as rebate offers, special plans, extra information to access, menus, on-line games, chat groups, on-line focus groups where people can review products and even help design them (a Ford innovation), and many others. They try to persuade people accessing a site for the first time to fill out an electronic form; those that tried to force people to do so quickly learned that they just move on to another site.

The general lesson here is that the Net is fundamentally a medium for interaction, whereas TV and print are one-way presentations. Advertising has to shift its thinking from the one-way mind set and find out how to create meaningful interaction. Companies—probably your own—need to take a look at their own Web sites and ask if they are just corporate PR. If so, that's a very expensive CPM to send a one-way message to the world.

QuickTime QuickTime is Apple's coder/decoder for video, now also available on PCs. Microsoft's more recent equivalent is called AVI (Audio Video Interleave), with a replacement called Action Movie ready for marketing. Both of these read and display data from storage devices such as CD-ROMs. Often, when you first install a CD-ROM, it will either require that QuickTime already be installed on your PC hard disk or include a version of it on the CD-ROM itself.

RAID "Redundant array of independent disks" is a complicated way of saying lots of reliable, low-cost storage. A RAID disk array is a connected set of smaller disk drives, which look as if they are a large single drive, just like the hard disk on a PC. Because the individual disks are smaller, they are faster. This may appear paradoxical, but the explanation is simple. Disks are exactly like a compact disc; they have a series of tracks. To locate track 200 and then track 1, the reader head has to move. The distance may be tiny, but it takes several thousandths of a second to start up, move, and stop. The smaller the disk, the less distance to move. In addition, having multiple disks allows simultaneous read/write operations. Having separate disks means that, if one drive fails, the others can continue; copies of the same data may be stored on several disks—"mirrored." There are different levels of RAID which offer different ways of ensuring data are protected.

Multidrive RAID arrays are increasingly being used on multimedia servers. These "stripe" a file across multiple drives: divide it up into separate components which can be processed at the same time instead of sequentially. Originally, the *I* in RAID stood for "*i*nexpensive." Today, it is less cost than protection of information that dominates firms' choice of storage devices. "Redundant" may be translated as "not having all your eggs in one basket" or "not having all your data on your PC hard drive, which you've forgotten to back up and which, when it crashes, loses every file you have on your machine."

RAID systems are servers on a network; they serve out data to PCs and other devices on the network. Multimedia sound and video files gobble up disk space at thousands of times the rate of electronic mail, word-processing, or spreadsheet applications. RAID helps solve the problem of storage, but the systems must be very fast. Otherwise, transferring a multimedia file is like watching a movie on a VCR and having it freeze every 10 seconds while it waits for the next movie frame. RAID systems for multimedia applications that store 8 GB (billion bytes) of data typically cost $12,000 to $20,000. A typical PC's hard disk stores from 250 to 500 MB and costs at most a few hundred dollars.

One of the almost immutable laws of computers has always been that data grow to overflow the storage capacity available; this is a variation on the famous Parkinson's law that work expands to fill the time available.

Resolution Resolution defines an image's degree of detail. For computer screens and disk storage, resolution is expressed in pixels—picture elements, the dots that form the displayed image—and for scanners and printers, it is measured in dots per inch. Obviously, the more pixels that are used to code an image and the more the dots per inch on the printout, the better the quality of the image, plus the more bits that are needed to store it. The digital coding has to capture each pixel's color, too. The more bits that are used to record the color, the more precisely it can be reproduced.

Any analog signal is continuous and provides smooth transitions. If you look at a blown-up photograph, you won't see any sharp gaps in a block of the same color, such as, say, a green wall. As you magnify the image, it will get fuzzy, but still without gaps. If you do the same with a digital image, you'll see the dots, exactly the same as the dots in a newspaper photograph under a magnifier. (The same difference applies with analog and digital music. The analog sound wave is continuous, but a CD breaks it up into separate, "discrete," subsecond units.) Each dot can represent only a single color, in the form of a number that uniquely identifies it. A one-bit coding can represent only two colors, such as black and white; this was the basis for the monochrome screens of early PCs. Later machines were advertised as providing 256 shades of gray; that was provided by coding each pixel with an 8-bit number. Now, 8-, 16-, 24-, and 32-bit color coding is available, and computer displays vary in the numbers of pixels per row and column, with 640 (rows) $\times$ 480 (columns) commonplace and 1,024 $\times$ 768 used on high-resolution monitors. Obviously, the size of the screen affects the number of pixels to fill it, and the size of the pixels affects the display, too. A 160 $\times$ 120 image looks acceptable if it is sized to 1/16 the size of the screen display, but dreadful on a 640 $\times$ 480 screen.

Resolution is a matter of bits. The more the better. It is also a matter of compressing those bits wherever practical. The simplest illustration of data compression is a stream of 100 bits that are all the same color number, say, 102. Rather than send and store 102, 102, 102, and so on for all 100, it makes more sense to analyze them and code them in the computer equivalent of "Next

100 all 102." Such compression is essential because high resolution means high storage demands. The uncompressed number of bits needed for 8-bit color on a 640 × 480 display is 2.3 million, equivalent to 100 printed pages. That for 24-bit color on a 1,024 × 768 screen, which is becoming the norm for multimedia applications, is 18.9 million, an increase of a factor of 8.

See also Data Compression; Monitor; Scanner

Scanner   Scanners read dots of light reflected from a document via what is termed "optical character recognition." Scanners are an essential multimedia tool, for the obvious reason that so many applications require that images be input. The quality of the scanned image is a function of the number of dots per inch (dpi) of the scanner's resolution. A low-end scanner uses 75 dpi, and a high-end one, 1,200. A black-and-white scanner that records up to 256 gray shades—the white to black hues of a picture—requires 8 bits per dot. Color typically takes 16 to 24 bits, with ultrahigh resolution using 32 bits. Obviously, the more bits used, the more processing that is needed and the more storage. That means that high resolution color scanners are slower than ones that are the digital equivalent of a fax machine, in terms of speed and quality, and they are obviously more expensive.

Scanners need software. Some software merely reads in and prints out images, with limited editing facilities. Others are designed to work with dominant multimedia software designs, such as Adobe's PhotoShop.

See also Image Processing; Resolution; TWAIN

SCSI   Small computer system interface (SCSI), pronounced "scuzzy," is one of the curses of adding devices to a standard PC. It is a way of stringing—"daisy chaining"—a bunch of tape backup drives, CD-ROM drives, and hard disks to the outside of a PC. You can get an idea of what this primitive though effective cabling system involves from the following very simple statement about it: "Devices on the SCSI daisy chain must have a unique ID, from 0 to 6. If a hard disk and CD-ROM have conflicting IDs, such as both being zero, the computer may not even start and will certainly not work properly. If a device is only partially connected or the daisy chain is unterminated, it will create data loss. You may get a spurious disk reading error or incorrect icons."

The main developments in multimedia hardware and PC operating systems are increasingly aimed at getting rid of such jumbles.

Search Engines   Search engines are software applications that search across the World Wide Web to locate Web pages—computer files—that meet the criteria in your request, which may be as simple as "Find all pages with the following word in them or on the following topic," or more complex ones, such as "Find those that include both of the following three words but do not include the fourth one." The latter are called "Boolean searches"; Boolean logic is basic to computer machine instructions and circuits, in resolving conditions involving *and, either, nor,* and the like. Search engines differ in how they work; some search only indexes and abstracts. The most powerful, Digital Equipment's Altavista, searches every word on every page. The claims for it are that it searches around 36 million documents. The problem is that this can return more information than you can use. In my own case, I test search engines by entering my own name. It makes a difference if I enter Peter Keen, Peter G. Keen, or Peter G. W. Keen. What comes back is literally thousands of references, some to Peter Keen, the coach of Britain's Olympic gold medal cyclist, some to college course reading lists that use one of my books. Some contain the word *Peter* somewhere in the article and *keen* somewhere else. Choosing and using a search engine demands some careful thought, especially in structuring requests.

Three widely used search engines are Webcrawler, Lycos, and Yahoo!, all of which are commercial products originally developed at universities for noncommercial use. Webcrawler is America Online's Internet search engine. It indexes the full text of Web

Lycos knows the location of over 90 percent of all Web sites around the world and sends out its spiders to bring back information from roughly 9 million of them.

pages but not of articles to which they point. It includes techniques for limiting the volume of matches it reports. Lycos is the first Internet search engine to use "spiders." It is named for a family of ground spiders that catch their prey by pursuit instead of by building a web and waiting. The Lycos software spiders are self-learning "knowbots" that wander around the Web and bring back 300,000 pages of abstracts every week. Yahoo! Is the most comprehensive and widely used search engine. Its data base organizes site names and descriptions by topic, reducing the chaff from the wheat. There are many other search engines on the market, and it is likely we will see many new ones for years to come.

Websight reports comparisons between them in its January–February issue, 1996:

	Webcrawler	Lycos	Yahoo!
Data base of Web pages	250,000	6,500,000	100,000
Type of indexing	individual words	title, key words	title, abstract, description
Results of searching for:			
"food"	5,962 hits	22,801	571
"Italian cuisine"	100	10,660	3

Secure Electronic Transactions (SET) Secure Electronic Transactions (SET) is a software standard for ensuring secure credit card transactions over the Internet, a facility that just about every observer sees as a key requirement for the Net to become the base for substantial volumes of electronic business. SET both scrambles the card and payment data before sending it over the Internet, where it is vulnerable to many, many skilled intruders, checks electronically and automatically with the issuing bank that the card is valid and the user the one authorized, and prevents even the merchant from being able to view or store the encrypted information. The standard, announced in early 1996, brought together two previously competing groups, one led by Microsoft and one by Netscape, the creator of the Internet browser with a 70 percent market share and thus the single largest software base for electronic transactions over the Net. Visa and MasterCard were the peacemakers. Everyone involved recognized that there must be a uniform standard, not incompatible and competing ones.

See also Business on the Internet

Security   Security is as much perception and emotion as reality. The Internet is widely seen as insecure by the very same people who give their credit card numbers over the phone. Experts' estimates of the likely rate of Internet fraud, given current security measures, are one dollar per thousand dollars of revenue. Even if that turns out to be too low, the Internet looks as safe as credit cards, where MasterCard reported $1.41 per $1,000, and much safer than toll calls ($16) and cellular phones ($41).

Many mechanisms are rapidly emerging to address what everyone involved in on-line services recognizes as a critical business requirement. Many of the agencies and individuals are part of the same communities that explicitly insisted that the Internet be kept as free of control and censorship as possible to ensure the open flow of information. Some of the major lines of attack are encryption of transactions, the new standard that embodies both encryption and formal procedures for safeguarding financial payments, and "firewalls," companies' installations of computer software and hardware that separate the firm's internal systems from the wide-open World Wide Web network and computers, including its own.

See also Secure Electronic Transactions

Passwords are recognized as the weakest link in network security. A survey of 172 corporations carried out in 1995 by Intrusion Detection, Inc., concluded that 85 percent do not require employees to change their password frequently, 23 percent allowed them to access company systems with ones that are easily guessed, and 6 percent did not require any password to be used.

Server   A server is a hardware-software combination that plays a key role in any telecommunications network that provides PCs with shared services. These services include information resources and communication management. A data base server stores data that the users on the network access; it is like a super library that passes out books as fast as people ask for them. Multimedia data base servers pass out books, pictures, data on CD-ROMs, and videos. Communication servers are electronic data air traffic controllers, managing the movement of bits, including error checking, accounting, and security.

Users of a PC and local area network are largely as unaware of servers as you are of electrical power plants, which are directly analogous to servers. They easily become a bottleneck if they lack speed, storage, and the ability to serve many users at the same time. Many of the delays on the Internet reflect overloaded servers. As a result, servers are getting bigger and faster, designed to meet the demands of multimedia. These superservers are either ultrafast PCs, arrays of linked hardware processors, or specially configured larger machines. They have to be extremely reliable. There are dozens of types of servers, as categorized by function. The terms are fairly self-evident: data base servers, Internet servers, communication servers, file servers, print servers, and others.

Multimedia servers will be a key, perhaps even *the* key, component of business multimedia. Today, the main growth in low-cost multimedia is through CD-ROMs, which are individually used on personal computers. A company can create a master disk, copy it for a dollar or so per unit, and distribute it to users. That's a simple and cheap process. However, more and more multimedia will be networked. Examples are videoconferencing; video mail; Internet traffic; on-demand video for training, marketing, and other applications; and intranets—servers accessible via the Internet that are used only within the firm. The new generation of servers are PCs on steroids. Called "*s*ymmetrical *m*ultiprocessor *s*ervers" (SMP), they are "scalable," a term that appears more and more frequently in the information technology field. Scalable means that you can scale up performance by adding extra components instead of either having to replace existing smaller units or buying extra and costly capacity in anticipation of growth. The cost is typically between $10,000 and $25,000.

Servers are basically souped-up PCs, but they play a different role in the business computing resource than PCs. Whereas most PCs use Microsoft's Windows operating system to access the Internet's World Wide Web, most Web sites don't: 32 percent use Sun Microsystem's Solaris, which is based on UNIX; 24 percent use another version of UNIX; 17 percent use Apple's OS; 14 percent use Windows; and just 1 percent use IBM's OS/2.

Silicon Graphics   Silicon Graphics (SGI) is the computer hard-ware manufacturer that has become as central to video develop-ment as Apple was to desktop publishing—the trendsetter and innovator and the choice of the trendsetters and innovators in the application of multimedia. Like Apple, it may become the much-respected but less-used victim of the economics of technol-ogy price and performance trends, left as the vehicle of choice for high-end multimedia and left behind as lower-end machines catch up with its power at a much lower price. Or it may build on its skills, reputation, user loyalty, and even user devotion.

Robert Johansen, one of the most insightful observers of computers and telecommunications, aptly captured in a personal comment to me that SGI is to multimedia what Apple has been to desktop publishing. Anyone who moved with the mainstream of Apple was in the vanguard of early multimedia. The same is now true of SGI. The firm faces very strong competition, and to survive, it must always be the technology leader. Otherwise, it will be unable to maintain its premium prices and fund its research and development. Its acquisition in early 1996 of the company that invented supercomputers, Cray Research, points up very clearly its intended direction.

SGI is almost synonymous with special effects in films. Holly-wood is its single main customer base. It is here that innovations in 3-D are applied, where new editing and postproduction tech-niques find fast acceptance, and where many of the most talented multimedia technicians and designers work. It will take time for this experience to filter down to developers of business training and marketing programs, but meanwhile, SGI's technology is one of the best benchmarks for assessing what we can expect on more standard machines two to four years from now.

Skills   Multimedia requires a complex mix of skills for which there is as yet no established education or career paths. Britain's Royal College of Arts is the leader in Europe in developing a master's program in interactive multimedia within the long-established arts tradition. It reached one conclusion in evolving and implementing the program: it's more effective to produce designers with computer skills than to teach design skills to technical people. The head of the college comments that "I would say that while it's possible to teach design concepts, really good design skills are intuitive." Pharmaceutical companies such as Merck similarly prefer to take those with training in biochemistry or physicians and teach them how to program.

I would say that, although it is practical to teach computer concepts and tools, really good computer design skills are intuitive, too. Anyone who is skilled in both is positioned for a fulfilling career; such people are hard to find, though skilled designers are rapidly picking up the computer side of interactive multimedia now that it is such a hot field everywhere. Skilled programmers are also pushing the limits of traditional design in ways the traditionalists may not be so adept at.

For business, the need for this new type of hybrid—the outstanding designer with pretty good computer skills and the superb technical person with pretty good design sense—is becoming already important and can only become more so. The new skills are needed to design the firm's Web pages, CD-ROMs used for marketing, and interactive training modules, to name just a few. Many of these skills will be obtained through freelance professionals, consulting firms, and universities. As multimedia merges with the mainstream of business, though, it will merge with the mainstream of business information systems, making it essential that the firm have these skills in house. For example, a system for customers to place their own orders for goods over the Internet, Microsoft Network, or CompuServe will involve creating an attractive, clean, easy-to-use interface, with graphics, sound, and some combination of animation, video, or 3-D. That interface will link to electronic forms for inputting the order; these require some clever programming of their own. These modules will in turn link to the firm's transaction-processing systems and data bases to complete the order and update records. The designer of

According to one very successful expert, people working on a multimedia project can never have too much of three things: (1) talent, with the combination of creativity and project management ability the rare ideal; (2) time to prototype, build, and test ideas before being pushed into the rush of production; and (3) hardware, especially data storage.

the graphics interface may rely on such tools as Macromedia, Netscape, and other products of the multimedia era. The designer of the forms and processing links may use Visual Basic and C++, products of the PC era. The people working on the transaction processing systems and data bases will use such tools as Oracle, COBOL, and SAP, products of the mainframe computing era.

It is no exaggeration to say that there is almost certainly not a single person on this planet who combines all these skills and knows how to use all these tools. It has taken well over a decade for companies to move their information systems developers' professional culture away from mainframe thinking and to build the attitudes, expertise, and experience needed for designing the new client-server systems that integrate PC, departmental, and mainframe software, hardware, and telecommunications. Now, they must begin extending the client-server culture to build the attitudes, expertise, and experience needed for designing multimedia client-server infrastructures and applications.

See also Authoring; Multimedia Development

Software Piracy   Software piracy is the copying of computer disks and CD-ROMs. It's a huge industry. One journalist who visited Asia to see just how much pirated software he could buy in the open market concluded that every leading software package and CD-ROM game is easily obtained. He estimated that he bought $2,500 of software for around $300.

Software is attractive to pirates for obvious reasons: it's portable and light, the reproduction cost is tiny and the margins high, and there's a massive demand. It is also hard to track down, though the industry and government agencies are committing more and more resources to tracking down pirated copies *and* the pirates. Multimedia software is a growing target because of its huge market worldwide. In March 1996, Disney released its *Pocahontas* video a few weeks early; pirated copies were already on the market.

According to the Software Publishers Association, the rate of piracy—illegal copying and sale of software—in the United States amounts to 25 percent of all software sales. The figure for China is 98 percent; for Russia, 95 percent; and for several Asian countries, 90 to 92 percent.

Sound   Digital sound is the fourth category of media to become part of multimedia. The first category was what typewriters used to produce: numbers and text. The second was images: electronic copies of documents and pictures. The third was video, without sound, in the form of the old home movie cameras. Sound is the fourth, with touch just beginning to be the fifth medium.

What is counterintuitive here is that the explosive growth in music and entertainment would naturally lead one to assume that digital sound is in the vanguard of multimedia use. That hasn't been the case. For several decades, it has been easier to provide first-rate video for videoconferencing than first-rate audio.

There are three types of digital audio:

1. *CD audio,* sometimes called "Red Book audio." CD audio is stored on compact discs and on the Red Book part of CD-ROMs (the other is the Yellow Book, used for digital video).

2. *Wave audio,* easily recognized on a PC by its being stored in a file with the suffix .WAV (JAZZ12.WAV, SAMBA.WAV, TALK.WAV, and the like).

3. *MIDI audio,* created and played by a synthesizer that uses the MIDI hardware standard for coding musical notes and instruments in digital form or turning digital music created on a PC back into the sound waves your ear hears.

The principles of digitizing sound—voice and music—are well established. The sound wave is sampled X times per second, with each sample converted to an 8-bit or 16-bit number. The more frequently the wave is sampled, the more accurately high and low frequencies are captured. An analogy is measuring traffic noise; if you sampled just once every 30 seconds, you'd miss the sound of a car backfiring. The more bits used, the more information you code about volume. For digital coding of speech over the phone, 8-bit 7,000 samples per second is fully adequate. That requires 56,000 bits for each second of speech, 2 printed page equivalents; when extra bits are added for error handling, this becomes 64,000 and matches one of the main units of telecommunications digital transmission speed provided by the long-distance phone service providers such as AT&T and MCI. An audio CD that plays high-fidelity music uses two channels of 44,100 16-bit numbers for each second of sound. That amounts to over 100 printed book equivalents (2.8 million bits). A minute of music takes almost six times more (17 million bits) to record and store. That is typically compressed by a factor of close to 20 (to 10 Mb (million *bytes*) on a hard disk. You can cut the storage requirements by 94 percent if you are willing to accept lower-quality mono (single-channel) sound. If your hard disk has 200 printed page equivalents of spare space (200 MB), a fairly typical figure, you can thus store 20 seconds of CD-quality sound or 32 minutes of fairly tinny sound.

Waveform audio permits a range of sampling speeds and bits per sample. The lowest practical speed for multimedia is 11,025 samples per second, with options for 22,050 and CD-quality 44,100.

CD and waveform audio are limited to playing sound from a single file and do not permit simultaneous sound effects. MIDI—"*M*usical *I*nstrument *D*igital *I*nterface"—was designed by a group of electronic musical instrument manufacturers to make their products able to communicate with each other. It is by far the preferred tool for computer applications of professional musicians. MIDI allows a computer to turn 16 different channels of audio on and off. The files are much smaller than for CD and waveform and can be manipulated to slow down or speed up play. A digital audio recording that takes megabytes of storage uses just a few kilobytes if MIDI is used instead. The drawback of MIDI to date is that they may sound entirely different depending on which specific sound board they use and whether or not the PC uses an external module, which adds cost. These enhance the reproduction and also eliminate the hisses generated by the MIDI interface card being inside the electromagnetically vibrant inside of a PC.

Sound Blaster   Sound Blaster is the trademarked name of a video card that has become a de facto standard. It is used in 70 percent of the multimedia PCs sold in 1995, with unit sales of 1 million per month. As has so often been the case in the telecommunications, PC, and multimedia fields, this dominant design came not from a committee or an established large company but from a start-up. Founded in 1981 in Singapore with $6,000 in capital, Creative Labs has grown to over $1 billion in revenues.

Sound Cards   Sound cards are, along with video cards, one of the add-on units of a personal computer that make it a multimedia PC. Sound cards are often called "sound boards"; the terms are interchangeable. They contain specialized computer chips that process audio sound waves, convert them to digital signals for recording sound, and convert them the other way for play back.

Spamming   Spamming is mass mailing unsolicited commercial ads to Internet users. It's a major breach of Net etiquette that can lead to the offender's Internet account being canceled by the person's service provider or a flood of abusive mass electronic mail messages flooding his or her Web site in order to overload and crash it. Spamming reflects the tension in the Internet community between protecting its openness to everyone and its pristine nonbusiness nature while also ensuring that openness is not misused. Since there is no formal controlling mechanism, only informal pressures can be brought to bear, plus withdrawal of services by commercial providers of Internet access. Spammers can find other service providers, though. There's no legal force preventing them from mass-mailing commercial messages any more than any legal force prevents objectors from mass-mailing abusive messages to the offender.

   See also Business on the Internet

Spyglass   Spyglass is the leading competitor to Netscape in providing the PC software that makes the Internet usable by nontechnical people. Whereas Netscape sells its software, in competition with such giants as Microsoft and Oracle, Spyglass licenses its systems to other software firms for a royalty fee. By the end of 1995, its Mosaic system was being put into the products of close to 40 software providers, including Microsoft, AT&T, IBM, CompuServe, and Oracle; that is, it is becoming an integral element of business computing and communications.

Both Spyglass's and Netscape's browsers originated at the University of Illinois, where in 1993 a team developed an Internet browsing program called Mosaic. Both were founded by members of the development group. When the university's licensing office was flooded with offers to commercialize the software, it decided to grant Spyglass the exclusive license. Netscape, which had tried to call itself Mosaic Communications but was prevented from doing so by the university, used programmers from the Mosaic group to build its own system.

The two software systems that have moved the Internet from a complex, arcane student, professor, and researcher niche tool all came out of academic institutions in the very early 1990s: the World Wide Web (a researcher at the Swiss CERN) and Mosaic. In both cases, the breakthrough was to make a useful tool, the Internet, usable. The marketplace response shows the degree to which the use of information technology is driven by usability.

See also Microsoft Network; Mosaic; Netscape; World Wide Web

The origin of the term surfing *reflects the origins of the Internet and the closeness of its original community. Vincent Cerf, the cocreator of the telecommunications protocol that is the very base of the Internet was asked by a California firm (Cerf taught at Stanford, and many of the early Internet pioneers were at Berkeley) if he minded their calling their firm California Educational Research Foundation Network. (Someone else had rights to the name surf.net.) It's a pity that Cerf's genius and geniality weren't rewarded by our cerfing the Web.*

Surfing   Surfing the Internet has become part of the vocabulary of everyday life. It means to use an Internet browser such as Netscape Navigator to locate information when you have no precise knowledge of what items you are looking for and absolutely no knowledge of where they are. The design of the World Wide Web encourages this flexible interaction. Search engines provide more focused identification of specific items. Other Internet services augment them. Usenet lets you join in thousands of discussion groups. FTP ("*File Transfer Protocol*") downloads files where you know which Internet server computer they are stored on.

See also Internet Service; Search Engine; World Wide Web

TAPI   TAPI stands for "*Telephony Application Program Interface.*" It is a set of conventions and tools—standards—for any type of Windows-based software application to send messages to software that handles telephone functions, such as automated paging; locating items in a data base and faxing them; identifying a customer's name from the number he or she is calling from; and bringing up account information automatically and immediately.

TAPI is part of what is termed "*computer telephony integration*" (CTI), one of the most promising business extensions of both phones and PCs. The rival standard to TAPI is TSAPI, "*Telephony Services API.*" API is the general term for the messages that allow different software packages to work together.

See also Application Program Interface, CTI

TCP/IP   TCP/IP is the telecommunications protocol that makes the Internet what it is, a network of networks. TCP/IP is the only protocol that is not in some way specific to a type of computer, operating system, or telecommunications environment. *It thus allows any computer in the world to talk to any other computer in the world.* That, rather than lofty words about the Information Superhighway, cyberspace, or the Web, revolutionized the entire world of computers and communications.

TCP/IP is by no means an elegant or efficient protocol. It was a very pragmatic result of computer science students' and professionals', centered at Berkeley, creating a means of sharing files across what was then the Arpanet. They focused on electronic mail message transfer and on moving large research files between university computers. They ignored security and all the complexities of network management that businesses were grappling with. For example, early versions had no facilities for error checking and correction. They simply dropped the short "packet" being transmitted (and still do). It's as if the principle was "On error, drop message" and "If you don't receive this message, let me know." For most applications, this is not a major problem. For multimedia, it means that a few frames of video or a subsecond part of an Internet radio or phone transmission are lost. For businesses, losing a packet may convert a funds transfer from millions to billions. TCP/IP was also designed to get information to its destination without worrying much about timing.

TCP/IP is in many ways less reliable and secure than other telecommunications protocols, but its capability of enabling any computer to communicate with any other computer has made it the fundamental building block of today's Internet and intranets. Intranets use TCP/IP to move information throughout firms and Web browser software to allow people to access that information.

See also Internet, Intranet

Telecommunications Legislation Telecommunications legislation in the United States is based on the technology, social priorities, industry structures, and economics of the early 1980s. In particular, it maintained very clear boundaries between fields that have now so converged that they cannot be kept apart. These include publishing media, from which phone companies were excluded; local and long-distance phone services, which were made into mutually exclusive businesses with strong barriers preventing firms crossing from one to the other; tight control of ownership of radio and television stations; and equally tight regulation of the cable TV industry and its prices.

All of this no longer applies to the realities of business, society, and technology. The multimedia industry that already exists even without new legislation permitting it includes alliances between publishers, local phone companies and cable TV firms; cable TV providers getting ready to add local phone calls to their use of cable; publishers eyeing the Internet as an opportunity or necessity for themselves to enter the on-line world; local phone companies getting ready to provide video films on demand down the phone lines; and megadeals among such firms as Time Warner, Viacom, CNN, TCI, and many others to gain an edge in either control of the delivery of TV and phone calls, or of the content on which those delivery systems rely, or of both delivery and content.

It has been clear for several years that new legislation was needed. June 1995 saw its initiation, with the Senate voting 81 to 18 in favor of almost total change. That change had been blocked by ferocious lobbying against such changes as local phone companies' being allowed into the long distance market, where MCI, whose aggressive arguments in favor of long distance competition led to the ending of AT&T's monopoly, now just as aggressively argued against competition, and where newspaper publishers used all their influence to keep out phone and cable firms. The stakes are immense. The technology is here and getting better and cheaper by the year. There will be big winners and equally big losers as everyone gets into everyone else's market.

The complete deregulation of telecommunications in the Senate proposal was passed into law in early 1996. There are five main innovations in the bill:

1. End the monopoly of local phone companies.

2. Remove the ban on local phone companies' entering the long-distance market.

3. Allow local phone companies to offer cable television programming and acquire cable TV companies in small cities.

4. Deregulate the cable TV industry.

5. Remove the limitations on how many radio and TV stations one individual or organization may own.

There were many other concessions and side deals, for small radio and TV stations who will be allowed to extend the life of their license to operate, with new rules making it harder for them to be challenged at renewal time, and for stations to use new channels previously set aside for high definition television (HDTV) and other services. The top official in the U.S. Department of Commerce in charge of the National Telecommunications and Information Administration summarized the Senate bill as "between horrific, bad and awful."

The Telecommunications Act of 1996 is essentially a multimedia bill. The fueling elements for multimedia to take off are: (1) massive bandwidth at low prices; (2) aggressive competition in meshing telecommunications delivery and information entertainment content; and (3) efficient and low-cost links into the home. Competition and technical innovation in telecommunications are ensuring that the bandwidth will be there within a very few years, whether via your phone line or television cable. Billions are being spent in mergers of delivery and content companies. An example is Disney's acquisition of ABC. Plenty of firms have paid plenty of money to position to be the second fueling force.

The third element is key: who controls the device in the home that is at the end of "the last mile," the link into the home from cable networks, TV broadcasters, the Internet, local and long-distance phone lines and other providers of multimedia information, entertainment, and other services. The battle is underway with or without legislative changes. The telecommunications reform bill makes the playing field bigger and the game faster.

One add-on to the bill will cause a great deal of debate and legal jostling for many years to come. It is the censorship of networks, something that either conflicts with First Amendment rights or meets the concerns of many citizens that the Internet has become far too much an invitation to pedophiles, pornographers, and child abusers to exploit the open communications and anonymity the Net provides. The legislation puts new controls on the dissemination of obscene material that may be accessed by juveniles. The very day the bill was signed into law, many Web sites displayed black, as a sign of protest and mourning for the loss of freedom of expression. Within a few months, much of its restrictive intent was struck down by federal courts as a violation of First Amendment rights.

See also Cable TV; Censorship; V-Chip

Touch Touch is the latest area of multimedia to move from the laboratory to the desktop and from multimillion-dollar research projects to low-cost products. Multimedia is fundamentally about using technology to match human senses. It has in turn addressed numbers, words, pictures, sound, movement and three-dimensionality—data, text, image, audio, video, and virtual reality. Touch adds a new dimension, illustrated by *Business Week's* description of the leading system, Phantom, developed at MIT and now moving into early commercial use: Dr. Krummel "slowly guided a biopsy needle into a small, hollow cone pressed against a skull. Pushing the needle in, he hit resistance, followed by a gentle pop as he pierced the outer skull. . . . Probing gently, Krummel felt a solid mass: a tumor. One firm poke, and he was inside it" (*Business Week,* 9 October 1995). This was not a real operation, of course. The skull was an image on the screen; the needle, a thimble on the end of his fingers through which Dr. Krummel controlled the needle on the screen and "felt" the resistance. He summarized the performance of Phantom: "The accuracy is excellent. It's truly awesome."

Phantom simulates touch through the combination of standard hardware chips (Intel Pentium) and special sensors which relay signals from the human's tiniest hand movement to motors that instruct the software how much pressure to apply to the thimble that translates to a sense of touch, at a rate of around 1,000 times per second. The cost of this system is under $20,000. What is perhaps more impressive is that the company that markets it is facing competition even lower in price. One rival has announced that it will ship a $200 joystick for computer games before the end of 1996. It would reproduce the vibrations of a tank on rough terrain and the feeling of the controls of a plane in a flight simulation (and, less appealing, whatever tactile violence the makers of the blood-and-destruction games that dominate the market may choose to offer and people choose to accept).

Training surgeons, even rehearsing operations, are obvious applications of touch technology, but there are many business opportunities, too. Chrysler expects to use it in designing cars: engineers will be able to run their hands over "virtual" buttons and controls. GTE uses it to mock up the panels of radar control devices. It seems likely that it will be used to train people in manufacturing and assembly activities and to provide users of many types of systems with the tactile feedback that is an everyday feature of the devices we use daily, including pencils. It may even be a feature of word-processing keyboards. Certainly, marketers will use it for customers to really feel the goods, such as the texture of materials and the comfort of machine controls.

At one level, Phantom is just another new item in the astonishing, almost daily record of technology breakthroughs. The main thesis of this guide is that multimedia is basically using computers to restore, instead of substitute for, the natural media of human understanding and living. Touch is part of this. Once digital touch is proven in early applications and this is followed by its price dropping into the business and mass market, then it should be on every manager's list of opportunities.

Direct labor costs now amount to less than 20 percent of sales in most manufacturing-based industries. In assessing the keys to becoming and staying world class, a widely respected book states that "the most

Training   Training is a "run, don't walk" target of opportunity for business multimedia. Studies consistently show that multimedia cuts training time in half and increases student retention by 20 to 40 percent. There are so many examples of successful use of multimedia for training that there is space to pick out only a few here:

- Union Pacific Railroad reports that it cut the costs of training by 35 percent, while reducing training time by 30 percent and increasing student retention by 40 percent.

- The Los Angeles Department of Power and Light slashed the time new customer service staff spend on training, from 13 weeks to 7. Rising demands for service and knowledge of products had led to training programs' ballooning in length. The costs were escalating as the increased time was nonrevenue generating. To spend a full quarter of their first year in the classroom was demotivating for staff, too. The investment in multimedia training via laser disc incorporated the training needed for 85 to 90 percent of on-the-job duties of reps. The analysis of what is a massive training program by any standards highlights the critical importance of visualization and role-playing simulations in adding something special to interactive training. In addition, the low cost of reproducing the self-paced material has enabled the organization to use it for remedial training as well as for new hires, and to use it across many other departments. The training paid for itself in a year.

- Lazarus Department Stores' "trainer in a box" both halved the time to train 250 new hires simultaneously and eliminated the need for constant one-on-one observation in learning its point-of-sale systems and procedures. Within an hour of being hired, an associate is walked into the training room by a sales manager and literally that manager says "let me introduce you to the company. Put on the headphones and touch the screen." The multimedia system added consistency in training across Lazarus' many stores, cut costs, added flexibility in recruitment, and boosted productivity. New hires are out on the floor in half the time.

Corporate training budgets in the United States now amount to well over $200 billion.

See also Education

important variable costs for an advanced manufacturing company may well be the costs of training and retraining people." If that's so, multimedia is a strategic tool for organizational advantage. Federal Express, for example, spent over $40 million to develop a laser-disc–based training kiosk installed in 800 of its 1,400 locations. It reports that the system cut training time by 60 percent. United Airlines' investment of $150,000 in CD-ROM training for flight attendants when the new Airbus A320 was brought into service cut training time from 8 to 3 hours and saved $9 million in travel, hotel, and other expenses. Holiday Inn, whose rapid employee turnover makes fast training of new hires essential, more than halved training time from 14 to 6 days in its property management operations.

TSAPI   TSAPI stands for "*T*elephony *S*ervices *A*pplication *P*rogram *I*nterface" and is one of the two main tools that allow software applications to include telephone functions as just another type of data, the same as a spreadsheet calculation or word-processed text. TSAPI is sponsored by AT&T, and its rival, TAPI, by Microsoft. They are the central components of what is termed computer telephony integration (CTI), one of the highest payoff areas of business multimedia for any firm.

See also CTI

TWAIN   TWAIN stands for "*t*echnology *w*ithout *a*n *i*mportant *n*ame," a charming contrast to the complex—and an implicit recognition that most of that complexity has little useful meaning and is close to unpronounceable (PCMCIA, for instance). TWAIN is a standard for software applications to interface with such input devices as digital cameras, scanners, and other multimedia devices. There are already plenty of established ways of interfacing with printers; TWAIN addresses the new generation of devices that generate a wide variety of digital "objects," including still images, video clips, and sound bites. TWAIN enables a software application to "acquire" a device and move objects to and from it through what are called application program interfaces (APIs).

See also API; Scanner

V-Chip   The V-chip is a device that owners of TV sets can use to block the reception of sexually explicit or violent programming. A 1996 federal law requires it to be installed in all televisions sold in the United States. By 1997, broadcasters and cable companies must come up with a rating system that transmits information directly to the V-chip. They will be free to produce and transmit programs of their choice, but parents now have a means of blocking all programs they regard as unsuitable for their family. The chip is part of an ongoing and fierce debate between those concerned for social, political, or religious reasons with "cyberporn" and civil libertarians opposed to any restriction of free speech.

The battleground is the Internet more than TV, and the wider law of which the V-chip is part makes it illegal to distribute over the Net "indecent" materials that could be accessed by anyone under 18.

The V-chip originated in Canada, where several cable TV companies include it in their services. Experience there suggests that even if the U.S. system is in place and the law is not overturned in the courts, this self-censorship mechanism will be more difficult to make work than appears at first sight. For instance, what type of violence will be censored: NFL games, news programs, war movies? In February 1996, executives from the leading television broadcasters announced that the industry would work together on a voluntary basis to develop a rating system.

Censorship of sexual material on the Internet and controlling viewing through the V-chip make for a political and social conflict whose resolution will have an immense effect on multimedia in general. First Amendment rights, "family values," religious organizations, and political platforms will all make this a turmoil of extreme positions, refusal to compromise, and court actions. Multimedia will be at the center of the conflict, for the obvious reason that it aims at immediacy, striking and emotionally vivid effects, and enhancing of reality. Much of it is targeted to entertainment and games. That naturally opens up the certainty of pornography. It is pictures more than words that is making this such an emotional issue, and the level of violence of more and more computer games surely shows the direction in which much multimedia will move. Here are extracts from two of the milder ads in a respectable video games magazine full of well-written articles: "Expect blood, expect visual nightmares, expect uncensored violence, but . . . expect no mercy." "If a mad scientist brings you back to life as a part-human, part-robotic killing machine, do you blow him away or call him Daddy?"

VGA VGA is a basic standard for personal computer display screens. It replaces the low-cost but also low-resolution screens that were fully adequate in the era when PCs were used almost entirely for word processing, electronic mail, data base management, and spreadsheets, where color was just an enhancement. The quality of multimedia rests on high quality color and resolution—the degree of detail provided by the display. VGA provides adequate quality and is found on most laptops and low cost multimedia PCs. SVGA (SuperVGA) is a variant of VGA that offers more colors.

Display Type	Pixels	Number of Colors	Memory Needed to Store 1 Image
CGA	320 × 200	4	16,000 bytes
EGA	640 × 350	16	112,000
VGA	640 × 480	256	224,000
SuperVGA	512 × 480	16,777,216	983,000
SVGA	800 × 600		1,440,000

Video Card Video cards are key add-on components to personal computers which determine their degree of multimedia capability, since video is by far their most demanding element in terms of needs for fast processing, amount of storage, and quality of display. There are many types of video cards and several different terms that are essentially interchangeable, such as *video card* or *accelerator.*

Videoconferencing is a well-established technology which has been in use for close to 30 years. It still isn't used by most people or most organizations. It is estimated that in 1993 there were 20,000 systems

Videoconference Videoconferences are electronic meetings, where people in different locations use real-time audio and video links to collaborate as if they are in the same room. Videoconferencing has been around for close to 30 years, as a very separate application from telephony, use of companies' telecommunications networks, and the mainstream of PC use. It remains fairly separate but over the next 2 to 5 years is almost sure to become part of the mainstream of business multimedia. The simple reason videoconferencing was separate is its difficulty. It was difficult to implement technically and difficult to operate socially. Now, it is much simpler in terms of both.

The technical difficulties are the same ones that are basic to all real-time video: huge processing and transmission demands. Historically, videoconferencing used its own technology base, using leased lines and equipment specially configured for it. It's gradually being moved onto the Internet and PC base of modern computing. Carnegie-Mellon's CU-See-me software is widely used on the Internet. Intel offers videoconferencing for Windows-based PCs.

Video Dial Tone   Video dial tone (sometimes referred to as soft video dial tone) is a recent development in telecommunications which makes it practical to run movies over the standard twisted pair phone lines in your house. This breakthrough in technology was indirectly a breakdown in the very structure of telecommunications and related industries, where "related" includes cable television. Until the development of a special ADSL chip ("*a*synchronous *d*igital *s*ubscriber *l*ink," the technical term for what makes soft video dial tone possible) in the early 1990s, most observers of the increasingly converging telecommunications and cable TV industries saw the phone companies' advantage being capital and presence in around 90 percent of all homes. The cable companies' advantage and phone service providers' corresponding disadvantage was the bandwidth—raw transmission speed and capacity. The phone lines now in place would need to be entirely upgraded to fiber optics.

Video on demand requires immense bandwidth. Films can be compressed and stored on large disks, reducing transmission requirements, but the files still consume at least a million bytes of storage for every second of content. That means that it would take a minute to transfer a second of film over the phone line. For this reason, until ADSL, most observers saw the cable TV companies as the likely winners in the race to wire the consumer home for multimedia. They had plenty of bandwidth available

installed in the United States. As desktop video on local area networks has become more available, easy to use, and low in price, it is likely but not guaranteed that videoconferencing will grow more rapidly. Kinko's, the national photocopying and printing service, offers videoconferencing services for around $150 an hour.

It would take days to download a copy of a movie the length of Jurassic Park *using the fastest speed obtainable over phone lines via a modem. Installing special ISDN lines in your home would speed that up to under a day. ADSL, the technology being piloted for video on demand over the existing copper wire phone lines in your house, makes it practical to send the two-hour movie at a speed at which it plays on your television set at VCR quality.*

There are faster transmission systems available but not yet deployed, which means it will take many years before the needed infrastructures are in place in more than a few major metropolitan areas. Cable modems, which of course cable companies are betting on, reduce the time to under an hour and fiber optics plus cable modems to 3 minutes. Phone companies are betting on ADSL, which has been in use in a thousand homes in Virginia since 1994.

through the coaxial cables that pass within 50 yards of 90 percent of U.S. homes and that could carry 500 channels of entertainment, leaving plenty of room to spare for phone calls. The phone companies would need to use their rich capital resources to buy their way into the market by acquiring cable firms.

ADSL and soft video dial tone change the balance of power. Bell Atlantic was the first to exploit this opportunity. It has been by far the most innovative of the notoriously lethargic regional Bell operating companies, the seven firms spun off from AT&T and given a soon-to-end monopoly over local phone service.

Virtual Reality   Virtual reality (VR) is the use of computers to create an artificial environment that appears to its users to be real. Virtual reality is at the same time one of the most far-fetched, hype-laden concepts in multimedia and one of its most practical emerging applications.

EDS, the giant IT service provider, opened a VR center in Detroit in mid-1995 to showcase under one roof all the available technology. Over 30 companies signed up, with others on a waiting list. One of the main aims is to dispel the notion that virtual reality is a toy whose future lies in entertainment. It is no coincidence that the center is located in Detroit. VR is well suited to many auto manufacturing activities, such as creating a mockup of a new plant that planners can "walk through" or engineers' evaluating the design of a proposed new model by sitting in a virtual car. NASA routinely uses VR for teams of astronauts to work together practicing repairs in space.

The costs of creating virtual reality systems are probably less than most managers realize. Software development tools cost under $1,000 (one $495 package offers "over 100 Sample Worlds" for an extra $99). VR helmets cost around $2,000, and data gloves, around $500. The main need is a really powerful computer at the core: $400 to $500,000.

For instance, a recent application of virtual reality sounds fairly humdrum but could well point to a widespread future use.

The Japanese government has made it mandatory, starting in September 1996, that applicants for a motorcycle driver's license take a test through a VR simulation. The rider wears a headset that gives an all-around display. Developed by a British company and marketed by Kawasaki, the simulation shows traffic to the left and the right, and the bike's "mirrors" show traffic coming up behind. As you move your head, it responds smoothly and realistically. The size of the market is estimated at around $50 million a year. Kawasaki will also market the developer's lightweight headset which plugs into a standard PC.

There are many obvious comparable applications of these tools: training and testing for work that involves operating machines, safety procedures, handling factory trucks, installing equipment, and so on.

One interesting and clever variation on VR is the BBC's virtual news studio. The British Broadcasting Corporation is one of the best-known national TV organizations in the world. BBC's daytime news studio looks very impressive, with an ornate, cut-glass giant globe carved with the "Beeb's" blue logo rotating above the news desk. The news desk itself is huge—wide enough to seat half a dozen journalists. It's three times the size of the newsroom it replaced in 1994. There are light grids everywhere and huge backdrop maps, and the ceiling is packed with cameras, lights, and other high-tech devices.

Of course, it's all fake. There's no desk, no ceiling, no lights, no backing, and no cut-glass globe. The only thing that is not generated by virtual reality software is the news reader and a single piece of backing directly behind him or her. The news reader is of course not in the studio. The studio isn't a studio. BBC's technicians built the virtual studio using tools for 3-D "rendering" to achieve the textured, cut-glass look. They added features that make it look as if light is being reflected as the globe rotates or as the camera angle changes, or rather seems to change.

BBC's purpose here is not just to provide the illusion of being in a huge newsroom, but also to contribute to its effort to re-

McDonnell Douglas is maintaining engines for a fighter plane that has not yet been built. Virtual reality linked to CAD/CAM software allows engineers to turn 3-D design simulation still images generated by that software into a fully animated aircraft. They wear VR helmets that allow them to enter a virtual world and use virtual tools to crack open an engine bay door, drop a new engine in, or unbolt engines. The system even includes a virtual trailer that enables the team to determine how quickly and easily maintenance mechanics can transport the engine to and from a shop.

establish its distinctive identity. This public funded service, for which every TV owner must pay a $150-a-year license fee, even if they never watch the BBC, has come under much attack. Its budget has been slashed and many staff laid off. Its managers are wrestling with how to change public perceptions, including "branding" its news programs. The virtual studio is intended to present a common front to the world through a family of visual designs that both stamp this as BBC and allow flexibility and diversity. A senior executive commented that the corporation wanted to avoid "the crude exercise of superimposing a logo on every frame of output, like CNN. The technology added class but also cut jobs. Robotic cameras replaced a dozen studio staff."

Visual Basic Visual Basic is a computer programming language for developing what are termed "client/applications." These are ones that combine PCs (clients), telecommunications networks, and remote computers of varying sizes (servers). It is well suited to streamlining the many, often tedious tasks inherent in making a system easy to use and interactive. These include the menus of options from which the user selects by clicking on an icon or list routines to clear the screen of unneeded items, links to other software applications, access to company data bases, security features, telecommunications linkages, and management of the screen cursor, to name just a few.

Visual Basic is one of the main options for programming client/server applications. Client/server computing is the emerging blueprint for business systems. The extremely complex Visual Basic is heavily supported by Microsoft, which announced in late 1995 a complete revamping of the language. Microsoft hopes to strengthen its position in the corporate marketplace and displace competitors like Sun who rely on the UNIX operating system and a language called C++ for client/server development. Microsoft's target is the large enterprise software developments that are the workhorse of business operations. The new version, called VB 4.0, provides powerful features for building and reusing libraries of program code, handling documents and images, designing forms, and, as the term *visual* implies, handling such multimedia "objects" as graphics.

The programming languages companies have used for decades were not designed to handle multimedia, PC graphical user interfaces, or client/server. The software that manages a PC user's interaction with a CD-ROM simply can't be built using them. However, a jazzy client/server application running on a PC may need to access old systems to search for data or update records. It may also need to link to several different telecommunications networks, such as a departmental local area network, the firm's "backbone" transaction processing network, and the Internet. Visual Basic and C++ offer the tools needed for this. Of course, skilled users of those tools are quite scarce.

An example of a fairly typical use of Visual Basic is a system developed in six months by two people, to help run auto repair garages. CarShop handles all aspects of customer relations, inventory control, estimates, pricing, scheduling of mechanics, and printing of reports. The heart of the application is the 79 forms in everyday use in the operation. The system has over 50 software modules. It would have taken at least five times the amount of time and staff it took to develop, had traditional tools been used. Another application developed for car repairs is the CD-ROM manual for the Lotus Esprit model, which is completely replacing Lotus's paper manuals. The Visual Basic application is built around 20 different forms. It also links to modules written in other programming languages, which produce code that runs faster than that generated by Visual Basic or that offer special features.

Given the profusion of software packages that you can unpack and run right away, with no programming needed, it's easy to forget that those packages have to be programmed and also that companies are constantly upgrading their existing systems to operate in a client/server environment, enhancing old ones and building new ones. If you were to use the Lotus Esprit CD-ROM manual, it is just another piece of easy-to-use packaged software. It took a year to build, and most of the effort went into making it easy to use. Software design and development is a complex art. Any tools that speed the process up and improve quality and productivity are a major business asset. Visual Basic is one of these tools. To date, there is no single dominant design, and competitors for VB 4.0 include Microsoft's own Visual C++, other companies' implementation of C++, Delphi Pascal, Perl, and, most recently, Java.

The choice of programming environment is a critical one for any large firm, because each of the implementations now on the market have their own special features and limitations or operate only with specific hardware and software operating systems. This means that, once chosen, it is hard to unchoose the tool on which the next generation of applications will be based. We are only just beginning the era of multimedia programming of applications which, for instance, provide customer service through kiosks, simplify staff handling of transactions, deliver interactive training, or provide executives with the most meaningful information they need to run the business. That new generation of applications will have a significant impact on the firm's effectiveness, efficiency, customer relations, flexibility, and organizational coordination. This makes the somewhat esoteric issues of C++, VB 4.0, OLE, DLL, RPCs, APIs, and DDE important business issues, too. With most central information systems departments under siege today, with business managers looking at outsourcing, budget slashing, and the death-of-the-mainframe syndrome, there is a distinct risk that these companies will miss out on the multimedia opportunity by not building up the new generation of IS professionals for the new generation of applications.

See also C++; Client-Server; Java

Voice Recognition—The Last Frontier   Voice recognition is the translation of spoken words to their correct written equivalent, taking into account the context of the words. Thus the system distinguishes between "Write a letter" and "Right this wrong." Efforts to develop efficient, reasonable-cost software and hardware for voice recognition have been underway for well over three decades, and progress has been continuous. There are plenty of systems in place, with limited applications, but there is no equivalent of word-processing or spreadsheet software. Only one in a thousand PC users will routinely use voice recognition. If you phone AT&T's universal credit card service, you have the option to speak your account number or enter it by pushing the buttons on the phone. Many handicapped workers and children who cannot move their hands rely on voice recognition and are willing to accept its slowness because they have no other choice. That said, this is still a technology that has a long way to go before it becomes part of the mainstream of multimedia. The over-800-page January 1996 issue of *Computer Shopper,* a magazine that is 95 percent ads, did not seem to include a single ad for voice recognition hardware or software.

It will do so in time. The most natural way to communicate is by speaking aloud. It is a natural medium for humans and our medium of choice. It is unnatural to use a keyboard or a mouse. We now take it for granted that anyone in business ought to be able to use a PC (though a 1993 survey by the Robert Half company found that 55 percent of executives in computer companies couldn't operate a PC). Just 10 years ago, this was called typing and was something very few people were proficient at. In a sense, the dominance of keyboards is a step backward rather than forward in making life more productive and convenient.

Voice recognition is part of a long-term move forward. Graphical user interfaces have reduced the typing load; you point and click on icons for many operations that previously required keyboard entries, but this is still unnatural. Pen-based computing moves another step forward in allowing you to enter information through handwriting; these systems are improving but are still quirky and not widely used.

The current state of the market is indicated by PowerSecretary, a software and hardware package that sells for around $2,500 and works with most standard word-processing software. It can be trained in a few hours. After about 20 hours, users typically achieve 40 words a minute of slightly robotic speech accurately converted into word-processed text on the screen. The upper limit claimed for the system is 55 words per minute. It has a dictionary of 120,000 words and can build a working dictionary of 30,000 to 60,000 words matched to your own voice and pronunciation. It becomes more accurate over time, as you correct its mistakes.

PowerSecretary requires a very powerful computer to run on, one with 24 to 32 MB of memory.

VRML   VRML ("*V*irtual *R*eality *M*odeling *L*anguage") is an extension of the tools used to develop World Wide Web pages for access over the Internet. The standard here is called HTML ("*H*yper*t*ext *M*arkup *L*anguage"). A brilliant innovation, which played the key role in making the Net usable by ordinary people as well as for those with computer expertise, HTML includes just about all the two-dimensional elements of multimedia. VRML (rhymes with "thermal") adds full three-dimensional features to Web pages. That may initially result in firms' adding too much that is jazzy and gimmicky, just as far too many HTML pages are a muddle of irrelevant graphics, flashy color, and "eye candy." That said, VRML and similar tools will change the metaphor of the World Wide Web from publishing and pages to touring and places. When you access the Web today, you get a page. It may include or provide hypertext links to images, radio, video, and photographs, but it is electronic Yellow Pages in conception. Read, click, read, click. The promise of VRML is to walk through a space, turn, click, enter, move, click. One commentator neatly captures this as "putting the *space* in cyberspace" (*Byte* magazine, March 1996). The writer asks, "The world isn't flat, so why should the World Wide Web be?" The creator of the Web comments that navigating 3-D space is more natural than clicking through hypertext-linked text pages.

VRML may well not be the 3-D replacement for 2-D HTML. It has many limitations. It does not yet include interaction; you can see a basketball bounce but you can't bounce it. It is slow because the adding the third dimension increases the processing required by a huge factor over HTML. VRML is more a signal of the direction of the World Wide Web than a tool to use now for business applications. But the direction is clear, and it's worthwhile for companies to experiment with it.

See also 3-D; Hypertext Markup Language; Virtual Reality

Web Browsers Web browsers are software packages that make the Internet easy for anyone to use. The original Internet required users to learn some quite arcane commands to invoke its services. Browsers generate the commands for you and also provide a growing variety of aids and services, ranging from ensuring security of messages and credit card transactions, locating sites, helping you organize searches for information, and many other features. They view Web pages. They handle electronic mail.

The leading browser is Netscape Navigator, which has around 70 percent of the PC market. Netscape has an even higher share of the corporate market for the necessarily more powerful software that processes requests to and traffic in and out of the Web sites that store files—pages—to be sent and displayed. There are many other browsers. Each major on-line information service like CompuServe and America Online, networked software vendor like IBM with Lotus Notes and Microsoft, and telecommunications companies like MCI and AT&T offers either its own products or adapted versions of ones like Netscape.

In the early 1990s, the main competitive battle in the PC field was for ownership of the desktop. Three companies competed— Apple with its Macintosh, Microsoft with Windows, and IBM with OS/2—with Microsoft the winner. The new battle is for ownership of the Internet access vehicle. A web browser like Netscape Navigator is really an Internet operating system. All of a sudden, Microsoft has become the underdog.

See also HotJava; Hypertext Markup Language; Java; Mosaic; Netscape; World Wide Web

Web Page A Web page is a computer file that can be any size that is formatted to appear on a PC or workstation as a page that can be scrolled through. The page may contain any type of multimedia and include what are called "hypertext links." Hypertext is the well-established enabling tool of the Web. It is why the request to access a Web page is preceded by http: This stands for "*hypertext transfer protocol*" and informs the Internet's processors how to handle the message. Hypertext is a way of linking information items. By clicking on highlighted text, addresses, words, or pictures you get information about the item, or rather the relevant Web pages are accessed. The brilliant insight of the Web's inventor, Tim Berners-Lee, a scientist working in Switzerland, was that hypertext would make it practical to build links between information resources without having to organize them in some formal system. They could then be located anywhere in the world on the Internet, making it a web of connections. By creating a very straightforward way of laying out a Web page, via the Hypertext Markup Language, he turned the Net from an environment where computer programming knowledge was needed to one where it was in effect a set of Yellow Pages. Look, click, browse around.

A home page is the one that is first displayed when a request is made to access a specific Web address. It may link to many other home pages anywhere on the Net. If you like or dislike a particular company or individual home page, you can create a Web page listing cool sites or worst sites on the Web and create hypertext links to them.

In late 1994, there were an estimated 250,000 Web pages

on the Internet. Now, there are well over 20 million. Although HTML remains the main tool for creating them, with on-line information service providers like CompuServe providing easy ways of designing them and with software companies like Microsoft including options for doing this even in word processing applications, there are newer tools that add more multimedia features, including virtual reality, 3-D, and animation. HTML looks almost like plain text, with special commands called "tags" that indicate where the text is a heading, where hypertext links are to be added, where forms are to be placed (for ordering goods, for instance), where a video clip should be displayed, and many other features.

Accessing a Web page is very simple. You need to send a message to the Internet that indicates its URL ("*unique resource locator*"). Web requests and sites have their own particular URL messages. A straightforward example is http://www.ml.tele.fii, which is the Web page for Telecom Finland. Some Web page URLs can be a long string of letters with characters like tildes, slashes, and dots (~, /, .) separating them. These all provide information to the Internet in general and to the Web in particular to find the exact pages you are requesting.

Web browsers handle all the chores of sending the request. They constitute a new breed of software as far-reaching in its impact in the era of the Internet as personal computer operating systems like MS.DOS and Windows were in their era.

Windows Windows, Microsoft's family of PC operating systems is the single most dominant force in the computer industry, except for the Intel chips on which it depends and whose sales in turn depend on it. The term *Wintel* is increasingly used by commentators to capture the symbiosis.

The evolution of DOS and Windows reflects Bill Gates's own vision for the movement of PCs toward an ever-more-glorious future, with tens of millions of PCs—all of them using Microsoft's products:

- *DOS* was the operating system for *personal* computers, standalone machines with minimal telecommunications capabilities. The spread of DOS, whose original success rested entirely on its being chosen by IBM for its personal computers, as the dominant design for all Intel-based machines, left Microsoft the winner over IBM, which has never since been able to establish its own operating systems as an effective rival to Microsoft's, especially in the consumer marketplace.

- The first versions of *Windows* were an effort to preempt Apple, whose Macintosh series of machines used an operating system that was in every way easier to use than DOS. Windows 3.1 was the version that eroded Apple's advantage, offering an adequate mimicking of the Mac "graphical user interface" for Intel CPU-based machines, whose prices and performance improved by 20 to 30 percent a year and even faster in periods of industry price wars. Windows left Apple out on the fringe of business computing though absolutely in the lead in multimedia. Until very recently, Apple owned the loyalty of probably 80 percent of self-employed professionals, writers, teachers, artists, and others who found—and still find—the Mac superior to Windows in every way, except price and availability of software. Apple gave away its market as much as Windows captured it.

- *Windows for Workgroups* announced Microsoft's move into an area where it did not have established strengths: business telecommunications. The PC now stood for more than just personal computing. Windows for Workgroups and Lotus Notes were part of the shift toward shared computing and communication. Lotus was thus the next major industry player to come head to head against Microsoft.

- *Windows NT* extended Microsoft's focus to the enterprise network and brought it head to head against Novell, the leader in the software that manages complex network links. NT also marked Microsoft's move into the world of 32 bits as the new base of PCs. It is an important part of Microsoft's armory in its battle against Netscape in the corporate network market for what are called intranets, company-specific World Wide Web sites that provide information and communication within the firm.

- *Windows 95* was a later move to tighten Microsoft's dominant hold on the consumer market. *It is the first true mass market multimedia operating system apart from Apple's.* Microsoft is positioning to be as dominant in multimedia software and telecommunications as it has been in word processing, spreadsheets, and other applications. (It has had failures en route, including its effort to develop what may be termed a user-cute rather than a user-friendly interface, called Bob, and several software packages that compete with Novell and Lotus Notes. But the juggernaut moves on unwounded.)

Gates recognized early that networks and multimedia are the future. Microsoft's CD-ROM encyclopedia, Encarta, was a late entry into a market dominated by Grolier and Compton but set a new standard of excellence, being a truly multimedia product rather than one that used multimedia to jazz up plain text. Its CD-ROM walking tour of and tutorial on the National Gallery of Art similarly was a step shift in multimedia, in terms of quality of content, presentation, and interaction.

When Microsoft launched its Windows 95 operating system in the late summer of 1995, it looked pretty invulnerable. That launch was either a triumph of marketing, a watershed moment in computing, egregious hype, or a nonevent, depending on how much you hate Microsoft (a company with many haters) or love Apple (a firm whose blunders were long forgiven by most of the multimedia development world). Whichever it was, it left Microsoft driving the entire direction of computing and its main growth areas of multimedia.

Within just four months, the cracks in the strategy showed almost like those from an earthquake tremor; the building may still stand or the Big One may come. Microsoft has had to reposition its entire business strategy, with Windows no longer the central sun around which all planets revolve. The Internet is now the sun, and Sun Microsystems, the big red planet closest to it except for Netscape. Microsoft is out in the colder orbits. The cross-references to other entries in this Glossary discuss the competitive issues. Simply summarized, there are now two fundamentally different and competing conceptions of computing. The new one is for $500 stripped-down computers marketed by companies like Oracle and Apple to use Sun's Java programming language to substitute applets for the reliance on ever more complex versions of the Windows family of operating systems. The other is a continued evolution of Wintel, with the PC doing most of the work. (Wintel is Windows plus Intel.)

The case for Windows is strong. Wintel is proven. Windows is everywhere. It can evolve to incorporate all the features and advantages of the Internet and is doing so rapidly. The competing Java–network computer view relies on very fast, low-cost telecommunications that are not yet widely practical for the mass market, let alone available. The case for the Sun/Netscape/Oracle model is also strong. The Internet is the new foundation of computing; that is, in the oft-stated phrase of Sun's chief executive, the network *is* the computer. Java is genius. Multimedia is the obvious demand on the Net and on PCs. PCs can't keep up with that demand and at the same time provide low cost and high reliability in both software and hardware. (Windows reliability has been such that, if PCs were cars, it would be called Microsoft Lemon.)

Windows 95 was exponentially more complex than its predecessors, and the 1998 and 2000 Windows and beyond will be more so. Dozens of hardware manufacturers can deliver a powerful device for, if not $500, then close to it.

Rather than avoid the issue of who is likely to win this battle for the soul of computing, I give my own opinion. My instincts are that Java will create a new mainstream; that after a few shaky years during which the Internet will crash and clog up even more than it does today, the basic conception of network-centric computing will be proven correct; that a firm like AT&T or Citibank or a cable television provider will just about give away network computers the way cellular phones are given away for $19.95 in order to capture the phone traffic. "Here's your free Internet/ home banking/interactive television box, and by the way the others come for free. You get top-of-the-line multimedia free, too. Do you really need to upgrade your PC again?"

But then I bet on the 49ers to win the 1996 Super Bowl instead of the Cowboys.

See also Intranet; Java; Network Computer; Operating System

Wired   *Wired* magazine is to multimedia what *Rolling Stone* has been to rock music, a widely read publication that is where the avant-garde and more radical figures in the field write and give interviews. *Wired* is essential material to at least glance at, if you are at all interested in the evolution of the multimedia industry and in getting a sense of the larger social, business, and political patterns it may or may not create. It's not essential *reading*, because it's very difficult to read, in its imitation of the glitz, frenetic tone, and graphics-rich hypertext of the on-line multimedia it covers. It is very much in touch with leading thinking and practice in the multimedia field and, unlike most of the multimedia press, covers issues relevant to business. Most comparable publications focus mainly on games and entertainment.

In addition, *Wired* captures well the emerging mainstreams of influential opinion about the cyberworld—cyberspace, cyber-sport, cyberselling, and the like. It is particularly useful in its frequent in-depth interviews with leaders in the telecommunications, software development, and computer industries. There is an emerging plurality of thought in the technical side of the multimedia community about what multimedia, telecommunications networks, and the Internet mean for business and society. It tends toward giant dreams of the breaking down of centralized systems and a loosening of government controls on both technology and individual life. In the interviews in *Wired,* many of the people most influencing multimedia thinking are given space to think out loud.

At the moment, there is no better window on the world of ideas that are shaping the innovators' priorities than *Wired.* For managers, it is less an issue of whether or not they agree with those ideas than it is worth their while to get a sense of what's happening in a field in constant flux. The year 1995 saw dramatic developments in the multimedia-related industries. Examples were the explosive success of Netscape, the Internet browser software; the sudden emergence of Sun Microsystems' Java software programming language as the most powerful challenge to the hegemony of Microsoft and Intel; and growing concerns about the Internet's pornography, censorship, and First Amendment implications. *Wired* covered these earlier and in more depth than the mainstream business press.

This summary of *Wired* is not intended as an endorsement. It's often a vapid and irritating publication. However, managers need to keep on top of leading multimedia trends, and this is a valuable place to browse.

Wireless   Wireless communications send and receive signals over the air, via broadcast radio waves, whereas wired systems use phone lines and cables; the latter are terrestrial systems, tied to physical lines. Multimedia is basically about making information natural and convenient; every development in the field moves in this direction. Wireless communications are basically about making communication natural and convenient. To date, the two have not converged. Multimedia is the domain of PCs, corporate networks, and the Internet. Wireless communications have been centered on cellular phones, satellite communication and TV broadcasting. This is changing, fueled by the same three forces that have driven telecommunications in the past decade: (1) deregulation, (2) technical innovation, and (3) information and communication access tools.

Historically, wireless communications have made inefficient use of the electromagnetic spectrum, the range of available frequency bands for sending communications, including AM and FM radio bands, TV signals, cellular phone systems, and many others. The foundation of telecommunications is to transfer information by changing the motion of an electrical charge. That charge is generated by vacuum tubes (radio, television, and navigation systems) and microchips. Wiggling, pushing, or vibrating it produces a wave that has a measure of energy. There are two determinants of the measure: how often the charge is manipulated—the frequency of the signal in wave cycles per second—and the distance between the waves that are generated—their wavelength. Wired communications send the waves down phone lines, television cables, and computer cables. Wireless ones send them through the air. They must operate at different frequencies from each other within a given area, so that the waves can be picked up by the receiving device tuned to them. Signals sent along a wire can be kept separate from those transmitted over another wire by insulating the cable. Wireless signals can't be isolated from each other and will cause interference if they are on the same frequency as another transmission.

This means that the scarce usable range of the radio spectrum has to be managed, especially the most crowded frequency range best suited to radio, television, and cellular phones. Historically, this was handled in almost every country through regulated allo-

Telecommunications industry estimates in 1983 were that fewer than 1 million Americans would pay to use cellular phones. By 1993, 10 million were. Annual rates of growth are 50 percent in North America, 60 percent in Europe and Asia, and 200 percent in Latin America. Cellular phones are just the starting point.

cation of licenses, which specify the frequency and range over which the devices or service may operate. That range is determined by the electrical power of the device sending the signal.

Increasingly, the spectrum is recognized as a prime economic good to be auctioned, with bids in many instances in the billions of dollars. In addition, the shift to digital transmission allows more data to be sent within the same frequency range. Data compression reduces the original digital signal by a factor of 25 to 100. More and more signals can be packed into the same channel. The higher the frequency, the tighter the channel and the faster the information transmission.

The main frequency ranges for wireless communications are:

- *AM radio.* 535 to 1635 KHz (kilohertz; thousands of cycles per second).

- *Cordless phones.* 44 to 49 MHz (megahertz; millions of cycles per second).

- *TV channels.* Channels 2–6: 54 to 88 MHz; Channels 7–13, 174 to 216 MHz; Channels 14–69 (UHF), 407 to 806 MHz.

- *Wireless modems.* 800 MHz.

- *Cellular phones.* 806–890 MHz.

- *Digital cordless phones.* 900 MHZ.

Computer chips operate on the same basis in transmitting information in and out. A standard Intel Pentium chip, for instance, runs at anywhere between 75 MHz and 120 MHz, with this year's speed demons offering 200 MHz.

At present, wireless digital communication speeds are too slow for multimedia. I've included wireless communications in this guide even though today the low speeds they offer mean that they are barely used for multimedia. They *will* be used more and more in the future, and more important, when they are, which is well within the next five years, they will open up immense new opportunities literally everywhere.

World Wide Web: Its Nature and Evolution The World Wide Web (WWW) is for many people equivalent to the Internet. More accurately, it is a form of publishing service within the Net that is comprised of "pages" that may contain a mix of formatted text and any type of multimedia. The pages are stored on Web servers—computers that, as the term implies, process requests for pages and serve them to client machines across the network. To access the pages, you use a Net browser—a piece of software that handles all the technical details and, more importantly, hides them so that "surfing" the Net becomes something anyone can do.

The pages are built on and made possible by a simple mini-programming language for describing the layout of the information to appear on a computer screen. The language is Hypertext Markup Language (HTML). There are newer languages, including ones that add 3-D and virtual reality capabilities to the static displays of HTML. The key concept they all share is hypertext, the provision of automatic cross-links to other information and other pages across the Web. By marking a word, phrase, picture, or some other item on the screen, the developer specifies a link to another Web page, which may be on any server on the Net. To find information, you follow a series of hypertext links. It is this that naturally coined the term *browser* for the software that manages the process for you.

The Internet allows any computer of any type anywhere in the world to communicate with any other anywhere else, through the use of a common telecommunications protocol called IP ("*In*ternet *p*rotocol"). The World Wide Web allows any human with access to the Web to communicate with any other human. The technology of the Internet standardizes and simplifies machine and software communication. The Web standardizes and simplifies human communication.

The Web is remarkably easy to use, but its value increasingly rests on the speed of the telecommunications links that move pages from the server to the screen. Slow speeds discourage use

Traffic on the World Wide Web grew an impressive 29,000 percent in 1992. In 1993, it grew by 290,000 percent. The cause was the release of Mosaic, the first novice-friendly software for browsing the Web. In mid-1992, the volume of Gopher traffic was about 500 times larger than that for the Web. By mid-1994, the Web had overtaken Gopher. In many ways, Gopher is a more efficient and effective vehicle for searching data bases and, like Mosaic, it relies on hypertext. It employs the now-outmoded menu approach to interaction between system and user. Mosaic has a graphical user. That made all the difference.

of multimedia. The race is on to exploit the multimedia capabilities of the Web. The most important move here has been the development of the Java programming language and its inclusion in the two Net browsers that account for 95 percent of Internet use (Netscape Navigator and Microsoft Express) and many others jostling for a position in the competitive on-line information services market. Java makes the Web a full computing and communications environment, rather than a publishing one. That makes it a powerful base for what are called "intranets," the most rapidly growing innovation in Internet use. Intranets are Web sites that may be accessed only within an organization, not by anyone on the Net. Java allows the development of transaction processing and complex information management applications, using the Web's protocols and browser. Essentially any application can now be put on the Web, on either an intranet or a Public Internet service.

There is a very small number of terms needed to understand the basics of the Web. The main ones, which summarize the organizational hierarchy of the Web, are:

- *Server.* A computer assigned the specific task of handling requests for Web pages. This is analogous to a physical library.

- *Site.* A collection of pages on a Web server. An indexed subsection of the library.

- *Home page.* The first or central page on the site about a particular topic or organization; the book jacket.

- *Web page.* A computer file that is formatted as a single page (that can be of any length) for formatting and displaying in the client's screen.

- *Browser.* The software running on a computer that searches for, requests, and displays the resulting pages. Browsers may also request non-Web Internet services.

- *HTTP.* The access method or protocol. The http: tag at the very start of the browser message signals to the Internet computers the protocol—telecommunications messaging formats and procedures to transfer Web pages. It stands for "*H*yper*t*ext *T*ransfer *P*rotocol." If the browser sent a message to the Internet that began with, say, ftp instead of http, the request would be to transfer a computer file using that protocol instead, which is designed for rapid transfer of large files.

- *WWW.* The World Wide Web, obviously. But it's not obvious to the Internet which of its many services the client is requesting. It might be Telnet ("dumb" terminal link to a computer for transaction processing or data base management) or Usenet electronic mail and discussion groups). "WWW" announces this is a Web request.

- *HTML.* The text-processing language the page is written in.

- *URL.* The message that puts together all the information the Internet needs to determine the access method, the service, the Web server, and the directory that lists the specific file name of the page it is requesting. Your browser generates this "*u*nique *r*esource *l*ocator" message for you. Here is the one for accessing the index to the pages about the international locations of a company called McKenzie and Thompson:

  http://www.mck&thom.com./international/index.html

This is interpreted as a request for the HTML file called index in the directory "international" on the Web server (www) named "mck&thom," which is registered by McKenzie and Thompson, a commercial organization (.com) using the HTTP protocol.

See also Hot Java; Hypertext Markup Language; Java

WWW *See* World Wide Web

Zipping To zip information is to combine a number of small files into a single, highly compressed one and to distribute it across a network or on diskettes to users who unzip it when they receive it. It is widely used on the Internet, more for sending and receiving software than for multimedia, using the basic principle that is perhaps the single most important tool in making it practical to move and store large amounts of information over networks: data compression. Zipping uses a relatively simple version of data compression. The zip and unzip programs, PKZIP and PKUNZIP, are included as part of many PC operating systems.

Without the data compression tools, which reduce the size of files, today's networks and storage mechanisms could not keep up with the demands of multimedia, especially using slow phone lines to access the Internet. Data compression uses mathematical algorithms or special-purpose hardware to scan data and compact it. A simple example is a message that contains a long string of the very same item, such as a stream of the number 106, 250 times in a row to indicate that the next part of, say, a photographic image is an expanse of the same light blue shirt. Through data compression, this is sent in the form Next 250 = 106.

Substantial hardware or software overhead is incurred in compressing and decompressing files. When the data are time-sensitive, such as full-motion video or interactive videoconferencing, or involves very high-resolution images (an extreme case are X rays to be interpreted by radiologists), the data compression tools are very sophisticated. Zipping and unzipping are used for data that are not time-sensitive, for which it doesn't matter if it takes a few seconds or even minutes to compress at the sending end and to decompress at the receiving end. When you send an electronic mail message over the Internet and want to attach a copy of a photographic image that takes up, say, 300,000 bytes of data, that takes at least 3 minutes using a standard modem connection. If you want to download a software program, such as the free upgrade of its Internet browser offered by Netscape in 1995, you may have to transfer around 1.3 million bytes of data, which adds up to almost 11 million bits. At 14,400 bits per second plus overhead, you're in for at least a 15-minute wait.

Zipping the data cuts all this by a factor of at least five. You need to unzip the data on your hard drive only once; even if this takes three or four minutes, you save time. Even if it took *longer* than transferring the uncompressed program, you'd still gain because your phone connection isn't tied up for as long. You can unzip the files off line.

See also Data Compression

Index

Primary glossary entry is indicated by boldface type.

About the Author

Peter G. W. Keen is the author of fifteen books on the link between information technology and business strategy, an international adviser to top managers, named by *Information Week* as one of the top ten consultants in the world, and a professor who has held positions at leading U.S. and European universities, including Harvard, Stanford, MIT, and Stockholm University. Companies with which Keen has worked on an ongoing, long-term basis include British Airways, Citibank, MCI Communications, Sweden Post, Cemex (Mexico), and the Royal Bank of Canada. All of his work focuses on bridging the worlds, cultures, and language of business and IT.